Elena Seibert

GILLIAN THOMAS is a senior staff attorney with the American Civil Liberties Union's (ACLU) Women's Rights Project. She previously litigated sex discrimination cases at the U.S. Equal Employment Opportunity Commission and Legal Momentum (formerly NOW Legal Defense and Education Fund). Her work has appeared in *The New York Times*, *Los Angeles Times*, *The Atlantic*, and *Slate*, and she has been interviewed by NPR and *The Wall Street Journal*, among others. She lives in Brooklyn.

gillianthomas.net

Additional Praise for *Because of Sex*

"A survey of Title VII cases about sex discrimination in the workplace might sound dry—if it weren't for Ms. Thomas's skills as a storyteller, as well as the drama inherent in the cases themselves."
—*The New York Times*

" 'Giving faces to the names of women who brought these cases,' says one reader, 'makes this book remarkable beyond the important historical perspective it offers.' "
—*Elle*

"Thomas grips her reader from the start. . . . [She] writes with a narrative style that makes reading legal cases accessible and enjoyable."
—Girl with Pen, thesocietypages.org

"Thomas chronicles court cases crucial to Title VII, and in doing so, illustrates the decision's enduring achievement."
—*Broadly*

"[Thomas's] book overflows with 'I can't believe he really said that' stories and 'head-shaking' moments—stories that would be unbelievable if they weren't true. . . . But the book is also full of strong women and their attorneys who fought back—and won."
—*Ms.* magazine

"Compulsively readable . . . A moving and informative account of a struggle for equality that remains incomplete."
—*Publishers Weekly*

"A riveting read, particularly for fans of Gail Collins's *When Everything Changed*."
—*Library Journal* (starred review)

"Eye-opening . . . Although the author's well-delineated examples will ring outrageous to modern-day ears, she reminds us how much there is still to be achieved."
—*Kirkus Reviews*

"It is because of sex that women are discriminated against in the workplace, and it is also because of sex that men are favored in language. Maybe it's time to follow Thomas's lead . . . and make that clear."
—A Little Feminist Blog on Language

"Thomas humanizes the fight against sex discrimination . . . by briskly introducing the reader to the women who litigated ten landmark Title VII cases."
—Law.com

"Elegantly written and vividly described, Gillian Thomas's *Because of Sex* tells the fascinating story of the transformation of the American workforce. It is a must-read for anyone—man or woman—who puts on a uniform, or a suit, and goes to work every day."

—Clara Bingham, coauthor of *Class Action:*
The Landmark Case that Changed Sexual Harassment Law

"In these gripping stories of the unsung women who helped lead the legal fight for gender equality, Gillian Thomas elegantly proves Justice Holmes's maxim, 'The life of the law has not been logic; it has been experience,' and she shows in vivid, painful detail how the brave battles of these plaintiffs made real life better for millions of their fellow Americans, women and men alike—if, sadly, not always for themselves." —Todd S. Purdum, author of
An Idea Whose Time Has Come:
Two Presidents, Two Parties, and the
Battle for the Civil Rights Act of 1964

"*Because of Sex* is the definitive and up-to-the-minute account of one of—if not the—most important achievements of the feminist revolution: legal equality in the workplace. Not only does Thomas tell this invaluable story, she brings the wronged women, their lawyers, and even the bad actors on the other side to life in the most engaging way. The reader comes to care for these largely unsung heroines deeply and to learn a lot of law along the way. Brava!"

—Linda Hirshman, author of *Sisters in Law:*
How Sandra Day O'Connor and Ruth Bader Ginsburg
Went to the Supreme Court and Changed the World

"A singularly important look into the relationship between women, the workplace, and the law. Gillian Thomas close-reads ten seminal cases. It's almost impossible to believe that this legal architecture didn't exist until so recently, or that women managed to work at all without it. This is a compelling, readable narrative about a law that changed everything, and the people who worked to spearhead a revolution."

—Dahlia Lithwick, *Slate*

because of sex

One Law, Ten Cases, and Fifty Years That Changed American Women's Lives at Work

Gillian Thomas

Picador
St. Martin's Press
New York

To my parents—
for everything.

picadorusa.com • picadorbookroom.tumblr.com
twitter.com/picadorusa • facebook.com/picadorusa

Picador® is a U.S. registered trademark and is used by Macmillan Publishing Group, LLC, under license from Pan Books Limited.

For book club information, please visit facebook.com/picadorbookclub or email marketing@picadorusa.com.

Portions of this book previously appeared in a December 1, 2014, article in *Slate*. Gillian Thomas, "Pregnancy Complication," *Slate*, December 1, 2014, http://www.slate.com/articles/double_x/doublex/2014/12/young_v_ups_the_supreme_court_takes_up_pregnant_workers_rights.html.

The Library of Congress has cataloged the St. Martin's Press edition as follows:

Thomas, Gillian, (lawyer), author.
   Because of sex : one law, ten cases, and fifty years that changed American women's lives at work / Gillian Thomas.
      p. cm.
   ISBN 978-1-137-28005-3 (hardcover)
   ISBN 978-1-4668-7897-6 (ebook)
   1. Sex discrimination in employment—Law and legislation—United States—Cases.   2. Sex discrimination against women—Law and legislation—United States—Cases.   3. Women's rights—United States—Cases.   I. Title.
   KF3467.T56 2016
   344.7301'4133—dc23   2015033086

Picador Paperback ISBN 978-1-250-13808-8

Our books may be purchased in bulk for promotional, educational, or business use. Please contact your local bookseller or the Macmillan Corporate and Premium Sales Department at 1-800-221-7945, extension 5442, or by email at MacmillanSpecialMarkets@macmillan.com.

First published by St. Martin's Press

First Picador Edition: August 2017

D   10   9   8

contents

acknowledgments

IT'S A CLICHÉ, BUT IN THIS CASE IT FITS: WRITING THIS book was a dream come true. It became a reality because so many people, when I asked for their help, said yes.

Above all, this project depended on the willingness of strangers to let me into their lives, in some cases their homes, to answer my questions about their personal histories. To a one they were gracious and generous, even when the memories were hard to revisit. Key among them are Teresa (Harris) Wilson and her lawyer, Irwin Venick, who nearly four years ago agreed to be interviewed when I cold-called them, told them I had an idea for a book, and explained I needed a sample chapter as a calling card for agents and publishers. I'm also indebted to the other women whose struggles are documented here: Lillian Garland, Ann Hopkins, Brenda Mieth, Kim Rawlinson, Sheila White, and Peggy Young; as well as three of Ida Phillips's children—Peggy Brandt, Alfred McAlister, and Vera Tharp (along with her husband, Mark Tharp)—who, through their memories, helped me get to know their mother. All of the women profiled in this book, along with the others I couldn't meet, are heroines to me, and it was a privilege to get to tell their stories. I hope they feel I served them well.

Also indispensable were the dedicated attorneys who took the time to recount their roles in these landmark cases: In addition to Irwin Venick they are Sam Bagenstos, Patricia Barry, Joan Bertin, Hon. John Carroll, Carin Clauss, Robert Dohrmann (who, miraculously, still had possession of the 40-year-old *Manhart* case files), Sharon Gustafson, Pam Horowitz, Miriam Horwitz, Doug Huron, Linda Krieger, Joe Levin, Judith Ludwic, Hon. John Marshall Meisburg, Jr., Reese Marshall, William Robinson, Patricia Shiu, and Marley Weiss. I loved hearing their blow-by-blow accounts, and how they came to recognize just how important each case might be. Dr. Susan Fiske was equally generous in recounting her experiences as an expert witness on behalf of Ann Hopkins.

I will never stop being grateful to my editor at St. Martin's Press, Elisabeth Dyssegaard, for taking a chance on me, a lawyer with one law review article to her name, and for her unflagging passion for making these stories known. Her assistant, Laura Apperson, helped me navigate this daunting process with calm and good cheer. The rest of the St. Martin's team, most notably the publicity and marketing fairy godparents Gabrielle Gantz, Laura Clark, Christine Catarino, and Chris Scheina, awed me with their energy. Production guru Alan Bradshaw and his crew were unflappable and eagle-eyed, not to mention positively saintly in their patience.

I'd be nowhere without my agent Rob McQuilkin, whose insights, razor-sharp pen, and endless supply of bons mots sustained me during the highs and lows of this experience. Everything he touched made the book better. Many thanks, as well, to his team at Lippincott Massie McQuilkin, especially Amanda Panitch, along with Clare Mao and Genevieve Buzo.

I also am grateful to the many people who assisted in my research, including Jay Barksdale and Melanie Locay of the New York Public Library. Sara Boswell of the U.S. District Court for the Middle District of Florida, Robyn Bradley Bryan of the Alabama Law Enforcement Agency, Emily Carr of the Library of Congress, Margaret Chisholm of the Yale Law School Library, Jennifer Hadley of Local 18 IBEW, Bob Horton of the Alabama Department of Corrections, Bryant Johnson of the U.S. District Court for the District of Columbia, David Tucker and Michelle Vaca with the U.S. Department of Labor Women's Bureau, and Penny Weaver at the Southern Poverty Law Center. Zoryana Bruher and Michelle Dubert transcribed hours of interviews with care and precision.

The daily ritual of putting fingers to keyboard was infinitely more productive due to the community of women writers at Powderkeg. A million thanks to Monique Truong for introducing me to this special place, and to co-founders Sharon Lerner and Holly Morris for welcoming me into the fold. My dear desk "neighbor" Lucie Whitehouse sustained me with mordant humor, sympathy, and above all, carbohydrates.

I am fortunate to know some exceptionally smart, insightful, kind people who took countless hours out of their busy lives to review these pages and offer not just their feedback, but their encouragement. Chief among them is Michele Host, whose dedication to this book rivaled my own. I can never repay the generosity she showed as a reader, and friend, during this process. David Franklin also read the full manuscript and managed to be both a ruthless and hilarious editor whose cuts were always kind. Jennifer Siegel and Maurice Samuels, both veteran authors (not to mention veteran friends), lent their brilliance, compassion, and discerning eyes at every turn, most memorably during our residency at the East Hampton Colony. Also indispensable readers and solid-gold spirit lifters were Eve Bowen, Joanna Grossman, Julie Kay, Sharon Lerner, Anna Pohl, Ghita Schwarz, Galen Sherwin, and Katrin Van Dam.

Other friends and colleagues have contributed to this project in myriad ways. Some have provided B&B services in my travels, while others have provided unstinting moral support, guidance on navigating this new world of writing and publishing, or lent their professional currency. They are Zoe Allen and Eric Hecker (of the Rebel Road and 666 Carroll Writers' Retreats), Jessica Arons, Melinda Arons, Dina Bakst, Konrad Batog, Daniel Bauman, Jessica Bennett, Julian Birnbaum, Julian Bond, Emily Bradford, Michael Cantwell, Dolores Caviglia-Fischer, Deborah Clark and Dan Kiefer, Kevin Cremin, Herbert Eisenberg, Jennifer Entine-Matz, Benjamin Feldman, Tony Fross, Jim Gatto, Martha Gatto, Melinda Gatto, Jason Glick, Janice Goodman, Gail Gove and Jordan Young, Marya Grandy and Matt Heimer, David Greenberg, Lynn Harris, Emily Houh, Sarah Ivry, Marjorie Jolles and Matthew Pearson, Lenora Lapidus, Tom Lepak, Dahlia Lithwick, P. David Lopez, Maggie Malloy, Miranda Massie, Louise Melling, Justin Mulaire, Daniel Mullkoff, Ginger Adams Otis, Maya Raghu, Jadhira Rivera, Alexandria Sage, Ami Sanghvi, Jill Savitt, Jennifer Schuessler, Laura Schnell, Elena Seibert, Jennifer Sheridan, Jacob Soll and Ellen Wayland-Smith, Amelia Tuminaro, Caroline Weber, Carolyn Wessling, Emily Whitfield, Verna Williams, Susan Williamson, and Sasha Zill.

My parents, John and Nancy Thomas, have always made me feel that anything is possible in my life, and have done everything to make it so. They came to love the stories told here as much as I do. Their pride in this book is my greatest reward.

Jeff Gatto lived this book with me from inception to completion, and he shares in its accomplishment. He played many roles—insightful reader, unflagging cheerleader, unparalleled mixologist, wise therapist, ergonomic expert, coordinator of not one but two apartment moves, financial consultant, and unparalleled mixologist (yes, I said it twice). I will always be grateful to him.

introduction

ON FEBRUARY 8, 1964, AN EIGHTY-YEAR-OLD SEGREGA-
tionist congressman named Howard Smith stepped onto the floor of
the House of Representatives and changed the lives of America's working women forever.

It was the eighth and last day of debate on a bill that would become the landmark 1964 Civil Rights Act, and Smith had a proposed
amendment to Title VII, the section dealing with equal employment
opportunity. The current draft already prohibited discrimination because of race, color, religion, and national origin, but Smith, a Democrat from Virginia, wanted to add one more category. The clerk read
Smith's proposal aloud. "After the word 'religion' insert 'sex' on pages
68, 69, 70 and 71 of the bill."[1]

Smith played his "little amendment"[2] for laughs, claiming to have
been inspired by a letter he had received from a female constituent.
She asked the government to "protect our spinster friends," who were
suffering from a shortage of eligible bachelors.[3] Over guffaws from his
virtually all-male audience, Smith concluded, "I read that letter just to
illustrate that women have some real grievances and some real rights
to be protected. I am serious about this thing."[4] Emanuel Celler of
New York, the bill's floor manager in the House, joined in the fun. "I
can say as a result of forty-nine years of experience—and I celebrate
my fiftieth wedding anniversary next year—that women, indeed, are
not in the minority in my house," he said. "I usually have the last two
words, and those words are, 'Yes, dear.'"[5]

Several of the House's twelve women representatives rose to try
to silence the laughter and advocate seriously for the amendment.
Martha Griffiths, Democrat of Michigan, was the one who finally
succeeded. "I presume that if there had been any necessity to point

out that women were a second-class sex," she said, "the laughter would have proved it."[6] Griffiths (who supported the bill) made a shrewd appeal to the Civil Rights Act's opponents, mainly Southern Democrats like Smith. By then, it looked inevitable that the law they hated had enough votes to pass. So she warned that without the sex provision, Title VII would afford more rights to black women than to white women.[7] "A vote against this amendment today by a white man is a vote against his wife, or his widow, or his daughter, or his sister."[8]

The session eventually dubbed "Ladies Day in the House"[9] had the hallmarks of an impromptu stunt by Smith to try to sink the Civil Rights Act.[10] Civil rights for African Americans might have been palatable to many white legislators now that the horrors of Bull Connor and Birmingham had become national news, but civil rights for women were, literally, a joke.

Though it might have seemed incongruous for an avowed enemy of civil rights, Howard Smith had a long history of supporting the Equal Rights Amendment. Under pressure from the ERA's supporters, he actually had been dropping hints for weeks that he intended to offer a "sex" amendment. (Most of the ERA's supporters were white, and many kept alive a legacy of not-so-subtly racist activism dating back a century that decried expanded legal protections for African American men, such as the right to vote, that were denied to women.)[11] As a friend to southern manufacturing interests, Smith also might have understood the human capital that would be freed up by a federal law nullifying widespread state law restrictions on women's ability to work as many hours as men.[12]

When Smith's amendment was put to a vote a few hours later, it passed 168 to 133, with the most votes in favor cast by Republicans and Southern Democrats.[13] From the gallery came a woman's shout, "We've won! We've won!" and then another's cry, "We made it! God bless America!"[14] After the bill moved to the Senate for consideration, Smith's amendment remained intact. When President Lyndon Johnson signed the Civil Rights Act into law on July 2, 1964, among its provisions was a ban on discrimination in employment "because of sex."[15]

TODAY MOST AMERICAN working women would probably be surprised to know that they have an unrepentantly racist, male octogenarian to thank for outlawing sex bias on the job. Although historians continue to debate Howard Smith's motives,[16] the law best known as a monumental achievement for African Americans' civil rights was a milestone in the struggle for sex equality too. Title VII started a revolution for women.

In the *Mad Men* world of 1964, fewer than half of American women were in the paid labor force, making up just one-third of workers. Most working women were concentrated in a few, low-paying jobs, such as secretary, waitress, and teacher[17]—no surprise, given that job advertisements were divided into "Help Wanted—Female" and "Help Wanted—Male." Male bosses' and coworkers' leers, touches, and propositions were as much part of the air working women breathed as cigarette smoke. Getting pregnant—and for some, even getting married—meant getting a pink slip.

Today, that "Jane Crow"[18] system no longer exists. Sixty percent of all women work outside the home, making up close to half of all American workers, and 70 percent of mothers work outside the home.[19] Women populate the highest ranks of politics, business, medicine, law, journalism, and academia, to name only a few. A third of the justices on the Supreme Court are women, and a woman president is inevitable, possibly imminent. The ubiquitous sexual conduct previously understood to be "just the way things are" now has a name: sexual harassment. Women routinely work until late in their pregnancies, and most return to work after having their babies.[20]

We never would have gotten from there to here without Title VII. But the law's enactment in 1964 was just the beginning. What happened next is where this book begins.

Women began stepping forward to use Title VII to get justice at work. The first women who sued under Title VII didn't always get a friendly hearing; in 1964, out of 422 federal judges in the nation, a paltry 3 were women.[21] And because Title VII's sex provision was added so late, there wasn't the usual history of congressional hearings and committee reports to define what discrimination "because of sex" even meant.

But with each favorable decision issued by each court, the contours of that definition began to emerge. A small fraction of these cases were propelled all the way to the Supreme Court, whose interpretation of Title VII then bound all of the nation's judges.

Most of the women whose legal battles made it to this rare pinnacle aren't well known: Ida Phillips, Brenda Mieth, Kim Rawlinson, the women of the Los Angeles Department of Water and Power, Mechelle Vinson, Lillian Garland, Ann Hopkins, the women of battery maker

Johnson Controls, Teresa Harris, Sheila White, and Peggy Young. Most were middle or working class, and most fought their cases alone for years, save for their dedicated attorneys and some supportive family and friends. None filed her lawsuit intending to end up before the nine justices. They all just wanted to work.

FOR MANY YEARS, individual litigants weren't just doing battle with biased employers or indifferent judges. The U.S. Equal Employment Opportunity Commission, the agency created by Title VII to enforce the statute, considered the sex amendment to be just as silly as Howard Smith's audience had. When a reporter asked the EEOC's first chair, Franklin Roosevelt, Jr., "What about sex?" he answered, "Don't get me started. I'm all for it,"[22] while one of the agency's first executive directors dismissed the sex provision as a "fluke" that was "conceived out of wedlock."[23] The hilarity of the notion that all jobs should be open to both sexes spawned a running joke, abetted by agency officials, that Title VII had created a "bunny problem"—as in requiring that hairy-legged men be hired as Playboy Bunnies.[24] Similarly confounding scenarios, wrote *The New York Times,* included "the woman who applies for a job as an attendant at a Turkish bath, a man who wants to clerk in a woman's corset shop, the woman who wants employment aboard a tug that has sleeping quarters only for men."[25]

Despite the fact that women filed one-third of the discrimination charges in the first year after the EEOC opened its doors,[26] the agency's chauvinism made it slow to address the myriad questions those charges posed. Thanks largely to the efforts of a small but determined cadre of women staff attorneys, along with protests launched by the National Organization of Women—which was founded in 1966 by activists furious at the EEOC's inattention to Title VII's sex provision—the agency eventually started taking more aggressive positions. It issued opinions ruling that sex-segregated want ads violated the law, that airlines' no-marriage policies for flight attendants unlawfully relegated them to the role of sex object, and that state "protective laws" limiting the weight women could lift or the hours they could work were preempted by Title VII and therefore null and void. When Title VII was amended in 1972 to give the EEOC power to bring litigation in its own name, those lawsuits became critical complements to the hundreds of individual cases already being litigated around the country.

THE SUCCESSES celebrated in this book are not meant to suggest that Title VII was or is a panacea for sex inequality at work. For one thing, the law does not even apply to employers with fewer than fifteen employees, which by one estimate leaves nearly one-fifth of the workforce, male *and* female, without the law's protections.[27]

Millions of women in this country labor in jobs that keep them in poverty, that endanger their health, that provide no retirement security or other benefits, that take no account of pregnancy or caregiving responsibilities or even the need to take an occasional sick day. Even for professional women, pregnancy and motherhood remain profoundly disruptive to career progression and spawn pernicious stereotypes about their commitment to their jobs.[28] Sexual harassment remains pervasive, especially in male-dominated fields and the low-wage and tipped workforces; e-mail, texts, and social media have given harassers new and sometimes terrifying ways of conveying unwelcome attention. Pay inequality, even when controlling for education and experience, has stalled. White women have inched up to making 78 cents for every male dollar, while the numbers for women of color are, predictably, far worse.[29] It's still a curiosity to see a female construction worker or a female firefighter (or, for that matter, a male nurse or a male secretary). Women also are chronically underrepresented in science, technology, engineering, and math (STEM) fields and the financial industries, and their numbers are also far too small in the top positions on the corporate ladder.[30]

Only some of these problems can be attributed to discrimination "because of sex." Others will have to be addressed by passing new laws, or amending old ones. Some will demand voluntary changes in employer policies, and still others will have to be left to the glacial process of cultural change. But even though it's easy to get discouraged about the glaring inequalities we see everywhere around us, there is some benefit to being reminded that it used to be so much worse.

ONE PROMINENT feminist lawyer wrote about her experience representing women in employment discrimination cases, "Because this road is so tough, I often hear clients say, 'Why me? Why did this have to happen to me? Why has my life been turned upside down by this

creep who had no right to do this to me?' And it is unfair. But the law
has been transformed by the many women who have bravely stepped
up and paved the way for the rest of us."[31]

This book aims to pay tribute to some of those women. They
achieved landmark legal victories that benefited millions, despite usually having very little to show for it themselves in the end. Many of the
rights established by the cases in this book have become so assimilated
into our reality that we don't even realize there was a time not very
long ago when they didn't exist.

I WAS INSPIRED to write this book by my own experiences representing women very much like those featured in its pages. Reflecting
on the tenacity shown by my own clients in trying to right the wrongs
done to them, often at considerable personal cost, I realized that the
women who had brought cases that wound up before the Supreme
Court had faced an additional challenge: They were breaking new legal ground entirely. While I had the benefit of citing to the precedent
they had helped to create, when *they* went to court, their predicaments
presented questions that the law had barely begun to address.

Forging ahead with a sex discrimination lawsuit where the odds
of a favorable outcome were so uncertain, and where the culture was
still so skeptical of working women, took a special brand of moxie. I
wanted to try to know these women, and to tell their stories.

one

women and
children last

Phillips v. Martin Marietta Corporation (1971)

ON A HOT FLORIDA NIGHT IN SEPTEMBER 1966, IDA
Phillips sat down at her kitchen table to write a letter. Her small frame
bowed over a tablecloth printed with green and orange flowers, she
quickly filled three small pages with her tidy cursive. "To the President
of the United States," she wrote. "As of this date, September 6, 1966 at
7 p.m., I answered an employment ad of Martin Co. of Orlando, Fla.
in which the co. seeks 100 assembly trainees. However after completing my application I was told by the receptionist that my application
could not be honored due to the fact that I have a pre-school child."[1]

A neighbor had alerted Phillips to the newspaper notice placed
by the Martin Marietta Corporation, a missile manufacturer with a
sprawling facility ten miles from downtown Orlando.[2] With a workforce numbering in the thousands, it was one of the largest employers
in the city.[3] Entry-level jobs on the assembly line paid up to $125 a
week,[4] more than double what Phillips was earning as a waitress at
the Donut Dinette.[5] Even better, the job came with a pension plan and
benefits, including insurance. "You'd better get down there early," the
neighbor advised. Because he worked at Martin Marietta, he told Phillips to list him as a reference. "There's gonna be a lot of people over
there looking for that job."

Phillips resolved to be one of them. Thirty-two years old and the mother of seven children ranging in age from three to sixteen, she was barely scraping by. Every day she counted up the tips that she'd made during her shift and decided what she could afford to buy for that night's supper; the little bit she had left over got tucked away to cover the bills. She certainly couldn't count on the wages her husband, Tom Phillips, got from working as a mechanic. Those he usually drank.

So Phillips, a vivacious, dimpled redhead, had driven the ten miles to the Martin Marietta facility on Kirkman Road to submit an application. When she got to the front of the line, the receptionist asked her if she had any preschool-age children. Hearing that Phillips had a three-year-old, the woman declined to let her apply. It didn't matter that Phillips's daughter was enrolled in day care[6] or that she also had plenty of backup child care, including a sister who lived nearby and the stay-at-home mother who lived just next door. The company simply wouldn't hire women with kids that young. "I felt like the world had caved in on me," Phillips recalled. "I had my hopes up so much for it."[7] She needed those wages, and her kids needed those benefits.

That's when Phillips decided to write President Lyndon Johnson. "My President, may I say that I believe that this is unjust from the policies that you have administered during your term of office," she implored. "As equal opportunities, as equal employment and consti-tutional rights."[8] Phillips hadn't grown up paying much attention to politics, but she had recently registered to vote and started "read[ing] the papers cover to cover."[9] She may not have known specifically about the 1964 Civil Rights Act, but she plainly suspected that Martin Mari-etta was doing something unlawful.

Phillips's daughter, Vera Tharp, remembered that when their neighbor stopped by that night to check how Phillips had made out, he was incredulous. After all, *he* had kids in preschool and the company had never objected. "You need to go back over there," he urged, "and you just ask them why." Phillips agreed and returned to the plant the following day, but the receptionist wasn't giving any explanations. She just repeated the rule: Women with small children were not eligible for hire.

Less than a week after she'd put her letter in the mail, Phillips got a response from the White House. Her complaint, she was told, had been forwarded to the U.S. Equal Employment Opportunity Commis-sion, the federal agency tasked with enforcing Title VII, for further investigation.[10]

The following summer, the EEOC issued a decision in Phillips's favor.[11] In November 1967, having tried unsuccessfully to convince the company to settle the case by giving Phillips the job she'd applied for,[12] the EEOC mailed a notice to Phillips, who by then had moved with her family to Jacksonville. The agency had done all it could, it said, but she had the right to continue the case on her own by filing a lawsuit in federal court.[13] Phillips definitely wanted to press on; she was too angry not to. Now she needed to find a lawyer.

THE FIRST ATTORNEY Phillips called told her, in her words, "he didn't think enough of the case to fool with it."[14] Undeterred, she said she got the idea she "should look for a Negro attorney, because [I] knew they knew more about civil rights."[15] A prominent African American attorney in town, Earl Johnson, was running for City Council, so Phillips met with him. Unfortunately, the campaign was taking up most of his time, he told her, and he referred her to a young black lawyer who'd just joined his law office, Reese Marshall.[16]

Then just a year out of Howard University Law School, Marshall was participating in the fledgling but already illustrious internship program at the NAACP Legal Defense and Educational Fund. Founded in 1940 by future Supreme Court Justice Thurgood Marshall, LDF was the country's preeminent litigation firm attacking the racial inequality that was still commonplace in American life—in education, voting, the criminal justice system, housing, public accommodations, and employment. LDF had devised and executed the litigation strategy attacking the "separate but equal" legal doctrine that had culminated in the Supreme Court's landmark *Brown v. Board of Education*[17] decision in 1954.

Recruiting and training foot soldiers to help wage the civil rights battle in the courts, the LDF internship program included a one-year stint in LDF's New York headquarters that Marshall had just completed, followed by three years litigating in the field under the tutelage of a more experienced attorney. Marshall was spending his three years with Johnson, one of LDF's national network of "cooperating attorneys," who represented Florida's NAACP chapter.

Today a solo practitioner in Jacksonville specializing in personal injury cases, Marshall has the sort of languid, sonorous voice, wide smile, and easy laugh that convey calm; but back in the 1960s, he handled cases that were anything but. Throughout Florida's Klan country, he represented indigent black defendants facing lengthy sentences for trumped-up "crimes" like spitting on the sidewalk.

Despite his professional focus on dismantling the Jim Crow regime and despite Ida Phillips's being white, Marshall felt a personal affinity for her story. Like Phillips, Marshall's mother had little formal education, having left school in the fourth grade. A single mother of four, she moved to New York City to try to make a better living when Marshall was still in elementary school. He and his two older brothers stayed in Fort Lauderdale with his grandparents, farmers who grew beans and eggplants. (His older sister was already away at college.) When Marshall contracted polio in the ninth grade, his mother, worried about the substandard medical care available to a black child in 1950s Florida, sent for him. Marshall and his brothers took a Greyhound bus to join her in the Bronx. In the years to come, he grew up watching his mother make ends meet alone while also managing to shepherd three of her four children to college graduation.

Marshall was intrigued by Phillips's case. Pulling out a statute book, he reread Title VII, which had gone into effect the prior year, and registered for the first time that on the list of protected characteristics was "sex." ("Sure enough," he later recalled, "I looked and said, yeah, there it is.") Martin Marietta's policy, it seemed to Marshall, presented a pretty straightforward case of sex discrimination: The company barred women with young children from working there, but not men in the same situation. If that wasn't discrimination "because of sex," what was? And Marshall liked Phillips. Her outrage at Martin Marietta, at its bald-faced denigration of working mothers, was contagious. "It wasn't just about her; it was about all the other women who were in her position who were thrown aside just because they had children," he explained. Marshall decided he was in. "Let's test the waters," he said.

As Marshall contemplated taking on a behemoth like Martin Marietta, including what would undoubtedly be an army of well-financed defense attorneys—he predicted he was "going to get the kitchen sink thrown" at him—he knew he could use some help. Marshall contacted LDF and a few other big names in the civil rights legal world. To his surprise, though, he couldn't get anyone interested in Phillips's case. At the time, there were few groups to call on devoted specifically to women's rights. The National Organization for Women had been founded just one year earlier, and as *New York Times* columnist Gail Collins would later report, making contact with its leadership was a "little like trying to find the early Christians."[18] Other now-illustrious national women's advocacy organizations—the American Civil Liberties Union's Women's Rights Project, for example, or the National Women's Law Center—simply didn't exist yet.

Nevertheless, convinced that Title VII had been violated and heartened by the EEOC's endorsement, Marshall plowed ahead alone. (His only hope for eventually getting paid rested with Title VII's requirement that if a plaintiff wins, the defendant has to cover her attorney's fees.) On December 12, 1967, he filed a complaint in the U.S. District Court for the Middle District of Florida, seeking an order finding the company in violation of Title VII, directing it to hire Phillips, and requiring it to pay her back wages. The case was assigned to Judge George Young, a recent appointee. Within weeks, it was clear how Phillips's claim was going to fare: In an unusual move, without any prompting from Martin Marietta, Young issued an order that eviscerated Phillips's claim. Declaring that discrimination against women with young children did not qualify as discrimination "because of sex," he deleted that part of Phillips's complaint. Instead, Young ruled, her complaint would proceed as if Phillips had alleged that the company's policy was not to hire any women at all.

That was a case that couldn't be made; Martin Marietta submitted ample evidence to Young that the vast majority of people hired as assembly trainees were women. A few months later, citing that evidence, Young found no evidence of sex discrimination and granted judgment to the company.[19] Although Martin Marietta hadn't denied that it hired men with preschool-age children, Young declared that fact irrelevant. "The responsibilities of men and women with small children are not the same," he opined, and "employers are entitled to recognize these different responsibilities in establishing hiring policies."[20]

To Reese Marshall, Young's dismissive treatment of Phillips's claim—"quick, fast, and in a hurry," as he ruefully described it—was simply "devastating." Yet he was steadfast in his belief that the case had "a good, right feel to it." Unquestionably, there was little legal authority for Marshall to cite; Title VII was so new that the Supreme Court had never had to consider what discrimination "because of sex" meant. Indeed, no other court had ever decided a case like Phillips's. The fact was that Martin Marietta's policy, not to mention Judge Young's rationale for endorsing it, was rooted in the stereotypical notion that women necessarily cared more about motherhood than about their jobs—exactly the kind of bias Title VII was surely meant to outlaw. Marshall resolved to appeal.

"I just felt like we would get a better ear in the appellate court," Marshall said. "Someone is going to see this and understand what we're talking about." Given that it was the Fifth Circuit that would be hearing the case, there was reason to be hopeful; although since that time it has come to be considered one of the most conservative courts in the country, in the late 1960s, the Fifth Circuit was one of the most liberal. Nicknamed the Supreme Court of Dixie,[21] owing to its jurisdiction over a wide swath of former Confederate states—Alabama, Florida, Georgia, Louisiana, Mississippi, and Texas—it had gained notoriety in the years following *Brown v. Board of Education* as fertile ground for civil rights litigators attacking Jim Crow.

Before filing Phillips's appeal, Marshall tried once more to interest national civil rights groups in the case, only to be rebuffed again; whatever doubts they might have had about using Phillips's claim to test the "because of sex" provision almost certainly had been confirmed by Judge Young's swift dismissal. So Marshall moved forward as the lone counsel. He did manage to secure the endorsement of the EEOC, which filed a brief as an *amicus,* or friend of the court. (Such submissions from outside interest groups help educate the court about the larger issues raised by the litigation and explain its potential wider impact on people beyond the individual parties involved in the case.)

In addition to having found in Phillips's favor, the EEOC had a larger agenda to promote. In 1965, the year Title VII went into effect, the agency had issued "Guidelines on Discrimination Because of Sex." Though lacking the force of law, the Guidelines informed employers, and judges, of the government's view of what Title VII's "sex" provision meant. One of the Guidelines' directives was that employers not refuse to hire a woman "based on assumptions of the comparative employment characteristics of women in general," such as "the assumption that the turnover rate among women is higher than among men."[22] Another provision stated that employers couldn't base their hiring decisions on "stereotyped characterizations of the sexes," including "that men are less capable of assembling intricate equipment; that women are less capable of aggressive salesmanship."[23]

Most pertinent, perhaps, was the Guidelines' provision about a different subset of women—those wearing wedding rings. "It does not seem to us relevant that [a] rule is not directed against all females, but only against married females," the Guidelines explained. "[S]o long as sex is a factor in the application of the rule, such application involves a discrimination based on sex."[24]

ALTHOUGH TWO YEARS had passed since Ida Phillips first applied to Martin Marietta, not much had changed in her life. Case documents filed with the Fifth Circuit include an affidavit attesting to a hardscrabble existence: Phillips was waiting tables at a restaurant called the Derby House, making $120 a month—roughly what she would have made in just one week at Martin Marietta. Phillips's kids helped their mom make ends meet by pitching in at the restaurant after school; Al, then thirteen, helped fill water glasses and wash dishes, as sisters Peggy and Vera had when they were his age, before they graduated to waiting tables. Brother Ronnie became a cook. In her affidavit, Phillips stated she had no savings or checking account.

It was a life very similar to what she'd experienced growing up during the Depression in rural South Carolina. Born Ida Watford, she was a sharecropper's daughter and one of eight children, with a few more who had died at birth or soon after. At fifteen, she met Fred McAlister, a long-distance truck driver and sometime mechanic; they wed after Ida learned she was pregnant. Although that baby died, by the time she was twenty-five, she had had six other children. The family had gone where McAlister found work, first in Bowie, Maryland, and Washington, DC, finally landing in Orlando in 1960.

During her years as Mrs. McAlister, Phillips had always helped to supplement her husband's income. When the kids were little, she sold Avon, Tupperware, and Sarah Coventry jewelry out of their home, and when they were older, she waited tables. In Florida, she worked for the first time in a factory, sorting citrus fruits into crates. Recalling their mother's speedy hands as the fruit came down the conveyor belt, her pay dependent on how many boxes she filled, her kids Peggy, Vera, and Al laughed at the similarity to the famous Lucille Ball candy factory sketch, right down to their mother's auburn hair. Coloring it had been one of their mother's few indulgences, if only out of a drugstore bottle.

The marriage was troubled, though; Fred McAlister had a drinking problem. He and Ida divorced, and she drifted into a relationship with a mechanic named Tom Phillips. It was with him that Phillips had her seventh child—Gracie, named after Ida's mother. Gracie was the one who was preschool age by the time Phillips tried to submit her application to Martin Marietta. Tom Phillips was decent at the beginning, but soon his true colors began to show. He beat Ida and the kids; Al was the only one who could talk him out of his rages. Ida Phillips was trapped in the marriage, terrorized and virtually penniless. To observers like Reese Marshall, Tom Phillips appeared to support Ida's lawsuit against Martin Marietta, but her kids always believed he was in it only because he thought it might yield a big payday. Not until the mid-1970s, when Tom was sent to prison for murdering a friend, would the family be free of him.

FROM THE BEGINNING of his oral argument before the Fifth Circuit, it was clear to Marshall that all three of the judges on the panel agreed with Judge Young. When they issued their written opinion in May 1969, then, it came as no surprise. They found that Martin Marietta hadn't discriminated "because of sex" because the company didn't exclude *all* women, just *some* women:

> Ida Phillips was not refused employment because she was a woman nor because she had pre-school age children. It is the coalescence of these two elements that denied her the position she desired.[25]

The court went on to specifically reject the EEOC's urged interpretation of Title VII. That interpretation, said the court, required believing that Congress had the "intent to exclude absolutely any consideration of the differences between the normal relationships of working fathers and working mothers to their pre-school age children, and to require that an employer treat the two exactly alike in the administration of its general hiring policies." Nonsense, the court concluded. "The common experience of Congressmen is surely not so far removed from that of mankind in general as to warrant our attributing to them such an irrational purpose in the formulation of this statute."[26]

Marshall and Phillips were still licking their wounds from the Fifth Circuit's resounding rejection when a curious letter arrived from the court's clerk. "Pending further order of the Court," it read, "the mandate heretofore issued is being recalled."[27] One of the other eleven judges on the court, Marshall learned, had proposed rehearing the case—but this time before all of them, not just a three-judge panel. Referred to as *en banc* review, such a procedure is reserved for those occasions where judges within the same court object to the outcome reached by their colleagues in a certain case. This was the first indication that Marshall's legal arguments weren't falling on deaf ears, and he was "elated." "That's what we were looking for," he said.

"Somebody who would look at this thing and understand where we were and what we were trying to say."

Three months later, though, he and Phillips got more bad news. Without any explanation, a majority of the court had decided against rehearing the case.[28] But included with this new denial by the Fifth Circuit, there was an impassioned dissent. Authored by Chief Judge John Brown—known for his progressive rulings throughout the civil rights maelstrom of the prior two decades—it was signed as well by two of his colleagues. "The case is simple. A woman with pre-school children may not be employed," but "a man with pre-school children may," Brown wrote. "The question then arises: Is this sex-related? To the simple query the answer is just as simple: Nobody—and this includes Judges, Solomonic or life tenured—has yet seen a male mother."[29]

Judge Brown sardonically dubbed the court's interpretation of Title VII the "sex plus" test: All an employer had to do was use sex "plus" another characteristic as its screening mechanism, and it could get a free pass to discriminate. As the judge explained, "sex plus" would cause the statute's death by a thousand cuts, freeing employers to disqualify ever-wider groups of women workers simply by including a "plus" characteristic in their policies that they didn't also apply to men—barring women who were below a certain weight, for instance, or whose biceps were too small.[30] He made a grave prediction: "If 'sex plus' stands, the Act is dead."[31]

IN THE FALL of 1969, a young African American lawyer at the NAACP Legal Defense and Educational Fund named Bill Robinson walked down the hall to see his boss, LDF's director-counsel, Jack Greenberg, to discuss whether they should take Ida Phillips's case to the Supreme Court. Former LDF intern Reese Marshall had called with news of the Fifth Circuit's ruling and Judge Brown's dissent. Tall and lanky, Robinson was just five years out of Columbia Law School, but he already headed LDF's burgeoning Title VII litigation team.

Using strategically selected race discrimination lawsuits around the country, LDF attorneys sought to use the new federal law to dismantle the machinery of segregation that kept African Americans out of high-paying manufacturing jobs. Based on information gathered with the help of civil rights field organizers, they had identified three main targets: rules for job applicants, such as aptitude tests or high school diploma requirements, that operated to keep blacks out (due to the poor education available to them in many parts of the country); seniority rules that assured they were the first fired in the event of a layoff (because white workers had been on the job longer); and openly biased practices by labor unions, including the refusal to refer them for work (assuming the union allowed blacks to join in the first place).

Sex discrimination cases had not been part of that strategy. But three years after Marshall had first tried to enlist support in litigating Phillips's case, he finally succeeded. The blistering dissent from Judge Brown, lending urgency to the wide range of issues at stake, could not have hurt. It was clear to both Greenberg and Robinson, in any event, that the case fit within LDF's mission. For one thing, statistics showed that working mothers, whether married or single, were more likely to be African American; as a matter of sheer demographics, then, the "sex plus" rule would inevitably affect black women disproportionately. Moreover, Greenberg and Robinson saw the Fifth Circuit's "sex plus" rationale as dangerous precedent. For it could just as easily be refashioned as "race plus"—not to mention "national origin plus" or "religion plus"—and used to exclude whole categories of workers, male *and* female.

Robinson called Reese Marshall and gave him the green light. Marshall, glad to have some good news to share with Ida Phillips, assured her that the LDF lawyers were "top notch" and would keep them both in the communication loop, rather than just taking over. "I think we're going to be all right," he told his client.

THE SUPREME COURT, unlike the federal appellate courts, doesn't accept appeals from just anyone who wants a hearing. The Court rejects the vast majority of requests—petitions for *certiorari*, or *cert* petitions for short—it receives every year. As Anthony Lewis put it in *Gideon's Trumpet,* his legendary account of the Court's 1963 *Gideon v. Wainwright*[32] decision establishing criminal defendants' right to counsel, "[O]ne of the most important duties of the Supreme Court has been to decide whether it will decide."[33] In the 1970s, an average of 4,000 petitions were submitted, and the Court granted just 4 percent of them.[34] (By 2004, the number of petitions had nearly doubled, to roughly 7,500, but the acceptance rate had decreased to just 1 percent.[35]) Although there are no hard-and-fast rules decreeing what cases the Court will and won't take, history has provided a few indicators: for instance, when it is necessary to settle a split in opinion among the federal courts of appeals, so as to assure uniform application of the law; or when the disputed legal issue is of such great importance—and the decision being appealed so grossly wrong—that it may be imperative the justices step in to make a correction. At least four of the nine justices must vote in favor of review for the writ of *certiorari* to be granted.

Given that Title VII was only four years old when the *Phillips* case came to the Supreme Court's attention and there were few cases interpreting its ban on sex discrimination, Robinson and his CDF team focused on trying to convince the justices that the Fifth Circuit had made a grave error. The law had barely been given a chance to work, for women or for anyone else, they argued, before being sharply and unfairly curtailed. Crafting the *cert* petition to magnify the issues at stake, the lawyers sought to convince the Court that the case was far bigger than just Ida Phillips or Martin Marietta.

To this end, they focused on two key arguments. The first was that "sex plus" was a flat misreading of Title VII. Refusing to hire subsets of women *was* discrimination "because of sex." Citing the EEOC Guidelines and the few lower court decisions interpreting the statute, LDF explained that "Title VII prohibits double standards, i.e., any practice which unequally restricts the job opportunities of women or imposes a burden on women not equally imposed on men."[36]

Here LDF had to be pragmatic, tackling head on the attitude expressed by Judge Young—and endorsed by the Fifth Circuit, and possibly by many Supreme Court justices too—that "the responsibilities of men and women with small children are not the same, and employers are entitled to recognize these different responsibilities."[37] It was a historical reality that women usually *had* been the primary caregivers in most American families. And it was a present-day reality that, even though more women now worked outside the home, mothers *still* shouldered more of the child care responsibilities. Undoubtedly, for some mothers, child rearing did get in the way of doing their job.

What Martin Marietta's policy did, though, was use these generalizations to assign certain traits—unreliability, lack of commitment— to *all* mothers. It took the stereotype that mothers cared more for their children than their jobs, and incorporated it into formal hiring criteria. LDF's challenge was to alert the Court that reliance on assumed group characteristics would "deal a serious blow to the objectives of Title VII." The law was supposed to treat applicants as individuals, not members of a group, the LDF team contended, giving them all an equal chance to get in the door. The *cert* petition explained:

> While it may be argued that because a woman might have special
> responsibilities toward her children she may be treated differently in
> hiring, this fails to take account of the situation where peculiar re-
> sponsibilities do not in fact affect job performance. . . . The Martin
> rule makes no attempt to assess family responsibility in any objec-
> tive way. The use of such stereotypes is, we submit, the essence of
> unlawful discrimination prohibited by Title VII.[38]

LDF reminded the Court that if an employer believed women were
incapable of doing a particular job, Title VII included a loophole.
Where an employer could show that it was "reasonably necessary to
the normal operation" of its business that a job be performed by one
sex, then sex would be deemed a bona fide occupational qualification, or BFOQ, for that job. LDF told the Court the BFOQ exception
arguably could be a way out for Martin Marietta, but only if it could
show that "mothers of pre-school children are poor performers on
the job."[39]

LDF also used statistical evidence to remind the Court that mothers weren't just working for "pin money." Their earnings were increas-
ingly critical to the survival of American families. There were 3.6
million mothers in the workforce who had at least one child under
age six. African American women were overrepresented in this group:
Among married women with small children, black women were nearly
twice as likely as white women to work.[40] Studies also showed that
mothers with small children were more likely to work because of economic need, either because they were the sole breadwinners or because
their husbands made too little for the family to survive.[41] The message was clear: If the Fifth Circuit's ruling was affirmed, millions of
women—and millions more children—could face crippling economic
consequences.

Finally, LDF also hoped to alarm the Court that discrimination
because of "sex plus" wasn't just a disaster for women. It led with
Judge Brown's warning that "[i]f 'sex plus' stands, the Act is dead."
Specifically, "race plus" couldn't be far behind. "[T]he sex plus rule
in this case sows the seeds for future discrimination against black
workers through making them meet extra standards not imposed on
whites."[42]

On March 2, 1970, Robinson got the call from the Court. The
justices had agreed to hear the case, and oral argument was scheduled
for December. It would be the first time the Court had ever considered the meaning of Title VII's "because of sex" provision. In fact, it

would be the first time the Court had considered the meaning of Title VII, period. Robinson made the trip down the hall to Director-Counsel Greenberg's office to tell him, naturally assuming that Greenberg would be the one presenting *Phillips* to the justices. Robinson had appeared before appellate courts but never the Supreme Court, whereas Greenberg was by now a Court veteran. And as the first Title VII case ever to reach the Court, *Phillips* was monumentally important. So Robinson was startled when Greenberg told him to get ready. He'd be the one arguing the case.

REESE MARSHALL remembered giving the news to Ida Phillips over the phone. They "hollered, screamed, and yelled" with joy. It was just the tonic needed to raise Phillips's flagging spirits. She was still waiting tables, earning a fraction of what she would have made on the assembly line, and still struggling every day to keep her head above water at home. She wanted to make a difference not only for her family but also for other women[43] and, so far, all she had to show for it was a lot of male judges telling her that Martin Marietta's policy was perfectly legal. But the experience had ignited a bit of an activist spirit in her. She'd recently joined the local chapter of the National Organization for Women and even dragged her eldest daughter, Peggy, to a women's rights rally in downtown Jacksonville. Not that she "[went] in for burning of bras and other silly things," she later told a reporter. To her, she said, "Women's Liberation means equal job opportunities."[44]

Whatever trouble Marshall had had garnering national interest in the case ended when the Court agreed to decide it. "High Court to Hear Sex Discrimination Test" read the headline in *The New York Times,* while Martha Griffiths, the Michigan congresswoman who had taken the lead in ensuring the "sex" provision was included in Title VII, was quoted registering her outrage about the case. "I'm going to move to impeach the entire court" if it affirms the Fifth Circuit, she proclaimed, "because they are obviously not enforcing the laws as they are written."[45]

Amicus briefs also started rolling in now. The U.S. solicitor general, the lawyer who represents the United States in legal matters, stepped forward to provide the federal government's support, as did the EEOC, while NOW—by then four years into its existence—and the American Civil Liberties Union and Human Rights for Women each filed a brief.

Those submissions sought to build on the *cert* petition, specifically by bringing the justices up to speed about the realities of the modern family. The stereotype of a two-parent household, in which the husband earned enough so that the wife could stay home with the kids, was simply a thing of the past. As of 1969, only about half of American families fit that mold, according to Department of Labor figures.[46] The reality was that nearly 40 percent of the nation's families were dependent on women's wages; in 30 percent of those families, both spouses worked, while in nearly 8 percent of them, a woman was the sole breadwinner.[47] Notably, 35 percent of those female-headed households were below the poverty line, and in African American families, women's wages were more important yet.[48] Indeed, the stereotype of a stay-at-home mother never had applied with equal force to black women.[49]

The *amicus* briefs also spelled out the sheer numbers of women who would face job loss were the Court to approve the "sex plus" doctrine and allow other employers around the country to follow suit. Of the 37 percent of women in the American workforce, a little more than a third were mothers of children age eighteen or under.[50] Of those more than ten million women, four million had children who were preschool age.[51] If additional "plus" factors were permitted by the Court, the numbers skyrocketed. As the ACLU pointed out, policies excluding various "plus" categories of women could be catastrophic. Excluding women whose "plus" factor was being married, for instance, would knock 17.5 million married women out of their jobs; sex "plus" being divorced would bar 1.6 million women from the workplace; sex "plus" being widowed would mean 2.6 million additional women were excluded.[52]

Nor was the ban on married women strictly hypothetical, as detailed in an *amicus* brief submitted by the Air Line Stewards and Stewardesses Association. The ALSSA was the labor union representing the flight attendants for seven of the nation's major airlines, totaling thirteen thousand people—twelve thousand of them women. Flight attendants had a great deal on the line in *Phillips*. After Title VII was enacted, female flight attendants were among the first to utilize the ban on sex discrimination, challenging the panoply of regulations from which their male colleagues were exempt: maximum weight restrictions, age limits (mandating retirement no later than age thirty-five), rules forbidding pregnancy, and marriage bans—all of them policies designed to reinforce flight attendants' image as sexually available eye candy for their (mostly male) passengers as they lit cigars, mixed Manhattans, and fluffed pillows.

As Gail Collins recounted in *When Everything Changed*, the average tenure of a flight attendant in the 1960s was just eighteen months, thanks to rules requiring women to quit if they got married.[53] Some airlines even used this turnover as a marketing ploy. An American Airlines ad from 1965 featured the caption, "People keep stealing our stewardesses," underneath a cartoon of a man furtively absconding with a flight attendant, mannequin stiff, his hand clamped over her mouth. "Within 2 years, most of our stewardesses will leave us for other men. This isn't surprising. A girl who can smile for 5½ hours is hard to find. Not to mention a wife who can remember what 124 people want for dinner. (And tell you all about meteorology and jets, if that's what you're looking for in a woman.)"[54] The ALSSA told the Court that an opinion upholding "sex plus" would be disastrous for its membership. It detailed all of the age, pregnancy, and marriage policies that the major airlines had rescinded after Title VII's enactment and warned that a ruling in Martin Marietta's favor could undo such progress.[55]

It was "like manna," said Reese Marshall, to have so many people weighing in on Phillips's side before the Court. "We were just so amazed that we had all of these great and wonderful people stepping in to help."

A SUPREME COURT oral argument is not a trial; there are no testifying witnesses, and only each party's lawyer, allotted just thirty minutes to cover all of the pertinent points, speaks to the nine justices. Nor is oral argument simply a matter of delivering a prepared speech. An attorney is lucky to get out a few opening remarks before the justices begin firing questions, teasing out the underpinnings of his or her argument, challenging those they find unpersuasive, and posing hypothetical scenarios to test the parameters of the urged legal principles. And all the while, the clock is running.

Whether oral argument affects the outcome of a Supreme Court case is a matter of much debate, with many advocates believing that it has little effect. But recent research has suggested that a high-quality argument *can* make a difference, even where the position advocated is contrary to a particular justice's ideological leanings. The justices themselves have also spoken of how oral argument may affect their view of a case. "[I]f an oral advocate is effective," Chief Justice William Rehnquist explained, "how he presents his position during oral arguments *will* have something to do with how the case comes out."

According to Justice William Brennan, "I have had too many occasions when my judgment of a decision has turned on what happened in oral argument," while Justice Harry Blackmun has said, "A good oralist can add a lot to a case and help us in our later analysis of what the case is all about. Many times confusion [in the brief] is clarified by what the lawyers have to say."[56]

A common component of an attorney's preparation for oral argument is the "moot court," a high-stakes dress rehearsal with various players—lawyers, professors, and other experts—acting the roles of the justices. The aim is to so thoroughly vet every angle of a case that a question never arises during the actual argument that the attorney has never heard before. For his first Supreme Court argument, Robinson underwent no fewer than three moot courts: one with his colleagues on LDF's Title VII team, one with Columbia Law students enrolled in a class Jack Greenberg was teaching, and a third composed of various attorneys drawn from outside LDF. It was a busy time at LDF; soon after the *cert* petition in *Phillips* was granted, the Court accepted another of the group's Title VII cases. That one, *Griggs v. Duke Power Company,* fit more squarely within LDF's core litigation strategy, challenging a utility company's requirements that applicants have a high school diploma and achieve a passing score on a general aptitude test.[57] The argument in *Griggs* was scheduled for just five days after *Phillips,* and Director-Counsel Greenberg would be arguing it.

On the morning of the December 9, 1970 argument in *Phillips,* Bill Robinson's wife was back in New York, due to give birth at any moment to their first child. But Robinson felt focused and ready. Reese Marshall and his wife were there, as were Ida and Tom Phillips, who had driven up from Florida.[58] They had brought with them Ida's daughter Vera and their daughter Gracie, though the girls stayed at Ida's sister's house during the argument itself. Marshall's law partner, Earl Johnson, rounded out the Florida contingent in the gallery. Ida Phillips's children recalled that she was "in awe" of being at the Supreme Court to hear *her* case argued. (She had been disappointed, though, to learn that she would only be allowed to observe. She had hoped for the opportunity to address the justices personally.) Phillips later told a reporter that she also got the added thrill of being treated as something of a celebrity before the argument: "There I was sitting in the courtroom and a teacher from Georgetown University was telling her class about sex discrimination and wondered whether Ida Phillips was in the courtroom," she remembered. "Can you imagine how I felt telling her I was Ida Phillips?"[59]

The nine justices filed in, with Chief Justice Warren Burger taking his place at the center of the bench, followed by the associate justices, who took their places on either side according to seniority. The most senior of them, Hugo Black, sat to Burger's immediate right, and William O. Douglas to Burger's immediate left. The remaining justices fanned down each side of the bench: To Black's right were Justices John Harlan, Potter Stewart, and Thurgood Marshall, and to Douglas's left were Justices William Brennan, Byron White, and the newest appointee, Harry Blackmun. Not for another decade would a woman be seated among them.

As the lawyer representing the party who had asked the Court to hear the case, Bill Robinson stepped to the lectern first. There were two lights perched on top: A white light would warn Robinson when he had only five minutes left in his thirty-minute argument; a red light would signal when time was up altogether.

"Mr. Chief Justice, and may it please the Court," began Robinson, speaking calmly and deliberately, betraying none of the nervousness one would expect of someone who was not only making his first Court appearance but also awaiting his baby's birth. After recounting the case's background—Phillips's original attempt to apply, Martin Marietta's rejection, and then the various lower court proceedings—Robinson moved into his three main reasons for reversing the Fifth Circuit. He was able to list them without interruption. First, the Fifth Circuit's ruling conflicted with the "basic purpose of Title VII," because it relied on a sex stereotype—"that the father goes out and works, the mother stays home and takes care of the children"—as a reason for not hiring women. Second, it contradicted Title VII's "plain language" forbidding discrimination "because of sex." Robinson cited the statistic included in LDF's *cert* petition (and again in its main brief submitted before the argument) that approximately four million mothers of small children would be left without job protection if "sex plus" were approved—and then noted the myriad "plus" factors that could be added to sex to further chip away at Title VII's protections. Such loopholes could not have been what Congress envisioned when enacting the "because of sex" provision, Robinson explained; indeed, during Senate debate on the statute, a proposal to amend the provision to read "*solely* because of sex" had been rejected.[60]

And last, argued Robinson, "sex plus" would erode Title VII beyond recognition. "[I]f the Act permits discrimination on the basis of sex-plus, it would also seem to permit discrimination on the basis of race plus, religion plus, or nationality plus."[61] Here Robinson used examples that, he later explained, were intentionally "ridiculous," so blatantly racist that no one would argue they comported with Title VII: "For example, an employer could then refuse to hire Negroes with chunky hair, or on the other hand Negroes with straight hair."[62] In this way, Robinson hoped to get past whatever hint of reasonableness the Court might see in Martin Marietta's policy and expose "sex plus" for what it was: an end run around federal antidiscrimination protections.

Although the justices didn't express outright hostility to Robinson's argument, there was a skeptical, even bemused tenor to several of their questions about the scope of Title VII's sex provision. For one thing, the notion that Title VII had done away with distinctions between "men's jobs" and "women's jobs" seemed to confound some of the justices. "Does the law require that the employer give the woman a job of digging ditches and things of that kind?" Justice Hugo Black asked Robinson, while Justice Harry Blackmun suggested that Robinson "educate me": "[S]uppose a hospital for years had employed nothing but female registered nurses. And then today after the passage of this Act, a male nurse applicant comes along. Do I understand your interpretation of the Act to be that just because they have always had female RNs and like them and got along well, they could not refuse to hire the male nurse, in the absence of [satisfying the BFOQ exception] in the statute?" Robinson told Blackmun that was correct. Chief Justice Burger piped up. "The same would be true with private secretaries who by and large, 99 percent plus are women?" Correct, answered Robinson.[63]

Burger appeared especially uneasy with Title VII's sex provision. Early in Robinson's argument, the chief justice interrupted to ask whether "if a federal judge as a matter of general policy would decline to hire a law clerk who had an infant child, a lady law clerk, but was willing to hire a man whose wife had infant children, they would be in violation of the statute, if the statute applied to them?" After Robinson explained that Title VII did not cover the federal courts (a gap that would be closed two years later, when government employers were added to the law), Burger got a laugh from the gallery with his relieved response: "I am sure, it doesn't apply to federal judges."[64] Then, after noting that Title VII's prohibition on sex discrimination "was added to the Bill at a later stage," Burger pressed Robinson to explain exactly how long had elapsed between the sex amendment and the vote approving the statute. But Robinson wouldn't bite; the question could only have been intended to suggest that the antidiscrimination protections for sex somehow applied with less force than those to do with race, national origin, or religion. "I think in interpreting the statute as lawyers and judges, we should interpret the sex provisions just as we do the others irrespective of when it was added," he said.[65] Burger didn't pursue the matter.

When Robinson sat down, a federal marshal handed him a note telling him to see the clerk after the argument. He knew what that meant; his wife had gone into labor. But he couldn't leave just yet. LDF had agreed to cede a few minutes of Robinson's allotted argument time to Lawrence Wallace, the U.S. solicitor general, after which Martin Marietta's attorney would argue for thirty minutes, in turn followed by two minutes of rebuttal by Robinson.

Rising to speak as the federal government's representative, Wallace echoed Robinson's characterization of "sex plus" as a fundamental misreading of the law. Just as a state regulation prohibiting women with preschool-age children from voting would violate the Nineteenth Amendment, so did Martin Marietta's rule violate Title VII. "You don't have to exclude all women in order to be discriminating against women," Wallace explained.[66]

Justice Black had a question about the contours of the BFOQ. Could an airline "decide that they only wanted to have the job position of stewardesses, that they didn't want to have a job, position of steward" because "customers like women better in that place, younger women obviously"?[67] Wallace answered that while the EEOC had formally disapproved of such rules, there still had not been a court decision on the issue.

Then other justices began asking about the kind of evidence that would satisfy the BFOQ exception in this case. Evidence that mothers were interrupting their work on the assembly line to make phone calls? Evidence of higher rates of absenteeism? Higher rates of accidents? Wallace strenuously argued that there would have to be a very strong group-related correlation between these kinds of performance problems and motherhood to justify a BFOQ. If a mother makes too many calls at work, misses too many days, or has too many accidents due to carelessness, she should be disciplined in the manner that a man would be; her failures, said Wallace, should be hers alone, and not imputed to *all* mothers as justification for a blanket ban on hiring them.[68]

Next up was Martin Marietta's attorney, Don Senterfitt. A former banker, Senterfitt was a partner in one of Florida's largest firms. Although the firm's client roster was overwhelmingly corporate, it also sometimes worked for the other end of the ideological spectrum. During the 1960s, for instance, the ACLU—aligned with Ida Phillips in this case—had been a client. Indeed, there were hints that Senterfitt might have been uncomfortable with Martin Marietta's stance in *Phillips*, too. Shortly before the oral argument, he had called Robinson to tell him he was going to be in New York and invited him to lunch. They met at the Four Seasons. The closest Senterfitt ever came to talking business was when he volunteered that on the first day Phillips had come to the Martin Marietta plant, company personnel had been overwhelmed by the number of applicants who had seen the newspaper ad. Hundreds of people had shown up. And so, in an ad hoc measure to make the process more manageable, Senterfitt explained, staff had come up with a number of eligibility criteria that would help thin the ranks—and not accepting applications from women with small children was one of them. Although Senterfitt never suggested Martin Marietta's willingness to give up the legal fight and settle, Robinson surmised that Senterfitt hoped somehow to temper the message that the "fire-breathing liberals" of LDF planned to present to the Court. Robinson recalled with a laugh that although he'd enjoyed his first lunch in a five-star restaurant, Senterfitt's pitch otherwise missed the mark.

Addressing the Court, Senterfitt tried a variation of his lunchtime message. The company didn't deny that its receptionist may have told Phillips that women with young children couldn't apply, but the company itself actually didn't have any such policy. In fact, Senterfitt went on, Martin Marietta didn't even agree with the Fifth Circuit's "sex plus" rationale. He argued, however, that the lower courts' rulings should stand because there wasn't sufficient evidence to determine why Ida Phillips herself was or wasn't denied a job. Judge Young had thrown the case out before that could be established.

But if the company *did* have a policy, the justices pressed him, it would be illegal, wouldn't it? Senterfitt resisted such absolutes. The most he would concede was that, should the Court decide that Phillips deserved the chance to prove she had been denied a job because she had a preschool-age child, then the company likewise should get the chance to advance the BFOQ defense. It was a strange argument: Martin Marietta did not ban mothers of small children, but if it had, it would have been legally justified in doing so.

Toward the end of Senterfitt's argument, Chief Justice Burger again took the opportunity to state his beliefs about women's inherent skill sets. When Senterfitt explained that the Martin Marietta assembly trainee job was not "heavy work" but rather "intricate work" involving "small electronic components," Burger stated matter-of-factly his assumption that that was precisely why women composed the bulk of the company's workforce. "[W]omen are manually much more adept than men and they do this work better," he said, adding, "Just the same reason that most men hire women as their secretaries, because they are better at it than men." Senterfitt responded, with evident relief that elicited laughter from the gallery, "I am so pleased. I couldn't say that because it appears to fall into this stereotype—preconception that the [EEOC] sees."[69]

That the chief justice of the Supreme Court felt comfortable opining on women's predisposition for secretarial work was dispiriting to observers from the women's rights community. As Bernice Sandler of the Women's Action League later described the argument to longtime women's activist (and coauthor of the ACLU's friend of the court brief in *Phillips*), Pauli Murray, "We have a long way to go."[70] It certainly would not have been considered funny if Burger had opined in open court about the inherent abilities of black versus white workers.

When Robinson returned to the lectern for his quick rebuttal, he urged the Court to take Martin Marietta's assurances with a grain of salt. After all, the EEOC had tried to broker a settlement between it and Phillips four years earlier, and the company had refused. If Ida Phillips had been turned away simply because a receptionist was misinformed about the company's policy, why hadn't the company agreed to hire Phillips once it knew about her claim—or, at the very least, allowed her to submit an application? Why had the company, instead, fought for its right to reject her all the way to the Supreme Court?[71]

When Robinson finished, he grabbed his belongings and headed to the clerk's office. His wife *was* in labor, he learned, but he couldn't get through to the hospital for any more news. With assurances from Jack Greenberg's wife that she would retrieve his luggage from their hotel, he caught a cab to the airport and boarded the next shuttle to New York. His daughter had been born hours earlier, he was told when he reached Mt. Sinai Hospital. According to the birth certificate, she had arrived precisely one minute before the start of the oral argument.

Back in Washington, all the other members of Phillips's legal team believed the argument had gone well. Robinson had managed to make his salient arguments without much interruption. Senterfitt must have read the justices the same way. When Reese Marshall made a quick trip to the courthouse men's room, he was startled when Senterfitt and his colleague William Akerman followed him in. Having apparently lost their appetite for waiting to see how the justices would rule, they wanted to talk settlement. "I told them I thought the bathroom was probably not a good place" to discuss it, recalled Marshall. He quickly excused himself and went to tell Ida Phillips about the overture. She wasn't interested. By then, said Reese Marshall, "she felt that [the] decision was more important than the money."[72]

ON JANUARY 25, 1971, Bill Robinson was home sick with the flu when the office telephoned: The *Phillips* ruling was in. In an opinion just a few paragraphs long, the Court had sided with Ida Phillips. Title VII "requires that persons of like qualifications be given employment opportunities irrespective of their sex," it wrote.[73] "The Court of Appeals therefore erred in reading this section as permitting one hiring policy for women and another for men—each having pre-school-age children." In other words, a policy that disadvantaged only women— even if not *all* women were harmed—was sex discrimination. "Sex plus" violated Title VII.

Reese Marshall, who by then had started working in Jacksonville's public defender's office, got a call from his former law partner, Earl Johnson, and then phoned Ida Phillips to tell her the news. After some celebratory whoops, Phillips began to cry. According to Marshall, it was especially sweet for both of them that the ruling had been unanimous.

Just one aspect of the Court's decision betrayed the ambivalence the justices had displayed during oral argument. The Court wasn't ready to say that Martin Marietta, or employers generally, could *never* take mothers' child care obligations into account. Companies would only have to produce evidence sufficient to satisfy the BFOQ loophole to Title VII—which in this case would mean showing that excluding mothers of young children was "reasonably necessary to the normal operation of that particular business or enterprise."[74] "The existence of such conflicting family obligations, if demonstrably more relevant to job performance for a woman than for a man," said the Court, "could arguably be a basis for distinction" under the BFOQ rule. The case would be sent back to Judge Young for a trial, so that Martin Marietta would be allowed to try to make that "demonstration."[75]

Justice Thurgood Marshall joined the Court's ruling but wrote a separate opinion that chastised the majority for even suggesting that a policy like Martin Marietta's might qualify for the BFOQ exception. The policy was based on "ancient canards about the proper role of women," and allowing the BFOQ to sanction such stereotypes was an invitation to employers to keep treating women as mothers first and workers second.[76] Citing comments during Congress's consideration of the provision and the EEOC Guidelines, Marshall argued that the BFOQ should be invoked only sparingly, limited to those "job situations that require specific physical characteristics necessarily possessed by only one sex," such as where a director is casting a performer to play a particular role that is necessarily sex-specific.[77]

Subsequent study of the internal colloquies that led to the *Phillips* ruling have confirmed that at least some of the justices, particularly Chief Justice Burger, were uneasy with giving a full-throated rebuke to Martin Marietta. In *The Brethren,* Bob Woodward and Scott Armstrong's behind-the-scenes account of the Court's deliberations in several seminal cases, the authors documented how Chief Justice Burger's own biases—which he'd hardly attempted to conceal at oral argument—played into the Court's deliberations. According to insiders, Burger "strongly supported" Martin Marietta's policy.

> "I will never hire a woman clerk," Burger told his clerks. A woman would have to leave work at 6 P.M. to go home and cook dinner for her husband. His first clerk back in 1956 at the Court of Appeals had been a woman, he told them. It had not worked out well at all. As far as he was concerned, an employer could fire whomever he wanted and for whatever reason. That was the boss's prerogative.
>
> When it was suggested that his position amounted to a declaration that part of the Civil Rights Act was unconstitutional, Burger angrily shut off the discussion. He didn't want to argue legal niceties. His experience showed him that women with young children just didn't work out as well as men in the same jobs. The employer was within his rights.[78]

Burger later told his clerks that he'd been outvoted at the justices' case conference. Keeping the door open for the company to fit its policy within the BFOQ exception was, he told them, "the best that I could do."[79] Burger wasn't the only one who hesitated before ruling against Martin Marietta. In her meticulously sourced history of how the legal theories of the civil rights movement have informed women's rights litigation, *Reasoning from Race,* Serena Mayeri quotes internal Court correspondence showing that Justice Blackmun believed "'discrimination [not] to hire a woman with pre-school age children has some rationality behind it,'" and later wrote the chief justice, "'I feel that the less we say by way of explanation, the better.'"[80]

AS IT TURNED OUT, Martin Marietta wasn't interested in a trial. It wasn't long after the Court's ruling before the company's attorneys wanted to talk again about settling the case—this time by phone. Phillips's lawyers worked with them to calculate what she would have earned if she'd been hired on September 6, 1966, and to negotiate an appropriate amount of back wages (in addition to a nominal amount to reimburse them for their fees).

Even in cases that reach the legal pinnacle of a Supreme Court victory, the grubby reality of tying up loose ends can be less than satisfying for the winner. In the intervening years, Martin Marietta had laid off a number of assembly line workers, including people hired in September 1966. This meant that even if Phillips had gotten the job, she wouldn't have kept it. She never would have earned those high wages and good benefits that she'd hoped for. So she kept working six days a week at the Ranchhouse, on the 6:30 a.m. to 2:00 p.m. shift.[81] ("All we know is work, honey," she told a reporter at the time, "work and come home and work some more."[82]) Moreover, the total wages that Phillips had earned in the meantime also were deducted from the settlement monies. As a result, the company paid Phillips just $13,507.[83] She used it to give her oldest daughter, Peggy, a down payment on a house, take her youngest daughter, Gracie, to Disneyworld, and install an air conditioner in her home—the first one she'd ever had.

IDA PHILLIPS worked as a waitress until 1985 when, at age fifty-one, she died from ovarian cancer. With health insurance a luxury she could not afford, the cancer went undiagnosed until after it had already spread to her lungs. Four years before her death, though, she did finally enjoy some happiness in her personal life: She met and married Ted Roberts, who proved a devoted caretaker. As luck would have it, after Phillips's death, Roberts and Fred McAlister, Ida's first husband—who by then had stopped drinking and renewed his relationship with his children—became good friends. They enjoyed referring to one another as "husbands-in-law."

Although Phillips was conscious of her case's wider significance—
"I feel like I've done my part in seeing women get their rights," she told
a reporter at the time[84]—she never became an outright activist while
her case made its way through the courts. Instead, she seemed content
to rely on Reese Marshall and her family for emotional sustenance.
She and Marshall had made somewhat of an odd pair in segregated
1960s Florida; after it was all over, they enjoyed remembering how
Martin Marietta's good old boy lawyers had "snickered and laughed"
when they saw Marshall at the courthouse because he was black and
had a limp due to his childhood bout with polio.[85]

Phillips herself also seemed to relish being underestimated. "I suppose," she said, "this is my way of letting people know I'm more than
just a dumb little waitress."[86]

two

breaking through
the thin blue line

Dothard v. Rawlinson (1977)

COLONEL E. C. DOTHARD, HEAD OF ALABAMA'S DE-
partment of Public Safety, would never hire a woman to be a state
trooper. That's what he was telling Brenda Mieth as she sat in his
plush, high-ceilinged office on a sunny day in early November 1975.
Flanked by the Alabama and United States flags and framed by the
enormous state seal on the wall behind him, Dothard explained that
the job of patrolling the state's highways was so dangerous that only
men could do it. This men-only rule was news to Mieth; the rejection
letter she had received in the mail mentioned only her failure to meet a
minimum weight threshold of 160 pounds.

Mieth, at 130 pounds, recognized that she was well under that.
She had sought the meeting with Dothard to try to convince him to
hire her anyway, hoping to impress him with her passion for the job,
not to mention her qualifications. After all, in order to qualify to take
the written state trooper exam, Alabama required only that applicants
be between twenty-one and thirty-six years old and have a high school
diploma or equivalent, along with a valid driver's license, no criminal
record, a clean bill of health, good vision, and "sound teeth." And
Mieth had much more: a business college degree, plus coursework toward a second bachelor's in criminal justice and psychology at local
Troy State College.

Her Troy State courses frequently were held at the Montgomery Police Academy, and she had struck up a friendship with two state troopers, Don Atwell and Jim Saunsaucie, who had encouraged her to apply for the trooper job, despite the fact that there were no other women on the force. In fact, so impressed was Atwell by Mieth's eagerness to learn that for weeks he had allowed her to join him on patrol, on one occasion even enlisting her to help arrest a woman for public intoxication. (The judge who later heard the woman's case was understandably nonplussed when the accused wondered aloud on the witness stand why Alabama state troopers "couldn't all be nice like that lady trooper.")

A redhead whose blue eyes and wide smile had once earned her an offer to be a model on the game show *The Price Is Right,* Mieth had always chafed at following rules. Growing up in 1950s Manassas, Virginia, the only child of a homemaker and a conductor on the Richmond, Fredericksburg & Potomac Railroad, she was troubled from an early age by the ubiquitous signs dividing the world into "white" and "colored." And when she considered her mother's life—which included looking the other way when Brenda's father had a child with another woman while stationed overseas during World War II—Mieth resolved, "I'm not gonna be like that."

Her ambition lacked focus, however, and she drifted through high school with spotty attendance, dreaming about being a country music star. After completing a one-year program at a local business college and getting married at age nineteen, she took a secretarial job at the Pentagon. She and her husband eventually divorced, and a few years later she married Ivan Mieth, an Air Force officer she'd met at work.

It was as a newlywed living in the Maryland suburbs of Washington, DC, that Mieth first got an inkling that she might like police work. A neighbor who was an FBI agent "would give me all of his FBI magazines, and then he would test me," recalled Mieth. "He'd say, 'Okay, what kind of fingerprint is this? Is this a tent, a loop, or a whorl?'" In 1973, the Mieths moved to Montgomery so Ivan could complete officer training at the Air War College on Maxwell Air Force Base. At his suggestion, Brenda decided to pursue her newfound interest in earnest, and she began taking night classes at Troy State.

Loving her coursework, just as she did shadowing the state troopers, Mieth felt that she'd finally found her calling. So when Troopers Atwell and Saunsaucie told her not to be deterred by the Department of Public Safety form rejection letter, Mieth called Dothard's office for an interview. On the appointed day, she pinned her long hair into a

French twist, put on her most professional outfit—an ivory linen suit and black pumps—and got a ride from Atwell to Dothard's office.

A trooper for nearly two decades, Dothard had done a stint on Governor George Wallace's personal security detail and was wounded in the 1972 assassination attempt that paralyzed Wallace.[1] From the start of his meeting with Mieth, it was clear his mind was already made up. "Now, Mrs. Mieth, I understand you want to be a state trooper," he drawled, leaning his bulky frame across his shiny, ornately carved wood desk. "Why in the world do you think a woman would be able to do a job like that?" Mieth told him that she thought women were just as capable as men.

"But you're not telling me *why* you think a woman could do the job," he persisted. Dothard's demeanor and body language intimidated Mieth, but she forced herself to lean forward in her chair too.

"I believe women are better at some skills required in policing, such as negotiating, and talking and reasoning with people," she answered. "And I think women could be equally adept at using a gun to protect themselves, as well as others."

Dothard leaned forward a little farther now. "How about in a fistfight?"

"Well, I've taken karate," Mieth answered sweetly, "so that might help."

Dothard, unimpressed, moved on to the 160-pound weight minimum, as well as the five-foot-nine-inch height minimum. At five feet six inches, Mieth didn't meet that either. "See, those are the requirements, and we can't change them just because you want to be a state trooper," he lectured. What Mieth didn't know, and Dothard didn't tell her, was that Alabama law actually *did* allow state officials to grant waivers of those thresholds, although they had never done so.

After twenty minutes, Dothard stood up. "I believe we're done here."

Startled but determined to remain polite, Mieth replied, "Yes, sir," and rose to leave.

But Dothard wasn't finished after all. With a flourish, he produced a certificate and handed it to her. It named Mieth an "Honorary State Trooper." "You have a nice day, Mrs. Mieth," Dothard called after her as she walked out.

Mieth was enraged. She had arrived hoping to convince Alabama's top police officer that she had a future in law enforcement and now was leaving with nothing more than the kind of souvenir typically

bestowed on schoolchildren. She practically ran out of the building
and into Atwell's waiting car.

Over drinks at a nearby bar, Mieth described Dothard's dismissive
treatment. "Are you gonna let him get by with this?" Atwell seethed.
"I want you to go down to the Southern Poverty Law Center."

Atwell no doubt recalled how, only a few years earlier, the SPLC
had brought a successful class action race discrimination lawsuit
against the state troopers. Mieth was aware that there was a federal
law prohibiting race discrimination, but it was news to her that women
might also receive protection from biased treatment. After talking it
over that night with her husband, Mieth called the SPLC the next day
and scheduled an appointment.

Dothard summoned Atwell to his office and told him he knew
Atwell had had something to do with "that woman" applying to be a
trooper. Atwell denied it, but he soon received word that he had been
transferred. His new post was one hundred miles away in Dothan,
Alabama, the self-proclaimed Peanut Capital of the World.[2]

ACROSS TOWN, another Montgomery woman was fuming over
her unsuccessful bid for an Alabama law enforcement job. Dianne
Rawlinson was twenty-two and a recent graduate of the University of
Alabama in Tuscaloosa. A year spent working as an assistant to four
professors conducting research in correctional psychology had fasci-
nated her. The nascent field studied the dynamics in prisons, between
and among inmates and guards. Rawlinson—who went by her middle
name, Kim—especially loved riding in a squad car with a police officer
from Tuscaloosa's juvenile division. She watched him make arrests,
conduct drug busts, and write reports about investigations. Becoming a prison guard might have seemed an unlikely goal for a book-
ish young woman so shy growing up that her neighbors hadn't even
known her two sisters had another sibling, but her exposure to law
enforcement "just ticked a box inside of me," she said. "It just went
'bing'—that's what I want to do."

With the help of the university's career services office, Rawlinson
had identified the one Board of Corrections job for which she was
qualified without a graduate degree: "correctional counselor"—or
prison guard. But she soon received a letter from Alabama's personnel director rejecting her application because, at 115 pounds,

she didn't meet the position's 120-pound weight requirement. (She did meet the height requirement; somehow, although state troopers needed to be five nine, prison guards only were required to be five two, and Rawlinson squeaked in at five three.) She later visited the Board of Corrections to protest, but to no avail. As with Mieth, no one told her that certain cutoffs could be waived.

"It pissed me off," recalled Rawlinson, who has a raucous laugh and a seen-it-all mellowness. "It was so arbitrary." Having grown up in Montgomery in the aftermath of the historic bus boycott, Rawlinson was aware of Title VII and the U.S. Equal Employment Opportunity Commission's role in enforcing it. She drove the two hours from Tuscaloosa to Birmingham, where the EEOC had an office, to file a charge of discrimination—the first step toward a lawsuit. The intake clerk warned her that it could be years before the agency took any action. Sure enough, in the year since Rawlinson had filed her charge, she had not heard a word.

Nothing else seemed to be going right in her life either. After she graduated from college in December 1974, Rawlinson and her boyfriend had broken up, sending her into a deep depression. She retreated to Montgomery, but her hometown brought no comfort. She had an uneasy relationship with her parents and sisters. Growing up in a home where everyone else casually called African Americans "niggers" and seemed oblivious to the civil rights movement, Rawlinson had often wondered, "Who dropped me off in this family?" Heartbroken, angry, and unsure what to do next, Rawlinson took a job shampooing hair at a local salon, A Kut Above.

The salon was the go-to place for haircuts for the staff of the Southern Poverty Law Center, among them a young attorney named Pam Horowitz. A Minnesota native propelled into law school by the civil rights and anti-Vietnam movements, Horowitz had moved to Prichard, Alabama, upon graduation two years earlier. She was drawn there by a job with the city's idealistic mayor, Algernon "Jay" Cooper, a civil rights lawyer and former aide to Robert Kennedy who in 1972 had gained national attention by becoming the first African American to unseat a white incumbent in Alabama. Then, after one of the SPLC's attorneys left to become a professor, Horowitz relocated to Montgomery and joined founders Joe Levin and Morris Dees as the third member of their legal team. (The SPLC's third cofounder, legendary civil rights activist Julian Bond, was its president; years later, he became Horowitz's husband.)

About a year into her tenure at the SPLC, Horowitz went for a trim and struck up a conversation with the woman washing her hair—Kim Rawlinson. "You're an attorney, aren't you?" Rawlinson asked. Fearing she was about to be embroiled in a stranger's tale of woe, Horowitz confirmed that she was. As Rawlinson explained her situation, Horowitz "listened with her mouth open," recalled Rawlinson. The coincidence *was* hard to believe: Horowitz had met with Brenda Mieth just that week and had agreed to take her case. Horowitz told Rawlinson that time was short; the SPLC was planning to file Mieth's lawsuit in days. If she was serious, she should come to the group's offices to sign the necessary paperwork and join in the case. By the end of the week, Rawlinson was the SPLC's client, too.

WHEN THE SPLC filed its lawsuit in December 1975, few women worked in law enforcement. Nationwide, women made up just 2.7 percent of police officers[3] and roughly 6 percent of correctional officers.[4] Only nine state trooper agencies had women on their forces.[5] And even when women managed to get hired, they typically were relegated to lower-status, lower-paid roles. They either pushed paperwork or handled the "softer" side of law enforcement, acting as quasi–social workers in juvenile units or the vice squad. The same was true for female correctional officers, who typically guarded women's penitentiaries, youth facilities, or minimum-security institutions. That women in law enforcement often were called "matrons" spoke volumes about their caretaking role.

Alabama was no exception. In 1975, its 659-officer state trooper force was all male. And although women worked in prisons in slightly higher numbers than the national average—making up approximately 13 percent of the state's 435 correctional counselors—the vast majority worked in the one women-only facility or in minimum-security youth and work release centers.

Minimum height requirements helped to keep law enforcement male-dominated. They were the rule in most jurisdictions, as were, though less commonly, weight minimums. As of 1974, forty-seven of the country's forty-nine state police agencies required applicants to be five feet eight inches or taller, as did the vast majority of the largest urban police departments.[6] The FBI also maintained a five-foot-seven-inch height minimum for its officers.[7] While such criteria differed from out-and-out bans on hiring women in that they were "gender-neutral," their effect was anything but. It didn't take an expert demographer to understand that considering only taller applicants would end up disqualifying more women than men.

Women's exclusion from law enforcement also reflected the overall division of the work world into "men's jobs" and "women's jobs," which had a legacy stretching back a century. From the late 1800s into the middle of the 1900s, state legislatures had enacted various "protective" labor laws that limited the number of hours women could work in a day, barred them from certain jobs or tasks deemed too hazardous, or granted them special privileges, such as rest breaks.[8]

Consensus did eventually coalesce around extending many of those protections to *all* workers through various laws, most notably the 1938 Fair Labor Standards Act. But the state laws remained in place, and their application to only one sex ensured women's second-class status on the job. In addition to denying women very tangible benefits, such as the higher wages and supervisory authority that came with overtime, nighttime shifts, and strenuous work, protective laws also reinforced the rigid cultural distinction between the sexes. White women were seen, above all, as stay-at-home wives and mothers whose bodies and abilities were unsuited to the vagaries of most work. (Women of color, in contrast, never were placed on such a pedestal; indeed, from slavery through subsequent generations, their labor made it possible for white women to stay home.)[9]

The Supreme Court gave protective labor laws its imprimatur on several occasions, each time reaffirming some variation on the theme that domesticity was the defining issue of womanhood itself. In 1872, for instance, the Court approved an Illinois law that barred women from practicing law, because "[t]he harmony . . . [of] the family institution is repugnant to the idea of a woman adopting a distinct and independent career from that of her husband."[10] In 1908's *Muller v. Oregon*, the Court approved a state law that imposed a ten-hour daily maximum for women laundry and factory workers. Although a few years earlier the Court had struck down a similar measure that regulated male bakers' hours, the Court in *Muller* reasoned that Oregon had a legitimate interest in protecting women from hard labor because women had a higher duty of "preserv[ing] the strength and vigor of the race."[11] And in 1948, just sixteen years before Title VII's enactment, the Court upheld a Michigan law banning women from working as bartenders unless their husband or father owned the bar.[12] "[B]artending by women may . . . give rise to moral and social problems against which [the legislature] may devise preventive measures," it explained. "Michigan evidently believes that the oversight assured through ownership of a bar by a barmaid's husband or father minimizes hazards that may confront a barmaid without such protecting oversight. This Court is certainly not in a position to gainsay such belief by the Michigan legislature."[13]

It was against this legal landscape that Congress passed Title VII in 1964. Although ultimately invalidating state protective laws, the statute did little at first to open up opportunities for women interested in police and prison work. As originally enacted, Title VII did not apply to the federal, state, and local governments, which operated law enforcement agencies. A few departments voluntarily changed their discriminatory policies,[14] but it wasn't until 1972, when Congress amended the law to cover government employers,[15] that women could file lawsuits to try to gain access to those jobs.

Thus, in 1975, there had been few opportunities for the courts to consider the vast array of rules that were keeping women out of law enforcement. It largely remained to be seen how Congress's mandate for equal employment opportunity would fare when pitted against deeply held beliefs like Colonel Dothard's. Indeed, many federal judges, not to mention much of the law enforcement community and the public, undoubtedly questioned whether women, of *any* size, were capable of breaking up street fights or keeping order in prisons.

The dearth of legal precedent meant that activist lawyers like Pam Horowitz and the Southern Poverty Law Center were on the lookout for women to begin challenging the status quo. Opening opportunities for women in male-dominated fields, Horowitz said later, "furthered the goals of the national women's movement" by defying stereotypes about what kind of work women could and should do. Such jobs also came with excellent pay and benefits, without requiring a college degree—a path to economic security that, said Horowitz, also "fit the Center's mission." Horowitz knew she'd gotten extremely lucky with Brenda Mieth and Kim Rawlinson—two highly qualified candidates, interested at the very same moment in two different branches of Montgomery law enforcement. When she met them, she already had filed a lawsuit against the Montgomery Police Department on behalf of three other women, challenging its refusal to assign them patrol duties; in 1976, she won a verdict in the women's favor.[16]

Horowitz and John Carroll, SPLC's newest lawyer and Horowitz's main co-counsel on the case, pursued two legal theories in their initial court complaint. Brenda Mieth's case against the state troopers

rested solely on the allegation that Alabama had violated her Fourteenth Amendment right to equal protection. (For reasons no one can
remember, her case was not filed initially with the EEOC, which is a
prerequisite for bringing a Title VII case.)

As for Kim Rawlinson's case to strike the Board of Corrections'
height and weight minimums, there was no evidence that those requirements were imposed with the intention of keeping women out
of the job. They only had the *effect* of disproportionately excluding
women. Still, based on a recent Supreme Court case, Horowitz and
Carroll were confident that that discriminatory effect alone violated
Title VII.

In that case, *Griggs v. Duke Power Company,*[17] a group of African American employees at a North Carolina utility plant had challenged the company's requirements that all applicants for initial hire
and for interdepartmental transfers have a high school diploma and
achieve a passing score on a general aptitude test[18]—rules that ended
up disqualifying most black candidates.[19]

In a ruling that vastly expanded Title VII's reach, the Supreme
Court found that employer policies that have an exclusionary *effect* can
be just as illegal as policies that are *intended* to exclude. Where a given
device has a "disparate impact" on a protected group, the Court explained—that is, where it's "fair in form, but discriminatory in operation"—Title VII demands that it be justified as a "business necessity."[20]

To prove "business necessity," said the Court, an employer must
prove that an applicant who passes the challenged test really will do
the job better than an applicant who doesn't.[21] And in *Griggs,* Duke
Power couldn't make that showing. The mostly white employees without diplomas or passing test scores who had been grandfathered in
at the time Duke Power adopted the policies had done just fine, performing satisfactorily and even receiving promotions.[22] To the Court's
eyes, this meant that the diploma and test requirements didn't actually
predict whether a worker would succeed at Duke Power; they merely
exposed the subpar educations available to most African Americans in
North Carolina at that time.[23] So the requirements weren't a "business
necessity" at all, and this made them illegal.

To win under Title VII, then, Horowitz and Carroll needed to
show that the Board of Corrections' height and weight requirements
were like Duke Power's diploma and test requirements: They kept
women out of prison jobs without actually yielding a more qualified
workforce. Of course, *Griggs* was a race discrimination case, whereas

this was a sex discrimination case. And the Supreme Court hadn't given any indication whether a neutral policy having a disparate impact against *women* was illegal. The good news for Horowitz and Carroll was that at least one federal court, in California, already had decided that issue. Citing *Griggs,* the court found the San Francisco Police Department's five-foot-six-inch height minimum had a disparate impact against women that couldn't be justified by business necessity.[24] The police department hadn't been able to produce sound data showing a link between officers' height and better job performance.[25]

BUT NO SOONER had Horowitz and Carroll decided on their two legal theories—equal protection for Mieth and Title VII disparate impact for Rawlinson—than the case got more complicated. In February 1976, the Alabama Board of Corrections issued a new regulation: Even if a woman was tall enough and weighed enough to be hired as a correctional counselor, she could not work in any of the state's maximum-security prisons in a job that required physical proximity to male inmates. From then on, these so-called contact positions—which encompassed duties such as patrolling showers, restrooms, and dormitories and conducting strip searches—would be for men only.

The effect of Regulation 204, as the new rule was known, was to bar women from virtually all of the prison guard jobs in Alabama. Although only four out of the state's fifteen correctional facilities were maximum-security male-only prisons, those four prisons employed fully three-quarters of the state's correctional counselors, and most jobs there qualified as contact positions.[26]

This development injected a brand-new legal question into Rawlinson's case. Regulation 204 explicitly, and intentionally, excluded women from a large number of jobs. Clearly, it violated Title VII. What could be more blatant discrimination "because of sex" than a rule designating certain jobs for men only? What was more, Horowitz and Carroll were confident that such a blanket ban, just like Colonel Dothard's male-only rule for state troopers, violated the equal protection clause.

The catch was that Alabama planned to argue that Regulation 204 fell within Title VII's loophole: the bona fide occupational qualification, or BFOQ, exception. If Alabama could prove that allowing only men in contact positions was reasonably necessary to the normal operation of its maximum-security facilities, then Regulation 204 would be allowed.

In the mid-1970s, Alabama's maximum-security penitentiaries were unquestionably very dangerous places to work, regardless of one's sex. They were laid out in an open-dormitory style, with even the most violent offenders unconfined to cells. Guards wore street clothes, not uniforms, and were unarmed, lest their own weapons be used against them. Since 1973, Board of Corrections Commissioner Judson Locke later testified, there had been forty attacks on correctional counselors, two of them fatal. (Rawlinson was unfazed by these hazards. During her deposition, she was presented with a series of photographs of the two dead officers, both stabbed by an inmate at Holman Prison, home to Alabama's death row. "Okay, Miss Rawlinson," the state's attorney challenged, pointing at the gruesome images. "You are so much smaller and you're a woman, and you want to go into *this* kind of environment. And you think that's not a safety concern?" To Rawlinson, the answer was obvious. She gestured at one of the pictures. "Sir, that's a large man, and *he's* dead. I don't know what your point is.")

The risks faced by guards working in Alabama's maximum-security penitentiaries were largely attributable to the state's glaring shortcomings in operating them. In January 1976, in another case litigated by the SPLC, Judge Frank Johnson, Jr. had issued an order finding conditions in Alabama's prisons so inhumane as to violate the Eighth Amendment's prohibition on cruel and unusual punishment.[27] (The prisons' chronic overcrowding[28] and administrators' gross neglect of inmates' medical needs[29] had been the subjects of other federal lawsuits and also had resulted in judgments against the Board of Corrections.) In addition to the facilities' being "wholly unfit for human habitation,"[30] Judge Johnson found that Alabama, troublingly, had no classification system for inmates. Violent prisoners and the mentally ill were dispersed among the general population, unidentified and untreated.[31]

Exacerbating this chaotic environment was the woeful understaffing of prisons; although close to seven hundred correctional counselors were needed to guard the inmates in the four maximum-security prisons, Alabama employed only 383. As a consequence, Judge Johnson observed, "rampant violence" prevailed, creating a "jungle atmosphere."[32]

Among the comprehensive measures that the judge mandated to remedy these conditions was to hire the requisite number of guards—essentially doubling the correctional counselor workforce. Alabama wasted no time, though, in making sure that women would not benefit from the court-ordered hiring boom. Within just a month of Judge Johnson's ruling, the state issued Regulation 204—seeking to use the very "rampant violence" and "jungle atmosphere" it had fostered in its prison system as the basis for banning women from most of the jobs in it.

GIVEN THAT TITLE VII was just a decade old, few courts had had the chance to consider what kinds of sex discrimination Congress had meant to outlaw, much less what kinds of sex discrimination it had intended to *permit* via the BFOQ exception. The EEOC, for its part, had issued regulations urging a "narrow" interpretation of the exception. It specifically disapproved of relying on sex stereotypes to justify it. Although the Supreme Court a few years earlier in *Phillips v. Martin Marietta Corporation* had seemed open to a more lenient standard, Justice Thurgood Marshall's separate opinion chastising the majority sent a mixed message about how the Court would rule in the future.[33]

Among the few lower courts to consider the BFOQ exception, a narrow interpretation had prevailed. Starting in the late 1960s, federal courts of appeals had refused to allow the BFOQ exception to excuse various job distinctions based on stereotypes about men's and women's respective abilities. These included Colgate-Palmolive's rule against women holding factory jobs that would require them to lift heavy equipment;[34] Southern Bell Telephone and Telegraph's policy restricting a maintenance job to men only, also due to the position's heavy lifting duties;[35] Pan Am Airways' women-only hiring policy for flight attendants, based on the stereotype that women were inherently better at "making flights as pleasurable as possible";[36] and Southern Pacific Railroad's refusal to hire women for a wide range of jobs for which the hours were deemed too long and the work too arduous.[37]

AN ESSENTIAL PHASE in any employment discrimination case is "discovery." That's when each side requests from the other the information needed to prove its claims and defenses. Documents are exchanged, witnesses are deposed, facts are confirmed or denied. All of the evidence amassed becomes the "record" of the case. When discovery began in *Mieth and Rawlinson v. Dothard, et al.,* Horowitz and Carroll soon learned that Alabama didn't have any concrete evidence to justify its policies.

For instance, the state had never looked into whether bigger officers actually made better ones. Colonel Dothard testified that he had no idea why the state trooper height and weight requirements had come into existence. He could merely state his personal belief that only someone of that size would have the strength necessary to perform job functions like "arresting an uncooperative individual, rescuing a person pinned underneath a car, or removing heavy objects obstructing the highway."[38] Equally in the dark as to why the board had imposed its height and weight requirements for correctional counselors was the Board of Corrections' star witness, Commissioner Locke. He too was unable to answer why prison guards were permitted to be a full seven inches shorter and forty pounds lighter than state troopers.[39]

Moreover, aside from making sure that applicants were tall enough and weighed enough, the state ignored their actual physical abilities. Were they strong? Fast? Agile? Did they have any self-defense skills? No tests were administered to find out. Nor did Alabama do any ongoing evaluation of officers' physical abilities after they were on the job. As John Carroll later noted with a laugh, "There were three-hundred-pound state troopers that could barely get out of the way of a tractor trailer truck that was about to run over them and they were still on the force."

When it came to Regulation 204, the "contact position" rule, Alabama didn't have any hard facts either. Horowitz still shakes her head at the state's "because we said so" approach to its defense. It was plain from Alabama officials' testimony that the rule rested mainly on their own attitudes about women—or their assumptions about the inmates' attitudes—rather than any empirical proof. "There is a basic difference," Commissioner Locke opined at his deposition, "between a female and a male, which renders her less capable of physically . . . protecting herself or subduing an inmate."[40]

Locke went on to hypothesize that seeing a woman guard would "incite inmates confined in an all-male environment with no heterosexual outlets. . . . [H]er mere physical presence, in my opinion, . . . would incite trouble and there is a sexual connotation which should go without saying. She is a sex object."[41] As evidence, he cited assaults on two women that had occurred in maximum-security facilities.[42] It turned out, though, that neither woman was a trained officer; one was a clerical worker and the other, a college student on a school tour.[43]

Because women had been serving in Alabama's minimum-security facilities since 1974, Horowitz and Carroll wanted to find out how they had performed in that setting. Bill Gilmore, director of Alabama's Frank Lee Youth Center for young men age twenty-three and under, admitted that six women had worked among the facility's sixteen contact positions without incident. Nonetheless, he stated his belief that the women guards' "performance as a whole [was] not as effective as" the male guards', and expressed "concern about their surveillance techniques, and the unwillingness of the male inmates to carry out their instructions."[44] (Gilmore didn't cite any actual incidents in which women guards had been demonstrably less "effective" or inmates had tried to "get away with more" with them.) He further opined, "It is synonymous with your mother-father situation," and ruminated, "Often times we will argue and sometimes can get away with more with our mothers. But when your father is involved, you tend to go ahead and fall in line earlier."[45]

To debunk all of these assumptions, Horowitz and Carroll looked to the small cadre of researchers and other professionals who, as of 1976, had formally examined what qualifications predicted success as a law enforcement officer. These experts were able to testify to the growing body of research that good judgment and interpersonal skills were more important than size, even in violent encounters; that women were no more susceptible to assault while on the job than men; and that, to the extent an officer might need to use physical force, technique trumped brute strength.[46]

One such expert was Peter Bloch, of the Urban Institute, whose work Horowitz previously had cited in making her winning sex discrimination case against the Montgomery Police Department. In 1974, Bloch had coauthored a landmark study of female officers' performance on the Washington, DC police force, which two years earlier had begun assigning women to patrol duties.[47] The report found that female officers performed as well as their male colleagues across many measures, including "handling angry or violent citizens," and that members of the public accorded "similar levels of respect" to officers of both sexes.[48] Women also were less likely than men to engage in "serious unbecoming conduct" and "aggressive" tactics.[49] To the extent that women's incorporation into the patrol ranks caused disruption, the study concluded that it was the negative "attitudes of male officers and police supervisors" that were to blame.[50]

In another study, Bloch had examined the effect of height on the performance of police officers in Nassau County, New York, and

Dallas, Texas, and found that police officers' height bore no significant relation to their on-the-job performance.[51] Instead, their success—or failure—was due mainly to the training they received during the probationary period and whether they got meaningful feedback from supervisors.[52]

Horowitz and Carroll also selected C. Robert Sarver, a professor at the Graduate School of Social Work at the University of Arkansas, who had served as commissioner for two state Departments of Corrections, first in West Virginia and then in Arkansas. He had testified as an expert on the SPLC's behalf in the recent Alabama prison conditions litigation. In his opinion, too, physical size didn't have any effect on a guard's performance.

The SPLC retained another expert on prison operations, Ray Nelson, the warden of Chicago's Metropolitan Correctional Center. The facility had a policy of hiring women to supervise male inmates; no height or weight restrictions were imposed on applicants, only the requirement that their height and weight be "proportional." Nelson would testify that these policies had not compromised safety at the MCC. He also would echo Sarver's opinion that women's presence in all-male institutions served a critical therapeutic function: "normalizing" the environment, so that inmates were better prepared for reentry into the general population after serving their sentences.[53]

———   ———

AS THE SPLC'S LAWYERS methodically built their case, Brenda Mieth and Kim Rawlinson tried to move forward with their lives. But Montgomery, Alabama, in 1976 was not an easy place to be a woman who didn't fit the traditional mold. Shortly after the case was filed, Mieth discovered a cross burning on her lawn. More than once, rocks were thrown at her car as she drove around town. Although Mieth's husband and closest friends were supportive, others in her social circle—mainly her husband's military colleagues and their wives—were conspicuously silent.[54]

Rawlinson was more willing to publicly embrace her new status as a civil rights litigant. She spoke to various reporters and allowed the SPLC to use her picture in its newsletters to publicize the case. After *The Alabama Journal*'s editorial page ridiculed her in a cartoon— depicting an inmate behind bars catcalling a woman guard, "Hey baby, you're just my size"—she wrote an impassioned letter in response: "[T]here should not be so much focus on how big and mean a person is, as on how able he or she is to handle the job, mentally as well as physically," she wrote. "And this, dear public, has nothing to do with inches, pounds or sex!"[55]

What was harder to take was her parents' reaction. Knowing that they wouldn't understand her dream of becoming a correctional counselor, she had never told them that she'd applied, much less that she'd filed an EEOC charge and retained a lawyer. Only after the case was filed, with press coverage imminent, was she forced to come clean. As predicted, "it didn't make any sense to them," Rawlinson later explained.

But if the Rawlinsons were puzzled by their daughter's enthusiasm for prison work, they found her decision to file a lawsuit appalling. For one thing, Rawlinson's father, Lamar, owned a real estate company, and both he and his wife, Virginia, worried the case would be bad for business. There was an even deeper transgression, though: As a woman challenging authority, Rawlinson was violating what she termed "Southern culture." "They said, 'I don't know why you're making all this trouble for everybody and you're bringing shame on us,'" Rawlinson recalled. "'They have the rules and regulations for a reason. They have the laws for a reason.'" Eventually, Rawlinson "just quit bringing it up."

BRENDA MIETH'S and Kim Rawlinson's consolidated cases were submitted to the U.S. District Court for the Middle District of Alabama in the spring of 1976. Because Title VII did not provide for jury trials until the law was amended in 1991, the case was to be decided by the court "on the papers"—that is, solely on the basis of the arguments contained in the lawyers' briefs. And because the case presented a constitutional claim, federal law provided that a panel of three judges, not the usual one judge, would decide the case.

Mieth and Rawlinson couldn't have gotten luckier with their panel; two of the three judges were giants of progressive civil rights jurisprudence. The first was Richard Rives, a Truman appointee who sat on the U.S. Court of Appeals for the Fifth Circuit, ground zero for civil rights litigators in the years following *Brown v. Board of Education*.[56] Rives, along with his colleagues Chief Judge Elbert Tuttle, Judge John Minor Wisdom, and Judge John Brown,[57] had issued so many rulings dismantling the Jim Crow South that one colleague bitterly dubbed them the "The Four"—as in the Four Horsemen of the Apocalypse.[58]

One of Rives's landmark decisions had been *Browder v. Gayle*,[59] which ended the historic Montgomery bus boycott by ruling that the city's segregated transit system was unconstitutional. He had authored that decision twenty years earlier with another member of Mieth's and Rawlinson's panel, Judge Frank Johnson, Jr. In addition to being the author of the recent blistering Alabama prison conditions decision, Johnson had presided over the SPLC's successful lawsuits to desegregate the Alabama state troopers and to admit women to the ranks of Montgomery's police officers, among others. Johnson's many civil rights rulings gave "true meaning to the word 'justice,'" in the estimation of Dr. Martin Luther King, Jr.[60] (Perhaps equally telling is Governor George Wallace's assessment of Johnson as an "integratin', carpetbaggin', scalawaggin', baldfaced liar."[61])

Mieth and Rawlinson didn't have to wait long to learn their fates. On June 28, 1976, the district court issued its decision. It was unanimous, and a clean sweep in the women's favor. "One lesson the women's rights movement has taught us," wrote the court, "is that many long-held conceptions regarding the sexes have been found to be erroneous when exposed to the light of empirical data and objectivity."[62]

The judges first dispensed with Mieth's constitutional challenge to the state troopers. Citing Peter Bloch's testimony and research, it concluded that the height and weight restrictions weren't "rationally related" to the goal of improving law enforcement. "Colonel Dothard contends that the exclusion of women for the job is intended for their protection and for protection of the public," it said. "Neither of these contentions is sound, however. First, women do not need protectors; they are capable of deciding whether it is in their best interest to take unromantic or dangerous jobs. In regard to the fear that the public will not be adequately protected, there is no evidence in the record that a woman cannot perform the duties of a patrol officer."[63]

The court used similar reasoning to reject, under Title VII, the height and weight requirements for correctional counselors. Noting that nearly 100 percent of men met the thresholds but that only 60 percent of women did,[64] the panel ruled that Alabama couldn't justify this "disparate impact" with any "business necessity," as required by the *Griggs* decision. "If strength is an important qualification for a prison guard, then the Board of Corrections should adopt a test for its applicants that does in fact measure strength," wrote the court. "The crude rule of thumb provided by height and weight levels impermissibly restricts qualified individuals without giving them an opportunity to demonstrate their merit."[65]

Finally, the court addressed Regulation 204. Alabama had failed to show that maleness was a BFOQ for contact jobs. "Labeling a job as 'strenuous' and then relying on stereotyped characterizations of women will not meet the burden," it said. "There must be some objective, demonstrable evidence that women cannot perform the duties associated with the job."[66] As it happened, the court observed, Alabama's evidence showed just the opposite because the state employed women in contact positions in minimum-security institutions, with no ill effects. They did everything the male guards did. Their presence had not incited male inmates to assault them. To the extent that inmates' right to privacy might demand a same-sex guard (such as for strip searches), it wasn't necessary to exclude women from the guards' ranks altogether. A male guard could be assigned to those few tasks.

Having found in Mieth's and Rawlinson's favor on all claims, the court turned to the question of remedies. It ordered Alabama to stop using the height and weight requirements for state troopers and correctional counselors and to suspend enforcement of Regulation 204. It also ordered the Department of Public Safety (DPS) and the Board of Corrections to launch recruitment campaigns aimed at encouraging women to apply for trooper and guard jobs within thirty days. There was some bad news, though, in the mix: The court refused to enter an order requiring that Mieth or Rawlinson be hired, as the SPLC had asked. The state had an established merit system for appointing public safety officers, and the court did not want to disrupt it with preferential hiring; if Mieth and Rawlinson still wanted the jobs they'd applied for, they'd have to start the process all over again.

"WELL, YOU MADE *The New York Times*," John Carroll told Brenda Mieth when he called to tell her that she'd won.

Mieth was ecstatic. "Oh, I was dancing and screaming and I called my husband at work," she recalled. "And he was all excited. So that night we went out and celebrated."

Mieth was disappointed, though, to learn that the court victory didn't mean she would automatically have a new job in Montgomery. For months she had been trying to get a job in law enforcement, first in Mobile, Alabama, and then in Maryland and Virginia, after returning to the Washington, DC, area with her husband. By the time of the court's ruling, she was killing time by continuing her criminal justice studies at a local community college and working as a detective at a clothing store, looking out for shoplifters. She also was pregnant with her first child.

Mieth and her husband already had wrestled with what they would do if the court case resulted in her getting hired as a state trooper. They had decided that she would take the position—"I said, 'Well, there's no way that after all this that I'm not taking the job'"—and they would figure out their family life from there; either her husband would try to find an Air Force assignment in Alabama or he would retire from the military. "That's how supportive he was of this lawsuit," Mieth marveled.

A few months after giving birth to a daughter, she flew back to Montgomery and sat for the state trooper entrance exam. "I don't remember it being difficult," she said. "I thought, 'I think I aced this test.'" When her score was tallied, however, Mieth was told she hadn't scored high enough to make it onto the eligibility list. Devastated, she called DPS and learned that the state had applied a five-point preference to the test scores of honorably discharged veterans and a ten-point preference for veterans who had service-related disabilities,[67] both of which had contributed to her lower placement among the candidates.[68]

By then Mieth was tired of fighting. She had a new baby and household responsibilities as a military wife. "I decided to let it go," she explained. "I went from women's rights advocate to all-American mom." Mieth had taken on Colonel Dothard and the state of Alabama, and she had won. Because of her, no other woman in the state ever would be denied a career as a state trooper just because of her sex. And for Brenda Mieth, that was enough.

The first female Alabama state trooper was finally hired a few years later, in 1979: an African American woman, Clara Zeigler.[69] Not many have followed in her footsteps, though; today, there are just 22 women out of 814 officers—just under 3 percent of the state trooper force.

KIM RAWLINSON WASN'T especially bothered that the court hadn't ordered the Board of Corrections to hire her. "I know how slow things can be, and big decisions are even slower. If somebody was willing to help me, I was going to hang in there," she explained. "So I did. I just felt very fortunate." By the time of the district court's decision, she had been working for a few months as an aide at the Department of Youth Services' juvenile corrections facility in Mt. Meigs, just outside Montgomery. Pam Horowitz had helped her get the job through a contact at the department, and Rawlinson was glad for the opportunity to finally put her psychology degree to use. She was reluctant to start all over again someplace new.

Then, just a few months after the victory before the district court, there was a new development, one that threatened to reverse the ruling in Rawlinson's favor: Alabama filed a petition for *certiorari* with the Supreme Court. For reasons that no one at the SPLC ever learned, the state only asked the Court to review the decision against the Board of Corrections, leaving undisturbed Mieth's win against the DPS.

Because there was a constitutional component to Rawlinson's case in addition to the Title VII claims, federal law at the time permitted the state to bypass the intermediate appeals court and seek review directly from the Supreme Court. Week after week, Horowitz recalled, the state's petition "sat there" in Washington, and she busied herself with other cases. And then "one day the phone rang and it was a reporter from the *Wall Street Journal* saying she would like a comment on the fact that the Court had taken the case, which was the first that I knew about it. And my comment was"—she let out a whoop—"Aaaaahhh!"

This was the second time in its five-year history that the Southern Poverty Law Center had a case reach the Supreme Court. The first had been in 1973, on behalf of another stereotype-defying female client, Sharron Frontiero. Frontiero was an Air Force lieutenant who challenged a military regulation that married servicewomen seeking various benefits to help them support a "dependent" spouse had to prove that their husbands were, in fact, financially dependent on them. Servicemen weren't required to make any such showing in order to get the benefits, which included a housing subsidy and health coverage; their wives were simply assumed to be "dependent." In a landmark victory for women's rights, *Frontiero v. Richardson,*[70] the Court struck down the military's rule as unconstitutional. While acknowledging that a male breadwinner–female dependent spouse model might still be the norm in many families, the justices ruled that that model shouldn't be the law's template.[71]

Joe Levin, one of the SPLC's cofounders and lead attorney on *Frontiero,* had emerged from his Supreme Court experience wary of the turf battles that can erupt when the justices grant a *cert* petition. The broad and lasting repercussions of a Supreme Court ruling often prompt a chorus of advice from attorneys around the country who feel invested in the outcome, and where the case concerns an undeveloped area of the law, the jockeying can be especially fierce. Only a few advocates in the early 1970s were taking on the monumental job of chipping away at more than a century of legal decisions enshrining women's second-class status. One of the most prominent among this small group was the American Civil Liberties Union Women's Rights Project, or ACLU WRP, cofounded and led at the time by now-Justice Ruth Bader Ginsburg. A few years earlier, Ginsburg had been the chief author of the winning brief in the first Supreme Court ruling to declare sex discrimination to be a violation of the Equal Protection clause.[72] (The case arose from an Idaho law that gave automatic preference to men in appointing estate administrators; a single mother named Sally Reed challenged the statute after her estranged husband was named to administer the estate of her teenage son, who had killed himself while in his father's custody.)

Although now recognized as one of the premier civil rights organizations in the country, SPLC was just a three-attorney operation at the time, only two years old. Levin and his colleagues initially were daunted by the prospect of shouldering a Supreme Court case alone, and asked the ACLU WRP for help. But a struggle for control soon erupted. The ACLU WRP feared that the SPLC was too conservative in its legal approach: Ginsburg and her colleagues wanted to push for a new, heightened review standard that treated sex and race discrimination as equal harms under the Constitution, but Levin and the SPLC felt their best chance to secure a win for their client was to stick with the existing standard, which only required them to prove the military regulation's distinction between servicemen and women lacked a "rational basis." There also was heated wrangling over who would handle the oral argument, not least because Ginsburg and her staff believed it was important, symbolically, for a woman to be at the podium. Ultimately, the SPLC retained the lead role on both the briefing and the oral argument. The ACLU WRP submitted a brief as a friend of the court, and Levin yielded ten minutes of his argument time to Ginsburg.[73]

The positive ruling in *Frontiero* may have helped smooth ruffled feathers, but the dust-up was still in Levin's mind when Pam Horowitz burst into his office to tell him that *Dothard v. Rawlinson* was headed for Washington. (The case caption retained Colonel Dothard's name even though the state trooper portion of the case wasn't being appealed.) Horowitz, Levin, and Dees agreed that the SPLC would keep the case, and that Horowitz would tackle the argument. As in *Frontiero*, but this time with considerably less friction, the parties agreed that the ACLU WRP's expertise would be put forward in an *amicus* brief authored by Ginsburg and her colleagues.[74]

For Horowitz, not even four years out of law school, the prospect of a Supreme Court oral argument was as terrifying as it was thrilling. Not that she didn't have a sense of humor about it. "I have always rather enjoyed the fact that I got to the Supreme Court via the hair salon," she would later chuckle. Over the five months she had to prepare, Horowitz consulted with the lawyers she knew and trusted most—Levin, Dees, and John Carroll at the SPLC, as well as the prominent Montgomery civil rights attorney Howard Mandell—and focused on becoming the "scholar of the case," knowing the factual record and legal precedents "backward and forward." Horowitz said, "I prepared a brief opening and then hoped that there would be enough questions that I didn't have to keep going!"

She also sought the advice of anyone she knew who had argued before the Court or seen an argument. She was surprised about the amount of attention paid to what she was going to wear; then again, as Horowitz wryly noted, "I was never particularly known for conservatism in my sartorial choices." She laughed, "Oh, [and] whether I was going to wear a bra, that was the *big* question!" Horowitz's friends were probably right to tell her to proceed with caution. Women appearing at the Court have always gotten a thorough once-over. Justice Harry Blackmun's notes of an oral argument four years before *Dothard* included the observation about one of the attorneys, "White dress, youngish, nice girl,"[75] and around the same time he commented about Ruth Bader Ginsburg's dress and hair accessory: "In red and red ribbon today."[76] As recently as the late 1990s, a female lawyer for the federal government who wore a brown skirt suit received a personal rebuke from Chief Justice Rehnquist for not wearing black.[77] Even women in the audience and press corps have been chastised for breaches ranging from sporting a hot pink sweater to failing to top off a businesslike ensemble with a blazer.[78]

Horowitz eventually opted for a conservative dress and blazer. And no bra.

ORAL ARGUMENT in *Dothard v. Rawlinson* was held on April 19, 1977. Horowitz was accompanied by Morris Dees and John Carroll, along with a few friends. Because she represented the respondent—the party that had won in the lower court and was "responding" to the appeal to the Supreme Court—she would be the second attorney to argue. The morning's first speaker was Assistant Attorney General for the State of Alabama, Danny Evans. Horowitz may have been green, but Evans—just two years out of law school—was positively wet behind the ears.

The justices emerged from behind the heavy velvet curtains to take their seats at the bench, with Chief Justice Warren Burger at the center and, at the end of the bench to his left, the Court's newest appointee, John Paul Stevens. Evans stepped up to begin his argument.

In his Alabama drawl, he outlined the state's main points. As to the height and weight requirements for prison guards, the district court's disparate impact finding was fatally flawed because it hadn't looked at how many female applicants had actually been screened out by the state's requirements. Instead, it only had looked at how many women in the U.S. population generally were excluded. That had artificially inflated the number of women actually harmed by the state's policy, Evans said. Although Evans didn't spell it out, the implication was that because there were so few women applying for prison guard jobs, the effect of the height and weight requirements was negligible and couldn't be the basis for a discrimination claim in the first place.[79]

Then he turned to Regulation 204. "If the bona fide occupational qualification is to be given anything more than an imaginary existence, certainly the facts of this case warrant it," said Evans. Those facts included "some peculiarities" of Alabama's penitentiaries, as Evans euphemistically termed them. Without referencing the fact that the state was under federal court order to remedy unconstitutional conditions in its prison system, Evans focused on painting the justices a scary picture: open dormitories, communal bathrooms allowing guards direct sight lines at naked inmates (and vice versa), prisoners with multiple offenses to their names (an estimated 20 percent of whom were sex offenders), and the "innate attraction of multiple offenders who have been long incarcerated to a female's presence." He also dismissed the expert testimony submitted to the lower court by C. Robert Sarver and Ray Nelson as being inapt; their experiences, after all, had been in facilities lacking Alabama's "peculiarities."[80]

Time was up, and it was Horowitz's turn. As she had hoped, she needed only to make a few opening statements before the questions started coming. The justices wanted to know her response to Evans's argument about statistics. "Why was not [evidence of the height/weight minimums' effect on actual applicants] presented?" asked Chief Justice Burger. "It is certainly available somewhere." Horowitz's answer—undoubtedly rehearsed many times before and delivered now in an assured voice whose flat vowels belied her Minnesota upbringing—ended that line of inquiry altogether:

> I would submit, Your Honor, that it is not easily available and that it should not be required as part of the plaintiff's evidentiary burden under Title VII. Because the height and weight requirement is a self-defining qualification . . . its evil is not only in the fact that it discriminates against anybody who applies and is rejected for being under the minimums, but it discriminates against all those who know of the minimums and do not apply because they do not meet them.[81]

Then Justice Marshall took things in a new direction. He wanted to know where Horowitz would draw the line for applicants, if not at five foot two and 120 pounds. "Don't you think they can put in a weight and height restriction of some sort?" he asked. "[C]ould they say that they will not hire anybody weighing more than 400 pounds? . . . Could they also say, 'We will not hire anybody over the age of 55'?" Chief Justice Burger chimed in. "What if they had said 100 pounds and 4'8"? That would be all right, wouldn't it?" But Horowitz refused to be pinned down. This case wasn't about defining absolute physical standards to be met by all prison guards. The pertinent legal issue under *Griggs,* she said, was whether an employer could justify its *chosen* selection device with evidence of its job relatedness—and Alabama couldn't do that.[82]

That also was Horowitz's message when it came to Regulation 204. "[We] do not argue that it is not permissible for the State of Alabama to want to have a safe and efficient workforce in its prisons," she emphasized. "The question then becomes whether or not Regulation 204 is necessary to the achievement of that objective. . . . The burden was on the state to offer factual objective data that women could not perform in this kind of prison setting, and that . . . proof is simply not in this record." She reminded the justices that the outside expert testimony had shown that "women were performing in this capacity elsewhere [in the country] in a satisfactory manner" and, moreover, that Judge Johnson was a member of the district court panel that had rejected Alabama's BFOQ argument. Having ruled on the earlier prison lawsuit, Johnson was "unusually familiar with conditions in the Alabama penitentiaries," Horowitz said. If he thought women could do the job in such an environment, the Court should defer to his judgment, not the state's.[83]

ON JUNE 27, 1977, Kim Rawlinson got the call. Pam Horowitz and John Carroll were both on the phone, and they had good news and bad news. The good news was that the Court had agreed with the district court about the five-foot-two/120-pound limit for all Board of Corrections staff: The *Griggs* "fair in form, discriminatory in operation" standard applied equally to sex discrimination cases, and Alabama had "failed to offer evidence of any kind" in support of its height and weight requirements—let alone evidence that would prove that they were a "business necessity."[84] The Court didn't care that the SPLC hadn't been able to show how many actual applicants were screened out by the height and weight threshold; it agreed that the "application process itself might not adequately reflect the actual potential applicant pool, since . . . [a] potential applicant could easily determine her height and weight and conclude that to make an application would be futile."[85] And while Alabama might well be reasonable in its stated desire for hiring correctional counselors who could demonstrate physical strength, it needed more accurate measurement if its disproportionate exclusion of women applicants were to be justified.[86] So Rawlinson should have been eligible for a prison guard job with the Board of Corrections.

But eligible for *what* job? And that was the bad news. Having taken Alabama to task for merely hypothesizing that height and weight correlated with strength, the Court, whose opinion was authored by Justice Potter Stewart, went on to embrace the state's hypotheses about women's susceptibility to attacks by inmates—and upheld Regulation 204 on those grounds:

> The likelihood that inmates would assault a woman because she was a woman would pose a real threat not only to the victim of the assault but also to the basic control of the penitentiary and protection of its inmates and the other security personnel. The employee's very womanhood would thus directly undermine her capacity to provide the security that is the essence of a correctional counselor's responsibility.[87]

Justice Thurgood Marshall filed a vociferous dissent to this portion of the ruling, joined by Justice William Brennan, blasting the majority for an analysis that "sounds distressingly like saying two wrongs make a right."[88] "A prison system operating in blatant violation of the Eighth Amendment" should not be the basis for "justifying conduct that would otherwise violate a statute intended to remedy age-old discrimination," he wrote.[89] As he had in *Phillips,* Marshall bemoaned using sex stereotypes to justify maleness as a BFOQ. He blasted the Court's willingness to accept "one of the most insidious of the old myths about women—that women, wittingly or not, are seductive sexual objects."[90] Sexually motivated attacks on women guards, Marshall argued, were just a small subset of the larger problem of inmate attacks on guards of either sex—a gender-neutral risk that didn't warrant women's outright exclusion from the workplace. "The proper response to inevitable attacks on both female and male guards is not to limit the employment opportunities of law-abiding women who wish to contribute to their community, but to take swift and sure punitive action against the inmate offenders."[91]

Although Horowitz and Carroll shared Justice Marshall's outrage at the majority's decision on Regulation 204, a silver lining cheered them: The Court took pains to emphasize that its decision on that point arose from the unusually barbaric environment in Alabama's prisons at the time and should not be read as giving carte blanche to exclude women from jobs as prison guards—or from other hazardous work—more generally; in all Title VII cases going forward, the BFOQ exception should be read narrowly. "In the usual case" it explained, "the argument that a particular job is too dangerous for women may appropriately be met by the rejoinder that it is the purpose of Title VII to allow the individual woman to make that choice for herself."[92]

What the Court's decision meant for Rawlinson was that she could work as a correctional counselor in one of Alabama's minimum-security facilities. It also meant that she was entitled to lost wages from the time she had been turned down by the Board of Corrections in the fall of 1974 to the present.

Rawlinson was disappointed that Regulation 204 would stand, but, to her, that part of the case was always secondary. She was thrilled to have succeeded in getting the height and weight minimums struck down. "That's what I wanted to do," she said—not just for herself, but also for "all the other tiny women out there."

RAWLINSON ULTIMATELY worked in corrections for only five years. It wasn't what she wanted, but it was just the way things turned

out. She first was a correctional counselor in the state's juvenile detention facility, the Frank Lee Youth Center. Despite her small stature,
Rawlinson said she never felt afraid. After all, she looked around her
and saw guards who were "incredibly old and decrepit and fat," she
remembered with a laugh. She also attributed her confidence to the
reaction she got from the inmates. "You could tell that it was so nice to
have a woman there because it made it more normal," she said. "They
would come [confide in me]. It was constant. I felt totally protected."

Less grateful for her presence were the other guards, all of whom
were men. Many came out of a military or police background, and had
never worked with a woman before. They knew about her case, and
weren't happy about her arrival. The head correctional counselor, for
instance, wreaked havoc with Rawlinson's schedule, assigning her a
shift of 6:00 a.m. to 2:00 p.m. one day, then 2:00 p.m. to 10:00 p.m.
the next, and then 10:00 p.m. to 6:00 a.m. the day after that.

After about two years, Rawlinson transferred to Montgomery's
Kilby Correctional Facility. Because it was a maximum-security
prison, Rawlinson couldn't hold a "contact" job; instead, she was a
classification officer helping to implement Judge Frank Johnson, Jr.'s,
1976 order that the state segregate the most violent prisoners from the
rest of the prison population. Working with a psychologist, Rawlinson
interviewed and evaluated inmates to decide where to place them, and
what supportive services they needed. For the woman who'd fallen for
the field of psychology as a college student, it was a perfect fit. "I really
loved that," she said. "I got to hear stories." While working at Kilby
during the day, at night Rawlinson attended Auburn University on a
scholarship, completing a master's degree in criminal justice.

Although she had dreams of using the advanced degree to move
into a more senior role, in early 1980 Rawlinson got derailed. For
reasons that never were explained to her—even after she hired an attorney to represent her—the Board of Corrections placed her under investigation. The probe never resulted in any charges being filed against
her, but her career was stalled. She couldn't get promoted, she couldn't
get a raise, and she couldn't transfer to another job. Devastated to
leave corrections work after all she'd done to get there, she nevertheless quit her job and got married to a fellow guard. Difficult years
followed, including a cancer diagnosis, bouts with substance abuse, a
divorce, a remarriage, and a second divorce. She excelled at whatever
job she tried, from selling Mary Kay—earning the famed pink Cadil-
lac—to being an executive secretary, but she never stopped regretting
that she didn't get to have the law enforcement career she wanted.

In 1998, Rawlinson moved back to Montgomery, her hometown. Through a renewed religious faith she found sobriety, and some measure of peace. And it's also through her church that she's been able to see the impact her case has had since that day in 1975 when she told her story to Pam Horowitz while washing her hair. For years, Rawlinson and other members of her congregation have made regular trips to Alabama's prisons to meet with inmates. With every visit, Rawlinson has seen more and more female guards—including women even shorter than she. (In 1985, her victory in opening prison guard jobs to applicants of any size was expanded when Alabama rescinded Regulation 204.) Women now compose 21 percent of the force in the state's all-male maximum-security penitentiaries, and a few of those facilities even have a female warden.[93] "I am so excited for the women that I see," she said. "I really think everybody kind of won."

Whenever she encounters a woman guard, Rawlinson strikes up a conversation. "'Is this what you always wanted to do?'" asks the woman whose family could never understand what she saw in such a job. "Most of them say yes. It's just amazing to me." She gave a boisterous laugh. "So I'm not the only crazy woman out here!"

three

live long(er)
and prosper

City of Los Angeles Department of
Water and Power v. Manhart (1978)

IN EARLY 1973, A UNION ORGANIZER NAMED RUTH
Blanco set her sights on the Los Angeles Department of Water and
Power. With 12,000 employees, the DWP was one of the city's largest
employers, charged with keeping the hot, arid city of roughly three
million supplied with water and electricity. Due to a recent change
in California law, those employees now were allowed to unionize for
the first time. In the feeding frenzy that ensued, unions big and small
had descended on the DWP's headquarters, a seventeen-story, steel-
and-concrete architectural landmark in L.A.'s Bunker Hill district, to
begin trying win the necessary votes to be named the employees' exclusive representative.

For close to a century, the DWP's engineers and technical workers
had belonged to their own craft union, Local 18 of the International
Brotherhood of Electrical Workers, and the union was eager to enlist
the new recruits. Blanco had been dispatched by the IBEW to woo the
DWP's two thousand mostly female clerical and administrative workers. Her biggest competitor was the American Federation of State,
County, and Municipal Employees. With teachers, nurses, librar-
ians, human resources professionals, and administrative staff among
its members, AFSCME was a female-dominated union. In order to

convince the women of the DWP to pledge allegiance to a union with "brotherhood" in its name, Blanco knew she needed a hook—some "razzle dazzle," as Local 18's attorney, Robert Dohrmann, later put it.

Blanco got to know Mary Born, the secretary to the DWP's five commissioners. The DWP's pension policy had long rankled female employees, Born told her. Promising retirees lifetime monthly benefits valued at a fixed percentage of their average earnings, the plan was funded by mandatory contributions from the DWP and from the employees themselves, in the form of deductions from each paycheck.

Like many of the pension plans of the early 1970s, though, the DWP plan relegated women to second-class status. Mortality tables showed that women lived, on average, five years longer than men, so the DWP made them contribute more from their paychecks to the pension program—15 percent more, to be exact. Those greater contributions didn't translate into greater pension benefits, though; female retirees still got the same monthly check as their male counterparts. But because women as a group collected benefits for a longer time, went the logic, women as a group were required to subsidize that difference out of their paychecks while they were still on the job.

Blanco was appalled that Local 18 had allowed the DWP to maintain such a policy, and for so long. No other department in Los Angeles's vast city government had a pension policy like it. Remedying the disparity was not only the fair thing to do—it would be a public relations boon to the IBEW's campaign to garner votes from women workers. With this strategy in mind, Blanco called attorney Dohrmann, whose firm had represented the union for years. "She yelled at me and swore at me," recalled Dohrmann with a laugh. "I thought she was the most obnoxious woman in the world." He admitted, though, that he'd never thought about the disparity between male and female contribution rates. It didn't take long for Blanco, in her trademark staccato delivery, to raise his consciousness. "They were mad," Dohrmann said of the DWP's women workers. "I don't blame them for being mad. Every paycheck, they saw the insult."

Under the DWP's plan, all of the other factors that affected an individual worker's longevity—smoking, drinking, weight, prior medical history, and so on—were pooled, and the risk was shared equally. So was race, even though African Americans had been shown to have shorter life expectancies than whites.[1] Sex was the only factor to be singled out. No matter how long each individual woman or man employed by the DWP might be expected to live based on all of those other factors, then, each individual woman still took home less each week than the man working next to her. That was less money for the mortgage, for food, for bills, and over the course of a career, it could amount to many thousands of dollars. Dohrmann agreed that something had to be done.

"Next thing I know," he marveled, "I'm part of the process."

"THE PROCESS" of agitating for change at the DWP already was well under way. Mary Born had gathered a coalition of women employees to establish the Committee to Protect Women's Retirement Benefits.

One of the committee's designated spokeswomen was Alice Muller, who a few years earlier had become the first woman at the DWP promoted to the position of chief clerk. At fifty-one, Muller had spent most of her working life at the DWP and was, in Dohrmann's description, a "striver." After earning an accounting degree from the University of California at Los Angeles and working for a few years in the public library, she was hired in 1942 by the DWP as a clerk in the Commercial Department. Within six months she was promoted to senior clerk. Beginning in the late 1940s, Muller took the test every year to win promotion to principal clerk in the Accounting Department; every year she received the top score, and every year she was denied an interview. Instead, she watched while men ranked below her on the list were promoted. "In those days, it would not have occurred to most of us women to file a grievance, if there had been such a process," Muller later wrote, "even when the men who were appointed ahead of us were less qualified than we were, because double standards in business were accepted as the norm."[2]

Muller finally was named principal clerk in 1958, the first woman at the DWP ever to earn the title, and a decade later she won the promotion to chief clerk.[3] By then she was in the Power Design and Construction Division, coordinating the logistics of construction projects throughout the DWP's ever-more-sprawling territory. "I have long dreamed of working on a power construction project," she wrote at the time of her promotion. "[M]y appointment to such a job seemed outside the realm of possibility." Muller's new responsibilities prompted her to resign her elected position as employee representative on the DWP retirement plan's board (where she had been the first woman to hold that job too).[4]

Her experience on the board gave her particular understanding of the ins and outs of the pension plan; "mid-Victorian," she later called it.[5] The lingering disparity in women's contribution levels was only the latest battle she had helped to fight. For instance, benefits paid to women's survivors were for years lower than those paid to men's survivors, based on the stereotype that men were the family's bread-winners and didn't need their late spouse's earnings, while women invariably did. Similarly, for decades the plan had offered women early retirement at age fifty-five, while their male colleagues couldn't take early retirement until age sixty. The plan's mandatory retirement also came five years earlier for women: at age sixty versus age sixty-five for men. The DWP characterized these provisions as "benevolent," with its board assuming that women didn't really want to work, and perhaps didn't even have to, thanks to their husbands. Few women availed themselves of the early retirement program, though, or were happy to be forced out once they turned sixty. The monthly pension checks paled next to what they could earn if they kept working. Nevertheless, the DWP for years required women to subsidize the "gift" of early retirement by contributing close to 50 percent more than their male coworkers. Even when these rules were finally abolished, none of the over- or underpayments were ever remedied.

After Alice Muller resigned from the retirement plan's board, she took a similarly active role on the Committee to Protect Women's Retirement Benefits. By early 1973, she had contributed nearly $18,000 to the pension plan; her male counterpart would have paid just $12,500. The day after meeting Ruth Blanco for the first time in May 1973, Muller wrote her, "[I]t really was great to meet you, and to share a little of your unquenchable enthusiasm. I envy that. I wish you lots of luck and success and fulfillment, in every way." Alerting Blanco to various rules of the DWP that governed the pension dispute, Muller also told her the schedule of meetings held by the board's administrators and the commissioners. "Maybe a chatty little column in your [IBEW] tabloid about these two meetings would generate an interest in the provider of the information," Muller proposed. "It would be so much more profitable if the ever-present grapevine got some of your true facts to mull over."[6]

Despite her fervor for reform and the DWP's "dishearten[ing]" treatment[7]—"I feel that I have given every bit as much of myself, my mind, my heart, my energy, to the Department as a male employee," she wrote at the time[8]—Muller believed the committee should be meticulous in separating its operations from the DWP's to avoid any appearance of impropriety. She paid for the group to rent a post office box to handle its correspondence and urged that members pay an outside vendor to print the committee's literature instead of using DWP copiers for the job. Muller also paid attention to the details that might turn off some of the women the committee was trying to attract. For an initial printing of 7,500 flyers, she wrote her colleagues: "Will we have it printed on a pale pink feminine paper or will we use an ugly unisex color?" She signed her note, "Love and $ucce$$, Alice."[9]

One of the committee's first tactics was a letter-writing campaign directed to the DWP's Board of Commissioners. Women with as many as thirty years of experience wrote to register their anger at having contributed so much more than their male colleagues without any guarantee that they'd live long enough to reap the benefits. They also noted that because of survivorship benefits, payouts for their male colleagues usually weren't any cheaper for the pension plan, when all was said and done. Indeed, as of late 1974, there were approximately four hundred widows of male DWP workers collecting under the pension plan and just three widowers of female employees.[10] "Sure, we live longer," wrote Margaret Davis, "but not that much longer, and the man may have a wife who lives longer and collects under his plan, so who is the winner?"[11]

"I am not for Women's Lib," Carol Rastall told the board, "but I do feel we, the women employees, have been discriminated against. . . . There should be no additional amount for female longevity, as the male employees usually ha[ve] a spouse that will have the same life span."[12]

Throughout the fall of 1972 and into early 1973, the committee also wrote the board directly to demand overhaul of the policy. Those appeals yielded a few meetings, but otherwise the women of the DWP were mainly met with silence.

It was around this time that organizer Ruth Blanco recruited Dohrmann to throw the IBEW's weight behind the committee's campaign. Title VII would be the primary vehicle. The law's amendment in 1972 had made government employers like members of the DWP subject to its prohibition on sex discrimination. In June 1973, Dohrmann submitted a charge of discrimination to the EEOC.

Local 18 business manager Walter "Red" Risse issued a press release announcing the filing. In a nod to the organizing effort being overseen by Blanco, Risse made clear that it was not only union members for whom the IBEW was going to bat: "Charges were filed against

DWP on behalf of all female members of Local 18. The charges filed, in addition, included all female employees of DWP." A few months later, the EEOC issued a right-to-sue letter, the green light to go to federal court.

———— ————

DOHRMANN SET about drafting the complaint, working with Katherine Stoll Burns, an attorney who had been enlisted by Mary Born to advise the committee and coordinate its appeals to the DWP. Burns had graduated from the University of Michigan Law School in 1937, when women lawyers were still a rarity; indeed, she had struggled to find a firm that would hire her and ultimately had settled into a solo practice, litigating personal injury and worker's compensation cases. But Burns also was passionate about women's rights, and she worked first with Born and then with Blanco to coordinate the committee's appeals to the DWP.

With Blanco guiding them, Burns and Dohrmann identified the DWP women who could serve as the "named plaintiffs" in the action—the ones whose names would appear on the court filing on behalf of the other 2,500 other current employees and retirees covered by the suit. They wanted a cross-section of women, diverse in race, departmental assignment and rank, tenure with the DWP and in the pension plan, and family status. They also wanted mostly women who were either retired or nearing retirement, so as to blunt the financial impact of any potential retaliation by the DWP. As Dohrmann noted, deciding who is in the best position to weather a potentially negative employer response "always goes on when you're . . . having employees stand up and be recognized and put in the limelight, and in peril, really." This decision was left largely to Blanco's judgment; she was the one who knew the DWP women best.

It was a given that Alice Muller would be named in the complaint; in addition to being committed to the cause, she had achieved a senior level in the Power Design and Construction Division and had thirty years of service at the DWP. Muller, who was white, also was unmarried, meaning there was no one else to receive the benefit of her overpayments to the pension fund once she died. Ethel Lehman, who was African American, worked in the Accounting Division and, like Muller, was nearing retirement, having contributed to the pension fund for twenty-nine years. Carolyn Mayshack, also African American, worked in the Commercial Division and had seventeen years of service; as a single mother of two and one of the lowest earners in the group, Mayshack starkly embodied the economic hardship caused by women's diminished take-home pay. Margerie Stoop, a white woman who worked in the Personnel Division, had the longest tenure of all the plaintiffs—she had been with the DWP since 1938—and was married to another DWP employee. Despite the fact that they had been at the company roughly the same number of years and she made substantially less than he did, to date she had contributed more to the pension plan than he had. Marie Manhart, also white, was the lone retiree in the group, having contributed to the plan for nearly twenty-five years. At the time of her retirement, she had contributed about $6,000 more to the fund than her male counterpart.[13]

On September 26, 1973, Burns and Dohrmann filed *Manhart v. City of Los Angeles Department of Water and Power* in the U.S. District Court for the Central District of California. The complaint sought a judgment declaring the DWP's unequal contribution policy illegal and ordering that the 2,500 women currently employed or retired be refunded all overpayments they'd made since March 24, 1972—the date Title VII became applicable to the DWP.

AT THE TIME that *Manhart* began its path through the lower courts, different treatment of men and women in retirement benefits programs still fell largely in the category of "just the way things are." Indeed, the EEOC's first annual report of its Title VII enforcement activities (issued in 1966) found that of the complaints filed by women, a full 30 percent concerned unequal employee benefits.[14]

Sex-based differences in retirement policies had long compounded the gender pay gap. Mandatory retirement policies, for instance, like the one maintained for years at the DWP, forced women off the job at younger ages than their male coworkers—despite the expectation that they would live longer—and their families received less after they died.[15] Pension plans also commonly imposed criteria that penalized women during their childbearing years by requiring workers to accrue significant time on the job before they were even eligible to enroll, and denying service credit to those who took time off for pregnancy (but not for other medical reasons).

By 1973, there had been some progress in equalizing the retirement landscape. Following omnibus hearings on gender convened before Congress's Joint Committee on Finance in 1968, the EEOC had amended its Guidelines on Discrimination Because of Sex to prohibit different mandatory retirement ages for men and for women. (The Age Discrimination in Employment Act, or ADEA, enacted in 1967, didn't outlaw mandatory retirement altogether for most workers until 1986.) And in 1972, the EEOC had supplemented its Guidelines with a far broader directive: "[I]t shall be an unlawful employment practice for an employer to have a pension or retirement plan . . . which differentiates in benefits on the basis of sex."[16] Notably, the agency had stated that "it shall not be a defense under Title [VII] to a charge of sex discrimination in benefits that the cost of such benefits is greater with respect to one sex than the other."

But no court had yet considered whether it violated Title VII for an employer to take women's longer life expectancies into account when structuring its pension plan. Depending on the plan, the disparity could be built into either end of the retirement equation—that is, at the contribution stage, while employees were still working, or later, after they had retired.

Some employers required women to contribute more to the plan while they worked, as the DWP did, but then paid women and men equal benefits upon retirement. These defined benefit plans typically based benefits on a percentage of an employee's average wages. More commonly, employers offered defined contribution plans, in which retirement funds collected equal contributions from men and women (and/or their employers) while they were still on the job but paid women lower monthly benefits to account for their longer average life expectancies once they were retired.

THE WOMEN of the DWP couldn't have gotten luckier with the judge assigned to their case. Appointed to the bench by President Johnson, Harry Pregerson was the son of a postal worker who had immigrated to Southern California from the Ukraine. At the time *Manhart* was filed, he had recently made headlines for blocking construction of the seventeen-mile Century Freeway running southeast from Los Angeles to Norwalk because of environmental hazards and disruption to local low-income residents. "While we are planning to move dirt and pour concrete," he said, "we've got to plan for the people whose lives are affected by it."[17] Pregerson later helped broker a settlement allowing the project to go forward, with mandates for training and hiring women and workers of color for the construction job and for building affordable housing. (A few years later, during his successful confirmation hearings for a seat on the U.S. Court of Appeals for the Ninth Circuit, Pregerson was asked how he would resolve the dilemma between following his conscience and following the law. "My conscience is a product of the Ten Commandments, the Bill of Rights, the Boy Scout Oath, and the Marine Corps Hymn," he told the Senate Judiciary Committee. "If I had to follow my conscience or the law, I would follow my conscience."[18])

Over the next year, as the DWP sought to get the case dismissed on various grounds, Pregerson proved an active presence. During one case conference, he bluntly told Dohrmann that some of the plaintiffs' claims—which attempted to hold the individual DWP commissioners personally liable—were distractions from the meat of the case, the Title VII argument, and should be abandoned. Burns and Dorhmann soon amended the complaint to reflect those and other suggested refinements. While preparing to file the new pleading in the summer of 1974, Dohrmann received an unusual phone call: Pregerson's clerk was on the line, alerting him to an editorial from *The Las Vegas Sun* that the judge had noticed and wanted Dohrmann to see. It reported on a decision recently issued by the EEOC in favor of a female city worker who had complained that she received lower monthly pension benefits than her male colleagues, based on sex-differentiated actuarial figures.

The *Sun* took a jocular tone—"Hell hath no fury like a woman's desire for pension benefits"[19]—but news of the ruling was a godsend to Dohrmann and Burns. Aside from the EEOC's Guidelines, they had little legal authority on which to rely, so new was Title VII. "We had to form an argument that nobody had ever taken to heart very much before," Dohrmann explained. "Women live longer than men. How do you respond to that? It's a statistical verity."

Although the EEOC decision, No. 74–118, concerned unequal retirement *benefits,* its reasoning was just as applicable to the unequal *contributions* at issue in *Manhart.* Women's overall longevity couldn't be the basis for crafting the terms of a pension plan. "The logic of this argument is that usually used to support discrimination: an appeal to the average characteristics of a particular sex, race, or other group protected under Title VII," the EEOC held.[20]

A few months later, Burns and Dohrmann used EEOC Decision 74–118 to try to convince Judge Pregerson to issue a preliminary injunction against the DWP. As its name suggests, a preliminary injunction is a way of getting early relief in a case, before all the evidence is in and its merits can be fully assessed. It forces the other party to do something (or to refrain from doing something, as the case may be) while the lawsuit is ongoing. Granted sparingly, preliminary injunctions depend to a large extent on whether the judge believes the party seeking the injunction is likely to win in the end. They also hinge on whether "irreparable injury" might result in the meantime. In this case, Burns and Dohrmann were asking Judge Pregerson to order the DWP to immediately stop deducting greater amounts from women's paychecks. The loss of income, they argued, would inflict irreparable financial harm on hundreds of DWP employees and their families.

. The DWP countered that its sex-differentiated contribution levels were perfectly legal under Title VII. Because they lived longer, women weren't being treated unequally at all—or as Judge Pregerson summarized the DWP's stance in his eventual decision, "Women should pay more to get more."[21] The DWP relied on a section of Title VII known as the Bennett Amendment, after the senator who had proposed adding it in 1964. The amendment had been drawn from the Equal Pay Act, enacted one year before Title VII. The EPA was more limited than Title VII in that it only addressed wage differences between men and women doing the same job; Title VII required no such equivalency. But the EPA did allow some wage differences when they could be justified by gender-neutral factors, such as seniority, a merit or incentive program, or—the catchall—"any other factor other than sex."

The Bennett Amendment to Title VII had incorporated these same exclusions. That meant an employer who was sued under Title VII for compensation discrimination could defend itself by claiming the disputed pay difference was actually due to "any other factor other than sex." Longevity, the DWP argued, was precisely that—a neutral factor that made its pension contribution scheme permissible under Title VII. For good measure, the DWP cited a Senate floor colloquy about the Bennett Amendment between West Virginia senator Jennings Randolph and the Civil Rights Act's floor manager, Senator Hubert Humphrey of Minnesota. In an exchange recorded after Title VII was enacted, Randolph asked for clarification: Did Title VII preserve employers' prerogative to treat men and women differently under their retirement plans, such as providing lesser benefits for widowers and earlier retirement ages for women? Yes, responded Humphrey. The Bennett Amendment made that "unmistakably clear."[22]

The DWP also brushed off EEOC Decision 74–118, arguing that it would inflict discrimination on men, whose contributions while working would not be fully repaid to them after retirement because of their shorter average life spans. Women, in contrast, would enjoy their benefits for an average of five more years. The DWP noted, correctly, that EEOC opinions aren't binding on the courts but merely advisory. Finally, it argued that the Department of Labor, which had authority for interpreting the Equal Pay Act, had issued decisions of its own that allowed for some sex differentiation in pension plans. That conflicting authority, the DWP urged, meant that the EEOC should not have the last word on the issue.

Shortly after New Year's in 1975, Judge Pregerson issued his decision granting the preliminary injunction. The plaintiffs were likely to succeed on the merits once all the evidence was in, he concluded, and therefore should begin getting relief *now*. EEOC Decision 74–118 provided his central authority. (To the extent that the Labor Department's decisions conflicted with the EEOC's, Pregerson said, the EEOC's interpretation should prevail, given that it was the agency responsible for enforcing Title VII.) Even though the decision concerned differential *benefits* and not differential *contributions*, "[i]n either case, the reason for this differential treatment is the actuarial fact of female longevity which, in effect, involves the application of characteristics that may be true of a class of people to individuals within the class for which the characterization may or may not be true," the judge concluded.[23]

To Judge Pregerson, this elevation of group identity over individual traits was illegal. "In passing Title VII, Congress established a policy that each person must be treated as an individual and not on the basis of characteristics generally, and often falsely, attributed to any racial, religious, or sex group," he wrote. "More particularly, Congress intended in regard to sexual discrimination cases to strike at the entire spectrum of disparate treatment of individual men and women resulting from sex stereotypes."[24]

Judge Pregerson also was unconvinced that the Bennett Amendment insulated the DWP's rule, scoffing at the notion that a policy premised on women's greater overall longevity could be considered a "factor other than sex."[25] As for the Randolph-Humphrey colloquy about the amendment, that did not even merit a mention. Pregerson then made quick work of the other factors required for a preliminary injunction. The plaintiffs would be "irreparably injured" by having to continue making larger pension contributions, he said, not only because of the loss of dollars and cents but also because of the "loss of human dignity which [civil rights] violations engender."[26] All of those factors, as well as the vast numbers of women affected by the DWP's policy, meant that the public interest—the final consideration in granting a preliminary injunction—would be best served by suspending the policy.

But if Judge Pregerson's ruling was a satisfying victory for the women of the DWP and for the IBEW, it was—for the moment—largely symbolic. A few weeks earlier, the DWP had adopted a resolution overhauling the pension plan and abandoning the higher contribution rates for women. It had done so to come into compliance with a newly passed California law that required pension plans for large cities to rely on sex-neutral actuarial tables. As of January 1, 1975, then, women with the DWP would see the same deductions from their paychecks as their male coworkers. Going forward, the DWP itself would pay the roughly $155,000 annually needed to make up the shortfall in contributions.

Even though the DWP had already changed its policy, Judge Pregerson's ruling was still an unhappy development for the department: It opened the door for the plaintiffs to recover past damages, namely reimbursement of their earlier overpayments to the pension plan. Indeed, six months later, Pregerson walked through that open door. After making his "preliminary" ruling into a final judgment, he ordered the DWP to return all of the women's excess contributions, plus 7 percent interest. Because Title VII hadn't started applying to government entities until early 1972, though, and the policy had been changed on December 31, 1974, the window of liability was relatively small—about thirty-three months' worth of overpayments.

Ruth Blanco trumpeted the victory in one of her broadsides to the women of the DWP: "For most of you, the refund that Judge Pregerson has now ordered will be substantial. For ALL of you, it is a tremendous moral victory, and, of course, it means more money in your pocket each month, as long as you work for DWP. That's REAL affirmative action!"[27] This was only the latest happy news for Blanco and the IBEW. A few months earlier, the vote on the DWP's unionization finally had been held. Local 18 had beaten every other contender, including AFSCME, by a landslide. It was a total vindication of Blanco's strategy, which over the prior year had included frequent updates to the DPW workforce about the IBEW's bankrolling of the *Manhart* litigation. Fighting for women's equality had proved to be an enormously successful union-building tactic.

Her work at the DWP completed, Ruth Blanco moved on to the next IBEW organizing campaign, and she and Bob Dohrmann lost touch. He heard through the grapevine, though, that she later put her considerable talents of persuasion to use in a new role at the union, mediating disputes between union members and management. She died in 2009.

———

ALTHOUGH THE PRICE TAG for reimbursing the women of the DWP was modest, it was still enough to motivate the company to continue the fight. In July 1975, it filed an appeal with the U.S. Court of Appeals for the Ninth Circuit, the appellate court with jurisdiction over California. The DWP asked for a stay of Judge Pregerson's order, which would excuse the DWP from complying with it while the appellate court considered the case. The Ninth Circuit agreed, and the stay was entered. The women of the DWP had won, but they wouldn't see evidence of it in their bank accounts anytime soon.

By now, *Manhart* was starting to attract some national attention. If other courts were to adopt Judge Pregerson's reasoning, it would not only invalidate the pension plans of countless employers, but arguably it could cast doubt on sex-based distinctions in other contexts, such as life, auto, and health insurance. When the parties submitted their briefs to the Ninth Circuit, the women of the DWP had some significant allies backing them up: Both the EEOC and the Department of Labor submitted friend of the court briefs declaring the DWP's policy a Title VII violation that did not qualify for exemption under the Bennett Amendment's "any other factor other than sex" language.

In November 1976, a three-judge panel of the Ninth Circuit affirmed Judge Pregerson's decision. Largely tracking his reasoning, the court concluded: "Setting retirement contribution rates solely on the basis of sex is a failure to treat each employee as an individual; it treats each employee only as a member of one sex."[28] The court also made quick work of the DWP's claim that the Bennett Amendment insulated its plan. "[I]t does not seem reasonable to us to say that an actuarial distinction based entirely on sex is 'based on any other factor other than sex.' Sex is exactly what it is based on."[29]

The court further affirmed Judge Pregerson's order directing the DWP to return the women's overpayments. Doing so, it explained, fulfilled Title VII's intent of "making whole" victims of discrimination. And the refund could be accomplished without unduly burdening the pension plan. The DWP could raise all participants' contributions, for instance, or raise its own matching percentage to the plan, or simply make a one-time lump payment to make up the difference.[30]

As reported by *The Los Angeles Times,* one of the city attorneys defending the DWP, David Oliphant, described the case as "a unique one with ramifications far beyond the DWP, leading to speculation that an appeal is probable."[31] Before that decision could be made, however, the Supreme Court threw both parties a curveball. Two weeks after the Ninth Circuit's *Manhart* ruling, the Supreme Court issued its now-infamous decision in *General Electric Co. v. Gilbert.*[32] GE's short-term disability plan paid reduced wages to employees who took time off work to recover from an illness or injury, but not to those who took time off to have a baby. The Court concluded that this exclusion wasn't discrimination "because of sex" because women otherwise received equal coverage under the GE plan for medical conditions experienced by both sexes—cancer, broken legs, and the like. Consequently, it regarded the pregnancy exclusion merely as a benign cost-cutting measure.

Even though the DWP's plan had nothing to do with pregnancy, lawyers for the company saw parallels between *Gilbert* and *Manhart.* If an employer could refuse to subsidize the cost of women's leaves of absence due to pregnancy, why couldn't an employer also refuse to subsidize the cost of women's longer retirements? The day after *Gilbert* was decided, the DWP announced it would ask the Ninth Circuit for a second bite at the apple by putting the *Manhart* case before all thirteen judges who sat on the court. Deputy City Attorney David Oliphant "expressed some optimism" that the full court would be willing to revisit the three-judge panel's ruling, in light of *Gilbert.*[33]

The Ninth Circuit refused to hear the case again. This time, however, the vote was not unanimous; one judge did feel *Gilbert* had sufficiently altered the landscape to warrant a second look at *Manhart.* But the two other judges were unpersuaded; whereas GE's refusal to cover pregnancy harmed only *some* women, the DWP's demand for higher contributions affected *all* of them.

The only route left to the DWP now was the Supreme Court. In the summer of 1977, it filed its petition for *certiorari,* and in October, the Court granted it. What had started as an effort to inject some "razzle dazzle" into a union organizing campaign at a single city department was headed to the nation's highest court.

———

NOT LONG AFTER the Court granted *cert,* Bob Dohrmann received a call from the ACLU Women's Rights Project. As he recalled, after praising Dohrmann and Burns for their stewardship of the case thus far, the ACLU WRP offered to take charge of presenting the case to the high court. As in the recent *Dothard* case, the group's eagerness (and likely anxiety) was understandable, given the high stakes; *Manhart* addressed an issue central to women's right to equal pay. A ruling for the DWP would give employers around the country the go-ahead to maintain all manner of sex differentials in benefits plans, and could even embolden pension plans that had switched to sex-neutral actuarial tables to switch back in the name of cost. Although Dohrmann's firm was not wholly inexperienced before the Supreme Court, it could not claim the pedigree of the ACLU WRP. Dohrmann himself had never argued a case before the justices.

Dohrmann was eager not to offend the "big, heavy hitters" of the ACLU WRP, but there was no way he was giving up the case. "What we said was, thank you, we'd appreciate the *amicus* [brief], but this is our case and our clients look to us to continue it and we want it," he said. To Dohrmann's relief, the conversation ended cordially.

The ACLU WRP did submit an *amicus* brief,[34] as did several other interest groups. According to Dohrmann, the support from friends of the court "came to us in droves." The EEOC weighed in again, as it had before the Ninth Circuit, to reiterate Title VII's proscription on allowing group characteristics to trump individual rights.[35] The United Auto Workers and the AFL-CIO filed a brief that told the Court most defined benefit plans no longer required higher contributions from women, nor paid them lower benefits at retirement, and were functioning just fine; the employers still relying on such plans, they noted, were mainly educational institutions and government employers.[36] A joint submission by the Women's Equity Action League and the Association for Women in Mathematics, which represented women statisticians, engineers, and accountants, explained that the DWP was overstating the actuarial significance of women's longer life expectancies.[37] Indeed, 84 percent of men and women who lived past age sixty-five, they noted, died at the same age. Yet all of the women of the DWP were being asked to pay a surcharge from which only 16 percent of them lived to benefit.[38]

A few of the friends of the court stood to gain more directly from a ruling in favor of the plaintiffs. The ACLU WRP was joined in its brief by the American Association of University Professors, many of whose members belonged to a pension plan operated by TIAA-CREF. TIAA-CREF provided pension, life insurance, and other benefits to personnel at 85 percent of private colleges and 45 percent of public schools. Both its pension and life insurance plans relied on sex-segregated mortality tables. Although employers made equal contributions on behalf of men and women enrolled in those plans, TIAA-CREF paid lower monthly annuity benefits to women based on their longer life expectancies. At the time it submitted its brief, the ACLU WRP was actively litigating one case against TIAA-CREF.[39] Another friend of the court, the American Nurses Association, also had a pending class action lawsuit against TIAA-CREF.[40]

Not surprisingly, TIAA-CREF itself also filed a friend of the court brief, but in support of the DWP.[41] Noting that it currently was fighting off six separate lawsuits—and likely there would be many more if sex-neutral actuarial tables were deemed mandatory under Title VII—the company warned of catastrophic consequences to the annuity industry: underfunded plans (if forced to equalize payments to women), increased costs for employers (who would have to make up any shortfalls out of their own coffers), and potentially higher rates for plan participants. A brief filed by the American Council of Life Insurance was similarly alarmist, warning that the "impact this Court's decision could have on the basic structure of the American life insurance industry" would cost American business "*billions* of dollars annually" and raise rates not only for men (in purchasing pension annuities) but for women (in purchasing life insurance, where their longevity had led to *lower* rates than for men).[42] Government entities, such as the State of Oregon, New York City, and the New York State Teachers Retirement System, filed briefs as well, all fearing for the futures of the sex-differentiated annuity plans maintained for their employees.[43]

ORAL ARGUMENT in *City of Los Angeles Department of Water and Power v. Manhart* was held on January 18, 1978, a cold and clear morning in the nation's capital. It was the second time in two days that Bob Dohrmann, his wife, and a few other guests had made the trip to the Court; argument originally was scheduled for January 17, but the case calendared before theirs had run long and the *Manhart* argument was put off until the next day. Dohrmann didn't mind; he felt ready, having participated in a vigorous mock argument convened at a DC law firm before a group of employment law experts, so he was able to enjoy the luxury of being witness to the highest-caliber legal advocacy in the country two days in a row.

When it was Dohrmann's turn at last, the justices filed in, with Chief Justice Warren Burger in the middle. It was the same group of justices as had heard *Dothard v. Rawlinson* the prior year, with one exception: The seat directly to Burger's right was empty; for reasons that were never explained, Justice William Brennan was not present.

David Oliphant was the first to take the lectern, arguing on behalf of the DWP. Dohrmann marveled that Los Angeles had put a rank-and-file deputy city attorney forward as its representative—an unlikely choice to submit to the glare of Court scrutiny. Oliphant followed two main themes. The first was well worn, having been the DWP's argument since its initial filings before Judge Pregerson: The DWP's plan was not discriminatory at all, because the Bennett Amendment allowed it to take account of longevity as a "factor other than sex." The Court's recent decision in *Gilbert,* Oliphant noted, was only the latest evidence that the cost of subsidizing such longevity was a valid, nondiscriminatory reason for different pension contributions. Oliphant's second theme was new, and reminded the justices of the practical consequences of their opinion: "[T]he impact of this decision will affect male employees, their spouses and a multitude of Retirement Systems across the country, as witnessed by the many *amicus* briefs that have been filed." Or as he put it later, "It seems to me this is one of those Gordian Knots that the Court is going to be faced with, with males on one side or the females on the other."[44]

The justices tried to tease out why sex-based longevity warranted separation from the other factors affecting mortality, which were otherwise pooled. Don't different races have different life expectancies? The Bennett Amendment allows sex to be treated differently from race, answered Oliphant. Don't males who don't live so long subsidize other males who live longer? Yes, but at the time they enroll in the pension program, they have the same general life expectancy, said Oliphant, and that can't be said of men and women. Doesn't the plan require smokers to subsidize nonsmokers? True, admitted Oliphant, but smoking is a risk factor that can't necessarily be known to the insurer, because it's within the control of an individual; but a participant's sex is evident.[45]

Bob Dohrmann was next at the lectern. During his mock argument, he'd received some advice that stuck in his mind, delivered by a hard-bitten female attorney from the EEOC. "Draw them a cartoon!" she had advised. "They're not that smart!" So Dohrmann kept his message simple: The choice was not between penalizing women or penalizing men but between treating the sexes "as statistics, rather than as individual workers." He didn't deny that mortality tables showed that women lived, as a group, longer than men. The problem arose when those tables "are used to apply the sole and only cost of longevity to one sex even though it bears only some co-relation to longevity, and not a complete one." Dohrmann also noted that the DWP had overstated the significance of sex in determining longevity; in fact, as had been noted in the brief by the Women's Equity Action League and female mathematicians, the vast majority of men and women lived to the same age. The better, fairer course, he argued, would be to assess longevity according to all of the relevant factors—smoking, drinking, weight, and the like, as well as gender.[46]

Here Justice William Rehnquist had a question. Assessing those other factors requires "a lot of forms to fill up" and depended on the honesty of the pension plan applicant. Wasn't it just easier to distinguish between men and women and be done with it? Dohrmann was taken aback. To prioritize administrative convenience over wage equality for women seemed to him breathtakingly cavalier. "[Sex] is readily identifiable but why is it identified and then used to penalize the person solely because she is a woman?" he answered, with obvious heat. "She receives fifteen percent less than a man in her paycheck and yet her rent is the same, her medical bills are the same, her bills at the supermarket are the same. . . . Why not pool all risk then, Mr. Justice Rehnquist, even as now, every other single risk is being pooled by this plan and a vast majority of plans in America. Why cannot we pool all risks? Why use sex?"

Here Chief Justice Burger stepped in. "It is a matter of choice," he answered.

"Yes, it is," said Dohrmann. "And we . . . contend that that choice is unlawful."[47]

The justices also wanted to know what Dohrmann had to say about the Bennett Amendment. Why wasn't longevity a neutral "factor other than sex"? Because it was only longevity *based on sex* that was being relied on, said Dohrmann. That was clearly not the kind of neutral factor intended by Congress to allow pay differentials under Title VII. Those factors, he explained, included merits systems, lifting requirements, and seniority systems.[48]

The rest of Dohrmann's argument was taken up with dissecting the evolution of the EEOC's position on the retirement benefits issue. Then, after a brief rebuttal from Oliphant—during which the justices mainly questioned him about the pension plan's mechanics[49]—the argument was over. Cautiously optimistic that the justices were leaning his way, Dohrmann boarded a flight back to Los Angeles with his wife.

THREE MONTHS LATER, the decision was in. "An employment practice that requires 2,000 individuals to contribute more money into a fund than 10,000 other employees simply because each of them is a woman, rather than a man, is in direct conflict with both the language and the policy of the Act," wrote Justice John Paul Stevens for a six to two majority.[50] (Only eight justices voted on the ruling, due to Justice Brennan's absence from oral argument.) "[T]he basic policy of the statute," Stevens explained, "requires that we focus on fairness to individuals rather than fairness to classes."[51] While women did, as a group, live longer than men, it was equally true that many women and men did not conform to that stereotype. "[W]hen insurance risks are grouped, the better risks always subsidize the poorer risks. . . . To insure the flabby and the fit as though they were equivalent risks may be more common than treating men and women alike; but nothing more than habit makes one 'subsidy' seem less fair than the other."[52]

As to the DWP's Bennett Amendment argument, the majority wasn't buying. Quoting the Ninth Circuit—"sex is exactly what [the city's policy] is based on"—the Court rejected the Equal Pay Act as a shield to the express gender differences in the pension plan.[53]

The majority also refused the city's plea that the recent *Gilbert* decision was a basis for approving the scheme. The Court's opinion in *Gilbert* had rested on the conclusion that the terms of GE's plan distinguished not between women and men but between pregnant and nonpregnant persons. In contrast, Los Angeles's policy expressly distinguished between men and women.[54]

Chief Justice Burger, joined by Justice Rehnquist, dissented. By enacting Title VII, he wrote, Congress had never intended "an effect upon pension plans so revolutionary and discriminatory—this time favorable to women at the expense of men." Echoing the colloquy between Justice Rehnquist and Bob Dohrmann at oral argument, Burger argued that the difficulty of tailoring a pension plan to take into account all individual variables should not preclude its taking into account the "reliable statistics" regarding male and female mortality.[55]

But Dohrmann's heart sank when he read the majority's ruling on the reimbursement issue. Reversing the Ninth Circuit by a vote of seven to one—only Justice Marshall dissented—the Court refused to order reimbursement of overpayments by the DWP women. The risk of jeopardizing the fund's fiscal health and the expectations of the thousands of retirees receiving benefits from it was too great, the Court found, to justify restitution—either by the DWP or, by implication, by any other fund found in the future to have violated Title VII as a result of the Court's ruling. "Retroactive liability could be devastating for a pension fund," it explained. "[T]he administrators of retirement plans must be given time to adjust gradually to Title VII's demands."

WITHIN FIVE YEARS of the *Manhart* ruling, twenty-four states had responded to it by adopting sex-neutral actuarial tables for their primary state workers' pension schemes, regardless of whether they were defined as benefit or defined as contribution plans, joining the thirteen that had done so before 1978.[56]

Finally, in 1983, the Court issued the ruling that *Manhart* had made all but inevitable: In *Arizona Governing Committee for Tax Deferred Annuity and Deferred Compensation Plans v. Norris*,[57] the Court struck down a public pension plan that used women's longer life expectancy as a reason for paying them lower annuity payments after they retired. Nathalie Norris, a fifty-three-year-old employee of Arizona's Department of Economic Security, filed the case after learning that she would receive $34 less a month than her male counterparts during retirement, even though she had contributed the same amount while working. "Even a true generalization about a class cannot justify class-based treatment," wrote Justice Thurgood Marshall. "[T]he classification of employees on the basis of sex is no more permissible at the pay-out stage than at the pay-in stage."[58] It made no difference, said the Court, that Norris didn't work for the private insurance company with which Arizona had contracted to provide pension benefits; her employer's use of a sex-differentiated plan, even via a third party, was still discriminatory.

As in *Manhart,* though, the Court reversed lower court rulings that had ordered reimbursement to women shortchanged by the disputed policy. Its mandate applied only to the plan's future operation.

As revolutionary as *Manhart* and then *Norris* were in equalizing retirement programs and life insurance policies offered by employers, they had no effect on the private insurance market. Again and again, efforts to enact federal legislation addressing gender inequities in that arena were beaten back by the insurance industry. "By the mid-1980s and into the 1990s," explained one scholar, "women's rights organizations turned their attention from passing proposed federal insurance non-discrimination legislation to achieving incremental gains in key states through legislative advocacy and litigation."[59] State equal rights amendments were one vehicle; insurance-specific legislation was another.[60]

DESPITE THE MIXED outcome of *Manhart,* Alice Muller always retained a special bond with Bob Dohrmann until her death in 1995. While the case was still pending, she enrolled at Cal State-Northridge and began working toward a journalism degree. After reading *Gideon's Trumpet* in her Law and Mass Media course, she mailed her heavily annotated copy to Dohrmann and commended it to him. She signed her letter "Success, always."

four
a hostile environment

Meritor Savings Bank, FSB v. Vinson (1986)

IN A TINY LAW OFFICE ABOVE A HARDWARE STORE AT A busy Georgetown intersection, Judith Ludwic's new client couldn't stop crying. It was September 1978, and Ludwic was meeting for the second time with Mechelle Vinson, a petite African American woman in her early twenties who wanted a divorce. Their first appointment had been a free fifteen-minute consultation, as promised by the newspaper ad placed by Rappaport and Associates. (The plural in the firm's name was a bit of posturing; Ludwic was the only "associate" at the firm, which specialized in low-cost divorces and wills.) Now Vinson had come back to sign the retainer agreement and pay Ludwic's $275 flat fee. Out of nowhere, as Ludwic stamped the firm's name on Vinson's receipt, the tears had started. Vinson was miserable at her job, she told Ludwic, and "couldn't take it anymore." Ludwic was puzzled. "Take what?"

And then, recalled Ludwic, "she started telling me. It was horrible. My jaw just dropped."[1]

As Vinson later testified, for more than three years, her supervisor at Capital City Federal Savings Bank, Sidney Taylor, had been sexually abusing her. When not forcing her to have intercourse or perform oral sex, Taylor would grope Vinson's breasts or buttocks or follow her into the restroom to expose his erect penis. He made vulgar comments about getting his "dick sucked" and would corner Vinson to warn her, "You are going to fuck me this evening."[2]

It all had started soon after Vinson was hired in the fall of 1974, when she was nineteen. Vinson had grown up in northeast Washington, DC, near the bank's Rhode Island Avenue branch, where she had a savings account. The bank was tiny, and Vinson had become friendly with the two tellers and with Taylor, the manager. After dropping out of high school at fifteen, she had held a series of part-time, low-wage jobs but wanted to work in a professional setting. One day she approached Taylor in the parking lot to ask whether he was hiring.[3] He gave her a job the next day as a teller trainee. Over the next four years, Vinson excelled, earning top evaluations, regular merit increases, and eventually a promotion to assistant manager.

When Vinson first started at the branch, Taylor had been "fatherly" toward her. Married with seven children and a deacon in his church, he appeared to fit the part. Taylor also was something of a success story in the local black community, having worked his way up from being the bank's janitor. He portrayed himself to Vinson as a mentor and encouraged her to confide in him about professional as well as personal matters. He lent her books about banking and paid her overtime that she hadn't earned, calling it a bonus for hard work. When Vinson told Taylor she was separating from her husband and was $120 short on the security deposit on a new apartment, Taylor gave the money to her. "[H]e tries to put on an air that he cares," Vinson told a reporter years later. "[L]ike he's here to help you."[4]

Vinson needed the help. Growing up, she'd had a troubled relationship with her father, a sanitation worker, and had run away so many times that her mother had tried to have her placed in foster care. It was in order to escape her troubled home that, at fifteen, she accepted an older family friend's marriage proposal, first getting pregnant so that she could legally wed despite being underage. She later miscarried after a fight with her new husband.[5]

After Vinson had worked at Capital City for about six months, she and Taylor went out to dinner at a Chinese restaurant, as they had on a few other occasions. According to Vinson, it was there that he propositioned her for the first time. Vinson refused but assured Taylor that she appreciated all he had done for her. "I don't want appreciation," he told her. "I want to go to bed with you. . . . Just like I hired you, I'll fire you, just like I made you, I'll break you, and if you don't do what I say then I'll have you killed."[6]

There was a motel connected to the restaurant, and Taylor got them a room. "I didn't know what to do," Vinson later told a reporter. "This is a man that I believed in. . . . And he kept saying to me I was a big girl now and he wasn't going to hurt me, and to take my clothes off. I just stood there. I didn't do anything. I was stiff like a board, almost like I was dead. Tears were running down my face. He wasn't saying anything. He just did what he wanted to do. He took my clothes off, he lay me down and that was it."[7]

Vinson had hoped that once Taylor got what he wanted, he would leave her alone, but the abuse escalated. (Not surprisingly, records show that Vinson took twenty-three days of sick leave that year.[8]) Vinson later testified that they had had intercourse forty to fifty more times, always at the bank after that first episode—in the basement and even on the floor of the bank vault.[9] Vinson felt powerless to escape. She needed her job. It was all she had to stay afloat financially. Moreover, she feared for her physical safety. Ever since that first night at the motel, Taylor had continued to threaten to kill her if she wasn't perfectly cooperative. When Vinson resisted his assaults, Taylor would use more violence in raping her. After at least one of these incidents, Vinson sought medical treatment for tears to her vagina.[10]

As Vinson later explained, "I had blinders on, I didn't see an outlet. I didn't have any support groups or anyone I could talk to about what I was going through. That's the reason I stayed in it so long. Out of fear."[11] And not surprisingly, after years of abuse by the men in her life, Vinson had begun doubting that there could be any other way to live. "You begin to accept what's happening to you," she reflected, "even though you know in your heart it's not right."[12] Vinson's body was certainly telling her that she was under extreme stress. Her hair was falling out, she couldn't eat, and she suffered from chronic insomnia.[13]

Judith Ludwic had no doubt that Vinson was telling the truth. She may only have been in her first year of legal practice, but she was twenty-nine, and, like Vinson, she had been essentially on her own since she was fifteen, working her way through high school, then Wayne State for college, and finally University of Detroit Mercy for law school. Through her years of babysitting, waitressing, working in retail, temping in an office, and teaching high-risk kids, Ludwic had seen a lot and experienced inappropriate sexual behavior more than a few times. But while Ludwic's experiences fending for herself had made her view human nature with something of a gimlet eye, Vinson was different. She was "not a hard, streetwise person," Ludwic observed, but rather had a "naivete"[14] about her, a quality of expecting the best in people. "As bizarre as everything was, she was a very, very credible person," Ludwic said. "It was very obvious. This was not a story. This was a *life*."

Ludwic knew she didn't have the expertise to handle Vinson's case and would need to refer her to another lawyer. For the time being, she told Vinson, "Do *not* go back to work. We'll figure this out."

"SEXUAL HARASSMENT" was not a phrase Ludwic had ever heard, but she was sure the kind of sexual abuse that Vinson described was a violation of Title VII. Recalling her idealism, she laughed. "[I] never had a clue," she said, "that the law would not protect you from that."

The behavior that we now call sexual harassment has been around as long as women have been working outside the home, but in the late 1970s, the term had just entered the popular lexicon and the law. As Fred Strebeigh details in his comprehensive legal history, *Equal: Women Reshape American Law,* "sexual harassment" was first coined by three professors at Cornell University's Human Affairs Program in early 1975. The program was devoted to a social justice curriculum and included a course in women and work taught by Lin Farley. Farley had been approached for help by a secretary at a university physics lab, Carmita Wood, who had resigned after three years of leers, gropes, and other sexual advances by her boss, the lab's director. Wood's claim for unemployment had been denied because the hearing officer found that she had left her job merely for "personal, noncompelling reasons."[15]

Farley and her colleagues, Susan Meyer and Karen Sauvigne, wanted to help Wood. They knew that her ordeal wasn't unique; they'd heard horror stories from their female students and personally had experienced such abuse in prior jobs. They were confounded, though, as to what they could do about it. In an appeal sent to roughly one hundred lawyers around the country, Farley, Meyer, and Sauvigne asked for guidance about building a legal case for Wood and a movement to support women like her. But they struggled with a shorthand to describe Wood's experience. After considering and discarding a number of phrases—including "sexual coercion," "sexual intimidation," and "sexual blackmail"—they found one that fit: "sexual harassment."[16]

Farley, Meyer, and Sauvigne's efforts on Wood's behalf had the desired effect. Eleanor Holmes Norton, then head of New York City's Human Rights Commission, held hearings in April 1975 about women's workplace rights, and Farley spoke about sexual harassment. "Most male superiors treat it as a joke. At best, it's 'not serious,'" Farley testified. "Even more frightening, the woman who speaks out against her tormentors runs the risk of suddenly being seen as a crazy, a weirdo, or even worse, a loose woman."[17] A month later, the Cornell Human Affairs Program convened a "speak-out" in Ithaca, New York, about sexual harassment. Roughly twenty women addressed the small crowd, detailing their experiences. The speak-out coalesced into a new organization, Working Women United (later renamed the Working Women's Institute and relocated to New York City).

The two events caught the attention of a *New York Times* reporter, Enid Nemy, and her resulting August 1975 article, "Women Begin to Speak Out Against Sexual Harassment at Work," is believed to be the first time the phrase "sexual harassment" appeared in a national publication.[18] (Not all women welcomed the pejorative new label: *Harper's* published a sarcastic rejoinder by a female copy editor at the magazine. Harassment, "or, as some of us call it, flirting," she wrote, "gives a woman a reason to be careful with her lipstick in the morning and a topic of conversation for the ladies' room at 4:30."[19]) Soon after, *The Wall Street Journal* published its first article about the issue,[20] and the same month, *Redbook* launched a survey asking its readers to document their encounters with sexual harassment.[21] A November 1976 article describing the survey's results declared a "pandemic" infecting "the executive suite, the steno pool [and] . . . the assembly line":[22] Out of more than 9,000 responses, over 90 percent claimed to have experienced one or more forms of harassing behavior.[23] "Both sexes arrive at work lugging the emotional baggage of a lifetime, all the childhood teachings about what's masculine and what's feminine, the cultural myths and social reflexes that make men and women behave as they do toward each other," it concluded. "We've just begun to unpack that baggage, to look at it and try to replace the worn-out, obsolete bits and pieces."[24]

Efforts by women to "unpack that baggage" through litigation yielded mixed results. Although racial harassment had been recognized as a variant of illegal race discrimination as early as 1971, sexual harassment had had trouble gaining traction. Judges were reluctant to apply the label "sex discrimination" to behavior that, to them, amounted to ill-advised come-ons. Consequently, throughout the 1970s, many courts responded to complaints about abusive bosses with a collective shrug that conveyed, "You can't blame a guy for trying."

These early cases were formulaic: Male supervisor propositions female subordinate; female subordinate refuses; male supervisor fires female subordinate. There was Paulette Barnes, a secretary at the Environmental Protection Agency in Washington, DC, whose job was eliminated after she rejected her boss's advances. The judge who dismissed her Title VII claim called it merely "a controversy underpinned by the subtleties of an inharmonious personal relationship."[25] Across the country in Arizona were Jane Corne and Geneva DeVane, clerical workers with eye-care giant Bausch & Lomb, who quit rather than continue to endure their supervisor's relentless verbal and physical harassment. The judge who dismissed their discrimination suit concluded that their supervisor's misconduct "appears to be nothing more than a personal proclivity, peculiarity or mannerism."[26]

A California judge rejected the Title VII claim brought by Margaret Miller, who was fired for refusing to be "cooperative" with her boss's sexual demands. Such demands couldn't be discrimination "because of sex," the judge concluded, because they were simply too pervasive to regulate. "The attraction of males to females and females to males is a natural sex phenomenon and it is probable that this attraction plays at least a subtle part in most personnel decisions."[27] And in New Jersey, a judge tossed the Title VII lawsuit filed by Adrienne Tomkins, also fired for rejecting her supervisor's propositions, because the law was not intended to "provide a federal [personal injury] remedy for what amounts to physical attack motivated by sexual desire . . . which happened to occur in a corporate corridor rather than a back alley."[28]

As these rulings illustrate, men treating women as sex objects (and then discarding them when they proved unwilling) was considered beyond the reach of Title VII. In contrast to other forms of discrimination that plainly stemmed from antipathy toward a particular group, sexual harassment was perceived by many to be motivated by attraction—a compliment, not an insult. Moreover, casting a supervisor's sexual advances as purely "personal" endeavors, outside the scope of his authorized job duties, also meant that his employer couldn't be held liable for them.

As feminist legal scholar Catharine MacKinnon detailed in her 1979 landmark work, *Sexual Harassment of Working Women*,[29] early sexual harassment jurisprudence considered the particular harasser and particular target in a vacuum. Unlike racial harassment, the law failed to see sexual harassment as occurring within a larger social framework—a framework in which men, as a group, still ran the world, and women, as a group, were still second-class citizens. As MacKinnon explained:

> [T]he fact that a sexual relation between a woman and a man is felt to be personal does not exempt it from helping to perpetuate women's subordinate place in the workplace and in society as a whole. . . . Once the "personal" is seen to conform to a hierarchical social pattern, it is no more unique to, and without meaning beyond, each individual than are race relations.[30]

MacKinnon explained that changing the law's treatment of sexual harassment required convincing courts of two overarching principles. First, harassing conduct was *not* just a matter of attraction by a particular man toward a particular woman. It was "because of sex," in that the victim's very womanhood was the reason for the harassment. And second, unwelcome sexual conduct in the employment context wasn't just personal. It directly—and adversely—affected the "terms, conditions or privileges" of a woman's employment in a way that most men never had to experience.[31]

The tide began to turn in 1976, when the first federal court recognized sexual harassment as sex discrimination, finding that it "created an artificial barrier to employment which was placed before one gender and not the other."[32] Over the next few years, a handful of other courts delivered similarly positive results for plaintiffs.[33] Even more encouraging was that Paulette Barnes, Jane Corne and Geneva DeVane, Margaret Miller, and Adrienne Tomkins eventually won reversals of their cases on appeal.[34]

What all of these successful cases had in common was that the women who brought them had rejected their bosses' sexual demands. There was no doubt that such overtures were unwanted and the women came to court with their "virtue" intact. Furthermore, they had been punished for their moral rectitude; all had been fired or forced to quit and as a result had suffered tangible economic harm.[35] Catharine MacKinnon gave a name to this kind of harassment: quid pro quo. Latin for "this for that," quid pro quo described sexual advances that were part of a proposed transaction: Submit to me, and you get to keep your job.[36]

But MacKinnon identified a second kind of harassment, which was—and remains—far more prevalent: "condition of work" harassment, now better known as hostile environment. She described the constellation of behaviors that fit this category:

Unwanted sexual advances, made simply because she has a woman's body, can be a daily part of a woman's work life. She may be constantly felt or pinched, visually undressed and stared at, surreptitiously kissed, commented upon, manipulated into being alone, and generally taken advantage of at work—but never explicitly connected with her job. . . . Sexual harassment as a working condition often does not require a decisive yes or no to further involvement. The threat of loss of work explicit in the quid pro quo may be only implicit without being any less coercive. . . . This requires "playing along," constant vigilance, skillful obsequiousness, and an ability to project the implication that there is a sexual dimension to, or sexual possibilities for, the relationship, while avoiding the explicit "how about it" that would force a refusal into the open.[37]

Mechelle Vinson's experience didn't fit neatly into either category. Although Vinson alleged that Sidney Taylor had linked his sexual demands with threats to fire her, a hallmark of quid pro quo harassment, unlike the supervisors of the women who had brought successful quid pro quo lawsuits, Taylor never actually followed through on those threats. He didn't have to, because Vinson gave in. And unlike those successful litigants, Vinson had not sustained any quantifiable financial damage. To the contrary, she had gotten top evaluations, merit-based raises, and promotions (all of which, the bank admitted throughout the eventual litigation, Vinson deserved).

In many ways, Vinson's depictions of Taylor's coercive sexual conduct—groping, leering, exposing himself—bore characteristics of "condition of work" harassment. During the workday, Taylor also would visit a go-go bar down the street and return to peruse pornographic magazines in front of Vinson and the bank's other female employees.[38] Even when Vinson wasn't being raped or touched or leered at, her work environment was sexualized.

No court had yet considered such a messy collection of facts. Indeed, at the time Judith Ludwic was puzzling over how to handle Mechelle Vinson's case, Catharine MacKinnon's book had yet to be published.

LUDWIC KNEW a lawyer in Washington who had experience with employment discrimination cases, John Marshall Meisburg, Jr., and asked him to meet with her and Vinson. For two hours, sometimes with Ludwic's gentle prodding, Vinson repeated the details of her ordeal. "I'll never forget that day because she was a very compelling person," said Meisburg. "She was very articulate, she was very beautiful, and very intelligent." Her story, he said, was "the most egregious thing I'd ever heard of."[39] Meisburg concluded, "If this isn't sexual harassment, nothing is."

However credible Vinson might have been, though, Meisburg knew the case would be stronger if it wasn't limited to "he said, she said" evidence. "I said, 'I'll make you this deal,'" he recalled years later. "'If you can give me affidavits from two other women in the bank that this was happening, I will file this lawsuit in federal court.'"

Vinson told Meisburg that there *were* other women at the bank whom Taylor had harassed. One was Christina Malone, the other teller when Vinson was hired in 1974. In her early days at the branch, Vinson had seen Taylor touch Malone inappropriately on a number of occasions and even chase her around the office. On another occasion, the two women were in the restroom when Taylor burst in and menaced Malone in a sexual way, shimmying his crotch at her.[40] Vinson never asked Malone about these incidents at the time, chalking them up to a soured romantic relationship and figuring it wasn't her place to ask.[41] Eventually Malone was fired. Malone later told Vinson that Taylor had pestered her for sex and had slapped her once.[42]

There was also former teller Mary Levarity, who testified that the day that Taylor hired her, he told her that he expected her to "pay up" and "do him a favor also"—a sentiment he repeatedly expressed throughout Levarity's employment. She also testified that Taylor had fondled her and had tried to catch glimpses down her dress. Levarity ultimately had been fired because, she believed, she refused to sleep with Taylor.[43]

Vinson held up her end of the bargain, reporting to Meisburg that Malone and Levarity had agreed to sign affidavits attesting to Taylor's misconduct. On September 22, 1978, Meisburg filed a complaint in U.S. District Court for the District of Columbia. Three weeks later, on November 1, 1978, Capital City fired Vinson, claiming she'd taken excessive sick leave.[44]

IN THE SUMMER of 1979, Meisburg accepted a job with the EEOC's office in Miami, which meant he'd have to hand the Vinson case over to someone else. The case would be ready for trial by the winter, and Meisburg felt protective of it, and of Mechelle Vinson. By then he'd taken Sidney Taylor's deposition. It lasted only around thirty minutes, Meisburg recalled, just long enough for Taylor to genially deny having anything other than a strictly professional relationship with Vinson. What was most memorable about the deposition, said Meisburg, was Taylor's "dapper" appearance: Tall, slender, and handsome, he wore a white suit with white shoes—looking, said Meisburg, "almost like a movie star."

Determined to leave the litigation in good hands, Meisburg contacted Patricia Barry, a solo practitioner who had built a reputation representing federal employees in employment discrimination cases. When Meisburg told Barry the details of Mechelle Vinson's case, she eagerly accepted, declaring it a "slam dunk." As she later told a reporter, she considered Vinson's story "a *Color Purple* set in the heart of Washington."[45] She had never handled a sexual harassment case before, but between the egregiousness of Taylor's alleged abuse, Vinson's credible demeanor, and evidence from the other women employees whom Meisburg had identified as witnesses, Barry thought she was set. And she was armed with her copy of MacKinnon's just-published *Sexual Harassment of Working Women,* which Barry described as "my Bible." The "condition of work" theory, otherwise known as hostile environment, was going to underpin Barry's strategy at trial— though at that point no court had yet accepted it.

As the trial date approached, Barry prepared to introduce evidence from Christine Malone and Mary Levarity to show that Taylor's behavior toward Vinson was part of a larger pattern or practice of harassment.[46] She also planned to call as a witness Wanda Brown, a part-time employee and college student to whom Taylor had allegedly made leering comments about her body's development ("My, you sure are getting some hips there"), and who had seen Taylor reading pornography in the office.[47] Those other women's voices would help transform Mechelle Vinson's case from "he said, she said" to "he said, she—and she and she and she—said."

TRIAL IN *Vinson v. Taylor* began on January 22, 1980, before Judge John Garrett Penn. Penn had been appointed to the federal bench the prior year by President Carter. He had entered law school the year that *Brown v. Board of Education*[48] was decided and claimed to have been inspired by the civil rights movement in pursuing a legal career (he was

African American),[49] but his resume did not reflect any particular affinity for victims of discrimination. For nearly a decade, he had served on the Washington, DC Superior Court, whose docket was heavy on criminal matters, and before that he was a lawyer in the Justice Department's Tax Division and General Litigation Section.

Over the next eleven days, Barry's trial strategy unraveled. It was, in her words, variously a "zoo," a "nightmare," and a "disaster." Over and over again, Judge Penn stopped the other women from testifying about the ways that Taylor had harassed them. "[W]hat Mr. Taylor did with this witness has nothing to do with what Mr. Taylor did with Miss Vinson," said the bank's lawyer in one of many objections that Penn sustained. On another occasion, Penn refused to allow Malone to describe instances where Taylor was "violent" with her. "[E]ven if he treats [women] violently, I'm not sure that is sexual discrimination necessarily," Penn said.[50] (He also wouldn't permit Barry to introduce a witness who would attest to Vinson's receiving medical treatment for vaginal tearing after Taylor raped her especially aggressively in May 1976.) Barry was left with only Mechelle Vinson's testimony about Taylor's sexual misconduct. It would be a "he said, she said" case after all.

When it was the bank's turn to put on its evidence, Sidney Taylor took the stand and denied all of Vinson's allegations. In fact, he said, it was *Vinson* who had come on to *him*, though he provided no specific examples of such overtures.[51] He did claim that Vinson's clothing was very revealing and that on one occasion he had had to send her home to change clothes.[52] He also stated his belief that Vinson's lawsuit was intended to exact revenge for his overruling her preference for a new head teller shortly before she stopped reporting to work.[53]

The bank also called two female bank employees to testify on its behalf. Teller Dorothea McCallum was the first. Although Vinson's filings with the court portrayed McCallum as a friend who confided her own unhappiness with Taylor's constant harassment,[54] McCallum denied she had had any problems. Instead, she described, in lurid detail, that Vinson "bragged about possessing voodoo powers, that she had told other bank employes [sic] about fantasies of sex and violence, including one in which she had sexual relations with a deceased grandfather."[55] The second was teller Yvette Peterson—whom Vinson testified she'd observed behaving flirtatiously with Taylor[56]—and who also claimed that Vinson "had a knack for talking of her sexual life quite a bit and her sexual activities," including "what she liked to do in bed with men, what she liked men to do with her."[57]

McCallum and Peterson also testified extensively about Vinson's wardrobe. McCallum said that her "dress wear was very exposive" [*sic*] and "most of the days she would come in with, if not a third of her breasts showing, about half of her breasts showing; and some days short dresses; or if she did wear a skirt, something that had a slit in it. It would really be split up."[58] Peterson added that Vinson's pants were especially tight, even by late 1970s standards.[59]

Barry objected vigorously to all of this testimony. But although Judge Penn had refused to admit any evidence about Sidney Taylor that didn't relate directly to his relationship with Mechelle Vinson, he permitted these wide-ranging discussions of Vinson's wardrobe and of her behavior and statements, none of which was alleged to have occurred in Taylor's presence. Nor did any of her alleged fantasies concern Taylor. (The rules of evidence in civil cases were amended in 1994 to limit testimony about the sexual history or behavior of victims of sex-based offenses—as is the case in criminal matters under so-called rape shield laws—but at the time of Vinson's trial, no such rule existed.[60])

Barry believes that Penn conducted the trial as he did because he considered Vinson to be a "slut." She characterized his attitude toward the bank's witnesses' inflammatory testimony about Vinson as, "Well, you've admitted to having sex, so—what do you want me to do about it?" In a defiant act of solidarity with her client, she bought a new suit to wear when delivering her closing argument. She made sure the skirt had a slit.

A LITTLE MORE than a month later, Penn issued his decision. Given how the trial had gone, it wasn't a surprise. "This Court after carefully considering the evidence offered by the parties has concluded that the plaintiff was not the victim of sexual harassment or sexual discrimination," Penn wrote.[61] In support of his ruling, Penn made a number of "findings of fact." Among them were that "[Vinson] was not required to grant Taylor or any other member of Capital sexual favors as a condition of either her employment or in order to obtain promotion" and that "[i]f [Vinson] and Taylor did engage in an intimate or sexual relationship during the time of [Vinson's] employment with Capital, that relationship was a voluntary one by plaintiff having nothing to do with her continued employment at Capital or her advancement or promotions at that institution."[62]

So Penn was doubly dismissive of Vinson: He was skeptical that she was telling the truth about whether sex had occurred at all—*"if"* there was a relationship—but if it had occurred, she was lying by claiming it wasn't voluntary. The notion that a woman might acquiesce in conduct by her supervisor that she didn't actually want wasn't part of his calculus. (Nor, apparently, were the parties' respective credibility. Sidney Taylor had denied any sexual contact with Vinson. Penn's conclusion that sex *might* have occurred also meant that Taylor *might* have committed perjury. But Penn made no finding of fact on this point.)

Even if Judge Penn had been willing to believe that the sex between Vinson and Taylor was *in*voluntary, though, he had another problem with her claim: She never had reported the harassment to anyone at the bank. Taylor's status as branch manager, Penn concluded, was not enough to make Capital City liable for his acts. The corporate entity had done nothing to facilitate or condone Taylor's conduct. After all, it had an equal employment opportunity policy that banned sex discrimination (though it was silent on the matter of sexual harassment).

Penn's implication was clear. This was just another "inharmonious personal relationship" caused by "personal proclivity, peculiarity or mannerism," a "natural sex phenomenon" that just "happened to occur in a corporate corridor rather than a back alley."

Barry was livid and immediately began preparing her appeal. She asked for help from New York City's Working Women's Institute, which in turn yielded interest from the San Francisco group Equal Rights Advocates and the Chicago-based Women Employed, all of which provided friend of the court briefs to supplement Barry's brief on the appeal's merits. They also secured an attorney, Ron Schechter, to represent them at the oral argument.[63]

Another stroke of luck came in March 1980, when the EEOC updated its Guidelines on Discrimination Because of Sex. For the first time, it declared that sexual harassment violated Title VII. Not coincidentally, the update came during the tenure of EEOC Chair Eleanor Holmes Norton, who, while heading the New York City Human Rights Commission in the 1970s, had given Cornell's Lin Farley her first public platform for describing, and decrying, sexual harassment.

The new Guidelines were a boon to Vinson's case in several ways. They held that an employee didn't sacrifice her claim by acquiescing to harassment. They provided for automatic employer liability when the harasser is a supervisor, regardless of whether the employee reported it.[64] And their definition of what kind of behavior is illegal was expansive and included harassment that created a "hostile environment":

> Unwelcome sexual advances, requests for sexual favors, and other verbal or physical conduct of a sexual nature constitute sexual harassment when (1) submission to such conduct is made either explicitly or implicitly a term or condition of an individual's employment, (2) submission to or rejection of such conduct by an individual is used as the basis for employment decisions affecting such individual, or (3) *such conduct has the purpose or effect of unreasonably interfering with an individual's work performance or creating an intimidating, hostile, or offensive working environment.*[65]

In early 1981, there was more good news. The D.C. Circuit—the very court that would decide Vinson's appeal—became the first federal court to recognize a hostile environment as sex discrimination under Title VII. In *Bundy v. Jackson,*[66] it ruled that prolonged harassment, in and of itself, was discrimination in the "terms, conditions, or privileges of employment." The court relied on the new EEOC Guidelines as well as MacKinnon's *Sexual Harassment of Working Women* and the by-then significant body of race, religion, and national origin hostile environment cases:

> Racial slurs, though intentional and directed at individuals, may still just be verbal insults, yet they too may create Title VII liability. How then can sexual harassment, which injects the most demeaning sexual stereotypes into the general work environment and which always represents an intentional assault on an individual's innermost privacy, not be illegal?[67]

BUNDY CEMENTED the D.C. Circuit's reputation as a "national leader in recent years in interpreting the law on sex discrimination."[68] Even for such a progressive court, though, the particular panel hearing Mechelle Vinson's appeal was something of a dream team. Two of the three judges were civil rights legends who understood the issue of sexual harassment. The first was Spottswood W. Robinson III. Among his other accomplishments before being appointed to the bench, Robinson had argued before the Supreme Court one of the four consolidated cases eventually decided as *Brown v. Board of Education.*[69] As a judge, he had authored the D.C. Circuit's opinion reversing the lower court decision against Paulette Barnes and holding that quid pro quo harassment is discrimination "because of sex."[70]

The other civil rights giant hearing Vinson's case was J. Skelly Wright. Before being elevated to the D.C. Circuit in 1962, Wright had been a district judge in his native Louisiana. During his tenure, he issued so many desegregation orders that he earned the nickname "Judas Wright."[71] After a cross was burned on his lawn and numerous threats were made on his life and his family, federal marshals provided round-the-clock protection.[72] (Justice Ruth Bader Ginsburg told an anecdote illustrating how accustomed Judge Wright's family became to living in the shadow of hatred: One night when the judge and his wife were out, their thirteen-year-old son received an anonymous phone call. "'Let me speak to that dirty nigger-loving Communist,' the voice demanded. Son James replied: 'He's not at home. May I take a message?'"[73]) But most important for Mechelle Vinson, Judge Wright also was the author of the recent *Bundy* decision.

DESPITE THESE auspicious circumstances, the February 1982 oral argument in *Vinson* was followed by prolonged silence from the court. Barry heard rumors that Judge Robinson was ill (which, it turned out, were true; he was diagnosed with colon cancer in the spring of 1982 and started a prolonged course of treatment[74]). She secretly feared that the delay signaled the court's distaste for the case and that it had put it on the back burner. "[Vinson] had talked about rape and she'd talked about having to have sex and I thought, it's too controversial," Barry recalled.

Whatever the reason, the appeals court's nearly three-year delay was hard on both Barry and Vinson. Barry was nearly broke, having spent much of her time since 1979 working on a case that so far had not yielded any legal fees. In the fall of 1982, she decided to move back to California to try her luck building a practice there. As for Vinson, since leaving Capital City in 1978, she had been unable to find work in the banking industry, so she had returned to the sort of itinerant jobs she'd done before, such as taking shifts at a plant store and selling newspapers and magazines.[75] She made a stab at attending nursing school but had to drop out because she couldn't afford it, and she eventually moved back in with her parents.[76]

Finally, in January 1985, the decision arrived: a complete reversal of Judge Penn. In a unanimous opinion authored by Judge Robinson, the court said that its recent decision in *Bundy* and the EEOC's updated Guidelines necessitated a new trial. Those authorities contradicted Penn's holding that because Vinson's career hadn't suffered, she hadn't experienced illegal harassment. What mattered, said the court, was whether Sidney Taylor "created or condoned a substantially discriminatory work *environment*, regardless of whether the complaining [employee] lost any tangible job benefits as a result of the discrimination."[77] That focus on the work environment also meant that it was incorrect to bar the testimony from Christina Malone, Mary Levarity, and Wanda Brown.[78]

The court was especially scornful of Penn's conclusion that any submission to sex by Vinson (that is, "if" there was any sex at all) was "voluntary": "A victim's 'voluntary' submission to unlawful discrimination of this sort can have no bearing in the pertinent inquiry: whether Taylor made Vinson's toleration of sexual harassment a condition of her employment."[79] In this vein, the court also castigated Penn for considering Vinson's wardrobe and alleged sexual fantasies. "Since . . . a woman does not waive her Title VII rights by her sartorial or whimsical proclivities, . . . that testimony had no place in this litigation."[80]

Finally, the court turned to the question of the bank's liability for Taylor's misconduct, even though Vinson had never gone over his head to complain. The bank had made Taylor its on-site representative and endowed him with authority to hire, fire, and control Capital City's employees' daily lives, said the court. That authority "carries attendant power to coerce, intimidate and harass," and "[f]or this reason, we think employers must answer for sexual harassment of any subordinate by any supervising superior."[81]

Four months later, the D.C. Circuit refused Capital City's request that all of the court's judges hear the case again. There were three dissenters, though, the only three Reagan appointees to the court, all of whom soon became household names: Judge Robert Bork, the author of the opinion, was joined by Antonin Scalia and Kenneth Starr. Scalia ascended to the Supreme Court a year later. The year after that, Bork famously was denied a seat on the Court, in part based on vociferous opposition by women's groups. His dissent in *Vinson* was among the precedents they cited as evidence of his unsuitability for confirmation.[82] Starr went on to serve as solicitor general under the first President Bush, then gained notoriety as the independent counsel overseeing investigation of the Monica Lewinsky–Bill Clinton affair.[83]

The *Vinson* dissenters were mostly preoccupied with how much more difficult it would become for supervisors to defend themselves against sexual harassment charges. "By depriving the charged person of any defenses, [the panel's conclusions] mean that sexual dalliance, however voluntarily engaged in, becomes harassment whenever an employee sees fit, after the fact, so to characterize it."[84] A twin concern, Bork wrote, was the ease with which a supervisor's actions could put an employer on the hook for harassment it was unaware of. "Though the employer has no way of preventing sexual relationships, he is defenseless and must pay if they occur and are then claimed to be harassment."[85]

Barry worried that the Bork-Scalia-Starr dissent gave the bank leverage to ask the Supreme Court to hear the case. (Indeed, Bork pointedly wrote, "The Supreme Court has never addressed the question of an employer's vicarious liability under Title VII."[86]) In October 1985, Barry's fears were confirmed. The Supreme Court agreed to consider the bank's appeal, with arguments to be heard in March 1986.

BY THE TIME the Court granted *certiorari* in Mechelle Vinson's case, ten years had passed since Lin Farley, Susan Meyer, and Karen Sauvigne had coined the term "sexual harassment." By then both the term and the concept had become widely known. Although the EEOC does not keep reliable statistics about charges filed before 1991, a 1986 article in *The Philadelphia Inquirer* reported that nearly 6,500 sexual harassment complaints had been filed with the agency the prior year.[87]

The publication of the EEOC's updated Guidelines on Discrimination Because of Sex and the growing number of supportive court cases had gone a long way toward educating employers and employees. Just six months after the agency issued an interim version of the Guidelines in 1980, for instance, *The New York Times* reported that Bell Telephone, IBM, and Time, Inc., had issued policy statements detailing the kinds of behavior that would no longer be tolerated and were conducting training for employees on how to avoid and report harassment.[88] Popular culture helped raise consciousness too; the 1980 female empowerment and revenge fantasy classic *9 to 5* was a box-office smash (and went on to become one of the highest-grossing comedies of all time).[89] Inspired in part by the true stories of members of 9to5, a Boston working women's collective, the movie resonated with female audiences.[90] A "sexist, egotistical, lying, hypocritical bigot" of a boss who gropes his secretary, starts rumors of an affair between them, and drops pencils on the floor so that she will have to bend over to pick them up would have been all too familiar to the women in the audience.

With wider awareness came intense interest in Mechelle Vinson's case (now known as *Meritor Savings Bank, FSB v. Vinson* because Capital City had been acquired by a larger bank). As one article put it, "Both those groups that support [Vinson] and those that have aligned themselves behind the bank share a common case of jitters over a variety of major issues that may be decided from a suit in which the facts are, as various legal observers have described them, 'incomplete,' 'tortured,' 'unclear,' and 'um, peculiar.'"[91] The notion that a work *environment* could be put on trial was especially unnerving to many observers. "*Vinson* is . . . the kind of case critics have in mind when they argue that the problem of sexual harassment doesn't belong in a court of law," said *The Washington Post*. "They envision hundreds, thousands of cases like Vinson's, cases filed by jilted lovers, disappointed mistresses, vengeful junior VPs, phalanxes of pink-collar Machiavellis seeking revenge and recompense."[92]

One of the entities that did not welcome *Vinson*'s consideration by the Supreme Court was the EEOC. Although the agency's 1980 Guidelines had been the basis for the D.C. Circuit's ruling in Mechelle Vinson's favor, the Reagan administration had since installed different leadership at the agency. Chair Clarence Thomas—later Supreme Court Justice Thomas—especially objected to the Guidelines' approving "hostile environment" claims and endorsing automatic employer liability for supervisors' harassment.[93]

When it came time to decide whether to submit a friend of the court brief in *Vinson,* Thomas and a majority of the five EEOC commissioners wanted to take the bank's side.[94] But using its *amicus* brief to renounce the Guidelines entirely would smack of political opportunism and damage the EEOC's authority as *the* interpreter of Title VII. So the agency split the baby: Its brief supported the D.C. Circuit's ruling that a hostile environment was illegal but attacked its conclusion that Mechelle Vinson had experienced one.

As Fred Strebeigh recounts, some vigorous dissenters within the EEOC felt that the agency should stand squarely behind its Guidelines and Mechelle Vinson. One was Clarence Thomas's top assistant, a young attorney named Anita Hill.[95] As a stunned nation learned six years later, Hill claimed to know from experience what a hostile work environment created by a supervisor felt like.

MUCH OF THE drama of Pat Barry's oral argument in *Meritor Savings Bank, FSB v. Vinson* occurred before she ever stepped into the courtroom. She came under intense pressure from the nation's most prominent progressive legal advocates to allow someone else to argue the case.

First she fended off Laurence Tribe, Harvard law professor and one of the giants of American constitutional law, who called her soon after the Court granted *certiorari* and offered to take over. She declined, although she later decided to ask Catharine MacKinnon to write the brief. (MacKinnon agreed.) Then, at a moot court session three weeks before the argument, Barry turned in a performance that was, by her own admission, a "bomb."

At Barry's moot court, the group of assembled experts included Carin Clauss, a law professor and former Solicitor of the Department of Labor; Marsha Berzon, cofounder of one of the nation's most prominent labor and employment law firms; Wendy Williams, a Georgetown Law School professor and leading expert on gender and the law; Sally Burns, assistant director of Georgetown Law School's Sex Discrimination Clinic (and also the point person for coordinating all of the supporting *amicus* briefs); and Catharine MacKinnon.

Barry arrived at the session totally unprepared. She claimed to have misunderstood the meeting's purpose, believing it to be a brainstorming session where "we would formulate as a group the best way to approach the argument."[96] The group was "jumping all over me," Barry recalled, as she failed to summon coherent answers to question after question. "They said, oh, we're going to lose the case." Her disastrous performance prompted calls for Barry to cede the argument to Clauss or Berzon,[97] while, according to Barry, MacKinnon pushed for Tribe.

The criticism definitely got under Barry's skin, but she wanted badly to appear before the Court. "I really wanted to be up there making the argument. I felt I had earned it," she said. "I was the blood, sweat, and tears behind [the case]." And after all, she had already argued one case before the Supreme Court five years earlier, on behalf of a federal employee with an age discrimination claim, and "no one said I bombed [that] time!" (The Court eventually ruled five to four against her client.[98]) Barry asked a lawyer friend to organize a second moot court for her. She went over for dinner, and afterward, the group of attorneys convened for the occasion grilled her. This time she was ready for it.

———— ▬ ————

WITH MINUTES to go before oral argument was to begin on the morning of March 25, 1986, Pat Barry was sitting in a taxi with her mother, crawling through Washington's rush hour. "Oh my god, I thought I was going to die," Barry recalled. "We were begging that cab driver, 'Please, please. We've got to make it. I'm arguing in the Supreme Court!'" She marveled that they actually made it in time. "I just barely squeaked in there."

Catharine MacKinnon and Sally Burns sat at counsel table with Pat Barry. In the packed gallery were Mechelle Vinson and attorney John Meisburg, who had flown in from Florida. At 10 a.m., the justices filed in. Chief Justice Warren Burger, serving in his final term on the Court, took the center seat. Notably, the Court hearing its first sexual harassment case now included a woman: Sandra Day O'Connor, the most recent appointee.

Robert Troll, the bank's attorney, was first at the lectern. His opening sentence said it all: He was going with the Bork-Scalia-Starr defense that employers shouldn't unwittingly be on the hook for sexual harassment. "The primary question in this case is whether a corporate employer is automatically liable under Title VII for a supervisor's sexual advances toward a subordinate even though the employer did not know about the advances and never had a chance to stop them."[99]

He got a skeptical reception from the Court's two liberal justices as well as its newest member. Justice Marshall wanted to know how an employee was supposed to put the employer on notice. Written notice? Oral notice? (The manner of notice is immaterial, said Troll. It just had to be given to someone with enough authority to fix it.) But Justices Stevens and O'Connor wondered why such notice was necessary. If quid pro quo harassment doesn't require notice to the employer, why is hostile environment any different? Troll said that in the quid pro quo context, the supervisor uses his authority to retaliate, such as by firing the employee. But how is that any different, asked Stevens, than a supervisor using his authority to make an employee's environment miserable? O'Connor added, "[The supervisor] is the person in place and who's in charge of trying to protect the work environment for the employees. That's part of the job."[100]

Justice O'Connor also pressed Troll about Vinson's entitlement to a new trial. Now that both the EEOC and the D.C. Circuit have recognized a hostile work environment as illegal discrimination, shouldn't Vinson get a chance to make that case? She also pushed Troll to explain why sexual harassment plaintiffs should have to prove that they experienced tangible harm beyond the "suffering" caused by a toxic environment. Shouldn't the same standard for racial harassment claims apply to sexual harassment claims? Troll tried pushing back, but it was futile. O'Connor repeated the question twice more—her gently steely voice never rising—and Troll caved. Yes, he admitted, the two standards should be the same. Quantifiable economic harm wasn't a prerequisite for a sexual harassment claim, after all.[101]

Troll's thirty minutes were almost up, so he circled back to his argument that, even assuming Sidney Taylor created a hostile work environment for Vinson, the bank wasn't liable for it:

> There is simply nothing unfair about requiring an employee to speak up when she perceives that her supervisor is harassing her. After all, sooner or later she'll have to make a complaint to someone if she wants Title VII relief. But there is something, we submit, very unfair about haling an innocent employer into court for a problem that it was unaware of and would have corrected voluntarily.[102]

Then it was Pat Barry's turn. Her opening remarks echoed Justice O'Connor's question to Troll: Vinson's case had not yet been tried under the new "hostile environment" framework, and it should be. The questioning then turned to the controversial conclusion by Judge Penn that Mechelle Vinson's participation in any sexual relationship had been "voluntary." "Voluntariness," Barry explained, doesn't take account of a victim's mere acquiescence, which could be under duress. Whether the conduct was "unwelcome" should be the touchstone.[103]

Justice Rehnquist spoke for the first time. Why aren't an employee's clothes and behavior relevant to whether sexual advances are "welcome" or not? With increasing incredulity, he pressed on. "So you say, then, that evidence of the complaining employee's work place dress and voluntary conduct is not admissible on the issue of whether or not the thing was unwelcome?" As Barry stammered a bit, Rehnquist interrupted, "Are you or are you not?" Barry rebounded by analogizing to rape cases, where a victim's behavior is irrelevant, except as to her behavior specifically toward the assailant—and there was no evidence in this case that Vinson ever made overtures to Taylor or discussed any of her (supposed) sexual fantasies with him.[104]

Barry was especially forceful when it came to explaining why it was critical for Judge Penn to try the case again, as suggested by Justice O'Connor. She recounted all of the evidence he had excluded because he wasn't concerned with whether there was a "noxious environment, poisoned with sexual innuendoes, insults, aggressive behavior that was unwanted."[105]

Barry ended on a high note. She addressed the bank's arguments about employer liability, arguing passionately that having invested a supervisor with authority to wield control over subordinates, the "employer"—not the harassed employee—"is in the best position to control the actions of the supervisors." And "with respect to the Northeast branch of . . . Capital City, Mr. Taylor *was* the bank for purposes of establishing the employer-employee relationship."

And then the red light on the lectern lit up. Her time was up. Pat Barry had gotten to argue the case she'd shepherded for seven years, and she hadn't bombed after all. One observer who'd been present at the disastrous moot court likened her transformation to Eliza Doolittle's.[106]

———— ————

ON JUNE 19, 1986, Justice Rehnquist delivered the opinion of a unanimous Court: "Without question, when a supervisor sexually harasses a subordinate because of the subordinate's sex, that supervisor 'discriminate[s]' on the basis of sex."[107] And harassment that causes purely emotional or psychological harm, he wrote, is just as illegal as harassment that results in tangible economic loss. In a callback to Justice O'Connor's questions at oral argument, Rehnquist analogized to racial harassment:

> Sexual harassment which creates a hostile or offensive environment for members of one sex is every bit the arbitrary barrier to sexual equality at the workplace that racial harassment is to racial equality. Surely, a requirement that a man or woman run a gauntlet of sexual abuse in return for the privilege of being allowed to work and make a living can be as demeaning and disconcerting as the harshest of racial epithets.[108]

Turning to exactly what kind of harassment rises to the level of illegality, Rehnquist articulated a new standard: The advances or other sexual behavior must be "sufficiently severe or pervasive to alter the conditions of [the victim's] employment and create an abusive working environment."[109]

Because Mechelle Vinson's allegations were "plainly sufficient" to meet that threshold,[110] the Court agreed with the D.C. Circuit that the case should go back to Judge Penn for a new trial. It also agreed that Penn was wrong in considering whether Vinson acted "voluntarily" and instead should consider whether Taylor's conduct was "unwelcome."[111]

But there were two caveats. First, as foreshadowed by Rehnquist's aggressive stance at oral argument, the Court held that Vinson's "provocative dress and publicly expressed sexual fantasies" were "obviously relevant" to whether Taylor's conduct was "unwelcome."[112] Second, a majority of the justices refused to find the bank liable for Taylor's misconduct solely because he was a supervisor. (Its most liberal wing, however, disagreed, and joined a separate opinion arguing that employers should be held automatically liable for a supervisors' harassment.) But the majority also rejected the bank's contention that unless an employee formally complains about a supervisor's harassment, she forfeits her right to later bring a lawsuit.

So on the issue of employer liability, Justices Rehnquist, Burger, White, Powell, Stevens, and O'Connor opted for the time-honored solution of punting: "We . . . decline the parties' invitation to issue a definitive rule on employer liability."[113] Instead, it held that liability would depend on the surrounding circumstances, such as how much control the harassing supervisor had over the employee's day-to-day life at work and whether an effective complaint mechanism was available. (Capital City's antidiscrimination policy, noted the Court, did not meet this standard; it neither mentioned harassment nor informed branch employees of other personnel to whom they could complain besides Taylor.[114])

And with that the Supreme Court returned the case to Judge Penn, with instructions to go back to the drawing board—and finish what Mechelle Vinson started in Judith Ludwic's office eight years earlier.

DESPITE THE DECISION'S few sour notes, the Court's ruling was met with jubilation by women's advocates and, as one reporter put it, "hailed by many as a victory for anyone who ever suffered a pinch, proposition or any other stunt perpetrated in the name of lust, piggishness or power."[115] Karen Sauvigne of the Working Women's Institute marveled at how far the law of sexual harassment had come in the decade since she and her colleagues gave it a name. It was especially striking, she observed, that the Supreme Court had issued such a landmark decision in a case involving someone who had "acquiesced, at least for a while," in the harassment. "That we won this case with those facts is very significant, because that's the least 'sympathetic' appellant."[116] (Sidney Taylor, for his part, remained unrepentant, telling a reporter shortly after the decision, "Right now I don't know if Ms. Vinson is a man or a woman. I have never had sex and don't intend to have sex with her."[117])

As for Vinson, she was "surprised and thrilled" by the decision.[118] People in her neighborhood whom she didn't even know congratulated her. "I've had a lot of women come up and say they've been harassed but just didn't have the guts to stand up," Vinson told *The Washington Post*. "One girl, 20 years old, came up and kissed me. She said she'd been abused but she didn't know what to do."[119]

But while *Vinson* may have revolutionized the law, it didn't revolutionize the culture. Five years after it was decided, the Senate was prepared to vote on the Supreme Court nomination of Clarence Thomas without even looking into Anita Hill's allegations that he had harassed her. (That he was accused of doing so at precisely the time he was in charge of enforcing Title VII—before and after *Vinson*—only made the claims more explosive.) It took a coalition of 120 women law professors writing each member of the Judiciary Committee, and seven congresswomen staging a photo op as they marched up the steps of the Capitol to demand a delay in the vote, for hearings to be held on Hill's allegations. As Judith Resnik, one of those 120 law professors, put it, "The Senate's initial disinterest in Anita Hill's information was a vivid reminder that not long before, disinterest in women's rights of all kinds was the norm."[120]

So it took another African American woman—coming forward to disclose her abuse by another powerful African American man—to fully galvanize a national conversation about sexual harassment. As Catharine MacKinnon later wrote:

> What happened in the Hill-Thomas hearings, among other things, was that sexual harassment became real to the world at large for the first time. My book of 1979, framing the legal claim in the way

that it became legally accepted, did not do this. The EEOC Guidelines of 1980 did not do this. Winning Mechelle Vinson's case in the Supreme Court in 1986 did not do this, although all these helped prepare the way. Anita Hill did this: her still, fully present, utterly lucid testimony, that ugly microphone stuck in her beautiful face, the unblinking camera gawking at her from point blank range.[121]

LIKE SO MANY cases that result in a Supreme Court victory, the aftermath of *Meritor Savings Bank, FSB v. Vinson* was anticlimactic. Upon being remanded to Judge Penn, the case languished for five more years, mired in disputes over discovery and procedural matters. Because Pat Barry had relocated to California, she didn't continue representing Vinson, so the Washington Lawyer's Committee for Civil Rights, an esteemed nonprofit legal group, took over. In the intervening years, Sidney Taylor was convicted of embezzling monies entrusted to him by an elderly bank customer and served time in federal prison.[122]

In 1991, before a new trial could occur in the case, the bank and Vinson, by then in her early thirties, reached a confidential settlement. With those funds, she was able to complete nursing school, and used it to pursue a career helping victims of abuse.[123]

In 2005, *Glamour* magazine celebrated Vinson in a feature entitled "These Women Changed *Your* Life." She described her victory as "the beginning" of concrete change, but cautioned, "[W]e still have a lot to do, such as teaching our sons to respect women and teaching our daughters"—and here she seemed to be speaking to her nineteen-year-old self—"let *no one* treat you that way.'"[124]

five

"a floor, not a ceiling"

California Federal Savings & Loan
Association v. Guerra (1987)

LILLIAN GARLAND WAS READY TO GET BACK TO WORK. After being on leave for close to three months with her newborn daughter, Kekere, she had started to go a little stir-crazy. She missed her job at Los Angeles' California Federal Savings and Loan, Cal Fed for short, where she was a receptionist for the commercial loan department. It was a perfect fit for Garland, an aspiring actress whose striking beauty and playful personality made her a favorite with the high-roller clients and executives alike. She called the bank bigwigs by their first names and teasingly reminded them to return their wives' phone calls.

So on April 20, 1982—one day ahead of her scheduled return date; she just couldn't wait—Garland put on her usual uniform of business suit and heels and rode the bus from her apartment in L.A.'s Baldwin Hills neighborhood to Cal Fed's headquarters on Wilshire Boulevard. She reported to the Personnel Department, expecting to fill out paperwork and take care of other formalities before going back to her desk. She was confused when she was told instead to go to the Legal Department. "They said, 'Your position is no longer available,'" recalled Garland. "'We hired the young lady that you trained in your place.' And I said, 'But I've been a loyal employee for over four years. What am I supposed to do now?'" Garland was told that the bank would let her know if something opened up, but otherwise, she should try to find a new job.

"I just felt faint, I was cold all over," said Garland. "I was in total shock."[1] She and her supervisor had discussed the starting and ending dates of her leave, so it never had occurred to Garland that there was any question of having a job to come back to. She'd been so dedicated to the bank, she said, that managers had had to scold her to take a vacation. Before Garland went out to have her baby, everyone had chipped in to buy her a crib, and the office had thrown her a shower. She hadn't known it was her good-bye party, too.

Garland was afraid to tell Wright Garner, her boyfriend and Kekere's father, about losing her job. To her surprise, he was supportive, and angry on her behalf. "He said, 'That's not right,'" recalled Garland, and urged her to go to the state's Department of Fair Employment and Housing. Soon after, she did.

She met with a lawyer there named Brian Hembacher. After detailing her situation, Garland asked if there was anything that she could do. Hembacher told her there was. He explained that in 1979, California had passed the Pregnancy Disability Leave law requiring employers to grant pregnant women up to four months' unpaid leave when they gave birth, and to reinstate them (or place them in a comparable position, if the same job was not available when they were ready to come back). Hembacher warned Garland, though, that the case against Cal Fed probably would be contentious. "Do you think you can handle it?" he asked. Garland was confident she could. At that point, she'd had close to a decade of experience acting onstage; she was comfortable being the center of attention. But, she later admitted, "I never dreamed that it was going to mushroom the way it did."

LILLIAN GARLAND grew up during the 1950s and 1960s in the segregated housing projects of Pittsburgh. She spent much of her childhood, though, in Finleyville, about fifteen miles south of downtown, on a farm that was owned by her great-grandmother, Garland's namesake. "Granny" was white, a former Ziegfeld Girl who had married a black man. She told Garland that she could be anything she wanted and not to let it get to her if anyone ever called her "nigger." "'Nigger' is only a word," she told Garland. "It only has as much power as you give it. Don't give it any power!"[2] It was a different message than Garland got from her mother, who was African American and had been raised picking cotton alongside her family in South Carolina, never attending school past kindergarten or learning to read or write. When Garland told her that she wanted to be a psychiatrist when she grew up, her mother told her not to dream of it. "Number one, you're black, and number two, you're a girl," she said. "So you can't."

Garland's father was very light-skinned—owing to Granny's race—and handsome. A "tanned Clark Gable" is how Garland described him, and his allure to women was only enhanced by his fluency in French. He had served in the Army in World War II, where Garland believed he had suffered "shell shock." It was that trauma that Garland blamed for his violent outbursts against her mother and her.

Garland's life in Pittsburgh was one of poverty, hand-me-downs and welfare checks, not enough food to go around. She was the eldest of six, and "I couldn't drink milk because I was one of the big kids," she recalled. "Only the little kids got milk and cheese and butter." Whenever she needed to be spoiled, she would escape to Granny's house.

By her early twenties, Garland was married and had two small children, a boy named Phillips and a girl named Pilar. She also knew she wanted to act. She had been regularly performing at the Pittsburgh Laboratory Theater—the first black actress to be accepted into the nascent company—and was itching to go to Los Angeles to try to make it on television or in movies. In 1975, she got a call to audition for a new show being developed by ABC, *Charlie's Angels*. Although the series didn't pan out for her, it was enough encouragement to move the family to L.A. Garland began taking acting classes and performing in small theaters at night (including at L.A. Connection, where she crossed paths with Whoopi Goldberg and Robin Williams), while working various jobs during the day.

In 1979, she signed up with an employment agency, which sent her to interview for the receptionist job at Cal Fed. The timing couldn't have been better; her husband had become so abusive she had fled, leaving her children behind. (After a period of estrangement, Garland repaired her relationship with the children, and today they are close.) The job at Cal Fed meant starting over, making $850 a month plus benefits, and getting a steady financial footing at last.

AS GARLAND'S complaint was investigated by the Department of Fair Employment and Housing over the next several months, her life took several traumatic turns. Her relationship with Garner took a turn for the worse, and he soon moved out. With $550 in rent due and a newborn to support, Garland frantically searched for work. Garner bought diapers and food for Kekere and sometimes cared for her on weekends but did little else.[3] Said Garland, "I had no money. I had no job. I had no car."[4] She sometimes went hungry or resorted to eating baby food.[5] Her job hunt was conducted by bus, with Kekere in her arms.[6] (When she was lucky enough to get an interview, she'd ask an obliging secretary to hold the baby until she was done.) Despite submitting applications all over the city, Garland couldn't get a job. Cal Fed did call a few times to offer her a position, but she turned the jobs down, either because they required secretarial skills that she didn't have—which she feared would give the bank a reason to fire her for poor performance—or because the assigned office was too far to commute on public transportation.

Garland eventually had a few friends move in with her to help pay the rent. She still fell behind, though, and in the fall of 1982, she was evicted. Although a friend who worked at Cal Fed was willing to let Garland sleep on her couch, she didn't have room for Kekere too. Because Garland's ex, Garner, had just bought a house with money his mother gave him, he took custody of their daughter. According to Garland, the arrangement was supposed to be temporary, just until she got back on her feet, but a few months later, Garner served her with papers seeking sole custody. She was in no position to pay for a lawyer, let alone convince a court that she could support a child. Devastated, Garland agreed to cede custody.[7] She'd lost her job because she'd had a child, and now she'd lost her child, too.

IN LATE NOVEMBER 1982, seven months after she'd tried to return to work, Cal Fed finally offered Garland a suitable job: She'd be a receptionist again, at her old salary, this time in the Accounting Department. But it soon became clear that her life at the bank would never be the same. Although no lawsuit had yet been filed on Garland's behalf by the DFEH, Cal Fed was aware of the agency's investigation. Like many employees who continue working for employers they've accused of discrimination, Garland was made to feel unwelcome. One friend warned her that coworkers had been told to spy on her. Someone stuck needles in her chair legs, so that when her calves brushed against them, they'd snag her stockings and leave scratches. She was assigned menial tasks, like filing, and others she couldn't do well, like typing. Eventually she was given chores such as cleaning out old storage rooms or crawling around under desks to inventory computer equipment. No longer was she the poised professional wearing a suit; she came to work in coveralls or jeans. The last straw was when she hurt her back moving boxes. That's when "I began studying for my real estate license," she said.[8]

About six months after Garland returned to Cal Fed, DFEH served a formal complaint on the bank. It alleged that Cal Fed's refusal to immediately reinstate Garland violated the state's pregnancy leave law. A hearing was scheduled for late summer 1983. But instead of responding to the DFEH complaint, Cal Fed filed a lawsuit of its own, this one in federal court. Joined by two business groups, the Merchants and Manufacturers Association and the California Chamber of Commerce, the bank argued that the state law was invalid under Title VII, which had been amended a few years earlier by the Pregnancy Discrimination Act. The PDA mandated that employers treat "women affected by pregnancy . . . the same for all employment-related purposes . . . as other persons not so affected but similar in their ability or inability to work."[9]

Cal Fed told the court that it *had* treated Garland "the same" as any other employee "similar in their ability or inability to work." The bank's temporary disability policy allowed employees an undefined period of "reasonable leave," and although it didn't guarantee they'd be returned to their old job (or a comparable one) at the end of it, it guaranteed the bank would try. Cal Fed said that Garland had simply been unlucky that there wasn't an available job right away; it claimed that 90 percent of its employees who went out on temporary disability did immediately get put back to work.

The bank further argued that the state law, by requiring that pregnant employees be treated *better* than others "similar in their ability or inability to work," violated Title VII. That is, by making the bank safeguard only pregnant workers' jobs, the state was requiring the bank to engage in sex discrimination against *men* who took leave for their temporary disabilities.

When Cal Fed's case was assigned to a judge on the U.S. District Court for the Central District of California, fortune was not smiling on Garland and her DFEH attorneys. Although Judge Manuel Real might have at one time seemed friendly to civil rights litigants—he'd been appointed by President Lyndon Johnson and gotten high marks for his early rulings desegregating Pasadena's schools[10]—he also had gained a reputation among lawyers for being "imperious,"[11] "mercurial,"[12] and a "bully."[13] One of his favorite sayings to those appearing before him was, "This isn't Burger King. We don't do it your way here."[14] Real also was on his way to gaining some measure of pop cultural infamy. At a hearing that took place just a few months before oral argument in Garland's case, Real sentenced *Hustler* publisher Larry Flynt to ever-longer jail terms for contempt—first six months, then twelve, then fifteen—as Flynt taunted him with epithets. ("Is that the best you can do, motherfucker?"[15]) Real eventually ordered that Flynt be gagged for part of the proceedings.[16] The contempt convictions were reversed on appeal,[17] but the scene still made it into the 1996 movie *The People vs. Larry Flynt*.[18]

Judge Real issued his opinion within two days of the March 19, 1983, oral argument. Invoking a legal doctrine known as preemption, under which federal laws generally trump conflicting state laws that concern the same subject matter, Real ruled in Cal Fed's favor.[19] He agreed that the state leave law's "preferential treatment" of pregnant workers violated Title VII's ban on sex discrimination and declared the statute "null, void, invalid, and inoperative."[20] Real ordered DFEH to cease enforcing it and specifically banned the agency from conducting any further proceedings "on the accusation issued on behalf of Lillian Garland."[21]

Speaking to the press after the ruling, DFEH's Brian Hembacher called the decision a "serious setback" that would force California women to choose "between having children and having a job."[22] Judge Real's ruling also left in limbo more than two hundred pending complaints at DFEH.[23] The Department was historically very progressive, and its attorneys were committed to appealing Judge Real's ruling. But the new California governor, George Deukmejian, was far more conservative than his predecessor, Jerry Brown. The rightward tilt of some of his appointments at other civil rights agencies prompted concerns among DFEH attorneys that they might not have permission to litigate the Garland case for much longer. (Hembacher later told Garland that Deukmejian had "called [him] on the carpet" for his statement to the press about Real's decision forcing women to choose "between having children and having a job.") At Hembacher's urging and with his help, Garland began looking for her own lawyer. Soon she'd found her: Linda Krieger.

IN 1983, Krieger was five years out of law school and a staff attorney with the Legal Aid Society-Employment Law Center of San Francisco. LAS-ELC was one of the most prominent legal advocacy groups serving low-income clients in California. Warm and low-key, Krieger was easy for Garland to bond with. "We just hit it off," Garland recalled. "She was almost like a sister. I trusted her totally."

In taking on the Garland case, Krieger was wading deeper into what she called a "serious controversy, one might even say a crisis, in the feminist legal community over the meaning of equality for women."[24] Krieger already was up to her neck in it, having just finished working on a Montana case similar to Garland's.

That case concerned Tamara Buley, hired in late 1979 by the Miller-Wohl chain of women's clothing stores. Buley, then pregnant, starting working in the company's Three Sisters store in Great Falls, earning minimum wage as a sales clerk. Due to severe morning sickness, Buley was absent several times during her first two weeks of work. She asked for a two-week leave of absence, which her doctor believed would be enough time for the worst of the nausea to subside. Instead, Miller-Wohl fired Buley, citing a company rule forbidding employees with less than a year of service to take any sick leave.[25]

The Montana fair employment agency filed a complaint against the company on Buley's behalf, citing its state law requiring employers to grant pregnant women a "reasonable leave of absence" when needed.[26] Miller-Wohl responded by filing suit in federal court. It claimed, as Cal Fed would a few years later, that the state law violated Title VII by mandating preferential treatment of pregnant women.

When Montana officials reached out to the preeminent women's legal organizations for their assistance in defending the law—such as the ACLU Women's Rights Project, the National Organization for Women, the National Women's Law Center, and the Women's Legal Defense Fund—they were surprised to learn that the groups agreed with Miller-Wohl. In fact, they planned to submit a friend of the court brief in support of the company.

These were the same advocates who had drafted and lobbied hard for passage of the PDA, in 1978. To them, the federal statute's focus on treating pregnant workers "the same" as those "similar in their ability or inability to work" was central to women's identity under the law. Known as "equal treatment" feminists, they worried that laws like Montana's were just a philosophical hop, skip, and jump away from the protective laws of the past century that treated women as mothers first and workers second. If history was any guide, they believed, that "special treatment" model could only damage women's status on the job. Indeed, singling out pregnancy for special mandates also made women more expensive to employ and could actually deter companies from hiring them at all.

Georgetown law professor Wendy Williams, one of the nation's foremost equal treatment scholars and a chief architect of the PDA, wrote a widely cited law review article about the questions raised by *Miller-Wohl*.[27] She argued that while the Montana legislators undoubtedly were well-meaning and while women like Tamara Buley undoubtedly would suffer hardship if the leave law never existed, the answer was not to privilege pregnancy. Such privilege was really a stigma, the stigma of "difference" from a male norm.

The preferable course, argued Williams, was for employers, and the law, to recognize that few women *or* men go through their working lives without some period of illness, injury, or disability. If pregnancy were understood as just one of many reasons an employee might need to take leave, its "difference" would be normalized:

> [T]he objective is to readjust the general rules for dealing with illness and disability to ensure that rules can fairly account for the whole range of workplace disabilities that confront employed people. Pregnancy does not create "special" needs, but rather exemplifies typical basic needs. . . . The solution . . . is to solve the underlying problem of inadequate fringe benefits rather than respond with measures designed especially for pregnant workers.[28]

When Montana officials asked Krieger if she would take on Buley's case, she agreed. (She later joked that she didn't mind being the B Team, after the ACLU WRP and other members of the feminist A Team had turned the state down.) She believed that the law's benefits to women outweighed the drawbacks. During a December 1984 *60 Minutes* segment about *Miller-Wohl*, Krieger defended Montana's approach. "Equality cannot be achieved by mandating that women and men will be treated exactly alike," she explained. "The reason for that is the simple fact that women get pregnant and men do not."[29]

That simple fact, said Krieger, translated into a greater need for job-protected leave. As she noted, roughly 80 percent of working women were of childbearing age, and nearly all of those women would have at least one child during their working lives.[30] That meant that the vast majority of women would need at least one temporary leave from work to recover from childbirth—on average, six weeks or fewer.[31] Other workers' potential need for disability leave simply didn't come close in terms of frequency or duration, so their risk of job loss wasn't comparable. Because there was no federal mandate for job-protected family or medical leave, pregnant women were at the whim of their employers when it came time to give birth.

The San Francisco women's rights group Equal Rights Advocates and the Los Angeles–based California Women's Law Center agreed with this approach. They submitted *amicus* briefs on Buley's behalf to counter those filed by the "equal treatment" groups, all of which were based on the east coast. To Krieger, this divide between east coast and west coast feminists was due primarily to their constituencies. The "client" of the former was, in a sense, the women's movement itself. Those organizations were "cause" lawyers who selected their clients and cases with a strategic eye. They also had close ties to academia, the laboratory where feminist thinkers could spot holes in judicial precedent and help litigators decide where to strike next. Having selected a legal problem that needed fixing, the cause lawyers then found a client to bring just the right case to illustrate the problem. Alternatively, they sought to change the law altogether through the often glacial legislative process. Ruth Bader Ginsburg's tenure at the ACLU WRP during the 1970s had been a master class in this kind of methodical litigation, working case by case to successfully dismantle the nation's second-class treatment of women in employment, education, public benefits, estate law, even criminal statutes.[32]

In contrast, Krieger, her colleagues at LAS-ELC, and the other west coast groups that joined in on Tamara Buley's behalf served, in Krieger's words, a "working class, pink collar client base." Many of them were women of color and single parents. They composed what Krieger termed a "secondary labor market," working in jobs occupied mostly by other women and "characterized by the absence of union representation, provisions for job security, or fringe benefits."[33] Their economic circumstances were precarious, their legal problems emergent. For these women, a no-leave policy was "tantamount to dismissal"[34] and had crippling economic consequences. They couldn't afford to wait for the universal solution to the disability leave issue advocated by the equal treatment camp. And in the view of Krieger and her colleagues, they shouldn't have to.

———————

THE DISPUTE between feminist groups about employment law's approach to pregnancy was so bitter because the stakes were so high. In the words of one scholar, "That women may and do become pregnant is the most significant single factor used to justify the countless laws and practices that have disadvantaged women for centuries."[35] It also had divided women's advocates for nearly a century.

The "protective" laws enacted in most of the states starting in the late 1800s were supported in large part by women's advocates. They saw such laws as a necessary check on the exploitative conditions endured by all workers on assembly lines and in other industrial settings. Because the Supreme Court appeared willing to allow such conditions to persist for men but not for women—as illustrated by its 1905 decision striking down a New York law that established maximum work hours for male bakers—while upholding such a law for female laundry workers in *Muller v. Oregon*[36] a few years later—social justice advocates decided that women-only protective laws were better than nothing.

One of the most outspoken advocates of this approach was Esther Peterson, whom President Kennedy appointed in 1961 to run the Labor Department's Women's Bureau. Peterson's perspective had been shaped by her years as a union organizer where, as described by Gail Collins, she had seen firsthand the "desperate women who were crippled by the physical demands of their jobs, sexually harassed by their supervisors, and deprived of enough time to be proper mothers to their undernourished children."[37]

Other activists, particularly those in the National Women's Party, contended that protective laws had the ancillary effect of stigmatizing women as weak, fragile, and otherwise undeserving of the best-paying jobs. The NWP had been forged in the battle for women's suffrage and thereafter took up the cause of the Equal Rights Amendment to the Constitution, which would erase legal distinctions between the sexes. Peterson dismissed these advocates as "elite, privileged old ladies" of the "Old Frontier" whose vision of equality didn't take account of the realities of class. As Peterson mused, "Are women better off being singled out for protection, or are they better served by erasing all legal distinctions between women and men? As the lettuce pickers and cafeteria workers know, it depends on your status."[38]

It was those "elite, privileged old ladies" who had successfully lobbied Representative Howard Smith to propose his "sex" amendment to Title VII. Indeed, when he first introduced it, Peterson had been an ardent opponent, fearing (accurately) that the law would strip away the state-law protections; to her mind, those laws were literally keeping women alive in the nation's factories and on its assembly lines.[39]

TITLE VII'S minimalist ban on discrimination "because of sex" did not answer "equality's riddle,"[40] as Wendy Williams accurately dubbed it: Because only women can become pregnant, what does "equality" between men and women even mean? Long after women had started shedding the stigma of protective laws—by gaining entry into "men's jobs," for instance, with *Dothard v. Rawlinson* and cases like it in the lower courts[41]—biological difference continued to pose a conundrum for employers and judges alike.

The EEOC didn't help matters in the early years after Title VII's enactment. Just as the agency was slow to grapple with overt sex classifications—such as separate job ads for men and women and airline rules that treated flight attendants like glorified cocktail waitresses—it clearly was stymied by how to deal with pregnancy.

Indeed, the EEOC's earliest pronouncements on pregnancy were all over the map.[42] In a 1966 letter to an employer asking for an advisory opinion as to whether it would violate Title VII to exclude pregnancy and childbirth from a guaranteed paid leave policy, the EEOC responded that it would not, "since maternity is a temporary disability unique to the female sex and more or less to be anticipated during the working life of most women employees."[43] A few weeks later, the agency also approved excluding pregnancy and childbirth from an employer's health insurance plan.[44] And while firing a woman outright upon learning of her pregnancy likely violated Title VII, said one early opinion, the agency's position was unclear as to whether it was lawful to freeze a pregnant woman's accumulation of seniority while she was out having her baby (even if workers who went out for injury or illness accumulated such credit while absent).[45]

It wasn't until 1972 that the EEOC issued official Guidelines about how pregnancy should be treated under Title VII. They came about largely due to tireless lobbying by the agency's first woman attorney, Sonia Pressman Fuentes, and another attorney hired soon after, Susan Deller Ross.[46] Among its provisions, the Guidelines expressly forbade firing or refusing to hire a woman because of pregnancy and required that any benefits extended to other employees with temporary disabilities—paid leave, health coverage, seniority credit during leave—had to be extended to pregnant workers too.[47]

The Supreme Court was equally inconsistent in its pregnancy rulings, both under Title VII and under the Constitution. (Until Title VII was amended in 1972 to cover employees of public entities claims under the Fourteenth Amendment were those workers' only recourse for on-the-job discrimination.) On one hand, in 1974, the Court rejected an Ohio school district's policy of forcing pregnant teachers off the job five months before their due dates, finding it violated their due process rights by presuming that they were incapable of working.[48] The following year, the Court struck down a Utah law that denied unemployment benefits to pregnant women during the twelve weeks before their due dates and during the six weeks after. Once again, the Court disapproved of the "presumption of incapacity and unavailability for employment" that underlay such a policy.[49] In 1977, the Court also rejected an employer's policy that erased women's accrued seniority whenever they went out on maternity leave while preserving it for workers who took other kinds of leave.[50]

As the saying goes, however, what one hand giveth, the other taketh away. While the Court was rejecting policies that overtly penalized pregnant women for simply being pregnant, it was approving measures that punished them more subtly, by ignoring pregnancy altogether.[51] Shortly after rejecting the Ohio forced leave policy for teachers, for instance, the Court *approved* a California law that excluded pregnant women from a short-term disability benefit program. (Wendy Williams was the lead attorney challenging the statute.) This meant that women who took leave to recover from childbirth didn't get paid while colleagues who were recovering from a broken leg or receiving cancer treatment did.[52] And a few years after that, in *Gilbert v. General Electric Co.*[53] the Court approved pregnant women's exclusion from a similar temporary disability policy in place at GE.

The reasoning for both decisions was the same: The disputed policies didn't disadvantage women "because of sex." Rather, pregnant women just happened to experience a particular medical condition that was unique to them. In all other respects, women received equal coverage; there was no medical condition experienced by men for which women wouldn't also receive disability benefits. The decision to exclude one particular medical condition unique to women, then, was simply a decision based on cost, which was a gender-neutral consideration. In the Court's memorable words, the plans distinguished not between men and women but between pregnant women and "non-pregnant persons."

Because the *Gilbert* decision approving GE's policy stemmed from the Court's interpretation of Title VII, an aggressive effort to amend the statute was launched literally within hours of the Court's decision. Cochaired by Susan Deller Ross, who had spearheaded the EEOC's adoption of an equal treatment approach in its 1972 Guidelines,[54] the Campaign to End Discrimination Against Pregnant Workers was a coalition of more than two hundred feminist, civil rights, and labor organizations.[55] Its leadership, including Williams and others from the east coast feminist groups, worked with like-minded congressional staffers to draft legislation nullifying *Gilbert*.

The campaign culminated in Congress's passage of the PDA in 1978. It amended Title VII to make explicit that discrimination "because of sex" meant discrimination "because of pregnancy."[56] And as a specific rebuke to the *Gilbert* decision, the PDA included the mandate that employers treat pregnant women the same as anyone else similarly able (or unable) to work.[57]

The PDA was a monumental achievement for women, not to mention a textbook example of governmental "checks and balances" in action. But it also left critical gaps. Justice Ruth Bader Ginsburg recently observed that "[a]lthough the PDA proscribed blatant discrimination on the basis of pregnancy, the Act is fairly described as a necessary, but not sufficient measure."[58] It did not require, for instance, that employers do anything for pregnant women that they were not already doing for other employees. Thus, it did not mandate that maternity leave, paid or unpaid, be available, unless others with temporary impairments also could take such time off. It did not require that a woman's job be held open for her after she had her baby, unless that protection was afforded to other workers who took leave. It did not require that a pregnant woman be allowed sick days to deal with the symptoms of pregnancy, whether it was severe morning sickness or a doctor's directive to go on bed rest, unless other workers could take intermittent time off of that sort. As prominent conservative judge Richard Posner once put it, under the PDA, "Employers can treat pregnant women as badly as they treat similarly affected but nonpregnant employees."[59]

It was as Congress was preparing to act on the PDA in October 1978 that the California legislature passed the Pregnancy Disability Leave law—the statute under which Lillian Garland's claim was raised. The state policymakers looked at the gaps in the federal bill that was about to become law and decided they wanted to do more. As one advocate put it, "The PDA did not go far enough, and we could do better in California and we did."[60]

This history had put women's advocates on a collision course. The Montana statute at issue in *Miller-Wohl* had been the first skirmish. Tamara Buley eventually won it in early 1984 when the Montana Supreme Court upheld the state's leave law as consistent with the PDA and awarded her close to $7,000 in lost wages.[61]

Within weeks of that decision, Judge Real struck down California's paid leave law and dismissed the state's lawsuit on behalf of Lillian Garland—assuring that the "crisis in the feminist legal community" wouldn't be over anytime soon.

THE NEXT STEP in Garland's case was to appeal Judge Real's ruling to the U.S. Court of Appeals for the Ninth Circuit. Lawyers for the state plowed ahead, despite early fears that they might give up the fight. But Krieger collaborated with the government on Garland's behalf and was the primary author of the brief defending the California law. Marian Johnston, an attorney in the civil rights unit of the state attorney general's office, would make the case at oral argument, scheduled for February 1985.

However unlucky Lillian Garland had been to draw Judge Real at the district court level, the panel assigned to hear the appeal was auspicious. It included Judge Harry Pregerson (who, while still a district court judge a decade earlier, had struck down the unequal pension contribution scheme in *Manhart v. City of Los Angeles Department of Water and Power*[62]) and Judge Warren Ferguson. As one of Ferguson's colleagues later described him, "He was concerned about people and about individual rights. He'd have a sense of outrage when he saw people unfairly treated by the justice system."[63] Rounding out the panel was Judge Earl Gilliam, a Carter appointee and the first African American judge named to the central California district court.[64]

On April 16, 1985, the Ninth Circuit issued its opinion reversing Judge Real's ruling. "We hold that the district court's conclusion that [California's pregnancy leave law] discriminates against men on the basis of pregnancy defies common sense, misinterprets case law, and flouts Title VII and the PDA."[65] The court criticized Judge Real's analysis of whether Title VII, as a federal law, preempted California's law.

It noted that Title VII contains its own provision specifying what state laws it does and doesn't preempt. Only state laws requiring employment practices that are "inconsistent" with the federal law's protections are trumped. The court explained that that provision was meant to nullify state statutes on the books that *limited* women's opportunities, not measures that *enhanced* women's opportunities.

Viewed in this light, said the court, the California law *complemented* the goals of Title VII (as amended by the PDA). It didn't contradict them. The PDA didn't only intend absolute parity between pregnant employees and their peers and no more, said the court. Federal law was "a floor beneath which pregnancy benefits may not drop—not a ceiling above which they may not rise."[66]

But Cal Fed wasn't giving up the fight. Nearly a year later, in January 1986, the Supreme Court took the case.

——— ———

BY THE TIME *California Federal Savings & Loan Association v. Guerra*[67] was heard by the Court in October 1986, Lillian Garland had put her ordeal at Cal Fed behind her. She'd gotten her real estate license, quit her job at the bank, and bought a realty franchise that she operated with her new husband. And she got to visit regularly with Kekere, although her ex retained custody.

She also had become something of a celebrity. In addition to her appearance on *60 Minutes* she'd been flown to Chicago for an appearance on *Oprah,* had been interviewed by Peter Jennings on *World News Tonight,* and had been featured in countless newspapers and magazines, from *U.S. News & World Report* to *People.* She'd met Gloria Steinem, Betty Friedan, and other feminist luminaries. (She took her first airplane ride sitting next to Steinem, who encouraged Garland to try her first Bloody Mary. Believing it to be Steinem's favorite accompaniment to air travel, she adopted it as her own ritual, too.) Garland's eloquence, her compelling personal story, and her regal beauty all made her a dream spokeswoman. As Linda Krieger put it, she was "everything a lawyer could wish a client could do in terms of [being] the public face of an important legal issue. She was really spectacular."

The equal treatment groups had not merely played defense while *Cal Fed* wound its way up to the nine justices. Shortly after Judge Real's 1984 decision striking down the California law, one of the law's original cosponsors, Howard Berman—formerly a state assemblyman, now a U.S. congressman—approached Donna Lenhoff of the Women's Legal Defense Fund to propose introducing a federal version of California's statute.[68] Staunch equal treatment advocate Lenhoff, along with Susan Deller Ross and Wendy Williams, already had been working on a gender-neutral version of the law to introduce in Congress, and the three convinced Berman to expand the proposed law's reach beyond pregnant women.[69] Two years later, when the Supreme Court heard oral argument in *Cal Fed,* the law that would eventually be named the Family and Medical Leave Act (FMLA) had been introduced in Congress twice, in various iterations, so far without success.

THE DAY OF the Supreme Court oral argument, Lillian Garland felt like "Judy Garland in the Wizard of Oz."[70] Once she and her lawyer, LAS-ELC's Patricia Shiu, made it into the majestic courtroom, Garland sat between Gloria Steinem and Betty Friedan. "I remember sitting there and I felt so small," said Garland, laughing as she remembered her surprise that the justices weren't wearing white powdered wigs.

When the justices filed in, there was a new face at the bench, sitting all the way to the far right of the spectators: Antonin Scalia, recently elevated from the D.C. Court of Appeals. The man sitting at the center of the bench, the chief justice, also was new. William Rehnquist had just been appointed to the position to replace Warren Burger, who had spent seventeen years as chief and just retired. For both Scalia and Rehnquist, it was their third day on the job.

Ted Olson, a former litigator in President Reagan's Justice Department and a partner with the corporate firm Gibson Dunn, would be arguing the case for Cal Fed. Although Olson went on to be one of the most prolific Supreme Court litigators, arguing more than sixty cases, *Cal Fed* marked just his third appearance. Olson also later served as solicitor general under George W. Bush, whom he had helped to become president by successfully arguing 2000's *Bush v. Gore.* (He recently broke conservative ranks, though, to help achieve a Supreme Court decision, *Hollingsworth v. Perry,*[71] that overturned California's Proposition 8, banning same-sex marriage. As law professor Kenji Yoshino described Olson in *Speak Now,* his definitive account of *Hollingsworth,* "Wherever one stands politically, it is next to impossible to dislike Olson. . . . Debating him is like debating a golden retriever with a genius IQ."[72])

Representing California was Marian Johnston, a senior attorney in the civil rights enforcement division of California's Office of the Attorney General. After starting her career representing farmworkers, Johnston had made her career in California government.

Olson went first, and he spent much of his time deflecting the suggestion that had been raised by the equality feminist groups: Why couldn't California just amend its law to make job-protected leave universal for anyone with a temporary disability? Olson told the justices that the California legislature was considering just such a measure—as was Congress, with the nascent FMLA—but that was an "end run" around the relevant issue. That issue, he emphasized, was whether the PDA permitted California to have a preferential pregnancy-only leave law. Olson noted that during congressional debate about the PDA, some lawmakers had debated whether to require employers to adopt pregnancy-specific leave policies and had decided not to include such a provision in the final law.[73]

Here Justice O'Connor jumped in. The PDA didn't include any provision *forbidding* employers from offering such leave either, did it? "I just don't think it's clear on the face of the statute how far it reaches," she said. Olson tried again to rely on the Congress's intentions in passing the PDA, this time reminding the Court that the law meant to dislodge the negative stereotypes about pregnant workers that were implicit in the "protective laws" of the past. California's law resurrected that sorry history, Olson argued, by appearing to confirm—and here he quoted the ACLU WRP brief—that "pregnancy renders women less reliable, less productive employees, absent more often, more expensive; that is to say, fundamentally different and handicapped."[74]

Marian Johnston was next at the lectern. She began with the statistics confirming the prevalence of pregnancy among working women and the near ubiquity of the need for job-protected leave. To ignore that need, she argued, would be tantamount to discrimination—precisely what the PDA forbade. "The flaw in Cal Fed's analysis, I think, is to equate pregnancy discrimination with discrimination against other disabilities," a practice that Congress had not yet outlawed, she said. (It finally did so four years later, with the 1990 Americans with Disabilities Act.). "[W]hat Title VII did is to equate pregnancy discrimination with sex discrimination," which Congress *had* made illegal in Title VII.[75]

Justice Powell wasn't convinced. He posed a hypothetical:

Let's assume that an employer had a man and a woman doing identical work, and that each on approximately the same day left the employment because of disability, the woman because of pregnancy or an operation or whatever, and they come back to work three months later on the same day. The woman is returned to her job. The man is told they're sorry, they've . . . filled his position with another satisfactory employee, so you go somewhere else. Your brief says that's perfectly fair. Is that your position today?

"No, I don't think it's perfectly fair," answered Johnston. "I think that it's not unlawful. And I think that there's a distinction, Your Honor."[76]

Pregnancy also shouldn't be compared to other physical impairments, Johnston argued, for the simple reason that it only affected women. Both male and female workers might want to start families, but only women bore the physical burden of that decision. "The male employee is going to keep his job when he has a child. There's no interruption of his work life," she explained. "So when it's viewed in that light, [the California law is] neither preferential nor prejudicial" but rather "simply an equalizer."[77]

Picking up on Justice O'Connor's earlier line of questioning with Olson, Johnston further reminded the Court that at the time Congress enacted the PDA, two states—Connecticut and Montana—already had their job-protected leave statutes on the books. Records showed that lawmakers knew about those laws and didn't disapprove them.

Johnston closed with that message. "[B]eing sure that pregnant employees keep their jobs," she said, "not only is not inconsistent, but we believe it's perfectly compatible and consistent with Title VII's goal of equality for both men and women, despite the fact that only women become pregnant."[78]

THREE MONTHS LATER, Lillian Garland was in the shower when the call came at seven-thirty in the morning. She jumped out to grab the phone, covered in soap and shampoo. It was a reporter, asking her how she felt about her win in the Supreme Court. "The first thing I did was scream," she said. "Then I said, 'Praise God, it's long overdue.'"[79]

The six to three opinion written by Justice Marshall was joined by Justices Brennan, Blackmun, Stevens, and O'Connor, along with

Scalia (who agreed with the outcome but wrote a separate opinion)—an unusually wide range of ideological slants. "[W]e agree with the [Ninth Circuit's] conclusion that Congress intended the PDA to be 'a floor beneath which pregnancy disability benefits may not drop—not a ceiling above which they may not rise.'"[80] Marshall continued, "By 'taking pregnancy into account,' California's pregnancy disability-leave statute allows women, as well as men, to have families without losing their jobs."[81]

The majority opinion concluded with some reassuring words to the equal treatment advocates. Marshall pointedly distinguished laws like California's that furthered pregnant women's employment opportunities from laws meant to diminish them.

> The statute is narrowly drawn to cover only the period of *actual physical disability* on account of pregnancy, childbirth, or related medical conditions. Accordingly, unlike the protective labor legislation prevalent earlier in this century, [California's law] does not reflect archaic or stereotypical notions about pregnancy and the abilities of pregnant workers. A statute based on such stereotypical assumptions would, of course, be inconsistent with Title VII's goal of equal employment opportunity.[82]

Marshall's words had the desired effect. NOW's President Eleanor Smeal called the decision a "solid victory" and was confident that it would not result in a "slippery slope" toward laws that restricted women's opportunities.[83] And Colorado congresswoman Pat Schroeder, one of the chief sponsors of the pending bill that later became the FMLA, remarked, "I think this decision gives us terrific momentum."[84] Less celebratory was Paula Connelly of the U.S. Chamber of Commerce, who was "disappointed and surprised by the decision."[85] She bemoaned the go-ahead that the Supreme Court had just given to other states to enact similar laws. "The way it is phrased," she said, "it seems to leave no limit on what the states can do . . . in terms of preferential treatment."[86]

SIX YEARS LATER, on February 5, 1993, just two weeks into his presidency, Bill Clinton presided over a ceremony in the White House's Rose Garden. Under an unseasonably warm sun, he signed the first law enacted on his watch: the Family and Medical Leave Act.[87] Surrounded by lawmakers and advocates and flanked by Vice President Al Gore and Vicki Yandle, an Atlanta woman who lost her job when she took time off to care for her cancer-stricken daughter,[88] Clinton told the assembled crowd, "Family and medical leave is a matter of pure common sense and a matter of common decency."[89] The law provided job-protected leave for workers of both sexes who needed to take care of a seriously ill family member, or to bond with a newborn or adopted baby, or for the worker's own serious medical condition, including pregnancy and recovery from childbirth.[90]

It had been a long time coming. Since California congressman Howard Berman and the "equal treatment" feminist leadership began their collaboration in 1984, some version of the FMLA had been introduced in Congress every year for nearly a decade. Twice the legislation had made it through both houses, only to be vetoed by President George H. W. Bush, citing the cost to businesses.[91]

The bill that Clinton signed showed the wear and tear of compromise. It granted just twelve weeks of leave. (The California law had provided up to sixteen weeks.) The time off was unpaid. The law covered only the largest employers, those with workforces numbering fifty or more. (California's applied to employers of five employees or more.) To be eligible for leave, an employee must have worked for the employer either for the entire prior year or for 1,250 hours, disqualifying many part-time workers, who are disproportionately women. (The California law had no such limitation.)

For all of these reasons, Clinton was more than a little overly optimistic when he proclaimed, "The FMLA will provide Americans what they need most: peace of mind. Never again will parents have to fear losing their jobs because of their families."[92] It was more accurate to say, as one women's advocate did, that "[t]his is just the first step in family protection. We're not saying this bill is the final answer. We've just built a foundation."[93]

LILLIAN GARLAND is now married to her childhood sweetheart, lives in the Virginia suburbs of Washington, DC, and is mainly retired. She puts her theatrical training to use as a Civil War reenactor and occasionally as a clown for civic events and children's parties.

After the Supreme Court decision, Garland's case returned to court in California. With the state law having been declared valid, there was no longer any question that Garland should have gotten her

job back after her pregnancy leave, so Cal Fed agreed to pay her a negotiated amount of lost wages. Given the devastating personal consequences of losing her job at the bank, not to mention how long she had
had to wait for a victory, Garland was disappointed at how small the
settlement check was. (The agreement's precise terms are confidential.)

Reflecting back on the detour her life took between that day in
April 1982 when she tried to go to work, and the far happier day in
January 1987 when she got the news of her Supreme Court victory,
Garland described it as "five years of hell." And yet, she was sure to
add, "even if it had taken twenty years I'd do it again."[94]

six

making
"lady partner"

Price Waterhouse v. Hopkins (1989)

IN 1978, ANN HOPKINS ACCEPTED A JOB IN THE NORTH-
ern Virginia office of Price Waterhouse, one of the "Big Eight" global
accounting firms. Hopkins joined the firm as a consultant in its Office
of Government Services, overseeing large-scale technology projects for
government clients. With a master's in mathematics, a stint at IBM
building computer systems for NASA, and close to four years at Touche Ross, another of the Big Eight, Hopkins was a veteran of male-
dominated environments.

She never gave her minority status much thought, though. A self-
described Army brat from Texas, she grasped at an early age how
to hit the ground running, even when she was the new kid in town.
"I have no understanding of people who are concerned about jerking
kids out of school," she said. "I thought of it as, 'Hey guys, what's
next?'"[1] Spending four years at an all-women's college also was for-
mative. According to Hopkins, "I learned to depend on myself and
on the analytical integrity of an answer to a question or a solution to
a problem before I was taught to depend on or defer to members of
the opposite sex or their point of view."[2] This didn't mean she felt any
affinity for the burgeoning feminist movement, though. "I have never
given a thought to the women's movement," she later said. "I just kind
of missed it."[3] Hopkins was raised wearing white gloves and attending

debutante balls,[4] but her personal style was, in her words, "wash and wear."[5] She also developed a fondness for motorcycles—even while wearing a suit and Ferragamo pumps, as she did when riding her Yamaha 175 to her first interview at Touche Ross in 1974.[6]

Over the next five years at Price Waterhouse, Hopkins set about positioning herself for partnership. (During that time, she had her third child, by Cesarian section. She returned to work within a few weeks, as she had with her two prior pregnancies, also by C-section. "I needed some rest and work offered more opportunity for rest than did staying home," she explained.[7]) Moving from consultant to senior manager, she amassed an impressive record, including winning roughly $40 million in contracts from the U.S. Departments of State and Agriculture. The Office of Government Services leadership later described this work as being "carried out virtually at the partner level." By the time she was put forward for promotion by the OGS in the summer of 1982, Hopkins had generated more business and billed more hours than any of the other eighty-seven candidates—all of them men.

In nominating Hopkins, the OGS partners wrote:

> In her five years at the firm, she has demonstrated conclusively that she has the capacity and the capability to contribute significantly to the growth and profitability of the firm. Her strong character, independence and integrity are well-recognized by her clients and her peers. Ms. Hopkins has outstanding oral and written communication skills. She has a good business sense, an ability to grasp and handle quickly the most complex issues, and strong leadership qualities.[8]

The partnership application process at Price Waterhouse was lengthy—roughly nine months—and elaborate. After each of the firm's ninety offices put forward its roster of nominees, all of the partners were permitted to submit individual evaluations. These evaluations were "long form" or "short form," depending on the partner's degree of personal contact with the candidate.[9] Those evaluations then were submitted to an Admissions Committee, which reviewed the comments and made recommendations to a Policy Board for a final decision. At the time of Hopkins's candidacy, just seven out of the firm's 662 partners were women—barely more than 1 percent. None of them sat on the Admissions Committee or Policy Board.

Price Waterhouse was not alone in its lack of gender diversity. The Big Eight were notoriously slow to accept women into their top ranks.[10] As one industry expert told *The New York Times* in the late 1980s, "The accounting firms are only now coming to the conclusion that women are as capable as men. They simply have not looked at women with the same open eye that they view men." At Deloitte Haskins & Sells, the firm with the best record of promoting women as of 1988, fewer than 6 percent of its partners—just 48 out of the firm's 850—were women. Arthur Andersen's partnership was just 3 percent female. But Price Waterhouse had the lowest numbers of the group. By the late 1980s, five years after Hopkins's candidacy, the number of women partners had crept up to a mere 2 percent.[11]

In April 1983, Lew Krulwich, an OGS senior partner, summoned Hopkins to his downtown Washington office to deliver the news. Although more than half the nominees had been promoted, Hopkins wasn't one of them. The Admissions Committee instead had recommended a "hold" on her candidacy, and the Policy Board had agreed. It wasn't an outright denial, but Hopkins would have to wait for the next year's cycle to begin, get renominated by OGS, and then go through the firm-wide evaluation process all over again. (So would the nineteen men who were also put on one-year holds.) Krulwich didn't have many answers for what had gone wrong, except for what he had been told by Hopkins's mentor in OGS, Tom Beyer, who was on vacation in the Cayman Islands: Hopkins had "consistently irritated senior partners of the firm."[12] When Beyer returned, that was all he could tell Hopkins too.[13] A few days later, she flew to New York to meet with the firm's senior partner, Joe Connor, to get more details.

Connor "was pleasant, but there was no warmth about him," Hopkins recalled.[14] She "listened in horror" as he read the remarks of the reviewers who had recommended denying or putting a hold on her application for partnership. None concerned the business she had generated or the clients she had managed. They were only about her interpersonal skills. Hopkins needed "a course in charm school." She was "overly aggressive, unduly harsh, difficult to work with and impatient with staff" and "overcompensated for being a woman."

Even her supporters' remarks lent credence to this unflattering picture. One wrote that Hopkins had "matured from a tough-talking somewhat masculine hard-nosed manager to an authoritative, formidable, but much more appealing lady partner candidate." Another acknowledged, "'Ann has a clearly different personality,'" but "'many male partners are worse than Ann (language and tough personality).'" The reviewer surmised that critics were focusing on her profanity "'because it's a lady using foul language.'" Another conceded that Hopkins

ross as "macho," but said, "'if you get around the
g she's at the top of the list or way above average.'"[15]

t Connor's office with little sense of what she could do
er when the new nomination cycle started up again in a
Back in Washington, she arranged a meeting with Tom
Bey, partner of OGS and her chief champion, to discuss how to
best position her candidacy. His advice? "Walk more femininely, talk
more femininely, dress more femininely, wear make-up, have your hair
styled, and wear jewelry."[16]

Hopkins later wrote of this period, "I was miserable, depressed,
furious, disconsolate, and inconsolable in cycles."[17] Her "normally un-
shakeable confidence," she said, "had been destroyed. I wondered how
I would tell my staff, friends, and colleagues. Five years of long hours,
hard work, and remarkable results were down the tubes." Nevertheless, she swallowed her humiliation and attended the office-wide cel-
ebrations for all of the new partners, "stoically and with all the dignity
I could muster." Her husband counseled a more combative stance. "Sue
the bastards" was his advice.[18] But Hopkins wasn't ready to declare
war. She would see how things played out the second time around.

She didn't have to wait long. Four months later, Hopkins learned
that two of the OGS partners who previously had supported her partnership had changed their minds. There wasn't going to be a second
time around, because she wasn't even going to be nominated by her
own department.[19]

Meanwhile, the men who had been placed on hold along with
Hopkins fared much better. Fifteen out of the nineteen were promoted
to partner that year.[20]

HOPKINS CONTACTED a friend who was a partner at the blue-
chip law firm of Arnold and Porter. He gave her a list of attorneys,
and because the first person on the list was out of town, she met with
the second one, Doug Huron.[21] Out of law school for little more than
a decade, Huron had already amassed an impressive resume working
for the federal government, first at the U.S. Department of Justice Civil
Rights Division—where, alongside the Southern Poverty Law Center,
he had helped to desegregate the Alabama state troopers—and then in
the White House Counsel's office during the Carter administration.
After leaving the White House, he'd opened a private practice with a
partner, Eileen Stein, in a modest Washington, DC, townhouse.

After hearing the basics of Hopkins's career at Price Waterhouse and the events leading up to the partnership denial, Huron wanted to know more about the overall environment at the firm. Hopkins realized that she hadn't given much thought to whether it was hostile to women. "I was either naïve or I wasn't paying attention," she later reflected.[22] Huron wanted to know about whether she had heard any sexist comments ("There were none that I could recall, but then, I infrequently recognized sexist comments" was Hopkins's response) and the statistical composition of the partners ("Other than to note that demographically they seemed to be a largely male, largely white population, I had too few facts to be informative").[23]

Although these blanks would need to be filled in, Huron had heard enough to conclude that Hopkins had experienced discrimination. There was something awry when a candidate who had brought in $40 million of business, won high marks from her clients, and earned the unanimous support of her department was turned down because eight men who barely knew her didn't like her personality. For her part, Hopkins was still getting used to the idea that "discrimination" even described her situation; she was still calling her partnership denial just a "bad business decision."[24] "The only context I had for discrimination and civil rights was what had taken place in Gadsden, Selma, Birmingham, and the like in my college years," she admitted. "The fact that the Civil Rights Act of 1964 might apply to me had only recently come to the forefront of my conscious thinking."[25]

It wasn't entirely clear in the spring of 1983 that Title VII, written to protect employees from employers' bias, would cover a denial of a partnership; unlike managers in a typical corporate entity, the Price Waterhouse partners all shared in the firm's collective decision making, including decisions about who would join their ranks. A case involving an Atlanta law firm's decision to deny a woman a partnership, *Hishon v. King & Spalding,* was pending review in the Supreme Court, but until *Hishon* was resolved, Doug Huron hedged his bets. He filed a lawsuit in DC Superior Court alleging violations of the local law against sex discrimination while also filing a charge with the EEOC to preserve the right to eventually file a Title VII lawsuit in federal court.

In the meantime, Hopkins was desperate to leave Price Waterhouse, but Huron told her to hold tight; if she quit, she couldn't recover any future lost wages unless she could claim she had been "constructively discharged." Constructive discharge was tough to prove. The prevailing legal standard required a plaintiff to show that her working conditions had been made so "intolerable" that she *had* to leave. Only then could she quit and still be treated, by law, as if she had been fired—which would entitle her to recover damages for losing her job. Hopkins may have been miserable about the nosedive her career had taken at Price Waterhouse, but that wasn't enough to make the job "intolerable." It was admittedly a murky line. Hopkins waited for Huron to tell her she had crossed it.[26]

It only took four more months. Soon after Hopkins consulted Huron, her mentor Tom Beyer told her she had three options: Get a new job, transfer to a different department within Price Waterhouse, or—Beyer's top recommendation—forget about making partner and accept a second-tier existence as a "career manager" at the firm.[27] Things deteriorated further when she got the results of a "quality control review" of her past work that, for the first time in her tenure, gave her low marks. Then one of the OGS partners who had withdrawn his support for Hopkins's renewed partnership bid began inserting himself into her newest project for the State Department, subjecting it to repeated, fine-tooth-comb audits. She returned from a work trip abroad to find her belongings packed up and moved to a new office, though no one could tell her where that was. By December 1983, Hopkins "was barely hanging on by my psychological fingernails" when Huron gave her the okay. In his judgment, she had reached the "intolerable" threshold that would qualify her for a constructive discharge claim. Hopkins resigned four days before Christmas.[28]

A few months later, the Supreme Court decided *Hishon,* unanimously ruling that Title VII did extend to decisions denying partnership. Huron obtained a right-to-sue notice from the EEOC and headed to federal court. *Hopkins v. Price Waterhouse* was filed in U.S. District Court for the District of Columbia in September 1984. In addition to seeking reimbursement of lost wages and attorneys' fees, the complaint asked the court for an order making Ann Hopkins a partner at Price Waterhouse.

—————

HOPKINS HAD TOLD Huron all she could remember about the negative comments relayed to her by the firm's top partner, Joe Connor. But in discovery, Huron was able to obtain copies of all of the long and short forms and read the comments for himself, word for word. He also got the forms submitted for the male candidates, to compare their qualifications, and the partners' assessments of their strengths and weaknesses, to Hopkins's. Huron made sure that Price Waterhouse's document production covered not only the promotion years in which Hopkins was a contender but also prior years, so that he could see how other female prospective partners had fared.

"I recall being struck by the discovery responses that Price Waterhouse gave us," said Huron. "I'm not sure I knew the word 'stereotyping,' but it was clear there was something peculiar going on." Like Hopkins, women who had gone up for partner in the prior years also had been described unflatteringly in distinctly gender-specific terms. Two unsuccessful candidates were pilloried for their perceived abrasiveness—one was written off as trying to be "one of the boys" and the other was dubbed "Ma Barker."[29] A third female candidate (who ultimately was promoted) was criticized for being a "women's libber." One male partner even stated categorically that he "could not consider any woman seriously as a partnership candidate and believed women were not even capable of functioning as senior managers."[30] Huron also identified male candidates whose crudeness, arrogance, and brusqueness had been remarked on but whom Price Waterhouse had promoted to partner anyway.

Another tool utilized during discovery is the deposition, when lawyers question witnesses from the opposing party under oath. When Huron took the deposition of Tom Beyer, he asked Beyer about his advice to Hopkins that she walk, talk, dress, and style herself more femininely. Even though Huron could tell that Beyer liked Hopkins and genuinely had wanted her to make partner, he was sure that Beyer's allegiance to Price Waterhouse would cause him to deny making the statement. But to Huron's surprise, he admitted it. Said Huron, "I remember thinking, 'Son of a bitch! We might win this case!'"

As obvious as it was to Huron that Hopkins's gender was the reason she had rubbed so many male partners the wrong way, though, there was no "smoking gun"; no one specifically had said, "We shouldn't promote Ms. Hopkins because she is a woman." The collective message of the comments was more accurately summed up as, "We shouldn't promote Ms. Hopkins because she is the *wrong kind* of woman." That Tom Beyer and others of Hopkins's supporters had expressed variations on that sentiment was a complicating factor. Although they hadn't held her womanhood against her in casting their votes, they were clearly treating Hopkins as a *woman* candidate.

Huron was aware of courts relying on social science literature that documented the various ways segregation had stigmatized African Americans, so he "wondered if that was true for sex." He called

Donna Lenhoff, a friend at the Women's Legal Defense Fund (now the National Partnership for Women and Families), and told her what he was looking for. Lenhoff knew that another prominent attorney in the Washington, DC, women's rights community, Sally Burns, had used a social psychology expert in an employment discrimination case she had recently settled, and referred Huron to her.

Huron called Burns's expert, a young psychology professor at Carnegie-Mellon University named Susan Fiske, and described Hopkins's situation. He also sent her the various long and short forms and other materials produced in discovery. Fiske's assessment was that Hopkins was being punished for not conforming to stereotype. Women were expected to be soft and tender, while men were expected to be assertive and competitive, even sharp-elbowed; because Hopkins was seen as behaving "like a man," she was judged more harshly. "I would not have taken the case unless I thought on the face of it that it was an injustice," Fiske explained. "My feeling was that if I was going to be doing this research, then I had to be willing to take it into the trenches, so to speak."

One thing she would not do, though, was meet Ann Hopkins in advance of the trial. What mattered was not how *Fiske* perceived Hopkins but how the *partners* had perceived her, and whether those perceptions showed stereotyping. Meeting and forming her own impressions would only muddy the waters.

Although social science literature on gender stereotyping had existed for more than a decade, Huron wasn't aware of expert testimony on the subject ever being introduced at an employment discrimination trial. He couldn't be sure whether Fiske's opinions would even be deemed admissible. He could only prepare Fiske thoroughly to take the stand and hope that the judge allowed her testimony into evidence.

TRIAL IN *Hopkins v. Price Waterhouse* began on March 25, 1985, before U.S. District Judge Gerhard Gesell. Gesell, a President Johnson appointee, was "widely regarded as the most agile and powerful mind on the D.C. bench."[31] As one lawyer who appeared before Gesell described him, "He's like God up there, with his white hair."[32]

Gesell was known for his liberal rulings, including, in the late 1960s, one of the nation's first decisions striking down an antiabortion law and, during the 1970s, rejecting the government's effort to stop *The Washington Post* from publishing the Pentagon Papers. He'd also presided over the trials of some of the Watergate burglars and several Nixon administration officials, at one point even threatening to find President Nixon himself in contempt of court.[33] Especially auspicious for Hopkins was the fact that Gesell's father, Arnold Gesell, was a renowned child psychologist who founded the Yale Clinic of Child Development.[34] Susan Fiske would be delivering her testimony to a judge who was no stranger to the tenets of psychology.

By the time Hopkins's case went to trial, Huron was no longer alone in going up against Price Waterhouse. After the retirement of his law partner the prior year, he'd joined the firm of Kator, Scott & Heller, and Jim Heller had become Huron's co-counsel on the matter. Heller, who died in 2001, was a veteran of Washington's progressive legal community. He'd spent his early career as a lawyer in the Johnson administration helping wage the "war on poverty" and later, as regional chief of the American Civil Liberties Union, had worked to get criminal charges dismissed against Vietnam War protestors arrested during Washington's 1971 "May Day" demonstrations.[35] "Jim and I had a unique relationship on the case—as close as I've ever come to joint control," Huron commented. "We did not have arguments."

The trial took place over five days. The theme of Huron and Heller's case was simple: If it weren't for her gender, Hopkins would've been a shoo-in for partner. In terms of generating business, "there was no comparison between Ann and any of the men," said Huron. She was "off the charts." In addition to eliciting this information from Hopkins herself, Heller and Huron called as witnesses two high-level officials at the State Department who had worked with her. One testified, "I would describe Ann as extremely competent, intelligent, a very capable person. Strong and forthright, very productive, energetic and creative."[36] Another praised her "intellectual clarity" and said that he had tried to convince her to come work for him.[37] Finally, Huron and Heller put Tom Beyer on the stand. He confirmed Hopkins's stellar performance evaluations over her five years at the firm. He also admitted, again, that he had advised her to behave more femininely and to change her hair, makeup, and accessories.

When it was their turn, Price Waterhouse's attorneys predictably focused on the negative reviews of Hopkins's personality. The written partner evaluations were only the half of it. Partner after partner took the stand to recount unpleasant run-ins with Hopkins. The main complaints were about Hopkins's relationships with Price Waterhouse partners and staff, not clients. "People testified about expletives I used, people I chewed out, work I reviewed and criticized, and they did so with the most negative spin they could come up with," recalled Hopkins.[38] She likened hearing partners' unvarnished comments about her to "being dissected like a diseased frog in the biology lab."[39] Huron and Heller attempted to show that Hopkins was the victim of a double standard. They got confirmation, for instance, that a male candidate was promoted despite comments such as "lack of maturity, wise guy attitude, abrasive, cocky,"[40] while another senior partner admitted, when asked if any men with "dirty mouths" had been made partner, "Oh, yes."[41]

Dr. Fiske was the star witness on rebuttal. She offered Judge Gesell an alternative reading of all the negative evaluations put forward by Price Waterhouse—that they were negative only because Hopkins was a woman who wasn't acting sufficiently "womanly." In her expert opinion, she said, sex stereotyping "played a major determining role" in the decision to deny Hopkins partnership.[42]

Fiske noted that there were various flaws in Price Waterhouse's promotion procedure that had allowed sex stereotyping to flourish. Because there were no other women among eighty-eight partnership candidates, Hopkins's gender became her most salient characteristic. The firm also relied too heavily on criteria that were in the eye of the beholder, such as whether a candidate had "an excellent reputation" or "outstanding attributes," as opposed to more quantifiable traits, such as how much business she or he brought in. The more subjective the criteria, Fiske explained, the more opportunity for the mind to default to stereotypic notions of what behavior is and isn't appropriate for a woman. Fiske also criticized the deference to comments from partners who had had little contact with Hopkins; when only a few encounters form the basis of an individual's opinion, she explained, it's easier for gender stereotypes to get in the way. Finally, Fiske observed that Price Waterhouse imposed no discernible "checks" on biased decision making, in that it had no written policy against discrimination and no training for partners in how to avoid stereotypes when evaluating candidates and had not reprimanded partners who submitted comments reflecting hostility to women.[43]

Price Waterhouse's attorney, Steve Tallent, rose to conduct his cross-examination. He questioned how Fiske could determine the intent of people she had never met. The stereotypes spoke for themselves, she responded. He asked Fiske to identify specific comments she saw as stereotyped. As Fiske went through the list and explained her reasoning, Tallent grew sarcastic. Aren't there some women who are just abrasive? he challenged. Rude? Arrogant? Fiske agreed that of course, women can have all of those qualities, just like men.[44]

Whatever skepticism Tallent had about Fiske's interpretation of the evidence, though, it didn't result in his challenging either her credentials as an expert or the validity of social psychology as a scientific discipline. At the end of the five-day trial, Gesell admitted Fiske's testimony into evidence.

After Fiske left the witness stand, Hopkins approached her outside the courtroom, shook her hand, and thanked her. "I finally understand what happened to me."

———

HURON WAS RIGHT about Judge Gesell's impressions of Susan Fiske. When he issued his opinion six months later, her conclusions were front and center. "The Court finds that the Policy Board's decision not to admit the plaintiff to partnership was tainted by discriminatory evaluations that were the direct result of its failure to address the evident problem of sexual stereotyping in partners' evaluations."[45] Although such stereotyping was unconscious on the part of the individual partners, Gesell explained, Price Waterhouse nevertheless had *consciously* used an evaluation system that allowed those stereotypes to carry the day. Fiske's testimony about the promotion process's flaws directly informed this conclusion:

> Neither a partnership nor any other employer can remain indifferent to indications that its evaluation system is subject to sex bias, as Price Waterhouse did in Plaintiff's case. Price Waterhouse's failure to take the steps necessary to alert partners to the possibility that their judgments may be biased, to discourage stereotyping, and to investigate and discard, where appropriate, comments that suggest a double standard constitutes a violation of Title VII in this instance.[46]

But then things got more complicated. Having agreed that gender bias played a role in the partners' criticism, Judge Gesell also concluded that many other of the complaints about Hopkins's interpersonal skills were *not* so tainted. He noted that even the staff who testified on her behalf during the rebuttal phase termed her management style "controversial" and said that it took "diplomacy, patience and guts" to work with her. Other records showed that in her years with the firm, Hopkins had been counseled about being "overly critical of others" and "impatient with her staff" and had not disputed those criticisms. In sum, Gesell wrote, "Plaintiff's conduct provided ample justification for the complaints that formed the basis of the Policy Board's decision."[47]

Judge Gesell had waded into an emerging area of Title VII law, the so-called mixed motive case. When an employer is motivated in part by bias and in part by a legitimate, job-related reason, where is the line between legal and illegal? Does *any* discriminatory animus automatically taint an otherwise fair decision? And is it the plaintiff's burden to show that the bias made the difference in the decision, or is it the employer's burden to show it would have made the same decision even absent the discrimination?

Gesell put the burden on Price Waterhouse: Once an employee shows that discrimination "played a role" in an employment decision, he wrote, the burden shifts to the employer to avoid liability. And at that point, the only way to do so is by proving by "clear and convincing evidence" that it would have taken the same action anyway. Title VII's goals were so important, Gesell said, that any uncertainty should be resolved against the employer, not the employee. In Hopkins's case, Price Waterhouse hadn't met the "clear and convincing" test; the evidence of stereotyping was just too strong to conclude that it would have denied partnership absent the biased comments.[48]

Gesell's opinion wasn't all good news for Hopkins, though. He ruled that she had not satisfied the legal test for proving that her decision to quit could be considered a constructive discharge. He cited a variety of factors necessary to meet the test—a "history of discrimination, humiliation or other aggravating factors that would have compelled her to resign"—and found them lacking. To the extent that she had been subjected to undue scrutiny in the months leading up to her resignation, Gesell found that Hopkins hadn't proved they were part of "an improper effort to pressure [her] to resign."[49]

As a result, Gesell ruled that Hopkins's legal entitlement to damages ended when she quit. He didn't even address the question of whether Hopkins was entitled to return to Price Waterhouse as a partner. Instead, she was entitled only to her lost partner-level compensation through December 1983, when she handed in her resignation. By Hopkins's estimate, that amount came to around $15,000.

BOTH SIDES immediately appealed the parts of Gesell's opinion that had gone against them: Price Waterhouse appealed the sex

discrimination ruling, while Hopkins challenged the constructive discharge decision.

The U.S. Court of Appeals for the D.C. Circuit heard the appeal
the following fall, in October 1986. From Hopkins's standpoint, it was
a promising panel. Judge Harry Edwards was a Carter appointee, as
was Joyce Hens Green (a district judge sitting in "by designation," as
sometimes occurs for scheduling reasons). Both had reputations as liberals, and Doug Huron and Jim Heller hoped that Green, as a woman,
would be especially receptive to Hopkins's case. The third and final
member of the panel, Stephen Williams, was a question mark, having
just been appointed to the bench a few months earlier by President
Reagan. In a way, though, it didn't matter if Williams went against
them; as Huron put it, "a 2–1 win would be fine."

In August 1987, the D.C. Circuit—in the two to one split predicted by Huron—gave Hopkins a total victory. In an opinion penned
by Judge Green, the court affirmed Judge Gesell's ruling on sex discrimination and reversed his constructive discharge decision. The
court agreed that the partners' comments about Hopkins and other
women candidates reflected unlawful stereotyping. The fact that even
Hopkins's supporters were responsible for using similarly stereotyped
language in *praising* Hopkins made no difference: "Stereotypical attitudes that sometimes work to the advantage of women, such as the
once unchallenged assumption that mothers are inherently superior
parents and thus nearly always entitled to custody of children in divorce actions, are no less the product of archaic thinking than those
attitudes that disadvantage women." The court further agreed that
Gesell was correct in finding that Price Waterhouse failed to show
by "clear and convincing evidence" that, absent its stereotyped assessments of Hopkins, it would have denied her partnership anyway.
Putting that burden of proof on the employee, said the court, would be
insurmountable for most litigants.[50]

As to constructive discharge, the panel found that Judge Gesell
had wrongly required Hopkins to prove Price Waterhouse *intended*
to make her working conditions so intolerable that she was driven
to quit. Instead, said the court, the appropriate question was simply
whether a "reasonable person" would have felt no choice but to resign.
And under that standard, Hopkins had made her case. "Price Waterhouse's decision to deny Hopkins partnership status, . . . coupled with
the OGS's failure to renominate her, would have been viewed by any
reasonable senior manager in her position as a career-ending action."[51]
Reversing this portion of Gesell's ruling, the court directed that the

case be sent back to him for a second go at devising an appropriate remedy for Hopkins. She could still hold out hope that he would order she be made a partner, after all.

——— ———

"ONE OF THE worst days of my life was when the Supreme Court took [my case],"[52] Ann Hopkins told *The New York Times*. After five years of litigation and a drumbeat of scathing commentary about her personality, she had hoped that the D.C. Circuit ruling meant the end was in sight. She was eager to get on with her life, which had new stresses to manage: She and her husband had recently separated, making her the primary caregiver for three kids. But Price Waterhouse sought review of the D.C. Circuit's ruling on sex discrimination, and in 1988, the justices agreed to hear the case. For reasons that were never clear to Huron, the firm didn't ask the Court to address the constructive discharge ruling.

Hopkins didn't share with Huron and Heller her personal heartbreak or her disappointment about the Supreme Court news; she was "unflappable" as always, said Huron. (When Hopkins did eventually confide in Huron about her separation, she learned that he had kept his own sad secret from her: He and his wife had split during the trial. He had been so disconsolate that he'd ceded the closing argument to Heller, which set the pattern for the rest of the case—Heller as oral advocate, Huron as chief brief writer.)

One of Huron's chief concerns was ensuring that the Supreme Court credited Dr. Fiske and her conclusions. Judge Williams of the D.C. Circuit had ridiculed both in his dissent. "In discussing sex stereotyping, the district court gave great weight to the testimony of Dr. Susan Fiske, a witness purporting to be an expert in that field," Williams wrote. Indeed, Judge Williams appeared to rate Fiske just above a dime-store psychic, lambasting Judge Gesell for giving credence to "the allegations of stereotyping floating in the Price Waterhouse ether and the remarkable intuitions of Dr. Fiske."[53]

Not surprisingly, Price Waterhouse relied extensively on Williams's dissent in its brief to the Supreme Court. When not quoting him directly, it echoed his sarcasm, such as describing Fiske's conclusions as "intuitive hunches" and consistently using quotation marks around "sex stereotyping" as if it were an idiosyncratic concept of Fiske's own invention.[54]

To lend heft to Fiske's conclusions, Heller and Huron secured a commitment from the American Psychological Association to submit a friend of the court brief. The APA sought to rebut Judge Williams's and Price Waterhouse's suggestion that those conclusions were based on pseudoscience by citing the reams of peer-reviewed studies about stereotyping. And it emphasized the role of stereotypes in straitjacketing all women:

> [S]ex stereotypes place women into a "double-bind" situation. If they are viewed "as women" they are frequently denied access to high power positions because their presumed attributes cause them to appear incapable or their performance is ascribed to something other than competence. . . . If, however, they are perceived as engaging in "masculine" behaviors deemed essential for the job, they are considered to be abrasive, or maladjusted. In many cases, then, the achievement oriented woman is caught—whatever her behavior, it bodes ill for her career.[55]

Among the three other *amicus* submissions on Hopkins's behalf was a brief from nineteen women's rights organizations. The groups noted that although *Hopkins* marked a "second generation" in cases alleging discrimination "because of sex"—in that it concerned biased *attitudes* toward women rather than formal *policies* that disadvantaged them—those attitudes were equally pernicious. To make their point, they quoted no less an establishment figure than President Reagan's Ambassador to the United Nations, Jeane Kirkpatrick: "When I have replied to criticisms of the United States (which is an important part of my job), I have frequently been described as 'confrontational.' . . . It was a while before I noticed that *none* of my male colleagues, who often delivered more 'confrontational' speeches than I, were labeled as 'confrontational.'"[56]

As the parties readied themselves for oral argument, Hopkins was at least able to find some pleasure in the case's continued prominence. "As the firm's appeal was going through the Supreme Court process, the media started to refer to it as a landmark," she later wrote. She met up with Betsy Hishon, whose successful partnership-denial case against King and Spalding had made it possible for Hopkins to sue under Title VII—a case also called a landmark. "Over grins and gins and tonics, we toasted each other as 'Landmark 1' and 'Landmark 2.'"[57]

THE SUPREME COURT heard oral argument in *Price Waterhouse v. Hopkins* on October 31, 1988. Hopkins filed into the courtroom with a large clan of supporters, including her sister and brother, friends, and her three children—Tela, twelve, Gilbert, ten, and Peter, eight.

As he had before the D.C. Circuit, Jim Heller would be arguing for Hopkins. Price Waterhouse, however, had new counsel. It would be represented before the justices by a partner at the white-shoe firm of Mayer Brown and a former deputy solicitor general, Kay Oberly.

As the party appealing the D.C. Circuit's ruling, Price Waterhouse went first, and Oberly took the lectern. Hopkins's case never should have been called "mixed motive" in the first place, she said. The evidence of bias against Hopkins really just came from Dr. Fiske, and that was simply too flimsy to qualify as a "motive" at all. While Oberly conceded that "there were a few sex-based comments about [Hopkins], and that those comments were inappropriate," she said, "they simply don't shed any light on the existence of a mixed motive." In contrast, Judge Gesell had found there was plenty of *un*biased evidence that Hopkins shouldn't have been made a partner.[58]

Because Hopkins didn't produce enough evidence of bias to "bring the ball over the 50-yard line," Oberly said, the burden never should have been on Price Waterhouse to show it would have made the same decision even without the biased comments in the mix.[59]

Oberly also tried to disavow the most direct evidence of gender bias in the partnership denial: Tom Beyer's advice that Hopkins "walk more femininely, talk more femininely," and so on. That remark, Oberly contended, should not be taken as an official directive of the firm but instead as a piece of personal advice from one friend to another.[60]

Oberly had not faced especially active questioning, but when it was Heller's turn, he got even less. He began by disputing Oberly's characterization of the weight of the stereotyping evidence found by Judge Gesell. "I think unfortunately Ms. Oberly has rather scanted what [Judge Gesell's] findings say," countered Heller. He quoted Gesell's conclusion that Hopkins "appears to have been a victim of . . . a system that made evaluations based on outmoded attitudes . . . *determinative*." Heller paused for emphasis. "Determinative. Hard to find a more decisive word."[61]

With that, Heller disputed Oberly's metaphor for the burden of proof on the plaintiff in a mixed motive case. "Now, this isn't a question of the 50-yard line," he said. "This is a question of two motives possibly playing a part, and what must the Plaintiff show." And all that was, he explained, was that bias was "[a] motivating factor, a substantial factor."[62]

Heller also rejected Oberly's effort to cast Tom Beyer's advice to Hopkins as not being attributable to the firm. Beyer was "the messenger from the policy board in the partnership." Indeed, Heller quoted another partner who at trial had testified, "I have no doubt that Tom Beyer . . . knew exactly what to tell her, where the problems lay."[63]

While most attorneys at oral argument struggle to reach the end of their prepared remarks within the allotted thirty minutes—given how much time typically is taken up by the justices' questions—Heller finished before his time was up. "If there are no other questions, I will then sit down," he said.[64]

For Hopkins, the argument had been "a disappointment"; her two young sons had alternately squirmed, chatted, and napped during the argument, all of which had drawn the attention of a vigilant marshal. Hopkins spent most of the hour in the courtroom keeping the kids awake, still, and quiet. "Between the dreadful acoustics and the badgering marshal, I barely heard the arguments," she wrote. But her friends who had better vantage points assured her that Heller was "calm, poised, eloquent, and articulate," while Oberly was "unpersuasive." Hopkins shepherded her three kids through the throng of reporters outside the Court and into a waiting cab. Then she went home and threw a big party.[65]

"EVEN THE CALENDAR knew *Price Waterhouse v. Hopkins* was not your ordinary case," commented Doug Huron. The case had been argued on Halloween, and the decision was issued on May Day—May 1, 1989. On that day, Huron was getting into a cab to go to court when Jim Heller appeared beside him. "The Supreme Court just decided *Hopkins*," Heller said, "and I think we won."

Heller called Hopkins and she raced to the law firm's offices. The vote was six to three in Hopkins's favor, but the six votes were contained in three separate opinions. As Heller read through the sheaf of pages trying to make sense of it all, Hopkins took her copy and drove home to read the opinion there, with a neighbor who was a law student to help translate.

Six justices—Brennan, Blackmun, Marshall, O'Connor, Stevens, and White—had ruled that gender stereotyping was sex discrimination. "An employer who objects to women being aggressive but whose positions require this trait places women in an intolerable and impermissible catch-22: out of a job if they behave aggressively and out of a job if they do not. Title VII lifts women out of this bind," wrote Justice Brennan. In Hopkins's case, the evidence showed both that the partners had engaged in sex stereotyping and that such stereotyping motivated her partnership denial. Indeed, the plurality found the gendered language of the partners' criticisms so blatant as to characterize Dr. Fiske's testimony as "merely icing on Hopkins's cake."

> It takes no special training to discern sex stereotyping in a description of an aggressive female employee as "requiring a course at charm school." Nor, turning to Thomas Beyer's memorable advice to Hopkins, does it require expertise in psychology to know that, if an employee's flawed "interpersonal skills" can be corrected by a soft-hued suit or a new shade of lipstick, perhaps it is the employee's sex and not her interpersonal skills that has drawn the criticism.

The same six justices also agreed that a plaintiff could win even when the proof showed the defendant had "mixed motives." That pronouncement would make it would considerably easier for employees to win discrimination cases in the future.[66]

There was one respect, however, in which the Court gave Price Waterhouse a win. Judge Gesell and the D.C. Circuit had held that the only way for the firm to avoid losing was to show by "clear and convincing evidence" that it would have denied Hopkins partnership even absent the stereotyped comments. But the Supreme Court found that that put the bar too high; Price Waterhouse should only have had to make that showing by a "preponderance of the evidence." Loosely translated, that means the firm had to show it was "more likely than not" that it would have made the same decision. Because Price Waterhouse was held at trial to the wrong standard of proof, the Court remanded the case back to Judge Gesell to decide if it could meet the less stringent standard.

Hopkins was confused by the multiple opinions and anxious about returning to the district court. "I could lose," she bluntly told one local reporter—earning a chiding from Jim Heller for expressing any doubt publicly.[67]

A week after the Supreme Court's ruling, Hopkins's divorce was finalized. With that chapter of her life closed, she girded for the next one. A new hearing before Judge Gesell was scheduled for November 1989, where he would apply the new, more lenient proof standard to Price Waterhouse. Trial on the issue of an appropriate remedy—including whether Price Waterhouse should be ordered to make her a partner—would take place in February of the following year.

"WELL, IT LOOKS like you're gonna be a partner," Jim Heller told Ann Hopkins over the phone. "Holy shit!" was her startled response.[68]

It was May 14, 1990, and Judge Gesell had just issued his opinion, giving Hopkins a wholesale win. Reexamining the evidence presented at the first trial, Gesell concluded that Price Waterhouse couldn't show by a preponderance of the evidence—just as it had failed to show by clear and convincing evidence the first time—that it would have denied Hopkins partnership even without the tainted evaluations.

That left the question of a remedy. It mystified Gesell, but Hopkins still wanted to be a partner at Price Waterhouse. As reported by *The New York Times,* "She said it would be fine to be a partner where, it had been established, for the record, that she was not wanted, because she was sure of her abilities as a management consultant and wanted a chance to use them at a top-notch concern."[69] Gesell rejected the possibility of requiring that Price Waterhouse just put Hopkins through the partnership consideration process all over again, calling it "futile and unjust." He explained, "[T]he deck is stacked against her. Price Waterhouse plainly does not want her and would not voluntarily admit her." For that reason, "[p]artnership, not simply a new vote, is the logical remedy."[70]

This was yet another historic turn in Hopkins's litigation against the firm. Although it was common for a successful discrimination litigant to be given the job wrongfully denied him or her, partnerships were unique, invitation-only institutions in which participants shared in decision making and profits. Gesell's ruling marked the first time a federal court ever had awarded partnership as a remedy in a discrimination case.

A few weeks later, Gesell entered a final order directing Price Waterhouse to admit Hopkins as a partner, effective July 1, 1990.

He also directed it to award her all the partnership shares she would have earned had she been promoted July 1, 1983, and pay her close to $400,000 in lost compensation plus interest, in addition to her attorneys' fees. Gesell further ordered that Price Waterhouse not retaliate in any way against Hopkins for having pursued her lawsuit.

The case didn't end there, though. Price Waterhouse made one more go at the D.C. Circuit, appealing both Gesell's discrimination finding and his award of partnership. As Hopkins ruefully told a reporter at the time, "My kids keep asking how many times we have to win this before it's over."[71]

On December 4, 1990, the appeals court unanimously affirmed Judge Gesell's order. As Hopkins later wrote with relief, "I could no longer lose."[72]

HOPKINS WAS RIGHT about the end of the court battle, but Price Waterhouse wasn't quite done trying to keep her out of the firm: Its lawyers told Heller and Huron that it would pay her up to $1 million if she would agree not to come back. Hopkins said that wasn't enough to make her give up after so long or to agree to any of the usual terms of settlement, such as promising never to speak ill of the firm again.[73] At that point, according to Doug Huron, Price Waterhouse "accepted its loss gracefully" and "worked constructively to make sure that Ann would be treated like any other partner."

In 1991, nearly a decade after she had first started trying to win partnership at Price Waterhouse, Hopkins rejoined the firm. She was forty-seven years old. "I was certainly nervous about going back," she admitted. "I'd missed eight years of experience."[74] People who had been junior to her during her prior tenure were now six or seven years into their partnerships. The proportion of women partners among the firm's partners had gone up since her 1984 departure, though. When she left, it was less than 1 percent. By the time of her return, it was 3 percent.[75] And upon her retirement from the firm in 2001—after the firm had merged with Coopers & Lybrand to form PriceWaterhouse Coopers—women composed approximately 12 percent of the partner ranks.[76]

Although Hopkins experienced a few snubs—at a new partner training, for instance, one colleague refused to shake her hand, while another snidely referred to her years of litigation as a "sabbatical"— overall she did not experience much in the way of outright hostility. As she later told one reporter, "The people who didn't like me still didn't like me," she said. "The people who liked me still liked me."[77]

She also relished a new role, one that would have been unthinkable during her first stint at the firm, when women's status wasn't even on her radar: She became an outspoken advocate for diversity. Today, with obvious pride, she can still list all of the diverse junior staff she personally mentored and shepherded to partnership. And given her high profile as a woman who took on institutional gender bias and won, she also became the go-to partner for anyone at the firm who believed they'd been wronged. Not that she always encouraged them to fight back. "You really have to decide if it's worth it," she said. "And unfortunately, all too frequently it's just not worth it."

But it was worth it to Hopkins. Indeed, winning allowed her the luxury, in her decade as a Price Waterhouse partner, of simply being herself. Hopkins recalled sitting in a meeting where the recruiting partner, upon being questioned about the firm's homogeneity, chalked it up to a lack of available talent. "You can't find sharks in a lake," he explained.

Hopkins wasn't buying it. "I said, 'Why don't you find a better body of water?'"

She laughed, imagining what all the male partners must have said about her insistence that she be made a partner at a place that had fought to keep her out for nine years. "'I don't know what we do with her, but you better enlist her, as opposed to screw around!'"

seven

potentially
pregnant

International Union, United Auto Workers of
America v. Johnson Controls, Inc. (1991)

IN AUGUST 1982, CAR BATTERY MANUFACTURER JOHN-
son Controls sent a memorandum to all of its Globe Battery Division
plants that dropped a bombshell: "[W]omen who are pregnant or who
are capable of bearing children will not be placed into jobs involving
lead exposure or which could expose them to lead through the exercise
of job bidding, bumping, transfer or promotion rights."[1]

At the time, about 275 women worked in the sixteen Johnson
Controls plants nationwide, making up fewer than 10 percent of the
company's workers.[2] Because the policy deemed a woman "capable of
bearing children" until she reached age seventy unless she provided
medical proof of infertility, it applied to most of those 275. And because lead is the key ingredient in batteries, most of the skilled jobs
in the factories were "jobs involving lead exposure." This meant that
even if a woman wasn't pregnant (and didn't plan on having a baby),
she still was barred from the best-paying jobs at the company.

Around the country, female Johnson Controls employees reacted
to their impending demotions with disbelief and rage. "Ridiculous
and degrading," said Elsie Nason, a welder in the company's Bennington, Vermont, factory, where she was one of just twelve women out

of approximately three hundred workers.[3] At the time the policy was announced, Nason was fifty years old and had been divorced for nine years. As a single mother of three, she had taken the Johnson Controls job when she and her husband separated. The factory paid Nason up to $20 an hour,[4] much more than what she could earn as a waitress, the only other job she'd ever held. Upon learning that she was to be transferred to a job sweeping floors with no eligibility for incentive pay, overtime, or promotion, Nason asked her doctor about getting sterilized. But when he told her the risks of the surgery, she grudgingly accepted the transfer. "They took me off my job for foolishness and I'll be mad about it, and the smutty jokes I had to hear from the men about an old lady like me still having her period, until the day I die," she said.[5]

A thousand miles away, Gloyce Qualls, who worked in the company's Milwaukee, Wisconsin, plant, made a different choice. When Johnson Controls told her about its new policy, Qualls was engaged to a man with four children and had just bought a new car and moved into a new apartment. Her job, welding lead posts into batteries, paid more than twice what she would make if she got transferred. Within a few weeks, Qualls underwent surgical sterilization. She was thirty-four years old. "I panicked," Qualls said. "My husband said, 'Don't let your job tell you what to do with your life.' But all I could see was that I couldn't afford to pay my bills," she explained. "I believe now that nobody can tell you what to do with your body. And if I had taken a little more time, I wouldn't have done it." (Notably, while the company didn't object to female employees' getting sterilized to comply with the new policy, male workers were a different story: When Doris Stone, who worked at the Milwaukee plant along with her husband, asked the personnel manager if she could keep her job if her husband "got himself taken care of," the answer was no. "In not so many words, he said that even if my husband had a vasectomy, it wouldn't stop me from getting pregnant," she said—the insinuation being that it wasn't just Stone's fertility but also her *fidelity* that the company considered a risk.)[6]

Across the country, twenty-eight-year-old Queen Elizabeth Foster applied for a job at the Johnson Controls plant in Fullerton, California. The position, as a member of a team assembling metal battery plates into bundles, paid twice what she was making as a bank teller. But as part of the application process, she needed to get a physical, and the company doctor told her about the company's new policy.[7] Although incumbent employees at least were offered transfers to (lower-paid, lower-skilled) jobs that didn't expose them to lead, Johnson Controls wouldn't hire *any* new female employees without proof of infertility. Foster didn't intend to have children but didn't want to have to undergo surgery either, so she didn't get the job.[8]

THE 1982 POLICY marked a radical change in how Johnson Controls addressed the issue of lead exposure among prospective mothers. Since 1977, the company had advised women workers about lead's potential risks to the fetus—likening them to smoking—but left it up to them how to respond to those risks. The company offered women the option of transferring out of lead-exposed jobs when they wanted to get pregnant, although it wouldn't guarantee that they'd be able to transfer back after having their babies.

In 1978, the federal Occupational Health and Safety Administration (OSHA) issued new regulations on a variety of hazardous workplace substances, including lead. The Final Standard for Occupational Exposure to Lead was the product of eleven weeks of hearings.[9] The standard confirmed that long-term lead exposure through inhalation and ingestion posed grave dangers to the central nervous system, blood's oxygenation process, kidneys, and urinary tract.[10] It recommended that to prevent such adverse effects, the lead content in the workplace environment not exceed 50 micrograms per cubic meter of air (50 ug/m^3) and that during an eight-hour workday, a worker's blood lead level not exceed 40 micrograms per 100 grams of whole blood (40 ug/100 g).[11]

As to the effect of lead on men's and women's reproductive systems, OSHA observed that "[n]o topic was covered in greater depth or from more vantage points [during the hearings] than the subject of women in the lead industry." Representatives from the Lead Industries Association in particular had urged that OSHA find fetal safety could be assured only if women were excluded outright from the workplace. OSHA rejected this proposal. It explained: "Exposure to lead has profoundly adverse effects on the course of reproduction in both males and females. . . . Given the data in this record, OSHA believes there is no basis whatsoever for the claim that women of childbearing age should be excluded from the workplace in order to protect the fetus or the course of pregnancy."[12]

Instead, the agency concluded that when a worker of either sex is contemplating a family, he or she could do so safely if his or her blood lead level was lowered to 30 ug/100 g. It recommended various protective measures that would not only benefit all workers' health but also, in concert, "should effectively minimize any risk to the fetus and newborn child."[13] These included proper ventilation, protective clothing and masks, personal hygiene procedures when leaving the workplace, "housekeeping" measures to keep work surfaces free of lead, and frequent monitoring of air and blood levels.[14]

According to Johnson Controls, in the four and a half years after its initial voluntary reproductive health policy was put in place, eight women had become pregnant while also, at some point, registering levels above 30 ug/100 g.[15] None of their babies showed any adverse health consequences. (One child did have some behavioral problems, but they never were conclusively linked to his mother's lead exposure.)[16]

Nevertheless, the company said that these developments, as well as advice from in-house medical advisors, prompted it to adopt its women-only fetal protection policy. Whatever OSHA had concluded about keeping potential parents safe in the workplace, and whatever choices employees were making for themselves about family planning, Johnson Controls claimed that it knew better. Even if it meant depriving women of their paychecks, it was for their own good.

JOHNSON CONTROLS was hardly unique in barring women from hazardous jobs in the name of protecting their potential offspring. In fact, by the time Johnson Controls adopted its new policy in 1982, Allied Chemical, B.F. Goodrich, Monsanto, Dow Chemical, DuPont, Eastman Kodak, Sun Oil, Gulf Oil, Union Carbide, and General Motors already had implemented some form of fetal protection policy to prevent exposure to a wide range of chemicals.[17] In 1979, such policies were conservatively estimated to affect 100,000 working women (though that number didn't take into account all of the higher-level jobs, through lines of progression, that also were foreclosed to them).[18]

While these policies were spun as benevolent, the reality was more complicated. Above all, as more and more women moved into jobs involving contact with toxic substances, companies feared for their bottom line. It was expensive to make workplaces safer. For instance, OSHA's rule for potential parents required extra monitoring (to ensure their levels did not go above 30 ug/100 g). Indeed, during the OSHA hearings that resulted in the final lead standard, Johnson Controls had been among the loudest industry advocates pushing for a minimum ambient air standard of 200 ug/m^3 rather than the 50 ug/m^3 that OSHA ultimately adopted.[19] Moreover, as *The Wall Street Journal* reported in 1979, "Corporations and their insurance carriers [were] more than a little worried about potential liability for a company if a malformed fetus [were] linked to exposure to toxins in the workplace."[20]

Yet such lawsuits were only hypothetical—no such case ever had been reported—while the harms of relegating women to low-paid jobs (or the unemployment line) were very real. As one commentator put it, "Keeping fertile women out of risky jobs may preserve them from one health risk only to expose them to others that are equally serious."[21] Poor housing, poor nutrition, and lack of health insurance all have demonstrable effects on the well-being of women and children. Women who are pregnant under such conditions are more likely to give birth to babies who are underweight and premature—two of the leading causes of infant mortality.[22]

It was no coincidence that fetal protection policies were most prevalent in well-paid, unionized industries from which women historically had been excluded. Indeed, they had been excluded precisely because they had been deemed physically unsuited for the dirty, sometimes strenuous work. Only under pressure from the federal government to comply with antidiscrimination laws did those businesses begin opening their ranks to women in the 1970s. It was in those years that the Department of Labor's Office of Federal Contract Compliance Programs had gotten serious about enforcing a 1967 Executive Order requiring federal contractors, such as automotive, aerospace, and electronics manufacturers, to adopt gender-neutral hiring practices. And in 1972, Title VII had been amended to give the EEOC the authority to bring discrimination lawsuits on the government's behalf. "As late as 1970, industry operated under the assumption that we could deny employment to individuals incompatible with the work," Allied Chemical's director of occupational safety groused in 1979. "Now laws dictate we must use women, the handicapped and others in shift work . . . which presents a series of new challenges."[23]

While kicking women out of jobs where they were in the minority didn't interfere with business as usual, it was a different story in workplaces that depended primarily on women's labor. There fetal protection policies were conspicuously absent. It certainly wasn't because those jobs were any safer than those on the assembly line. Carbon disulfide and benzene, routinely used by dry cleaners and laundries,[24] have been linked to birth defects, miscarriage, low birth weight, and preterm birth.[25] Ethylene glycol, a solvent used in making electronics (one of the few female-dominated manufacturing fields), is known to cause birth defects and miscarriage.[26] Health care workers and staff in dental offices are regularly exposed to radiation and mercury, which are associated with a range of harms, from miscarriage to developmental disorders to childhood cancers.[27] Salon workers inhaling nail polish and hair-processing chemicals and clerical workers staring at computer screens also face similarly grave reproductive hazards from workplace carcinogens.[28]

Indeed, when the full range of workplace toxins that may harm reproductive capacity was taken into account, by the mid-1980s, the government estimated that fifteen to twenty million jobs were at issue.[29] In female-dominated fields, though, fetal protection policies made no business sense; they effectively would gut the workforce. That reality apparently trumped any hypothetical harm to employees' future pregnancies.

This history made fetal protection policies look less like humane measures that put employees first and more like a backdoor strategy for resegregating the workforce. For its part, Johnson Controls didn't hire its first female employee until 1972. When women began arriving at its plants, the company showed little interest in making them feel welcome. Jean Jones, the first woman to get a job at the Bennington plant, observed, "The men were nasty. A lot of the women didn't last. They could do the work, sure, but they couldn't take the comments."[30] The only reason Jones was spared the worst abuse, she said, was because her husband also worked at the plant.[31] Elsie Nason, also among the early hires at Bennington, was harassed mercilessly by her male coworkers, who told her that she was taking a job away from a man with a family to support. (That she was the sole provider for three children apparently didn't count.)

Those coworkers were gloating ten years later when the company began banishing women from the production line all over again. Jones recalled grimly, "They had a good laugh when [the policy] came down. They said, 'Well, you girls burned your bras and look what you got. You're pushing brooms and washing respirators. Just like housework.'"[32]

Manufacturers' stated concern for their employees' future children also would have appeared more sincere had they made an effort to protect male employees from dangers to their reproductive capacity as well. By focusing solely on potential damage to the developing fetus—"teratogenesis"—companies were ignoring the proven role of industrial toxins in "mutagenesis," that is, genetic damage to men's (as well as women's) reproductive cells.[33] One OSHA study of fetal protection policies found that twenty-one of the twenty-six chemicals at issue under such policies also caused sterility or damage to sperm.[34] Because the male body's creation of sperm is an ongoing process—as opposed to women's generation of eggs, which occurs before women are born—there may actually be *more* opportunities for damage to occur over time the longer a man is exposed to a particular toxin. In the vivid words of one doctor quoted by *The New York Times* in 1981, the male reproductive process is "'a garbage disposal system' where substances like lead and cadmium may collect for future elimination."[35]

As to lead specifically, during the 1978 hearings, OSHA had made extensive findings about its dangers to men's reproductive capacities, and research in subsequent years only bolstered these conclusions. Indeed, long before women began working in toxic jobs, evidence of lead's damage to male workers' children had been documented. Miscarriages, stillbirths, and birth defects caused by mutations in the sperm all were demonstrated effects, as were infertility, low sperm count, and low sperm motility.[36] And during the same period that the eight female Johnson Controls' employees with elevated blood lead levels had given birth, nearly sixty male employees had filed worker's compensation claims for various adverse lead reactions. Such overexposure signaled, at the very least, a *risk* of reproductive damage, but if Johnson Controls had responded by excluding all the fertile men from lead-exposed jobs, production would have come to a standstill. It was much easier just to cut the small number of women workers.

So Johnson Controls' male employees continued to labor in the lead-exposed areas from which all fertile women had been expelled. Those who sought to avoid such reproductive risks encountered outright hostility. In the spring of 1984, Donald Penney, a production worker in a high-lead area of the Middletown, Delaware, plant, met with the personnel manager. He and his wife, Anna Mae—who also worked at the factory but whose job didn't involve exposure to lead—wanted to start a family. Because the level of lead in the blood diminishes during periods of nonexposure, Donald Penney asked for a three-month leave of absence so that his level could go down, and he and his wife could safely try to conceive. The personnel manager, John Frey, was openly hostile to Penney and urged him to quit. At the end of the meeting, Penney resigned.[37]

AT UNITED AUTO WORKERS headquarters in Detroit, known as Solidarity House, attorney Marley Weiss began hearing from the union's field representatives about Johnson Controls' new policy. A number of UAW members at various plants had filed grievances challenging it, but the union was getting nowhere with the company.

Although Weiss had encountered fetal protection policies at some other companies where the UAW represented the workers, those policies had affected only a few women. "Most of the employers where this was an issue had only very small areas that were exposed to lead or cadmium," she explained in her rat-a-tat delivery. "You were talking about [women] just not doing this set of six jobs in a particular plant." But what Johnson Controls had done, she said, was to "wholesale exclude women because their plants were basically total lead exposure plants. So there were a handful of jobs that *weren't* lead exposure jobs rather than the other way around."

The union had an unwritten policy of using the weapon of litigation sparingly, so as not to alienate employers and make future dealings, such as contract negotiations and grievance resolutions, more contentious. But Weiss had no trouble convincing the UAW leadership that the Johnson Controls policy was an ideal litigation vehicle. It applied in all fourteen of the company's plants, in all departments, and defined a woman "capable of becoming pregnant" so broadly that it risked wiping out the female workforce. That a lawsuit might attract new women members to the union only made it more appealing to the UAW leadership.

Weiss began asking local union representatives to identify women affected by the policy who would be willing to serve as plaintiffs in a lawsuit. She wanted a cross-section of employees from various facilities who could demonstrate the policy's many negative effects, such as an older woman who, if not yet menopausal, at least was done with her childbearing; a younger, fertile woman who didn't want children; and a younger, fertile woman who *did* want to start having children.

Weiss and her UAW colleagues also saw the importance of including a male plaintiff in a Title VII sex discrimination case. It was a strategy pioneered by Ruth Bader Ginsburg during her tenure at the ACLU Women's Rights Project in the 1970s: attack the law's discriminatory stereotypes about women by identifying *men* who also defy gender stereotypes.[38] In Johnson Controls' case, the premise of its policy was that women, by virtue of their ability to bear children, were uniquely vulnerable to lead's dangers. But science showed that men were just as vulnerable. Excluding men from any protective policy, then, stigmatized women as mothers first and workers second while also belittling men's commitment to becoming parents.

Ultimately, Weiss filed Title VII charges of discrimination on behalf of eight employees. They included Elsie Nason, the fifty-year-old divorced mother of three who had no plans for more children but still was transferred to a janitorial job; Donald Penney, the man who unsuccessfully sought a leave of absence to begin trying to start a family with his wife; Anna Mae Penney, Donald Penney's wife, who worked in a low-lead exposure area but nevertheless was required to wear a heavy, uncomfortable respirator while her male colleagues were not; and Mary Craig, who had worked for the company more than fourteen years and underwent sterilization rather than lose her job. Rounding out the group were Linda Burdick and Mary Schmitt, denied promotions because the new jobs were in lead-exposure areas, and Lois Sweetman and Shirley Mackey, who were transferred from lead-exposed areas to lower-paying jobs.[39]

Before signing the eight on as the plaintiffs, Weiss was brutally frank with them about the inherent risks of suing one's employer. "'You need to realize that they might take your deposition, and they might come after you, and it might be very unpleasant,'" Weiss told them. "'And if you go to find other work, . . . this could be used by another employer. It may be illegal, but that doesn't mean it wouldn't happen.'" Weiss later explained, "I think it's only fair to let people know that the law is supposed to protect them against retaliation, but it doesn't always work."

None of the eight turned Weiss down. They were in.

A FEW YEARS before the UAW filed its lawsuit against Johnson Controls, women's advocates had begun strategizing about ways of combating the rise in fetal protection policies. In 1979, they coalesced into the Coalition for Reproductive Rights of Workers, a group of close to fifty women's advocates and labor leaders, including Marley Weiss. Many of CRROW's members previously had allied to successfully campaign for enactment of the Pregnancy Discrimination Act in 1978. They also had friendly ears within the federal government.

OSHA, the EEOC, and lawyers with the Department of Labor all were sympathetic to CRROW's objectives.

The group saw fetal protection policies as the next looming challenge to women's workplace equality. The policies smacked of the "protective" labor legislation that had kept women confined for generations to a small universe of low-paid, low-status jobs. Those laws had had as their premise that women's reproductive capacity interfered with the rigors of work, and vice versa. And at the time that fetal protection policies were on the rise, it hadn't been long since the Supreme Court equivocated about whether motherhood was compatible with work (in Ida Phillips's 1971 case against Martin Marietta) and whether women were physically suited to be guards in maximum-security prisons (in Kim Rawlinson's lawsuit against Alabama's Board of Corrections, decided in 1977).

Although the PDA had reaffirmed that Title VII prohibited pregnancy discrimination and mandated that pregnant workers be treated "the same" as those "similar in their ability or inability to work," the law did not explicitly address the legality of fetal protection policies. Indeed, many of the activists spearheading the campaign against such policies perceived the same "special treatment" slant that they were bitterly opposing in Montana's *Miller-Wohl* litigation (and later in *Cal Fed*), cases that arose from state laws giving job protection to women who took maternity leave but to no one else who took time off.

Policies like Johnson Controls' also were considered a step backward because they privileged women's potential motherhood over any other role they might see for themselves. They treated all women as "potentially pregnant," no matter their plans as to when, or even whether, they would have children. "I was struck, from the first time I read of this case," wrote syndicated columnist Ellen Goodman, "by a company policy that assumed every woman was a pregnancy waiting to happen. The life of this policy didn't begin at conception; it began at menses and ended at menopause or sterility."[40]

Finally, women's advocates saw in fetal protection rules the same tenets underpinning the escalating antiabortion movement. Despite the Supreme Court's 1973 decision in *Roe v. Wade*,[41] abortion opponents continued their fight using a variety of strategies, including an (unsuccessful) push in 1974 for a constitutional amendment outlawing abortion and then the (successful) campaign in 1976 to ban Medicaid funding for abortions. That movement, which only intensified during the 1980s, spawning restrictive state legislation and radical groups such as Operation Rescue, elevated the interests of the fetus—indeed, the embryo—above those of the woman.

Corporate industry's rhetoric around fetal protection policies pushed the same emotional buttons as the antiabortion rhetoric. It cast women as irresponsible about their bodies and uncaring toward their potential children—only in these cases it was a woman's employer, not the legislature, that sought to make reproductive decisions for her.

THE SPECIFIC EVENT that had galvanized CRROW's formation took place in a depressed region in West Virginia along the Ohio River. Willow Bay was the site of an enormous production facility operated by American Cyanamid, a manufacturer of everything from household cleaners to vitamins to shampoo to fertilizer. As Susan Faludi documented in *Backlash: The Undeclared War on American Women,* when federal investigators discovered in 1973 that the company didn't employ any women, American Cyanamid launched a two-year hiring blitz.[42] But just a few years later, the company issued its first fetal protection policy, barring any woman under age fifty from working in the pigments division—the one division in which workers were exposed to lead—unless she could prove infertility. Corporate managers further insinuated that the policy would be expanded to cover all women in the plant's production units, who by then numbered just seventeen.[43]

Ultimately, five of the seven women in the pigments division chose to be sterilized so as to keep their production line jobs. (When the five women returned to work after their surgeries, male coworkers taunted them for getting "spayed."[44]) The two who refused were transferred to the janitorial department, where they made $50 less a week and had no chance to earn overtime and other extra pay.[45]

Under pressure from the women's union, the Oil, Chemical & Atomic Workers International, OSHA began an investigation and concluded that the policy violated the federal occupational safety law's requirement that a workplace be free of "recognized hazards" because it coerced women into sterilizations.[46] But American Cyanamid appealed and ultimately won a reversal. In a 1984 opinion authored by Judge Robert Bork (and joined by future Supreme Court Justice Antonin Scalia), the U.S. Court of Appeals for the D.C. Circuit ruled that American Cyanamid's policy didn't meet the law's definition of "hazard" because the actual harm—sterilization—happened off the job, not on it.[47]

As OSHA's lawsuit was winding its way through the courts, the American Civil Liberties Union's Women's Rights Project brought a companion lawsuit. While the OSHA case concerned whether American Cyanamid had violated the women's right to a safe workplace, the ACLU WRP case claimed it had violated their right to equal employment opportunity. Because the company used women's capacity to become pregnant as a reason for denying them jobs, went the argument, it had violated Title VII.[48]

After a few years of bruising litigation—the company had "multiple times our resources," former ACLU WRP attorney Joan Bertin said—the case settled in 1984. The company agreed to abandon the fetal protection policy, and the women were paid $200,000 to divide among themselves. Bertin ruefully called it a "Pyrrhic victory," given the extreme suffering and stress endured by the five women and their colleagues. Indeed, shortly after OSHA had cited the company for its policy and the resulting sterilizations, American Cyanamid closed the pigments division. The women had sacrificed their fertility for nothing.

But even though the case had never progressed far enough to force a ruling on the policy's legality under Title VII, it had created another kind of precedent. As Bertin put it, the American Cyanamid litigation had created a "template" for all of ACLU WRP's legal challenges to fetal protection cases. Bertin and her colleagues had assembled a group of like-minded medical and scientific professionals who would continue to serve as a loose coalition of advisors, expert witnesses, and authors of friend of the court briefs. They tutored the attorneys in the science of lead's effect on the human body. They helped them pronounce multiconsonant chemical names. They confirmed that while in utero exposure certainly wasn't any less dangerous to a fetus than it was to an adult, it hadn't been proven at exactly what level it becomes *more* dangerous, either.

This new alliance between scientists and advocates was a critical development. The 1980 election of Ronald Reagan meant that the federal government would no longer be an active partner in the multipronged advocacy effort by women's groups, unions, and government agencies that had coalesced during the 1970s. Not only did top government personnel change, but regulatory policies took a pronounced tilt toward business interests and away from workers' rights.[49] Indeed, the leadership of the outgoing Carter administration at the Office of Federal Contract Compliance Programs and the EEOC scrapped their draft guidelines on fetal protection policies altogether rather than risk handing them off to the Reagan administration for retooling.[50]

Without vigorous government enforcement of federal civil rights and occupational safety laws, it would fall to individual Title VII lawsuits to beat back the rising tide of fetal protection policies—to say nothing of holding on to the little ground women had gained in male-dominated fields. The litigation template would be deployed case by case, policy by policy, company by company. As a result of that methodical campaign, the courts either would reach consensus or would fall into disarray. And disarray could propel the issue all the way to the Supreme Court.

THE UAW'S CASE against Johnson Controls was filed on April 6, 1984, in federal court in Milwaukee.[51] A few months after the complaint was filed, the court certified the case as a class action. That meant that in addition to the eight named plaintiffs, the case was filed on behalf of "all past, present and future production and maintenance employees" in the nine Johnson Controls plants represented by the UAW who "have been and continue to be affected by [the company's] Fetal Protection Policy implemented in 1982."

The case was assigned to Judge Robert Warren, whom President Nixon had nominated to the bench shortly before resigning in 1974.[52] After extensive discovery of each side's scientific evidence and dueling expert depositions, Johnson Controls filed a motion to dismiss the case. Miriam Horwitz, the UAW's lead attorney in Milwaukee, wasn't optimistic. She remembered discussing the chances of winning with a senior partner at her firm who had experience in front of Judge Warren. "'Don't expect it,'" the partner told Horwitz. "'He's not gonna like this case.'"

He didn't. On January 21, 1988, Judge Warren sided with Johnson Controls. The company had argued that its policy actually was sex-*neutral,* in that it intended to protect the future children of all its employees, men and women alike. The policy just happened to fall more heavily on women, in the same way that Alabama's height and weight requirements just happened to disqualify most women from being state troopers or correctional officers in *Dothard v. Rawlinson.* This argument already had been endorsed by three federal appeals courts, and it worked with Judge Warren too. He went on to rule that Johnson Controls' fetal protection policy was justified by "business necessity." In the process, he credited the company's experts and discounted the UAW's, finding lead's harm to male reproductive processes to be speculative while its harm to fetuses was not. "Society has an interest in protecting fetal safety," he wrote. "Lead poses a substantial risk of harm to the fetus. This risk is born [*sic*] only by women who are pregnant or will become pregnant. . . . Stillbirths, reduced birth weight and gestational age, and retarded cognitive development are abnormalities too serious for this Court to find unimportant."

There was no question that the UAW would appeal. The union wanted an experienced appellate litigator to argue the case before the Seventh Circuit. Carin Clauss, the former Solicitor of the Department of Labor, who had been at the forefront of the government's prior efforts to combat fetal protection policies and by the time of Judge Warren's decision was a law professor at the University of Wisconsin, signed on as counsel for the appeal.

An unwelcome development came a few months later in October 1988, when the EEOC finally issued its first policy statement about fetal protection policies. As the CRROW advocates and their government partners had feared, the shift to a Republican White House in 1980 also had effected a change in EEOC's orientation. The Policy Statement on Reproductive and Fetal Hazards stated that fetal protection cases "do not fit neatly into the traditional Title VII analytical framework and, therefore, must be regarded as a class unto themselves."[53] Citing the three federal courts of appeals that had reached the same conclusion, the agency approved a business necessity defense in such cases too and didn't require the stricter bona fide occupational qualification (BFOQ) analysis.[54] For the nation's top enforcer of Title VII to suggest that it could be legal to deny women hazardous jobs just because they *might* become pregnant was, to say the least, disheartening.

The Seventh Circuit's consideration of *Johnson Controls* dragged on for nearly a year. In September 1988, Clauss had appeared for oral argument before a three-judge panel—Judge John Coffey, Judge Joel Flaum, and Judge Frank Easterbrook, all Reagan appointees—and sensed they were on her side. But after six months of waiting for a ruling came discouraging news: The court had decided that all eleven judges on the Seventh Circuit would consider the case. A second oral argument was scheduled. In Bertin's pessimistic assessment, it was a sign that "defeat [had been] snatched from the jaws of victory."

She was right. On September 26, 1989, the court ruled in Johnson Controls' favor by a vote of seven to four. The majority opinion was authored by Judge Coffey, known as an "unyielding conservative voice"[55] who had made his prejudices known at the outset of the second oral argument: He leaned over the bench and declared, "This is about the women who want to hurt their fetuses."[56]

In addition to upholding the business necessity framework for assessing fetal protection policies—and concluding that Johnson Controls' policy met that test—the Seventh Circuit went even further. It became the first federal appeals court to rule that a fetal protection policy satisfied the stringent BFOQ test too—that is, that it was "reasonably necessary to the normal operation of the company's business" to have only men or infertile women working with lead.

It was by tweaking the definition of Johnson Controls' "business" that the court made such a leap. The company's business wasn't just limited to making batteries it concluded, but also encompassed ensuring "industrial safety (preventing hazards to health)":[57]

> The evidence presented concerning the lingering effects of lead in a
> woman's body, combined with the magnitude of medical difficulties
> in detecting and diagnosing early pregnancy, lead us to conclude
> that an extension of this policy to all fertile women is proper and
> reasonably necessary to further the industrial safety concern of pre-
> venting the unborn child's exposure to lead.[58]

The majority dismissed the notion that it was up to the individual woman, not the company, to decide what level of "industrial safety" she could tolerate. The court analogized to *Dothard,* where the Supreme Court had found maleness a BFOQ for prison guards in "contact" positions. The Court had reasoned that third parties—the inmate population—could be endangered if a female guard were assaulted, so the decision to assume the job's risks was not the guard's alone to make. Substitute fetuses for prisoners, said the Seventh Circuit, and the same result follows.

The four judges who disagreed with the majority filed three dissenting opinions. All of them rejected the notion that Johnson Controls' policy could be called sex-neutral or justified by business necessity. The company's policy clearly discriminated against women, they said, and could be justified only under the stringent BFOQ standard. (The UAW was especially heartened that one of the dissenters, Judge Posner—an influential conservative voice—thought the case should go back to Judge Warren for a trial, where all the relevant scientific evidence could be explored fully.)

It was the dissent by Judge Frank Easterbrook that made Joan Bertin say, "Finally, someone has gotten this right!" Easterbrook declared the case "likely the most important sex-discrimination case in any court" since Title VII's enactment, noting that if the majority's opinion were to be adopted by courts nationwide, "by one estimate 20 million industrial jobs could be closed to women, for many substances in addition to lead pose fetal risks."[59]

Easterbrook and Judge Flaum, who joined his opinion, were the only two dissenters who didn't think a trial was necessary, because a fetal protection policy could *never* qualify for the BFOQ exception, no matter what scientific evidence was put forward. The reason, explained Easterbrook, was the false underlying premise that fetal protection was "reasonably necessary to the normal operation" of Johnson Controls' battery-making business. He was especially scornful of the company's claim that it was "morally required to protect children from their parents' mistakes."[60] That justification, Easterbrook scoffed, was "redolent of *Muller v. Oregon,*" the infamous Supreme Court maximum work hours case. "Statutes of the sort sustained in *Muller,* supported by the justifications advanced in *Muller,*" scoffed Easterbrook, "are museum pieces, reminders of wrong turns in the law."[61]

WHEN THE UAW filed its petition in January 1990 seeking Supreme Court review, the time was ripe for the high court to weigh in. At that point, four courts of appeals had ruled on fetal protection policies, with wildly divergent outcomes. The Posner and Easterbrook dissents were especially noteworthy, coming from two such stalwart conservative voices who couldn't even agree with one another, let alone with their seven colleagues in the majority.

Moreover, in January 1990, the EEOC updated its approach to fetal protection policies, in response to the Seventh Circuit's decision in *Johnson Controls.*[62] Criticizing the court's conclusions, it directed its staff in all other jurisdictions to treat fetal protection policies as facially discriminatory, allowable only if a BFOQ defense could be shown. The EEOC specifically noted that the cost of potential personal injury lawsuits would not qualify such policies for the BFOQ exception. The timing of the EEOC's action—just two days before the UAW filed its *certiorari* petition—prompted one observer to dub the new Guidelines a "*de facto* substitute for an *amicus* brief" in favor of the UAW's petition seeking Supreme Court review.[63]

Given these circumstances, it came as no surprise on March 29, 1990, that the Court agreed to hear *Johnson Controls*. Oral argument was scheduled for the fall.

That brought up the question of who would argue the case for the UAW. The union's parent entity, the AFL-CIO, selected Marsha Berzon, its assistant general counsel. Berzon, today a judge on the U.S. Court of Appeals for the Ninth Circuit, had served as Justice William Brennan's first female law clerk and had extensive experience before the Court, both as an oral advocate and author of *amicus* briefs. She had served in her AFL-CIO role while running one of the top labor law firms in the country with her husband. She also was one of the primary authors of the PDA, expertise that made her an especially authoritative advocate against Johnson Controls' reading of the law and of Title VII's BFOQ exception in the pregnancy context.

For the women's organizations, the Supreme Court's consideration of *Johnson Controls* offered a welcome opportunity to present a united front in a pregnancy discrimination case; the rift in the feminist community caused by *Cal Fed* was still a fresh memory. ("It left a lot of wounds," said one of the lawyers who had represented Lillian Garland, the woman at the heart of the dispute.) But fetal protection, they could all agree, was the old-fashioned kind of "special treatment" that contradicted, rather than furthered, the PDA's objectives. This time, east and west coast feminist groups collaborated on a single *amicus* brief.[64]

THE DAY OF the oral argument in *Johnson Controls,* Carin Clauss and Joan Bertin arrived together. As they walked up the front steps of the courthouse and prepared to enter through the side door designated for attorneys, they were approached by two anxious-looking middle-aged women. Both worked at Johnson Controls' Bennington, Vermont, plant: The shorter of the two, Ginny Green, had been demoted as a result of the company's policy, while the taller, Joanne Leard, had been denied a transfer into a better-paying lead-exposed job.[65] Green and Leard had traveled to Washington to hear the argument but hadn't been able to get into the packed courtroom. Clauss and Bertin found Berzon inside the building and asked if there was anything that could be done. Berzon told them to wait, and then disappeared for a few minutes. The former clerk for Justice Brennan managed to quickly pull some strings, and she returned with two tickets. Ginny Green and

Joanne Leard listened to the oral arguments from seats reserved for guests of the justices.

BERZON WAS FIRST at the lectern. Directly in front of her was Chief Justice Rehnquist, flanked by Justices Byron White and Thurgood Marshall, the two most senior justices. The justice sitting the farthest to the right as Berzon faced the bench was David Souter, who had been sworn in just two days earlier.

Berzon spoke for lengthy stretches without interruption, a luxury not often enjoyed during oral argument. "[T]he issue here," she declared, "is not whether fetal health is going to be protected, but how and by whom." Would it be protected by women, with the help of government agencies like OSHA that monitored workplace safety? Or was it going to be by the managers at Johnson Controls?[66]

Berzon emphasized that Johnson Controls' policy actually did very little to advance fetal health. Most of the women excluded from the workplace posed no risk of fetal harm, Berzon explained, because they didn't want children, or were done having children, or—if they did want children—would either remove themselves from lead-exposed jobs or manage their exposure through OSHA-approved hygiene methods. Men, however, were ignored by the policy, despite the demonstrated harm to fetal health that their lead exposure might cause.[67]

What the policy did do, Berzon argued, was violate both the letter and the spirit of Title VII by fostering a "negative behavioral stereotype" about women's trustworthiness in managing their own reproductive lives. It publicized women's "private reproductive functions" to coworkers and supervisors. It "relegate[d] women in general to a second-class status" in the workplace by barring them from the best-paying jobs.[68]

And finally, given the number of workplace toxins that might pose risk to fetal health, Berzon told the justices that upholding Johnson Controls' policy would give all manner of employers permission to bar women from all manner of jobs. Its "net effect," declared Berzon, "would be to sanction the resegregation of the work force" and "cut the heart out of Title VII and the Pregnancy Discrimination Act."[69]

The issue on which Berzon faced her most aggressive questioning was the question of future lawsuits against the company by lead-exposed children of its workers. "I don't think it's bizarre to assume that a State court in a [personal injury] suit would impose very severe liability on an employer for knowingly placing a woman in the position where the fetus is injured if the fetus is actually injured," said one justice.[70] Only if an employer were *negligent* in maintaining worker safety, responded Berzon, could it be held liable for such harm. If an employer satisfied its obligations to keep lead exposure at OSHA-approved levels, she said, then that wouldn't rise to negligence. "It's as if the employer said I would rather not hire blacks," she said, "because if I hire them I'm going to have to . . . act toward them in a nonnegligent fashion."[71]

Johnson Controls' attorney, Stanley Jaspan, was next. He faced far more skepticism from the justices. He had barely begun when he was interrupted by Justice Stevens and asked to quantify the risk posed by lead to fetuses, based on the company's own experience.

"How often does this happen? Does the record tell us?" Stevens asked. "[T]he record doesn't tell us how many cases there are, how many work in the factory, or what the history has been, does it?"

Jaspan tried to find his footing. "No, the record does show that the company attempted a voluntary program. Approximately 1977 to 1982, the company advised women of the—"

Stevens was not going to let him off the hook. "How many women?"

Jaspan finally admitted, "The exact number isn't in the record."[72]

The justices also grilled Jaspan about how Johnson Controls' policy could possibly be squared with antidiscrimination law. Justice O'Connor was first. "Mr. Jaspan, I"—she paused, and sighed audibly—"it seems to me that you are not coming to grips with the effect of the Pregnancy Discrimination Act . . . which says that female employees affected by pregnancy shall be treated the same for all employment-related purposes as other persons similar in their ability or inability to work." Jaspan responded that the PDA's "ability to work" language meant "ability to work *safely*."[73]

Now it was Justice Scalia's turn. By taking into account the fetus's health, wasn't Johnson Controls making a "dead letter" of the PDA? "That was always the justification for discriminating against pregnant women, that they shouldn't work extra long hours because it would be bad for the fetus," he said. "You're making it a ridiculous piece of legislation."[74]

But before Jaspan could get any traction, a prolonged line of questioning began about why Johnson Controls was insisting on zero risk of fetal harm when the rest of the workplace was not a zero-risk environment. Justice Scalia took the lead.

"[Pregnant women] should not smoke cigarettes and drink substantial amounts of alcohol, either, but the Government does not have laws that take the judgment of whether to do it or not away from them," he observed. Jaspan answered that there was a difference between the government *prohibiting* certain harmful conduct and *mandating* that an employer enable it.[75]

Scalia continued. "[H]ow is a court to determine how careful the employer may be without violating Title VII?" He got explicit. "I'm talking about how many deformities is worth letting women work in the department. How many is worth it?" he asked. "One in a million?"[76]

But Jaspan—wisely—wouldn't be pinned down by a precise number. Instead, he closed by reiterating that Title VII's BFOQ exception allowed Johnson Controls to "protect against injury from [a] hazard" that it had created and appealed to the justices "not to leave common sense at the doorstep when interpreting Title VII."[77]

FIVE MONTHS LATER, the Supreme Court issued its unanimous opinion: Johnson Controls' policy violated Title VII. "The bias in Johnson Controls' policy is obvious," wrote Justice Harry Blackmun. "[W]omen as capable of doing their jobs as their male counterparts may not be forced to choose between having a child and having a job."[78] For this reason, said the Court, the Seventh Circuit was wrong to consider the policy "neutral" and justify it using the "business necessity" defense. "[T]he absence of a malevolent motive," Blackmun explained, "does not convert a facially discriminatory policy into a neutral policy."[79]

The only way for Johnson Controls' policy to survive, then, was if women's infertility could be deemed a BFOQ. Justices Blackmun, Marshall, Stevens, O'Connor, and the Court's newest member, Justice Souter, concluded—as Judge Easterbrook had eighteen months earlier—that it *never* could, no matter how a company tried to justify it. They focused on the "O" in BFOQ: occupational. What was necessary to get the job done? "Fertile women, as far as appears in the record, participate in the manufacture of batteries as efficiently as anyone else,"[80] they concluded. "No one can disregard the possibility of injury to future children; the B.F.O.Q., however, is not so broad that it transforms this deep social concern into an essential aspect of battery making."[81]

The remaining four justices believed, like Judge Posner, that the BFOQ exception was slightly more expansive than that, and that a more narrowly tailored fetal protection policy could satisfy it. Justice Scalia filed a separate concurrence, showing a libertarian streak: "By reason of the Pregnancy Discrimination Act, it would not matter if all pregnant women placed their children at risk in taking these jobs. . . . As Judge Easterbrook put it in his dissent below, 'Title VII gives parents the power to make occupational decisions affecting their families.'"[82] Scalia did agree, though, that cost considerations posed by fetal risks could justify a BFOQ, if an employer could make that case.[83] But Johnson Controls, in his view, couldn't.

JOHNSON CONTROLS marked the end of *Muller v. Oregon*'s "mothers first, workers second" framing of American womanhood. As *Muller* put it in 1908, women's reproductive health was "an object of public interest":

> [B]y abundant testimony of the medical fraternity continuance for a long time on her feet at work, repeating this from day to day, tends to injurious effects upon [a woman's] body, and as healthy mothers are essential to vigorous offspring, the physical well-being of woman becomes an object of public interest and care in order to preserve the strength and vigor of the race.

But with *Johnson Controls,* no longer was a woman's biology to be *society's* destiny; thanks to Title VII, it was returned to her, at least when it came to decisions about how and where she earned a paycheck:

> It is no more appropriate for the courts than it is for the individual employers to decide whether a woman's reproductive role is more important to herself and her family than to her economic role. Congress has left this choice to the woman as hers to make.[84]

eight

taking it all the way to "sandra fucking day o'connor"

Harris v. Forklift Systems, Inc. (1993)

ON A HOT NASHVILLE AFTERNOON IN AUGUST 1987, TE-resa Harris put a small tape machine in her purse, pressed "record," and walked into her boss's office to quit. It was the last thing she wanted to do; Harris loved her job. As rental manager at Forklift Systems, she negotiated deals with contractors to lease the company's fleet of cranes, trucks, and other equipment—the rare woman in the male-dominated world of construction. Harris was a Nashville native and the eldest of five children. Although as a girl she had harbored dreams of becoming a lawyer like Atticus Finch in *To Kill a Mockingbird*, Harris had been working since she graduated from high school. After starting out in the customer service department of a shoe manufacturer, she switched to sales, first selling boats and other watercraft and then construction equipment. In the spring of 1985, eager to escape from her job with a company whose co-owners were in the middle of an acrimonious divorce, Harris accepted a job offer from Charles Hardy, Forklift Systems' owner. With a passing resemblance to Ava Gardner and a quick, salty wit, Harris was a born saleswoman, and in her first year on the job, she doubled the company's rental revenue.

But Harris's success masked a more disturbing reality. Almost as soon as she arrived at Forklift Systems, Hardy began showing his true colors. He constantly commented on women employees' clothing and appraised their bodies. He told Harris that she had a "racehorse ass" and advised her not to wear a bikini "because your ass is so big, if you did there would be an eclipse and no one could get any sun." He would approach Harris while jingling change in his front pants pocket. As Harris recalled, he liked to tease, "Teresa, I have a quarter way down there. Would you get that out of my pocket?" He told Harris that they should start "screwing around" and joked that they should go to a Holiday Inn to negotiate her raise (although by the time he made that proposal he had cut her commissions in half because, in his words, she "made too much damn money for a woman"). Hardy dropped pens and papers on the floor and asked women employees to pick them up, then suggested what kinds of necklines would better show off their breasts. He turned the air conditioner down to make the office colder, jovially voicing his hope that the women's nipples would start to show.[1]

Beyond this barrage of sexual comments, Hardy insulted Harris's competence on a regular basis, often in front of her male peers. One of two women among six managers, Harris was the only one who worked on the business side of Forklift Systems; the other female manager, Hardy's daughter, handled administrative matters, such as ordering office supplies and paying the company's bills. "You're a woman, what do you know?" Hardy would sneer when Harris spoke up at management meetings. He often told Harris to shut up, called her a "dumb-ass woman," and said that the company needed a man in her job. Not surprisingly, Harris's male colleagues parroted Hardy's opinions and used the same sort of disparaging language.[2]

Hardy's harassment had a profound impact on Harris. Having worked mostly among men for years and grown used to hearing (and using) some profanity at work, Harris felt humiliated by Hardy's constant appraisals of her body. Worse yet were Hardy's statements about her competence. She was proud of her career and the reputation she had earned in Nashville as a savvy businesswoman, without the benefit of a college degree. "The comments about my ability to do my job and that I was stupid and I was dumb devastated me," Harris later testified at her trial. "I hated walking in there. Everybody made fun of me because Charles Hardy did that. And I was supposed to laugh about it, and it wasn't funny." Harris developed chronic insomnia, and would "get drunk every night so I would go to sleep so I could get up and go to work the next day." Her heavy drinking strained her family life, especially her relationships with her two sons. She cried "all the time." She was often short of breath and would sit in her office, shaking uncontrollably. When she went to her doctor for help, he found nothing physically wrong with her and sent her away with prescriptions for tranquilizers and sleeping pills.[3]

Harris had always considered herself a feminist, and Hardy's mistreatment enraged her. She suspected it might even be illegal. But she didn't feel she could quit, let alone file a lawsuit. Hardy was prominent in the Nashville construction business, the field in which Harris had the most experience. As a single parent and the main source of support for her ailing grandmother, she needed a job. And although she married while working for Hardy, that did nothing to alleviate the potential financial fallout were she to resign; Forklift Systems was a major customer in a business owned by Harris's new husband, Larry. Not only did his company sell batteries to Forklift Systems for use in its equipment, but Hardy also had made a loan to Larry to help finance the business. Were Harris to quit, she feared her husband's livelihood would be ruined along with her own. Given these realities, Harris says, "it really was a no-brainer to just shut up."

But by August 1987, after putting up with two years of abuse, Harris had had enough. She scheduled a meeting with Hardy to hand in her resignation. Bringing the tape recorder was a lawyer friend's idea; if Harris caught Hardy admitting to the harassment on tape, she might have some ammunition to ensure that he wouldn't blackball her. But when Harris told Hardy she was leaving and explained why, Hardy insisted that he had only been kidding and just was trying to make her feel like "one of the boys." He apologized and swore that from then on, he would treat her with respect. Reassured, if wary, Harris agreed to stay.

Whether or not Hardy genuinely intended to change his ways, he didn't keep his promise for long, as Harris later testified. A few weeks after their meeting, when Harris told him in front of a group of co-workers that she had landed a big client, Hardy asked, "What did you do, Teresa? Promise the guy some bugger on Saturday night?" It was the last straw. "He was embarrassing me to *me*, because I was taking it," Harris said. "I didn't want to anymore." She quit a few days later. Within a week, Hardy canceled Forklift Systems' account with Larry Harris's company and sued Larry Harris to recover the balance of his loan. A friend referred Teresa Harris to an attorney.

———

HARRIS DIDN'T know it, but in 1986, a little more than a year before she quit her job, the Supreme Court had issued its landmark ruling in *Meritor Savings Bank, FSB v. Vinson*.[4] Groundbreaking as *Vinson* was in declaring sexual harassment to be sex discrimination, it fell short in one respect. The Court didn't explain at what point harassing conduct stopped being merely offensive and became illegal—or, in the Court's words, at what point the harassment became so "severe or pervasive" that it "created an abusive working environment."[5]

Mechelle Vinson had alleged far more egregious harassment at the hands of her boss, Sidney Taylor, including violent physical and sexual abuse—indeed, most of what she'd accused him of had been criminal—so the Court hadn't needed to articulate any particular legal test in order to find Vinson's work environment "abusive." But as Teresa Harris's experience illustrated, women face myriad other kinds of harassment on the job that do not reach that outer boundary, ranging from unwanted touching or leering commentary about their bodies to propositions, vulgar jokes, and graphic discussions of sexual exploits, to name just a few indignities. Then there is the conduct that is nonverbal yet nonetheless capable of "altering" a work environment for the worse, like displays of obscene graffiti, pornography, or calendars featuring a different bikini-clad woman each month.

After *Vinson*, then, how were employers, women, and courts supposed to assess whether harassment was bad enough to be illegal? Was it enough if the victim testified that she personally perceived the environment as abusive? Or did she need to show more quantifiable (if not financial) harm, such as psychiatric treatment for her distress or a demonstrable decline in her job performance? The skepticism leveled at Anita Hill during Clarence Thomas's 1991 confirmation hearings reflected this tension. Even if Thomas *had* discussed pornography and bestiality and pubic hairs on Cokes, was that enough to violate the law? Hill did not allege that Thomas had touched her inappropriately or otherwise intimidated her, such as by threatening to fire her if she reported him. And Hill not only had managed to continue doing her job throughout the period when Thomas supposedly harassed her, she had followed him from the Department of Education to another job at (ironically) the EEOC. Indeed, even after they stopped working together, she had maintained contact with him by speaking on the phone and sharing the occasional meal.

Skeptics claimed that if Thomas had behaved as grotesquely as Hill later said he did, how was she able to keep working for him? And why, after they no longer worked together, did she continue to cultivate a professional relationship with him? Surely the harassment couldn't have been as bad as she said it was. Surely she must not have been all *that* bothered by it.

——— ———

AFTER QUITTING Forklift Systems in late 1987, Teresa Harris met with attorney Irwin Venick. A wry, bearded New York native who had moved to Nashville to attend law school at Vanderbilt and never left, Venick was in his late thirties and roughly ten years into his legal career; he had a diverse civil litigation practice that included a bit of work in the area of employment law on behalf of the state's civil service employees' union as well as a few trials. Although he was well aware of the *Vinson* decision, he had never litigated a sexual harassment case. Still, after talking with Harris, listening to her recorded conversation with Hardy, and getting corroboration of Hardy's behavior from another woman who had worked at Forklift Systems, he concluded that Harris's case fit within *Vinson*'s amorphous definition of a hostile environment.

The key obstacle was a decision handed down the prior year by the U.S. Court of Appeals for the Sixth Circuit, the federal appellate court whose interpretations of the law are binding on courts in Tennessee. That case, *Rabidue v. Osceola Refining Company*,[6] was similar to Harris's: As recounted in the court's decision, a male manager frequently made obscene comments to the women in his office, calling them "whores," "cunts," "pussy," and "tits," often directing his abuse specifically at the female manager who eventually brought suit, Vivienne Rabidue. He called Rabidue a "fat ass" and told her coworkers that "all that bitch needs is a good lay." Rabidue's male coworkers also had a habit of displaying pictures of naked women in the office.[7]

After the trial court dismissed Rabidue's claim and her lawyer appealed, the Sixth Circuit became the first of the nation's twelve federal appellate courts to apply *Vinson*. Agreeing with the trial judge, the court upheld the dismissal. Rabidue, it maintained, had not shown the work environment to be sufficiently abusive to qualify as a hostile one in the legal sense defined by *Vinson*. It reached that conclusion by imposing an additional evidentiary burden: Not only did Rabidue have to show that the environment was abusive, but she also had to show that it was so abusive as to "seriously affect [her] psychological well-being." After all, the court noted, "sexual jokes, sexual conversations and girlie magazines" were always going to be part of the American workplace, and Title VII was not meant to change that.[8] In essence, *Rabidue* held that a woman can't expect her work environment to be free of *all* harassment, just harassment so severe that it damages her mental health.

Venick knew it would be an uphill battle for Harris to satisfy the new *Rabidue* standard. Harris undeniably had suffered extreme distress, which manifested itself in her behavior (insomnia, heavy drinking, and disrupted family relationships) and her physical symptoms (shortness of breath, crying, and shaking). But she had not seen a counselor, her primary care doctor had found nothing wrong with her, and she had been able to continue doing her job—even excelling at it. Nevertheless, Harris spoke so compellingly about her emotional deterioration, and Hardy's harassment so clearly fell within *Vinson*'s parameters as being "unwelcome" and "severe or pervasive," that Venick believed they had a good enough chance of winning to take the case. Aware of these caveats, Harris agreed to go forward. "I wanted to take Charles Hardy to court and prove that he had done these things," she says. "I had no expectation as far as finances, money goes. That never played into it at all. Primarily it was to *win*."

TERESA HARRIS'S trial began on July 23, 1990, in federal district court in Nashville and lasted close to a week. Harris took the stand to describe Hardy's abuse as well as the toll it took on her. Venick also called as witnesses a female Forklift Systems employee and two male employees who attested to Hardy's offensiveness. Hardy, for his part, did not deny any of the behavior attributed to him and merely claimed that he had been joking. He damaged his credibility, though, with a ham-fisted attempt to manufacture damaging evidence against Harris. He produced handwritten notes from his calendar showing that employees had lodged complaints against her, prompting Venick to put on an expert witness who analyzed the ink from those notes and declared it too recent to be authentic.

The company did manage to find three women employees, all in their early twenties and holding low-level clerical positions that put them in less frequent contact with Hardy, who testified that they weren't bothered by Hardy's behavior. The defense also focused on the soured business relationship between Charles Hardy and Larry Harris as the real motivating factor in Teresa Harris's resignation and lawsuit. Nevertheless, after all the testimony ended and the closing statements had been delivered, Harris and Venick felt the totality of the evidence weighed in their favor and were optimistic that the judge would rule for Harris.

A few months later, the decision was in. The judge agreed that Hardy had in fact subjected Harris to "a continuing pattern of sex-based derogatory conduct." He further held that Hardy was "a vulgar man" who "demean[ed] the female employees at his work place."[9] But he didn't think Hardy's behavior met the onerous new *Rabidue* standard of "seriously affecting [Harris's] psychological well-being." Just as Venick had feared, Harris's emotional strength in the face of Hardy's abuse proved her undoing: "Although Hardy may at times have genuinely offended [Harris]," wrote the judge, "I do not believe that he created a working environment so poisoned as to be intimidating or abusive to [her]."[10] Harris was furious. "How can a judge say, 'This man did everything you said. He's a vulgar man who demeans women in the workplace, but so what,'" she fumed to one reporter. "That eats me up inside. That can't be. That has to change."[11]

Venick filed an appeal with the Sixth Circuit. This put Harris's case in front of the same court that had decided *Rabidue;* now the court could either rescind the requirement that a harassment plaintiff show psychological harm or conclude that Harris had met that test when she testified at her trial about her heavy drinking, insomnia, and other symptoms. But the court did neither. Not deeming the case worthy of a full written opinion, on September 17, 1992, it merely issued a statement affirming the district court judge's decision.[12]

Although her chances before the appeals court had been slim because of its prior decision in *Rabidue,* the ruling hit Teresa Harris hard. The case was over, and she had lost. And what had her decision to fight Charles Hardy gotten her? Whether Hardy had pressured competitors to blackball her or her lawsuit simply had branded her as a troublemaker, Harris now could not get a job. By this point, she had been unemployed for five years. For the first time in her life, she had fallen behind in paying her bills, seriously damaging her credit. Her electricity had been cut off twice. Officials had shown up in her driveway to repossess her car. She had had to sell her house just to pay her bills. Harris, who had always been proud of her professional success and her spotless credit, describes her slide into financial hardship as "very humiliating."

Ultimately, she had decided to embark upon a new professional life as a nurse, and returned to school—but that only brought a new round of bills to pay, and it would be another year before she received her degree. Her personal life was no better; she and Larry Harris were divorcing. After learning of her loss before the Sixth Circuit, Teresa Harris called her cousin and went out to get drunk. She spent the rest of the night sick to her stomach, furious at herself for letting Charles Hardy make her miserable yet again.

Venick called Harris the next day to tell her that they had a decision to make: Should he file a petition with the Supreme Court to review the case? If he was going to do it, he needed to do it soon. Harris was dubious. She felt demoralized, even hopeless. She was looking forward to starting her career in nursing; maybe she should just embrace this new chapter and leave all things related to Forklift Systems behind.

As Harris told it, the answer came to her that night while taking a bath. She thought back to an encounter she had had with Hardy a few weeks before the trial. A former coworker had called her to say that Hardy wanted to meet with her. Without telling Venick, Harris reluctantly agreed, thinking that if she could manage to negotiate an end to the case, it would be best for everyone. She met with Hardy and the former coworker—whom she had insisted also be present—at a local restaurant. Hardy was solicitous and gave her his best good ol' boy smile.

"Now, Teresa, what'll it take for you to drop this case?"

Harris told Hardy she needed to pay Venick's fees and to recover some of the income she had lost as a result of having to quit her job, and asked for $25,000. This figure must have been higher than Hardy was expecting, because he grew enraged. "He told me that he was going to wear me out in court," Harris recalled, "that I did not have enough money to fight him. And of course, he insulted me, got nasty with me. He told me he was going to ruin me."

Harris was no less surprised by her own reaction: "I said to him, 'I will sell every fucking thing I own, I will not stop.' And I looked at him and I said, 'I'm talking Sandra Fucking Day O'Connor!'"

Harris laughed as she told the story. ("I don't think he knew who that was!") With that flourish, Harris grabbed her belongings and marched out of the restaurant. Then she sat for a while in her car in the parking lot, alternately berating herself for making such an outrageous threat and feeling even more livid at Hardy's arrogance than when she arrived.

Lying in the bathtub the night after her bender, Harris realized that she did not need to think at all about whether to appeal to the Supreme Court. She called Venick at home that night. "I told Charles Hardy that I was taking his ass all the way," she told Venick, "and I am not a liar. We're doing it. What are our chances?"

Venick's rueful response still tickles her: "I don't think we have a snowball's chance in hell."

"That's okay," Harris told him. "We're doing it. I said I was going to do it—and we're going to do it!"

IN PREPARING to ask the Supreme Court to review Harris's case, Venick knew he needed guidance. He consulted with Bob Belton, a Vanderbilt law professor who, during his tenure as an attorney with the NAACP Legal Defense and Education Fund, had been part of the team that presented the landmark Title VII case, *Griggs v. Duke Power Company*,[13] to the Supreme Court. Two of Belton's Vanderbilt colleagues, each of whom had clerked for a Supreme Court justice and had wisdom to share about the process, also pitched in.

A few months later, in December 1992, Venick submitted the petition for *certiorari*. Noting that the *Meritor* decision "provided limited guidance regarding the necessary elements of proof for a successful claim," Venick asked the Court to clarify it. He told the Court that the question posed by Teresa Harris's case—"Is a plaintiff in a sexual harassment case also required to prove, in order to prevail, that she suffered severe psychological injury?"—had been answered in contradictory ways by various federal courts of appeals. After the Sixth Circuit decided *Rabidue*, the Seventh and Eleventh Circuits had followed suit and imposed the "severe psychological injury" standard while the Third, Eighth, and Ninth had rejected *Rabidue* and required only that a plaintiff show that she was offended by the harassment (and that she was "reasonable" in having that reaction).[14]

By noting this so-called circuit split, Venick hoped to convince the justices that their intervention was necessary to ensure fair and uniform application of Title VII to harassment cases around the country. By the time of Venick's petition, the number of sexual harassment complaint filings was skyrocketing. Although the EEOC didn't keep reliable statistics on the number of charges filed prior to 1991, between the 1991 and 1992 fiscal years, sexual harassment charges filed with federal and state officials rose by a whopping 40 percent, from approximately 7,000 to more than 10,000.

What had occurred in the intervening year? The Anita Hill–Clarence Thomas hearings. The *Vinson* case may have given women a legal remedy for sexual harassment in 1986, but it was the October 1991 hearings on Clarence Thomas's Supreme Court nomination that started a national conversation about how sexual harassment plays out in real life: Harassers usually don't look like drooling perverts, the harassed usually don't look like helpless victims, and harassment, even if it's only words, can be traumatic. For those women who already knew all of this—who listened to Hill and thought, "It happened to me too"—it was a galvanizing moment. "It's hard to overstate [the hearings'] importance," Marcia Greenberger, copresident of the National Women's Law Center, later wrote. "The issue of sexual harassment was out of the shadows. . . . Pundits speculated that the Anita Hill testimony would forever intimidate women from ever coming forward again, but the opposite happened."[15]

Another, more prosaic factor likely driving the uptick in charges was a recent change in the law. The 1991 Civil Rights Act had made it possible for workers who prevailed on their claims to recover damages for intangible harms, such as emotional distress, as well as punitive damages. Prior to Title VII's amendment, workers could win reimbursement only for tangible economic losses, so they tended to bring harassment claims only if they could show—as Teresa Harris had alleged—that the abuse was so bad they'd been forced to quit. In those "constructive discharge" cases, lost wages could be recovered. But after 1991, the availability of damages for emotional harm meant that a woman could seek compensation even if she'd managed to keep working; such damages provided some measure of reimbursement, however inexact, for having gone through the indignity of working in a sexualized environment.

In March 1993, three months after Venick filed his petition for *certiorari*, he had his answer: The Court would hear the case. Oral argument was scheduled for October.

WHILE PREPARING for a Supreme Court argument is a Herculean task for anyone, Venick felt significant added pressure. He was, in his words, a "rinky dink lawyer from nowhere." *Harris* also was his first sexual harassment case. Venick knew that scores of women's advocacy organizations were deeply invested in the outcome of Harris's case. A ruling from the Supreme Court that only serious psychological harm could trigger Title VII liability would make the courts available to only a fraction of harassment victims. Were this to happen, countless other women—women who, like Teresa Harris, managed to continue performing their jobs despite egregious harassment, or who, like countless others, simply left their jobs before the harassment could damage their emotional well-being—would have no legal recourse.

These high stakes weighed on Venick in the months leading up to the argument. He was especially intimidated by the moot court convened in Washington, DC, by leading women's groups and civil rights organizations. It took place at a conference table surrounded by roughly twenty of the heaviest hitters in the women's rights movement. Venick spent hours fielding questions from attorneys who had litigated harassment cases for years both before and after *Vinson*. Although still a Washington outsider when he left that conference room, Venick was at least less of an unknown quantity, which boosted his confidence. After returning to Nashville, he also underwent another moot court, this one convened by Bob Belton.

It wasn't only women's rights organizations that were invested in the outcome of *Harris*. Nearly a dozen *amicus* briefs were filed on behalf of more than forty groups claiming an interest in the outcome of the case, including labor unions; women's and civil rights organizations; and professional organizations of employers, attorneys, social workers, psychologists, and even police officers, who claimed an interest in the case due to the pervasive sexual harassment in their male-dominated ranks. Of these, only one organization, the Equal Employment Advisory Council—whose membership comprised 270 corporations and related business-oriented entities—weighed in on behalf of Forklift Systems.

One of the most significant voices among the *amici* was the EEOC, which also submitted an *amicus* brief on Harris's behalf. Although the EEOC had taken a stand against sexual harassment for the first time in 1980, six years before *Vinson* was decided, in 1990 it issued a new set of Guidelines approving that decision. In *Harris*, the EEOC urged the Court to expressly reject the psychological harm requirement in favor of requiring only that the harassment "interfere with the work performance" of a "reasonable person." The agency also specifically noted that verbal harassment alone can be sufficient to meet that standard.[16]

The American Psychological Association, which had featured so prominently among the *Price Waterhouse v. Hopkins amici,* also filed a brief. Unlike its *Hopkins* brief about sex stereotyping, in which it overtly took the side not just of Ann Hopkins but of its colleague Dr. Susan Fiske, the APA's brief in *Harris* didn't explicitly support either party. Its evidence was unquestionably more helpful to Teresa Harris, though. It offered a survey of the "growing body of social science data" developed since the 1970s showing that sexual harassment has many deleterious effects without causing "serious psychological harm." Indeed, many of harassment's harms are not psychological at all, the APA noted, but instead consist of the disruptions to victims' careers as they adopt coping strategies to avoid the harasser: They change jobs, request transfers, abandon efforts to win promotion, and turn down opportunities that could yield greater pay, seniority, and access to professional networks.[17]

Especially noteworthy for Harris's case was the APA's recitation of research confirming that different women react differently to harassment. Consequently, focusing on the victim's individual response does not say much about whether the harasser's conduct crossed the threshold into illegality. Rather, the "psychological injury requirement shifts the focus of Title VII's protection to the victim's psychological wherewithal to sustain abuse, rather than the nature of the harasser's conduct." Studies showed that women with high self-esteem and supportive networks of friends and family are better able to "insulate" themselves from harassment's worst effects.[18] Teresa Harris exemplified this kind of resilient woman: She had continued performing her job well, despite the inner turmoil she experienced while at the office and the self-destructive behavior she engaged in when she went home at night. In other words, although she might not have shown it, she unquestionably was experiencing an "abusive working environment."

THE MORNING OF the oral argument before the Supreme Court on October 13, 1993, six years after she'd quit Forklift Systems, Teresa Harris was overcome with nausea. "I was so scared, at the same time I was excited," she recalled. "I knew, *this is it.* If it don't play here, there's no place to go."

Although Harris had arrived in Washington a few days early to do some sightseeing—she brought along her mother, sister, brother-in-law, and a friend—she had not visited the Court. Walking up those famed marble steps and entering the chambers where the case would be argued was "overwhelming. I mean, it's awesome, I'd never seen anything like it. It was unbelievable." Charles Hardy did not attend.

Because seven years had gone by since Mechelle Vinson's case was decided by the Court, more than half of the justices hearing *Harris*—Ruth Bader Ginsburg, Anthony Kennedy, Antonin Scalia, David Souter, and Clarence Thomas—would be deciding the issue of sexual harassment for the first time. The perspectives of the newest members of the Court, Justices Ginsburg and Thomas, could not have been more different: Justice Ginsburg had spent her career litigating landmark women's rights cases while Justice Thomas recently had been accused of precisely the same kind of lewd conduct that Harris attributed to Hardy. It was hard to imagine an odder couple of colleagues.

Irwin Venick was the first lawyer to step to the lectern. He was able to speak at some length about the wrongheadedness of the "serious psychological harm" standard itself. The Court was more interested in the potential alternatives: If a woman didn't have to show psychological distress to prove a violation of Title VII, what *did* she have to show? Should the Court require that the harassment "interfere" with a woman's work performance, as the EEOC urged in its *amicus* brief? And if so, that raised other questions: Did "interfere" mean that the harassment made the work environment merely "unpleasant," or did it have to "make the job more difficult"? Did a woman have to show that her work performance diminished in some quantifiable way—such as increased absenteeism, or missed deadlines, or lower performance ratings?

Venick argued against applying an "interference" test because, like the psychological harm requirement, it focused on the woman's reaction to the harassment rather than the harassment itself, while Title VII was intended to address the employer's misconduct. Venick told the Court that so long as a woman can show that the harassment was unwelcome, as *Vinson* required, she has proved that the "terms and conditions" of her employment were "altered," at which point examination of her subjective response should end. Justice Ginsburg agreed, observing "If you take a similarly situated man and a woman, and the woman is constantly told, you're a woman, you think like a woman, and her coworker is not told those things, doesn't that make their job more difficult? Do you need anything further than that? Is it really more complex? The terms and conditions [of employment] aren't equal if one is being called names and the other isn't."[19]

The bulk of the Court's examination, Venick argued, should be on whether a hypothetical "reasonable person" would experience the environment as abusive, in the legal sense. Venick argued that meeting this more objective standard would depend on all of the factors that the Court had laid out in *Vinson* when assessing whether harassment is severe or pervasive: "How often does the conduct occur, who's perpetrating the conduct, who else was exposed to the conduct, who else joined in the conduct?"

But that standard was just as vague, interjected Justice Scalia. "'[S]ufficiently severe or pervasive to alter the conditions of employment.' That is utterly meaningless to me," he said, "I don't care if we did say it." Over laughter from the gallery, he continued, growing more exercised. "All right, there are all of those factors, but how many of them do you need to alter the conditions? How can you tell? What magic event says, oh, the harassment has risen to the level of severity to alter the [working] conditions? . . . Now, the test that says, it affects your work performance, ah, that's something I can identify!"[20] Venick parried for a few more minutes, staunchly contending that Justice Scalia's proposed standard was too high, and then his time was up.

When Stanley Chernau, the Nashville attorney who had represented Forklift Systems since the start of the case, stepped forward, he had some explaining to do. In the legal brief he had filed in advance of the argument, Chernau had taken the peculiar step of disavowing the *Rabidue* "psychological injury" requirement that had been the basis for his client's victory in the Sixth Circuit. Instead, he had argued that the EEOC "interference" standard was the correct one. And because Harris could not show a tangible decline in her work performance, she couldn't prove that the harassment "interfered" with her ability to do her job—so the ruling in favor of Forklift Systems should stand.[21]

Chernau's argument did not go well. Justices Souter and Ginsburg took the lead, confronting the attorney with quotes from the Sixth Circuit's written opinion in which it stated that psychological harm was a prerequisite for any claim. If the Sixth Circuit had applied the wrong standard of proof—a standard that even Chernau now conceded was incorrect—wasn't the Court, then, obligated to reverse the Sixth Circuit's ruling? Chernau responded that the Sixth Circuit's opinion implied that it would have reached the same result under the "interference" test, so the Court could simply affirm the decision on those grounds instead.[22] But the justices were not persuaded.

Justice Ginsburg proceeded to read from the portions of the trial court's opinion in which the judge agreed that Harris had been subjected to a "continuing pattern of derogatory conduct." Then she posed a hypothetical to Chernau: "I'm curious, . . . if [the derogatory conduct] had been race-based or religion-based or national origin, and we had a similar inventory of continuous behavior, would your analysis be any different?"

"I think that when you try to—in order to answer—that is a very difficult question to ask—to answer," Chernau stammered, before finally conceding that no, sex-based harassment and harassment based on any other characteristic should be analyzed the same way.[23]

When the justices questioned Chernau about his interpretation of what a victim must show in order to satisfy the "interference" test, he declared, "I don't believe that it is necessary to specifically assert and prove interference with your work performance to be successful" on a harassment claim.

"Oh, well, that's new!" exclaimed Justice Scalia. "That's new to me then. You're changing your position that was in your brief."[24] Chernau floundered for a few more minutes under questioning from Ginsburg and Stevens about the "reasonable person" standard and then his time was up.[25]

Teresa Harris was thrilled. To her, Venick had emerged the clear winner of the argument. "The difference between what Irwin did and what Chernau did was just like night and day," she said. "It was unbelievable. I got the vibe of course from Judge Ginsburg—you could tell she was on board—but I got good vibes about [the whole thing]."

After the argument, Venick and Harris headed to the headquarters of the NOW Legal Defense and Education Fund, where they were the guests of honor at a reception attended by women's rights advocates and civil rights luminaries. If there had been any apprehension among the Washington insiders about Venick's ability to rise to the occasion, it surely had dissipated; the mood was decidedly celebratory.

ALTHOUGH VENICK may have given the superior performance, it was hard to tell which way the Court was leaning. The reliably liberal justices—Ginsburg and Stevens—had been active participants during the argument, but several justices considered "swing" or conservative votes—such as Kennedy, Rehnquist, and Thomas—had remained silent or asked just a few questions. It was all but impossible to tell what they were thinking about the parties' arguments.

It didn't take long to find out. Typically the Court deliberates for at least a few months, but with *Harris v. Forklift Systems* the Court took just twenty-seven days. Harris got a call from Venick: They had won—and it was unanimous.

"Title VII comes into play before the harassing conduct leads to a nervous breakdown," wrote the Court.[26] In a line that could have been lifted from the APA's *amicus* brief, it explained: "A discriminatorily abusive work environment, even one that does not seriously affect employees' psychological well-being, can and often will detract from employees' job performance, discourage employees from remaining on the job, or keep them from advancing in their careers. Moreover"—and here the opinion echoed Justice Ginsburg's observations at oral argument—"even without regard to these tangible effects, the very fact that the discriminatory conduct was so severe or pervasive that it created a work environment abusive to employees because of their race, gender, religion or national origin offends Title VII's broad rule of workplace equality."[27] (Justice Ginsburg submitted a concurrence amplifying even further her conviction that sex-based disadvantage is no less pernicious than race-based harm—a conviction that had animated her career as a litigator, too.[28])

Having rejected the Sixth Circuit's "serious psychological injury" standard, the Court laid out its chosen alternative. After reaffirming *Vinson*'s ban on harassing conduct that is "sufficiently severe or pervasive to alter the conditions of the victim's employment and create an abusive working environment," it noted that the "appalling conduct" by Sidney Taylor toward Mechelle Vinson in that case did not "mark the boundary" of what is illegal.

That boundary instead was the point at which a hypothetical reasonable person would find the work environment hostile or abusive. The Court cautioned that there was no "mathematically precise test" for meeting that standard and conceded that its ruling asked the lower courts to, in effect, make up as they went along the kinds of circumstances that a reasonable person might find harassing:

> We need not answer today all the potential questions [our decision] raises. . . . But we can say that whether an environment is "hostile" or "abusive" can be determined only by looking at all the circumstances. These may include the frequency of the discriminatory

conduct; its severity; whether it is physically threatening or humiliating, or a mere offensive utterance; and whether it unreasonably
interferes with an employee's work performance.[29]

(Despite the lengthy questioning at oral argument as to how to prove
such "interference," the Court did not address this in the opinion.)
The Court concluded by emphasizing that although "psychological
harm, like any other factor, may be taken into account" when assessing whether a work environment is illegally hostile, "no single factor
is required."[30]

In practical terms, the *Harris* ruling invalidated the Sixth Circuit's
decision in *Rabidue* as well as any other appeals court decisions that
had followed it by imposing the "psychological harm" requirement in
harassment cases. By extension, the Court also overturned the Sixth
Circuit's decision upholding the trial court's ruling in Forklift Systems'
favor. Because Harris should not have had to prove Charles Hardy's
harassment caused psychological harm, the justices directed that her
case return to the district court for renewed consideration.

A jubilant Harris immediately joined Venick at his office, where
they read the faxed opinion together and sat for multiple interviews
with local and national news outlets. "And then," Venick recalled with
a smile, "we went downtown and had a drink."

Harris was hailed by civil rights advocates around the country for
her bravery in coming forward and making the Court's ruling possible.
She even got a congratulatory phone call from Anita Hill, whose testimony during the Thomas confirmation hearings Harris had watched
vigilantly and with mounting anger at the Senate Judiciary Committee
questioners. ("I mean, just based on my own experience, who would
make up something like that? Where does it get you?") The realization
that she had helped millions of women she would never meet was hard
to comprehend, but gratifying. "[P]eople would be pretty naïve to believe that women don't get harassed in the workplace, because they do,
and there's still a lot of bigotry in the workplace, and all those sorts of
things," she said. "However, I think that my case probably makes it
easier for women to do something about it. And for that I'm grateful,
and I'm glad."

AFTER THE SUPREME COURT sent Teresa Harris's case back to
the trial court in Tennessee, the judge issued a new ruling, this time in

Harris's favor. He ordered Forklift Systems to pay her \$151,435, representing her lost income after Hardy's harassment forced her to quit, as well as her accumulated legal fees. He also ordered the company to put in place a written policy against sexual harassment. Harris and Venick disagreed with the way the judge calculated her back wages, considering them too low, while Forklift Systems disagreed with the ruling entirely. But rather than spend more time and money on an appeal, the parties agreed to settle the case for an undisclosed amount.

By the time of the Supreme Court's decision, Harris had graduated from nursing school and been working in the bone marrow transplant unit at Vanderbilt Hospital for close to a year. She had not told her coworkers about the case, even when she took time off to travel to Washington for the oral argument. But when the decision came out and Harris's name and photograph were all over the news, her colleagues were supportive, to her pleasant surprise, offering congratulations and teasingly scolding her for having kept the case to herself for so long.

There was one aspect of the Supreme Court's decision that Harris savored privately, though, one that was especially sweet, given her secret pretrial meeting with Charles Hardy three years earlier. The author of the Court's opinion in *Harris v. Forklift Systems* was Justice Sandra Day O'Connor.

nine

don't shoot the messenger

Burlington Northern & Santa Fe
Railway Company v. White (2006)

IN THE SUMMER OF 1997, SHEILA WHITE DROVE FROM her home in the Whitehaven neighborhood of Memphis to a job interview at a sprawling rail yard operated by Burlington Northern & Santa Fe Railway, fifteen miles southeast of downtown. White, then forty-one and a single mother of three, had been out of work for close to a year, laid off during a downsizing from her machine operator job with pharmaceutical giant Schering-Plough. In that position and prior jobs, she had learned to operate a forklift, a fact that came as good news to one of White's interviewers, Marvin Brown, Road Master of the Memphis rail yard.

Although White had applied to be a track laborer, whose primary duties were to repair and maintain rail lines throughout BNSF's freight system, Brown needed someone who could work the Memphis Yard's forklift; the man who had been doing the job had recently taken a different position with the company. After a successful second interview and passing the company physical, White reported for duty on July 2, 1997. She was the only woman out of roughly one hundred employees in her department.

White had grown up in Memphis, the elder of two daughters. Petite and effusive, with a round face framed by close-cropped platinum blond hair, White speaks deliberately, with a pronounced Southern accent and polite precision. She credits her parents, Leon, a high school history teacher, and Ruby, a social worker, with instilling in her a social conscience. Like any African American of her generation who grew up in the South, White remembers the routine indignities of being relegated to the back of the city bus and forced to shop in the basement "colored" section of clothing stores. Her high school was integrated in name only; white students bullied White and her friends, and the Fairley High yearbook featured two sets of couples crowned as "Miss and Mister Fairley." (The African American couple's photograph was black and white while the white couple's was in color.) Although White's parents supported the civil rights movement that roiled the city throughout White's preteen and teenage years, they were eager for her to stay safely on the sidelines, so the few times she joined demonstrations to protest segregated shops and restaurants in downtown Memphis, she had to sneak out of the house.

White had her first child, a daughter, in her senior year, and married her high school sweetheart. They stayed together for four more years, having a second daughter before divorcing. She eventually married again and had her third child, a son. By the time White began working at BNSF in the summer of 1997, her second marriage had ended and she had built a life around her children, church, friends, and volunteer activities. (One of her favorites was sewing the uniforms for the flag bearers for Fairley High's marching band.) Both daughters were in college, and her son was in high school. White was thrilled to have secured a job paying close to $15.00 an hour, with generous benefits, such as health coverage and a pension plan. She saw it as a job that would see all three kids through their college educations and provide for a comfortable retirement.[1]

White's direct supervisor in the Memphis Yard was longtime BNSF employee Bill Joiner. On her first day, White was stunned when Joiner interrupted an orientation speech he was delivering to her and five other workers to address her specifically. "Sheila, when you come on your period, you let somebody know so we can make your job lighter on you." Nearly two decades later, White was still incredulous recalling that moment. "I froze, because I couldn't believe that he would say that." It was the first time she ever had been treated differently on the job because she was a woman. "And so something told me, you better be careful."

White's intuition was right. Joiner constantly told her that the railroad was "no place for a woman" and that she should find another job. He wouldn't give her any overtime hours, while men with the same or less seniority as White routinely were assigned after-hours work. Joiner refused to provide her with a company-issued raincoat, even though her male coworkers received theirs and she frequently was called on to work in inclement weather. And he told White that Road Master Marvin Brown—despite having just helped make the decision to hire White—wanted Joiner to find a reason to fire her within her sixty-day probationary period, before the protections afforded by her union contract could take effect.

Joiner was not the only man making White's life miserable at work. As one supervisor later described it, there was a "general anti-woman feeling" at the Memphis Yard.[2] Perhaps emboldened by their openly biased boss, other coworkers also told her that a woman shouldn't be working there. The road crews reported their sexual exploits while traveling to far-flung locations to work on track lines. The only bathroom at the Memphis Yard was unisex and didn't have a working lock; after being walked in on one too many times by her coworkers, White asked for the lock to be repaired, but no one was interested in fixing it. She started borrowing a sympathetic coworker's truck to drive to a nearby BNSF office where there was a women's restroom; if she didn't have to stop for train crossings, she could usually make it there and back in about five minutes.

On September 10, 1997, White was called in the middle of the night to the site of a train derailment. When Bill Joiner arrived on the scene, he summoned her to the other side of one of the rail cars, away from her huddled group of coworkers. "And he said, 'Come here, Sheila. Shine that flashlight on me so I can see where I'ma pee at,'" recalled White. "I thought that was very disgusting. You're exposing yourself and want me to shine the light on you? I told him I wasn't gonna do nothing like that."

White filed a complaint with BNSF. In a handwritten statement, she said that "foreman Joiner has a problem working with coworkers of the opposite sex" and described the various ways he had singled her out for mistreatment over the past two and a half months. Later that day, she met with Marvin Brown and his supervisor. The two men read over the statement—chuckling together when they got to the urination incident—and promised White they would submit the complaint to BNSF's human resources department for investigation.

Ten days later, Brown called White into a meeting. This time, an HR representative was with him. Brown told White that the company's inquiry had confirmed that Joiner had harassed her and that he was going to be suspended for ten days without pay and required to attend sensitivity training. A letter of reprimand would also be placed in his permanent personnel file. Unfortunately, that wasn't all. Brown explained that because some male coworkers interviewed during the investigation had complained that White's job, as forklift operator, was easier than theirs, she no longer would hold that position. Instead, it would be reassigned to the man who previously held the job, and White would be performing the usual track laborer duties. What's more, Joiner would still be her direct supervisor after he returned from his suspension. "I started crying," White recalled. "I told [them they were] wrong for doing me like that because that wasn't right. They found Bill Joiner guilty, and why should they take me off the forklift because they found him guilty?" White told the men that she thought the change in her duties was retaliatory, but they were unmoved.

White was disconsolate. She loved working on the forklift, the skill it took and the satisfaction she got from doing it well. And as evidenced by her coworkers' grumbling, it was a coveted position; regular track laborer duties were much more difficult. Under the hot Tennessee sun, workers dismantled and assembled rail lines, loaded and unloaded heavy equipment from trucks, cleared brush, and cleaned up waste that blocked the tracks. The job required them to get much dirtier, using oil to lubricate tools and machinery, inhaling dust from the rocks used to line the tracks, and sometimes working on their hands and knees. They also were often required to leave their families behind and travel to distant locations, working multiple overtime shifts for days or even weeks at a time. (White cited the common wisdom around the Memphis Yard: "First thing a man going to ask you on that job, 'Are you married?' You say, 'Yes.' 'Well you gon' be divorced.'") Even though the job paid the same wages as working on the forklift, White was convinced that the transfer was intended as punishment for complaining.

A woman at White's church worked for the EEOC and told her to visit the office to file a charge. White followed her advice, taking with her the pile of pocket notebooks she had been filling with scribblings about her life at BNSF since her first day on the job, and explained her story to the EEOC investigator.

White had been fairly sure that Joiner's comments about her period and his hostility toward having a female employee were against the law, but she didn't know whether her removal from the forklift was. The EEOC investigator, though, told her that Title VII also forbids retaliation against an employee who has complained about discrimination. Protecting individuals from retaliation goes hand in glove with advancing Title VII's broader goal of ending discrimination; if employees are too afraid to report biased treatment because they can be punished with impunity, such treatment will continue to flourish.

The investigator told White that she believed the transfer off the forklift was illegal retaliation for having filed a written complaint about Joiner. On October 10, 1997, White filed a charge alleging just that.

WHITE WAS FLYING blind in her new position on the tracks. "I didn't know the first thing about how to do the work," she said. Ignorance was dangerous when handling equipment that could weigh more than a hundred pounds—"You could easily get killed or hurt out there"[3]—so she got up to speed by watching her coworkers and enlisting the friendlier ones as her tutors. She enjoyed the collaboration and learning new skills, such as how to use a jackhammer to drill spikes that would join tracks, plates, and rail ties.

But according to White, BNSF did everything it could to isolate her and force her to quit. After all, at that point she had filed not only an internal complaint but a formal charge with a federal agency. She often was assigned to do tasks by herself that could be done safely only by two or more people. If she got along too well with her crew, White would suddenly find herself transferred to a new assignment, often out of town and even out of state. On those trips, White frequently was partnered with BNSF workers and supervisors from all over the region. Her reputation preceded her. "Each state I worked in, they knew who I was. I had a foreman [who] said, 'You're Sheila White.' I didn't even have to introduce myself. He said, 'You gonna follow rules and do what I say do.'"

At least White didn't have to keep working with Bill Joiner. Shortly after returning from his suspension—which he laughingly declared a "vacation" and claimed he had been paid for his time off—Joiner was granted a transfer to an Arkansas post. A young African American man named Percy Sharkey took over as White's foreman. It was clear from the outset, though, that Sharkey was not going to make White's life any easier. "You're going to do what I tell you to do and don't ask any questions," he told her. Sharkey also reported to White that Marvin Brown thought she was a "troublemaker" and wanted to "get rid" of her. White remembered, "Mr. Brown was calling Sharkey every day. He wanted to know my whereabouts, what I be doing and what time I got there, what time I was leaving."

White learned that other supervisors also were under orders from Brown to scrutinize her every move, in the hope of catching her in a fireable offense; she even heard a rumor that whoever succeeded would get assigned a brand-new company truck. Sometimes Brown conducted his own surveillance. "He would come down in his truck and sit there on my job site and just stare at me while I was working," said White. Of course, having a target on her back didn't endear White to her coworkers. Just riding in a truck with her meant getting stopped by the foreman to check that everyone was wearing a seat belt.

The strain of being under the microscope began to get to White. As fall turned to winter in 1997, she retreated into what she called a "deep shell depression." She "couldn't hardly think, couldn't hardly drive." Despite being constantly fatigued, she couldn't sleep either. She stopped socializing with friends and family and dropped her church and volunteer activities. She struggled with headaches and bouts of crying that she couldn't control. White's older daughter, Monica, later testified at trial that her mother became "isolated" and "withdrawn," prompting her to come home from college in Knoxville at least twice a month to try to cheer White up. "She used to be my best friend, my sister," Monica said. "But [now she] wasn't."[4]

On December 4, 1997, White filed a new EEOC charge claiming that the company's increased scrutiny was retaliatory. One week later, White was dispatched with a Memphis crew to do track work in Blytheville, Arkansas. When the morning's assignments were distributed, Sharkey told one of the Memphis workers, Greg Nelson, to ride along with him and directed White to join a group headed by a foreman from the local rail yard. White went to join the Memphis foreman's truck, as she'd been told, but he refused to let her in. Instead, Greg Nelson got in the foreman's truck, and the convoy drove off without her. When White returned to the staging area and told Sharkey what had happened, he was irate. After making a phone call to Marvin Brown, Sharkey informed White that she had been insubordinate and was suspended without pay, effective immediately, and should return to Memphis. Greg Nelson, however, was not disciplined.

White filed yet another EEOC charge, alleging that the suspension constituted further retaliation. She also contacted her union representative, who initiated the company grievance procedure, seeking to rescind the suspension. But then all she could do was wait. It was the worst possible time to be without income; Christmas was just two weeks away, and White had no idea when—or if—she would get another paycheck. She later testified at her trial about that holiday season, "That was the worst Christmas I had out of my life. No income, no money, and that made all of us feel bad. . . . I got very depressed because . . . I couldn't even have a Christmas dinner, a meal. . . . I was anxious, couldn't sleep at all, and I was just destroyed."[5] With a new school semester about to begin in January, White couldn't make her daughters' college tuition payments and had to ask her parents for money. They and White's friends stepped in to help with groceries and other necessities, and with their assistance she was able to stay afloat financially.

White knew she needed help coping with the emotional fallout of her job as well. In early January 1998, she began seeing a psychiatrist. After her first visit, she got some good news: She had won her grievance and could return to her job. The insubordination charge was unwarranted, and the suspension was unjust. She also would be reimbursed for all of the pay she'd lost during the thirty-seven days she was out of work.

Although relieved to have her economic safety net restored, White found that nothing had changed when she returned to the Memphis Yard. With a sexual harassment complaint, three EEOC charges, and now a union grievance to her name, White was more of a "troublemaker" than ever.

After a little more than a month back on the job, White's psychiatrist instructed her to take a disability leave until the summer, pronouncing her "unable to work at this time."[6] When that leave expired, the psychiatrist prescribed more time off. In a note to BNSF dated November 4, 1998, she described White as having post-traumatic stress disorder and major depressive disorder, with symptoms including depression, anxiety, flashbacks, poor memory, and inability to concentrate. "Patient remains anxious," she wrote. "Unable to function and cope with stress." As for an estimated date White would be able to return to work, the doctor stated, "Unknown."[7]

AS IT TURNED OUT, by the time trial began in *White v. Burlington Northern & Santa Fe Railway* nearly two years later in August 2000, White still had not returned to the Memphis Yard. Her psychiatrist didn't deem her ready to work until June 1999, but by then, BNSF had

had to temporarily lay off a number of track laborers for lack of work; White didn't have the seniority to avoid being one of them. She wasn't fired, but she wasn't working either.

At trial, White was represented by Don Donati, an experienced Memphis employment attorney, and his stepson Billy Ryan, who had been out of law school for just over a year. BNSF's attorneys were also related, a father and son duo named Everett and Ralph Gibson. For a railway company second only to Union Pacific in its size and with deep pockets to match, BNSF had made an odd choice in the Gibsons. Their small firm primarily handled DUI defense, personal injury, and divorce cases, not employment litigation defense.

The judge was Jon McCalla, a former Army lieutenant who had been appointed to the bench by President George H. W. Bush. McCalla had earned some infamy in Memphis legal circles for being "erratic,"[8] prompting several attorney complaints, an official investigation of his conduct, and—just a few months prior to the start of White's trial—a rebuke from the federal appeals court for his "intemperate behavior" toward an attorney during a sentencing hearing.[9] White didn't know this history, but she didn't like the "edge" she perceived in how McCalla talked to potential women jurors. And the composition of the jury concerned her too; all but one of them were white, there were more men than women, and most of the jurors looked to White like they wouldn't be able to relate to her—too "corporate," she said.

White brought three claims. The first was that Joiner's conduct had created a hostile work environment for her. The other two claims were for retaliation. First, did White's removal from the forklift job constitute retaliation for complaining about Joiner's harassment? And second, was the decision to suspend her for insubordination intended as legitimate discipline, or was it intended as retaliation for filing EEOC charges?

For three days, the jury heard from nine witnesses, including White herself and the main players from BNSF: Bill Joiner, Marvin Brown, and Percy Sharkey. They confirmed that operating the forklift was an easier, cleaner, and more desirable assignment than the usual track laborer's job. Brown also admitted that male workers had been griping about White's assignment to such a "pud" job long before she complained about Joiner, yet it was only after she lodged that complaint that he made the transfer decision.[10] He further admitted, as did Joiner, that White had done the job well and there was nothing in her performance that warranted removing her.[11] When it came to the discredited charge of insubordination against White that had triggered her suspension, Brown and Sharkey couldn't get their stories straight about who had made the decision or why.[12]

White's two retaliation claims were hardly slam dunks, and not just because juries are always unpredictable. Title VII's antiretaliation provision is bare bones, with no congressional committee testimony or other legislative history to give it shape. It merely makes it illegal to "discriminate" against someone for opposing biased treatment but doesn't define what retaliatory "discrimination" means. In contrast, the law's section banning employment discrimination includes all sorts of language spelling out what kinds of employer conduct are prohibited because of sex (as well as race, national origin, color, and religion). That provision explains it's unlawful "to fail or refuse to hire" someone, to "discharge" that person, to treat the person differently "with respect to his compensation, terms, conditions, or privileges of employment," or to "limit, segregate, or classify . . . employees or applicants for employment in any way which would deprive or tend to deprive any individual of employment opportunities or otherwise adversely affect his status as an employee."[13]

So it had been left up to the courts to decide what it meant to "discriminate" against someone for complaining about perceived bias. All of the courts that had considered the issue by then had established a basic test: An employee had to show that he or she had complained about perceived discrimination and that the complaint had caused the employer to take an "adverse action." But how "adverse" was *illegally* adverse?

Federal judges couldn't agree on an answer. Among the twelve federal courts of appeals, no fewer than three standards were in use. Some courts thought retaliation claims should be limited to only the most serious kinds of punishment for lodging a complaint, such as discharge or demotion. Others thought retaliation should be much easier to prove and should encompass employer actions that might seem minor but were clearly meant as retribution—say, closely monitoring an employee's arrival and departure times or rescinding a previously granted vacation request.

In the middle was the Sixth Circuit—the circuit that included Tennessee as well as Kentucky, Michigan, and Ohio—which analyzed retaliation claims the same way it analyzed any other Title VII claims: An employee must show her complaint resulted in a "materially adverse change" in the "terms and conditions of [her] employment." "Materially adverse" was a definition that included, as one court explained, not just actions that had economic consequences to the employee, such as firing her or cutting her pay. It also included job changes like "a less distinguished title, a material loss of benefits, significantly diminished material responsibilities, or"—and here was the catchall that White and her attorneys hoped the jury would find applied to her—"other indices that might be unique to a particular situation."[14]

BNSF argued that neither the job transfer nor the suspension met the Sixth Circuit's "materially adverse" test. Although the usual track laborer duties might have been more strenuous than operating the forklift, track laborer was the job for which White applied, interviewed, and was hired. Nor had White's transfer resulted in a cut in her pay, loss of seniority, or any other tangible harm. She just didn't like it as much, and that, went the argument, wasn't "material" enough to violate the law. The same went for White's suspension: She had been reinstated and had received all of the back pay, seniority, and other benefits that she'd lost during the thirty-seven days her grievance was pending. So she didn't have any out-of-pocket losses, and she still had her job. While it had undeniably been stressful to be in limbo for a little over a month, that also wasn't a "material" enough harm to qualify as illegal retaliation.

After just a few hours of deliberation, the jury had its verdict: It found in White's favor on both retaliation claims. (For reasons that are unknown—juries aren't required to explain their decisions—it ruled against White on her third claim, for a hostile work environment.) It awarded her legal fees, $3,250 as reimbursement for her out-of-pocket medical bills arising from her treatment for depression, and $40,000 as compensation for her overall emotional distress.

WHEN A JURY reaches a decision that a litigant doesn't like, the unhappy party has two options: Challenge the way the trial was run—such as by arguing that certain evidence was wrongly excluded, or that the jury instructions describing the applicable legal standards were defective—or ask the trial judge to set aside the verdict. BNSF did the latter. Although Judge McCalla had conceded during an on-the-record colloquy at trial that the case was treading on new ground—"This is an area that the Sixth Circuit might end up writing something on," he mused[15]—he quickly denied BNSF's motion. White's transfer and suspension were "material" enough to support the verdict, he found, according to the "indices" that were "unique to [her] situation": The harsh realities of track labor made it, for all intents and purposes, a demotion, despite its paying the same wage as forklift work, while the thirty-seven-day suspension left White without income and, if not for her union's intervention, would have become a permanent discharge.[16]

McCalla couldn't have been more prescient; the Sixth Circuit did end up writing a great deal about the case. The first time was in the fall of 2002, after BNSF appealed McCalla's decision denying a new trial. By a vote of two to one, the court ruled that the evidence did not support the verdicts in her favor. "We fail to see how White suffered an adverse employment action by being directed to do a job duty for which Burlington Northern had hired her,"[17] it wrote. "Additionally, the district court's reasoning ignores the inescapable fact that Burlington Northern ultimately reversed White's suspension and reinstated her with full back pay and overtime."[18] When she learned that her trial victory had been nullified, White said, "I felt like I had been hit by a bomb."[19]

Donati then filed the appellate equivalent of a motion for a new trial: He asked all of the Sixth Circuit's judges to consider the case. Donati won his motion, and the case was argued before the full court in the summer of 2003. For that argument, BNSF had replaced its local legal team with a heavier hitter, the Dallas office of corporate firm Thompson & Knight.

Donati stayed put as White's counsel, but the case had attracted some attention in high places. The EEOC filed a friend of the court brief on White's behalf. The agency not only supported White; it also urged the court to dispense with the "materially adverse" requirement altogether and to adopt the more employee-friendly standard contained in the EEOC's Guidelines (which three other courts of appeals also had adopted). Under that standard, an employer violated Title VII if it took punitive action against the complaining employee that—if the worker had known to expect it in advance—would likely have deterred her from complaining at all.[20] The Guidelines contained an example. Suppose an employee lodged a complaint about her boss's decision to deny her a promotion. Within days, the boss then told the complaining employee not to bother coming to the weekly lunch that everyone else in the department attended. According to the EEOC, the boss's action likely was illegal retaliation: Because most employees would not want to be publicly shunned by their boss, they wouldn't risk it by complaining about the lost promotion—that is, the shunning would have been "reasonably likely to deter" the worker from complaining.[21] The theory was that there were many ways of punishing a worker besides firing her or cutting her pay, and Title VII should protect employees from those subtler forms of retaliation, too.

In April 2004, the Sixth Circuit's decision came down. The thirteen judges weren't able to agree on a single standard for "adverse action." Eight voted to stay with the "materially adverse" standard, while five voted for the more generous one advocated by the EEOC. But the one thing that all of them *could* agree on was that the prior panel's ruling should be reversed, and White's jury verdict should be reinstated. BNSF's decisions to remove her from the forklift and to suspend her for insubordination were illegal "adverse actions," whatever the definition.

Because BNSF had fought White's claims through three EEOC charges, a trial, a motion for a new trial, and two Sixth Circuit hearings, it came as no surprise to White that, after its loss, BNSF filed a petition for *certiorari* with the Supreme Court. ("I knew that they were going to appeal anything with my name," said Sheila White with a sigh. "They hated my name.")

On December 5, 2005, the answer came: *cert* granted.

——— ———

"IT MAY SOUND odd to say that we were not surprised that the Supreme Court agreed to hear this case, but that is how we felt," Don Donati later wrote.[22] He recognized that the fissure among the federal courts on the retaliation question was just the sort of classic "circuit split" that can prompt the Supreme Court to hear one of the thousands of petitions it receives each year. A patchwork of legal standards means confusion for employers, employees, and courts alike.

The split was a problem with a relatively recent origin. One cause had been the 1991 Civil Rights Act, which expanded Title VII to allow recovery of emotional distress damages and punitive damages, in addition to reimbursement for out-of-pocket losses, such as back pay and attorneys' fees. As courts had begun to grapple with claims like Sheila White's—that their employers' retaliation didn't have economic repercussions but had caused emotional harm—they had adopted conflicting standards for assessing them.

The Supreme Court itself also was responsible, if indirectly so, for the rise in retaliation claims. In a 1997 decision, it had ruled that Title VII's ban on retaliation protected not just current employees but former ones too. In that case, a former Shell Oil sales representative named Charles Robinson alleged that after he was downsized and filed a race discrimination charge with the EEOC, Shell interfered with his efforts to get a new job by bad-mouthing him to a prospective employer. The Court found that Title VII allowed Robinson's claim, even though he no longer worked for Shell when it allegedly spoke ill of him. Protecting former employees from retaliation, reasoned the Court, was essential to preserving Title VII's underlying purpose of remedying discrimination. If the price of complaining about a racially motivated firing was blackballing, undoubtedly many former employees wouldn't want to pay it. The fired employee wouldn't complain, and the employer would be free to keep discriminating.

The Court assured that the pool of retaliation plaintiffs only got deeper and wider when, in 1998, it issued opinions in two landmark sexual harassment cases. In those rulings, the justices finally answered the question on which they had punted in Mechelle Vinson's case a decade earlier: Is an employer liable for a supervisor's harassment even if it never knew about it?

The first case concerned Beth Ann Faragher, who had worked as a lifeguard at the beach in Boca Raton, Florida. In a case that *The Wall Street Journal* jovially described as having "shades of 'Baywatch' and 'Law and Order,'"[23] Faragher alleged that she had been subjected to constant harassment by her direct supervisors. The two men constantly touched her sexually, made crude appraisals of her body ("If you had tits I would do you in a minute"),[24] mimed sexual acts, and made vulgar propositions. One of them warned Faragher, "Date me or clean the toilets for a year."[25]

The second case was brought by Kim Ellerth. As a sales representative for textile giant Burlington Industries, Ellerth had endured a steady stream of lechery from her boss's boss. He gave her breasts lingering stares, touched her suggestively, greeted her phone calls with sexual innuendo ("How are those legs of yours, Kim?"), and regaled her with dirty jokes about dumb blondes.[26] On a business trip, the man pressured Ellerth to join him for drinks, then remarked on the size of her breasts, told her to "loosen up," and advised, "You know, Kim, I could make your life very hard or very easy at Burlington."

Despite arising out of vastly different workplaces, the cases were essentially the same. Each woman alleged she'd been harassed so relentlessly by a supervisor that she'd been forced to quit, but neither one had ever filed a formal complaint with her employer.

In dual opinions issued on the same day,[27] the Court laid out its new rules for holding companies liable under Title VII for a supervisor's harassment. If a harasser uses his authority to take some sort of tangible action against an employee, such as firing or demoting her, then the company is automatically liable. But if the harasser merely creates an abusive environment—as it did in Faragher's and Ellerth's cases (and in Mechelle Vinson's case as well)—then the employer can defeat a lawsuit by showing that it implemented preventive measures, such as a complaint procedure, and the complaining employee didn't use them.

The intention, said the Court, was to spur employees to report harassment so that employers could remedy it before it turned—literally—into a federal case. Because Boca Raton had no such preventive mechanisms, a lower court ruling in Faragher's favor was allowed to stand; Ellerth's case was sent back to the trial court for new consideration, given that Burlington Industries did have an antiharassment policy in place during the relevant time frame.

Even though most people have never heard of it, much of the working public likely has personally experienced the effects of the so-called *Faragher/Ellerth* defense. Nearly two decades after its creation, sexual harassment policies, "sensitivity training," and company complaint hotlines are as much a part of many Americans' work lives as e-mail; with such mechanisms, employers hope to insulate themselves from at least some varieties of sexual harassment lawsuits. In practice, of course, once companies adopted such measures, employees actually began using them to file harassment complaints. More complaints meant more opportunities to retaliate. So although Title VII's retaliation provision protects employees who allege any kind of discrimination—not just discrimination "because of sex"—the *Faragher* and *Ellerth* decisions amplified the provision's pertinence for women workers, who were the ones bringing the vast majority of sexual harassment complaints.[28]

In combination, all of these developments during the 1990s increased not just confusion among the courts about what constituted illegal retaliation but the sheer number of claims being filed: By the time the Supreme Court agreed to hear White's case, roughly a third of the 75,000 charges filed annually with the EEOC alleged retaliation.[29]

THE COURT HEARD oral argument in *Burlington Northern & Santa Fe Railway v. White* on a rainy April morning in 2006. Sheila White had traveled from Memphis to attend, along with her husband, Andrew Parrish. Nearly a decade had passed since she first interviewed for her job with BNSF; now she was disabled from the "wear and tear" of track laborer work and getting by on disability benefits. Still, White told a local reporter a few days before the argument, "It makes me feel good to know that someone out there is concerned about me and especially the decision and the law."[30] That stormy day, White savored the experience of walking up the Court's steps and through its marble columns—as a litigant, not a tourist. "That was a great experience for me," she marveled. "Many people don't get a chance to do that." To White's astonishment, as she found her way to her seat in the packed courtroom, people in the gallery began recognizing her. Some even asked for her autograph.

After more than a decade without any changes to the Court, the lineup had undergone a dramatic shift. Chief Justice John Roberts was just a little over six months into his tenure, having replaced Justice William Rehnquist, while Justice Samuel Alito had recently taken the seat of Sandra Day O'Connor. Justice O'Connor's retirement had left the Court with just one woman, Justice Ruth Bader Ginsburg. Between the Court's new gender composition and the addition of two conservatives—both of whose nominations had been opposed by broad coalitions of women's and civil rights groups—it was even harder than usual to predict how an employment discrimination case would fare.

Arguing the case for BNSF was Carter Phillips, a veteran litigator with Sidley Austin, one of the largest firms in the country. A former assistant to the solicitor general and law clerk to Chief Justice Warren Burger, Phillips was making his fiftieth appearance before the Court with *Burlington Northern*.

Don Donati would be arguing White's case. Although Donati was an experienced trial lawyer by Memphis standards, his practice had not taken him anywhere close to the national stage represented by a Supreme Court argument. Consequently, soon after the grant of *certiorari*, he had enlisted the assistance of Eric Schnapper, one of the nation's most prominent Supreme Court advocates. Schnapper, who had spent twenty-five years at the NAACP Legal Defense and Education Fund before becoming a law professor at the University of Washington, had twelve arguments and eighty briefs to his name, mainly in the employment law arena.[31] Schnapper assumed primary responsibility for drafting the arguments in the briefs while Donati prepared himself for a grilling by the nine justices.[32] He participated in two moot courts—one comprising counsel from some of the forty-odd women's rights and related groups that had submitted *amicus* briefs in White's favor and another through Georgetown Law School's esteemed Supreme Court Institute.[33]

From the outset of Carter Phillips's argument, his message to the justices was clear: Consider the "real-life" implications of your decision. In the second sentence of his opening argument, he reminded the Court that "the number of these claims has increased by more than 100 percent over the course of the last decade, more than 30 percent of the EEOC's docket is now made up of retaliation claims, and the cost of an average contested retaliation claim exceeds \$130,000 per case." The only way to avoid increasing the number of claims by "another 100 percent" was to adhere to the "materially adverse" standard.[34] Moreover, argued Phillips, the Court should find, as the Sixth Circuit did when it first considered Sheila White's case, that BNSF's actions toward her were not "material" enough to meet that test.[35]

The problem for Phillips was that most of the justices seemed to understand just how easy it is for an employer to make its employees' daily lives difficult. Justice Breyer was the first out of the gate. "Congress is worried that people won't complain," he said. "And there are millions ways of harassing people. . . . You do all kinds of things. You freeze them out. You insult them." A few minutes later he observed, "[T]here are many possible ways of seriously injuring a person . . . to stop them from complaining."[36] Justice Ginsburg posed the hypothetical of a supervisor who punishes a female employee who's lodged a complaint by changing her work hours, knowing that doing so will disrupt her child care schedule.[37] And Justice Scalia noted that being without a salary for just two weeks, let alone the thirty-seven days that White was, could be "for some people, a real hardship," even if the pay subsequently was restored.[38]

Whenever Phillips tried vainly to focus on the ultimate "economic effect" of an employer's alleged retaliation—such as pointing out that White's transfer from forklift to track labor had none—Justice Kennedy chimed in, "Well, it has an effect on your back."[39] Justice Souter spoke up. "[I]f your argument is sound, Mr. Phillips, then . . . any employer is well advised to define job categories by having one really nice job within the category and one really rotten job within the category," he said. So long as both jobs paid the same, Souter argued, punishing an employee by transferring her to the one really rotten job wouldn't be illegal. "I mean, that would seem to me . . . an end run around the whole concept of retaliation," he observed.[40]

Soon it was Don Donati's turn. With his earnest, almost folksy demeanor, Donati presented a stark contrast to Phillips (who was so self-assured that he corrected Justice Scalia when he mistakenly referred to the "severe or persuasive" test for harassment rather than "severe or pervasive"). Donati was prone to complimenting the justices for asking a "great question,"[41] or a "legitimate question,"[42] or for being "exactly correct."[43] And he struggled throughout his argument to articulate a clear demarcation between illegal retaliation and merely trivial slights, such as where—in a hypothetical posed by Justice Scalia—a supervisor accused of discrimination is "not as friendly" anymore to the subordinate who lodged the complaint. "[R]etaliation is only as varied as the human imagination," said Donati. "Yes, I worry about that," parried Scalia. "Juries can have wonderful imaginations."[44]

But Donati savvily focused the justices—just as Phillips had—on the "real-life" effects of the Court's ruling in the case. As Schnapper had tutored him in advance of the argument,[45] Donati explained how the rulings in *Faragher* and *Ellerth* were playing out in employees' everyday lives. Within his first moments at the lectern, he said, "You have a . . . woman here who did exactly what this Court asked her to do in *Ellerth*," he said. "She complained internally about sexual harassment. . . . Because she complained about sexual harassment, . . . she was removed from the forklift."[46] Twenty-five minutes later, he closed with a similar message. *Faragher* and *Ellerth* told employees to use their employers' complaint procedures rather than go straight to court with their sexual harassment claims; if you force employees to complain, then fail to protect them if and when their employer punishes them, they'll eventually stop speaking up altogether.[47]

White and Donati left the courthouse together and arrived at a bank of microphones at the base of the steps. It was still raining, recalled White, and "I was drenched, but never mind—this was my day. I felt good. I felt relieved. I felt vindicated."[48] She also felt optimistic. "I felt that they were leaning our way," she said. What she hadn't expected, though, was the wide variation in demeanor among the justices. As she summarized it, there had been "one talker and one napper" hearing her case that day. (The first was Justice Scalia. The second was Justice Thomas.)

"SHEILA! WE WON! We won!" Sheila White was still waking up as she struggled to take in the news from Don Donati, calling her from his office. "Didn't you hear me? You need to be jumping up hollering!" What White felt, though, was peaceful. "This was one time in my life that I felt joy and relief from all the tension that had built up," she later wrote.[49]

It was a unanimous victory. The jury verdict for White would stand. Better yet, the Court had rejected the "materially adverse" standard for future cases. Instead, it adopted the standard contained in the EEOC Guidelines. From now on, an employee seeking to prove retaliation need only show that the employer took adverse action that would have "dissuaded a reasonable worker from making or supporting a charge of discrimination."[50] And the Court, in an opinion authored by Justice Breyer, emphasized that that would vary depending on the particular workplace. "We phrase the standard in general terms because the significance of any given act of retaliation will often depend upon the particular circumstances. Context matters."

Here Breyer addressed some of the examples raised during oral argument. "A schedule change in an employee's work schedule may make little difference to many workers, but may matter enormously to a young mother with school age children," he wrote. Referencing the example in the Guidelines, he continued, "A supervisor's refusal to invite an employee to lunch is normally trivial, a nonactionable petty slight. But to retaliate by excluding an employee from a weekly training lunch that contributes significantly to the employee's professional advancement might well deter a reasonable employee from complaining about discrimination."

The Court rejected the idea that an employee didn't have a retaliation claim unless and until she was demoted, or fired, or otherwise tangibly harmed. It recognized, instead, that employers can, when they put their minds to it, exact virtually limitless forms of punishment.

IT TOOK SEVERAL months for White to absorb just how significant the Court's ruling was. Part of the problem was that, for her, the case wasn't actually over: Up next was a trial on the issue of punitive damages, which had been ordered by the Sixth Circuit but put on hold during the Supreme Court phase of the case. Before that could happen, BNSF approached Donati with a settlement offer. White didn't feel it fairly compensated her, but she knew the risk that a jury might see the facts differently and award her even less. Rather than take her chances, she decided to accept the offer and move on.

With time, she was able to appreciate what she'd accomplished. "I came to realize that this action would have far-reaching results that would overshadow my own difficulties," she later wrote. "I was thrilled that the Court's decision would touch so many people."[51]

White is often a featured speaker before groups of lawyers, unions, and other advocates around the country, a role she revels in. Nearly a decade after the ruling, audience members still tell her how far her case went in making employees feel a bit safer speaking up.

"This decision vindicated me," she said. "No one can take away this sense of accomplishment and feeling of satisfaction."[52]

ten

"everyone deserves a safe delivery"

Young v. United Parcel Service, Inc. (2015)

BY EIGHT O'CLOCK ON THE MORNING OF DECEMBER 3, 2014, the crowds had begun to gather in front of the Supreme Court. Under a pale, steely sky that matched the gray and white marble of the Court's famed façade, clusters of mostly female spectators huddled against the chill. They clutched signs—some of them handwritten in brightly colored markers, others mass-produced and bearing the names of various women's advocacy groups—that proclaimed "Stand with Pregnant Workers," "Protect People, *Not* Packages," and "Everyone Deserves a Safe Delivery."

The oral argument scheduled to begin two hours later would mark the first time in nearly a quarter century that the Supreme Court had considered the issue of on-the-job pregnancy discrimination. The last time had been in 1991, when the women of Johnson Controls had asked the Court to invalidate the company's "fetal protection policy" that kept women out of the best-paying jobs unless they could prove infertility. The Court's unanimous decision in women's favor had been hailed as another step toward equality, vesting women—not their employers—with responsibility for safely managing their reproductive lives.

But more than twenty years later, the Court was faced with a question that was something of a bookend to *Johnson Controls:* If safely managing a pregnancy meant that a woman wanted to temporarily avoid the hazards of her workplace, what rights did she have? And what were her employer's obligations?

To judge by the palpable emotion among the demonstrators on the Supreme Court steps that December morning and the ubiquitous press coverage in the preceding weeks, the case had galvanized collective frustration with the status quo—both for pregnant women and for mothers in this country. More than thirty-five years after the Pregnancy Discrimination Act became law and twenty years after the Family and Medical Leave Act was enacted, women were still losing income, if not their jobs, because of pregnancy. As one commentator wrote at the time, "[T]he simple—and celebrated—act of having a baby turns out to be a stunningly precarious economic and professional choice."[1]

The woman at the center of the maelstrom on the courthouse steps, an earnest, bubbly single mother named Peggy Young, was stunned to find herself there, surrounded by signs displaying the Twitter hashtag "#IStandWithPeggy." A "private, to-myself kind of person," Young had unwittingly launched her journey onto the national stage eight years earlier, while working as an "air driver" for shipping giant United Parcel Service. Each morning starting at 6:30, Young delivered packages that had arrived overnight by air at UPS's Landover, Maryland, facility, driving a route covering Annapolis and the surrounding area. After making those deliveries, she would punch out, and at 11:00 a.m., she'd begin working at her other job, delivering flowers for a company named Floral Express.

Beginning in the summer of 2005, Young and her husband began trying to have a baby by in vitro fertilization. The first attempt resulted in a pregnancy, but Young miscarried shortly thereafter. A second attempt failed too. But in July of 2006, while on a leave of absence, Young got pregnant. At the end of her first trimester, she contacted Carol Martin, UPS's occupational safety and health manager for her district, to discuss resuming her duties.

Young was perplexed when Martin instructed her to obtain a note from her medical provider outlining her "restrictions." Young hadn't been told she had any restrictions, and her pregnancy wasn't high risk (nor were two prior pregnancies she had carried to term). Her job wasn't particularly strenuous either; because air shipping is more expensive, by weight, than ground, the packages Young delivered were small and light, usually ten- by thirteen-inch envelopes that fit on the passenger seat next to her. Indeed, throughout her second full-term pregnancy, she'd regularly lifted and carried far heavier—namely, her three-year-old son—and had worked right up until the moment she went into labor.

But in an effort to be agreeable—"I didn't know any better," she said later—Young relayed Martin's request to her midwife. "I explained to her what I did for a living: I drove a minivan, I delivered small envelopes." Young recalled her midwife's puzzled response. "Why do you need a note? There's nothing wrong with you physically." So that Young could comply with UPS's directive, though, she proposed a compromise. "She said, 'I'll write you a note *recommending* you not lift over twenty [pounds].'"

Young rarely had to lift packages that heavy, much less the seventy pounds that her job description listed as the maximum weight that air drivers should be able to carry. In any event, because she shared territory with another driver, on those few occasions when a heavy package was in the day's shipment, Young's coworker didn't mind delivering it.

But health and safety manager Martin told Young that under UPS's policy, she could not continue to work at all with her lifting "restriction" in place. That policy, contained in UPS's collective bargaining agreement with Young's union, allowed for employees to be temporarily reassigned to "light duty" work or desk jobs—in just three circumstances—none of which applied to pregnancy: when a worker's impairment was due to an on-the-job injury; when it qualified him or her for a "reasonable accommodation" under the Americans with Disabilities Act; or if he or she became ineligible, under Department of Transportation regulations, to hold a commercial driver's license (which could result from any number of medical conditions but also if the employee had a conviction for driving under the influence).

Young begged to return to work, assuring Martin that she was willing to perform at full capacity without an accommodation, but Martin refused. Desperate, Young then approached the senior manager at the Landover facility, Myron Williams. She explained her situation and her eagerness to resume her job without limitation. According to Young, Williams told her "not to come back in the building until she was no longer pregnant because she was way too much of a liability." Another supervisor to whom she pleaded her case told her the same thing.

By the end of 2006, Young was out of options. Just fourteen weeks pregnant, she went out on an unpaid leave of absence for the rest of her pregnancy. Although UPS coded her in its personnel system as "disabled," she couldn't collect any disability benefits unless she got a new note from her midwife that would declare her unfit for *any* work. That simply wasn't true; in fact, Young continued to perform her duties with Floral Express without any modifications right up until her due date. In addition to losing between $400 and $500 a week in wages from UPS, she stopped accruing pension credit, and lost her health benefits. Although Young was lucky enough to get medical coverage through her husband's military insurance, it wasn't anywhere near the gold standard offered by UPS; she had to switch providers and deliver her baby at a hospital more than two hours from her home, instead of at the one fifteen miles away, where UPS insurance was accepted. Young delivered her daughter, Triniti, in late April 2007, and in late June, after being without her UPS paycheck for roughly six months, she went back to work. By then, she had a lawyer.

BORN IN SOUTH DAKOTA in 1971, Young is the youngest of five children. When she was a girl, her carpenter father and homemaker mother moved the family to the tiny east Texas farming community of Scurry, Texas—population: three hundred—so that Young's father could join one of her older brothers in his woodworking business.

By the age of fifteen, Young was working in a sandwich shop and had a paper route; by seventeen, she had dropped out of high school, married, and moved with her husband, an Army serviceman, to a base in Germany; at nineteen, she became pregnant. Although Young found it exciting to live abroad and enjoyed traveling around Europe in the first few years they were there, her pregnancy coincided with her husband's deployment to Iraq during the first Gulf War. Overwhelmed by the prospect of becoming a mother for the first time by herself, she moved back to Texas to be near her parents.

When her son Chase was three months old, Young's husband returned from the front lines. He was assigned first to North Carolina, then back to Germany; Young went with him and while overseas had a second child, a daughter they named Cassie. But when yet another reassignment came through for her husband—this time to Korea and without permission for his family to come along—Young returned to Texas with her children. The geographical distance took its toll, and the couple grew apart. They soon divorced.

Now a single mother of two, Young needed a job that paid well and had good benefits. She eventually found it at UPS, in 1999 taking a part-time position on the sunrise shift at Dallas–Fort Worth

Airport, where she drove a vehicle that moved large cargo canisters on and off airplanes. She also held down second job as a bartender at a go-kart track. It was there that she met her second husband, a recording engineer with the U.S. Marine Corps band, which was performing at the state fair in Dallas. After a whirlwind romance, the couple married and, in 2002, Young and her children joined him in the DC area. Luckily, she was able not only to keep her part-time job with UPS— which she considered a "great place" to work—but also to retain the seniority she'd accrued over the past three years. Soon Young and her husband decided to have a child of their own. They were overjoyed when they finally succeeded, after the heartbreak of two unsuccessful rounds of *in vitro* fertilization.

But as Young later testified, "What should have been a very happy pregnancy was instead one of the most stressful times of my life."[2] For the next six months, the couple scrimped to make do without her UPS salary. "I was very, very worried about our finances because we were getting behind financially," Young said at her deposition. "I experienced trouble sleeping at night. When I woke up, this was the thing on my mind. I was emotionally very fragile."[3] She also was incredulous that UPS had essentially engineered her removal from the job, first by forcing her to obtain a note identifying her pregnancy-related "restrictions" (which even her medical provider did not believe her to have) and then, when her provider made a "recommendation," refusing to accommodate it—despite making such accommodations for other employees with temporary impairments. "This was wrong. Flat out wrong," Young later said. "I wanted to work. I wanted to earn my benefits and I wanted to earn my wages. Like I always had." To be made to feel useless because she was pregnant was especially unnerving. "I believed I was being discriminated against because of my pregnancy, and I was beside myself over this," she testified. "I could not think straight. I felt sick to my stomach."[4]

Desperate to get at least temporary disability benefits while on her forced leave of absence, Young felt she had no choice but to seek legal help. She got the name of a law firm from a friend. Lawyers there told Young they were too busy to represent her but referred her to an Arlington solo practitioner, Sharon Gustafson. Young met with her soon after, in Gustafson's tiny office in a converted garage behind her house. Young was pregnant, and Gustafson was nursing her newborn daughter, Sigrid—her ninth child.

"I really wasn't in the mood to take on another pregnancy discrimination case," recalled Gustafson with a laugh. A tall, vivacious blond whose speech is still sprinkled with the telltale vowels of a native Michigander, Gustafson had started her law career at a large DC firm representing employers in discrimination cases. She had decided to switch sides after working on an especially ugly sexual harassment case, and for more than a decade, Gustafson had had her own practice, primarily representing employees. As a plaintiff's attorney, she explained, "you get to wear the white hat. You get to go after the bad guys who are breaking the law."

Young's situation was unlike any Gustafson had encountered. She had represented women with more straightforward pregnancy claims—woman discloses pregnancy, woman gets fired—but never a refusal to accommodate a physical limitation related to pregnancy. So while Gustafson went to work trying to negotiate with UPS to get Young covered by the company's temporary disability plan (an effort that ultimately was unsuccessful), she also began researching the question of whether it was legal for the company not to extend its light-duty policy to pregnant employees. What she found convinced her that while Young's case would be an uphill battle, the law was on her side.

IN A CULTURE like ours that fetishizes the "baby bump," it can be easy to forget that pregnancy is a major medical event. Joints loosen, muscles spasm, blood pressure spikes, legs swell. Even an uncomplicated pregnancy can cause nausea, migraines, urinary tract infections, carpal tunnel syndrome, back pain, shortness of breath, dizziness, and chronic fatigue, while more serious conditions include diabetes, deep vein thrombosis, placenta previa, and preeclampsia.

All of these conditions might necessitate some time off of work or, at the least, some modification of duties—be it a schedule change (to accommodate severe morning sickness), a work station closer to the restroom (to deal with nausea or dizziness at other times of day), a stool to sit on occasionally (if the job requires standing for long periods, such as a retail clerk or cashier), or a water bottle to carry (to stave off dehydration and urinary tract infections). And although Peggy Young's "restrictions" had more to do with UPS's assumptions about her pregnancy than her midwife's medical opinions, countless pregnant women work in jobs that *do* pose actual risk to pregnancy, because of the hazardous environmental conditions (fumes, toxins, excessive noise), physical activity required (stooping, climbing, lifting), or irregular hours (night work, overtime), and require some modification to facilitate a healthy pregnancy.

Coupled with these medical realities are some demographic ones. Close to 60 percent of all women now work.[5] Three-quarters of working women will be pregnant at least once during their working lives.[6] Most pregnant women stay on the job right up until their due dates; according to a U.S. Census Bureau study, the number of women working into their ninth month has more than doubled in the past forty years, with a whopping 87 percent who had their first baby between 2006 and 2008 working fulltime into their ninth month.[7] The fields that pose the most hazards to pregnancy are the ones dominated by women (especially women of color), such as nursing, housekeeping, retail, and service jobs, and the ones dominated by men, such as law enforcement, firefighting, and construction.[8]

Many employers, like UPS, have resisted making the job modifications pregnant women need to keep working safely. Some of these employers are household names—Wal-Mart,[9] Pier One,[10] and Old Navy[11]—and many more are small employers few have ever heard of.[12] A recent study by the National Partnership for Women & Families estimated that more than 250,000 women a year have their accommodation requests denied.[13] These women are left with the Hobson's choice of risking their pregnancies or having to leave their jobs. While Peggy Young was lucky enough to keep hers—allowed to take extended leave of absence, albeit unpaid, under the terms of her union contract—countless others are simply fired for absenteeism. For an expectant mother to lose a paycheck just as she's about to have another mouth to feed is a devastating outcome.

These realities have converged to cause an explosion of pregnancy discrimination charges filed with the EEOC and its state counterparts. Charges filed with those agencies increased by nearly 50 percent between 1997 and 2011,[14] and recent statistics confirm that women in low-wage and historically male-dominated jobs[15] are filing most of those claims.

Regardless of what kind of work a woman does, then, her pregnancy is likely to interfere at some point, to some extent. The questions are by how much, and what her employer is required (or allowed) to do about it.

The Pregnancy Discrimination Act has two clauses. The first makes it explicit that discrimination "because of sex" means discrimination "because of pregnancy."[16] The second clause mandates that employers treat pregnant women the same as anyone "similar in their ability or inability to work."[17] Under the PDA, if an employer has a policy that helps employees through times of temporary impairment—such as by paying them some portion of their salary or by imparting some other benefit, like holding their jobs open for them or allowing them to keep their health benefits while they aren't working—then the employer has to extend that benefit to pregnant workers.

ALTHOUGH THE PDA would seem to have been Peggy Young's ace in the hole—after all, UPS admitted that it offered modified work to three separate categories of other employees who couldn't perform all of their job duties—Sharon Gustafson discovered that most of the federal courts of appeals were not reading the statute that way. "[T]he more I got into reading how the courts have handled these things," she said, "I realized: oh, my word." Included in this mixed legal bag was the fact that impairments caused by pregnancy, even life-threatening ones, were not generally considered to be disabilities entitling a woman to an "accommodation" under the Americans with Disabilities Act; because they were temporary, they didn't qualify.

Most of the PDA failure-to-accommodate cases had arisen in the context of employers that, like UPS, offered light duty to employees with impairments caused by *on*-the-job injuries but not those that arose *off* the job, including pregnancy. (This trend arose because many state workers' compensation laws required employers to provide such accommodations as a way of minimizing benefits claims. Even absent a legal obligation to do so, many employers sought to minimize their worker's comp liability by providing modified duty.)

Three federal appeals courts had considered such cases and ruled in favor of the employers. They concluded that workers injured on the job weren't sufficiently "similar" to pregnant workers to trigger the PDA's mandate that they be treated "the same." Instead, they reasoned, pregnant workers were in fact "similar" only to workers whose illnesses or injuries occurred off the job and need only be treated "the same" as those workers—that is, by not getting any accommodation at all. But one appeals court, the Sixth Circuit, had better precedent; a decade earlier, it had decided a case in which an employer accommodated workers with on-the-job injuries and had ruled that the PDA required accommodating pregnant employees too. It found that what mattered was the similarity of a coworker's impairment to pregnancy-related limitations, not similarity in *how* the coworker became impaired.[18]

Gustafson was heartened by the Sixth Circuit's decision and the fact that the Fourth Circuit, the appellate court with jurisdiction over Maryland, hadn't yet ruled on the question of whether the PDA mandated accommodation of a pregnancy-related impairment. And she was convinced that UPS's provision of alternative work for employees who had lost their driver's license made Young's case stronger than any others she'd read about, even in the circuits with "bad" law. UPS's policy meant that whole swaths of workers with off-the-job injuries and illnesses were getting light-duty work and desk jobs, while pregnant employees still were excluded. Indeed, a representative from Young's union marveled to Gustafson that, in her experience, the only workers UPS ever had refused to accommodate were the pregnant ones. "[T]he statute says you have to be treated the same as others similar in their ability or inability to work, and she is the same as *hundreds* of these other people that UPS [was] accommodating all the time," Gustafson said.

Gustafson filed a lawsuit on Young's behalf in federal court in the fall of 2008. After an arduous year and a half of discovery, UPS filed a motion to dismiss the case, and nearly a year after that, the motion was granted—on Valentine's Day, 2011. There was no pregnancy discrimination, the judge found, because pregnant workers weren't singled out for harsh treatment. Instead, they were part of a larger group of employees "similar in their ability or inability to work" who also were denied accommodations—namely, those with off-the-job injuries.

Gustafson was dispirited and exhausted; her family urged her not to pursue the case any further. But she left the decision in Young's hands, and Young wanted to move forward. "I just didn't want them to get away with it," she recalled. "It was a little bit scary. I felt like this little person going against this giant company, but that's how [they] keep getting away with it, is because nobody is willing to take a stand."

Continuing the fight was a little easier because Young was no longer working at UPS. After nearly two more years on the job following Triniti's birth, she decided to quit in the summer of 2009. Her routes were getting longer, her delivery distances more difficult to complete in a single shift—issues arguably not blatant enough to make a formal retaliation charge worthwhile but tough enough to make daily life a grind. As the litigation dragged on for months and then passed the one-year mark, the stress of being someplace she felt unwanted became too much. She had left the flower delivery job, but had two waitressing jobs—one at Olive Garden and another at the restaurant on the Fort Myer Army Base—so Young felt financially secure enough to quit.

Gustafson left for a family trip to Europe. In an unorthodox move, she gave Young instructions about how to file the appeal with the Fourth Circuit Court of Appeals, believing that whether she followed through would be a litmus test of her commitment. While abroad, Gustafson checked her e-mail and saw a notice from the court: appeal docketed.

BEFORE SHE EVEN finished her oral argument at the Fourth Circuit, Sharon Gustafson knew she'd lost. Two of the three judges were plainly against her, and that was all UPS needed to win. One of them, J. Harvie Wilkinson III, was a Reagan appointee whom President George W. Bush had considered a few years earlier to replace Justice Sandra Day O'Connor, though he ultimately nominated John Roberts. (Wilkinson later gave details about his interview with Bush to a reporter for *The New York Times,* an indiscretion rumored to have "all but killed his chances" of being put forward again a few months later when Chief Justice Rehnquist died and Roberts became the nominee for that job.[19]) Judge Wilkinson took up a chunk of Gustafson's argument time to catalog the rulings from other appeals courts that supported UPS's position. Not a good sign.

As Gustafson watched her minutes count down, fretting about getting all of her arguments on the record, Judge Allyson Kay Duncan—a George W. Bush appointee—chimed in. She reminded Gustafson that she had been an attorney with the EEOC in the late 1970s after the PDA was enacted. (Duncan had briefly made an appearance, if only in name, in the drama surrounding Anita Hill's sexual harassment allegations against Clarence Thomas: In his autobiography, Thomas claimed that when he promoted Duncan over Hill to be his chief of staff, Hill "stormed out of my office . . . complaining I preferred light-complexioned women."[20] Hill, for her part, told the Senate that Duncan's appointment eased the daily stress of working for Thomas, because "most of my work was then funneled through her and I had contact with Clarence Thomas mostly in staff meetings."[21]) Judge Duncan opined that the law was never intended to guarantee the "special treatment" that Young was seeking. "I knew when I heard 'special treatment' I'd lost her vote," recalled Gustafson grimly. The third member of the panel, Judge Roger Gregory, a Clinton appointee and the first African American judge to serve on the Fourth Circuit, was fairly quiet during the argument. Gustafson couldn't read which way he was leaning.

She got her answer when the decision came down a few months later, on January 9, 2013. In an opinion penned by Judge Duncan and joined by both Judges Wilkinson and Gregory, the court sided with UPS. The court concluded that Young actually wasn't "similar" to any of the three categories of workers to whom UPS granted modified duties, so she wasn't entitled to be treated the "same" as they were. The logic supporting these conclusions was decidedly circular. She wasn't "similar" to employees accommodated under the Americans with Disabilities Act because she herself did not have an ADA-qualifying disability. She wasn't "similar" to employees disqualified from driving by the Department of Transportation because she was not "legally disabled from operating a vehicle." Finally, Young wasn't "similar" to employees injured on the job because, well, she wasn't injured on the job. And because all of these rationales were "pregnancy-blind"—in that they all were gender-neutral—then they didn't intentionally discriminate against pregnant workers.

Gustafson called Young to break the news. "I could tell it in her voice," Young remembered. "I answered the phone, and I knew." They had a dispiriting conversation about their few remaining options, which at that point were to seek a rehearing from the full Fourth Circuit or to ask the Supreme Court to hear the case—an option that seemed as likely as if they wished on a star. Young thanked Gustafson for her efforts and for making a good fight out of it.

But the next day, Gustafson called Young again. Young told her, "I don't know what's happened, but your voice sounds really different!" Something *had* happened. Help was on the way.

SAM BAGENSTOS was in his office at the University of Michigan Law School when he read about the Fourth Circuit's opinion in *Young v. UPS*. As a nationally recognized expert on the ADA, "I pretty much read every ADA case a court of appeals decides within a day or so of it deciding it," he said. (In Young's case, Gustafson had from the start included an ADA claim as an alternative cause of action, arguing that UPS had violated a provision in the law forbidding employers from discriminating against an employee who is not disabled but whom the employer *believes* to be disabled. That claim also had failed before the district court and the Fourth Circuit.) Because the ADA had been dramatically expanded since the time Young's case was filed, though, that aspect of the Fourth Circuit's ruling would have little impact on future cases. But the PDA piece of the decision caught Bagenstos's eye.

"I read the opinion and I read the statute," said Bagenstos, "and I said, this just seems totally wrong to me." A review of the other circuits' PDA accommodation cases convinced him that those courts also were getting it completely wrong too—so wrong, he thought, that the otherwise conservative Roberts Court might be receptive to making a correction. Bagenstos suspected that Young's case would be an especially appealing vehicle because of UPS's generous accommodation of workers who had lost their driving certifications. That group included not just workers who had impairments that arose off the job, as hers did, but who didn't even *have* an impairment, such as those with DUI convictions. The Fourth Circuit's refusal to find pregnant women entitled to the same benefits as able-bodied drunk drivers made its reading of the PDA seem even more wrongheaded.

Bagenstos was particularly well equipped to predict the Court's inclinations; in addition to teaching constitutional and civil rights litigation for more than a decade and having recently served as the number two official in the Justice Department's Civil Rights Division, he had clerked for Justice Ruth Bader Ginsburg and argued two prior cases before the Court. "I think [the Roberts Court] is a Court that's not very favorable to civil rights generally, so I'm usually the person who's calling people saying, don't, don't, don't, don't, *don't* file a *cert* petition," Bagenstos said. The danger is that the Court agrees to hear the case, then uses it as an occasion to affirm the bad opinion and make it applicable nationwide. But in Young's case, Bagenstos said, "It seemed to me, why not?"

Bagenstos called Gustafson. "He asked if I wanted help, and I was like, '*Do I want help?*'" She laughed. After litigating the case alone for nearly six years and suffering losses at every turn, the answer was clear. "Yes! That would be a *yes!*"

AT THE TIME Bagenstos and Gustafson filed Young's petition for *certiorari* in April 2013, similar cases had been on the radar of women's legal advocates for some time. A year earlier, the EEOC had held a widely publicized hearing about the most prevalent kinds of discrimination against pregnant workers, and numerous speakers cited employers' failure to accommodate their physical limitations—and courts' misreading of the PDA's protections on the issue—as pressing concerns. Representatives from the National Women's Law Center[22] and the National Partnership for Women and Families (formerly the Women's Legal Defense Fund),[23] as well as advocates for low-wage workers,[24] organized labor,[25] and academia[26] had all echoed the same theme. Just two months after Peggy Young's *cert* petition was filed, two prominent organizations issued a widely cited report drawn from interviews with "dozens of women across the country and across the economic spectrum" who reported "job loss, diminished income, or pregnancy complications or loss after their employers refused to make reasonable job adjustments while they were pregnant, even as they accommodated workers with limitations arising out of disability or injury."[27]

Yet many of these advocates tried to dissuade Bagenstos and Gustafson from seeking Supreme Court review. Although there was uniform agreement that the Fourth Circuit was dead wrong, it came down to tactics. The Roberts Court had issued several rulings unfriendly to employees generally and to women specifically—the 2007 decision tossing out Lilly Ledbetter's jury verdict against Goodyear Tire for pay discrimination was infamous[28]—and advocates were gun shy. They feared a wholesale evisceration of the PDA if the chief justice and Justices Scalia, Thomas, Kennedy, and Alito got their hands on it. They felt that it was safer to pursue pregnancy accommodation cases in circuits that hadn't yet decided the issue, to try to rack up some favorable precedent that could help turn the negative tide created by the Fourth Circuit and other appeals courts; a bad ruling by the Supreme Court would short-circuit any of those potential gains and make matters worse for a lot more women.

Advocates also were optimistic that pregnant women might start to win legal claims that their physical limitations qualified, under the newly broadened ADA, as "disabilities"—triggering that law's explicit right to "reasonable accommodation" instead. There also was hope of a legislative solution: The Pregnant Workers Fairness Act, which had been introduced for the first time in 2012, would establish an independent right of accommodation for pregnancy—that is, a right that doesn't tether the fates of pregnant workers to those who are "similar in their ability or inability to work." Many states and some cities already had some version of the act in place, enacted with broad bipartisan support.

But for Bagenstos (and Gustafson), the risk-taking calculus came out a different way. "The other cases might wash out, they might get bad case law. . . . There could be all kinds of reasons why the other strategy might mean five or six years of further litigation and nothing good coming of it," Bagenstos explained. "We had, I thought, a very good vehicle for going to the Supreme Court right now and a decent chance of prevailing." So it was that on April 8, 2013, he and Gustafson filed the petition for *certiorari*, supported by just one *amicus* brief—a passionate and scholarly one authored by two law professors on behalf of two women's legal organizations, a social justice organization, and numerous other professors.

A few months later, a bit of smoke came out of the conclave's chimney. The Court asked U.S. Solicitor General Donald Verrilli, to weigh in. Should the Court take the case or let the Fourth Circuit ruling stand? (Bagenstos considered this a positive sign; if the Court asks the solicitor general for its views, "that dramatically increases the chance that *cert* will be granted.") After several months of deliberation, though, in May 2014, Verrilli submitted his (rather circuitous) answer: The Fourth Circuit was dead wrong, as were all of the other federal appellate courts that had adopted similar reasoning. But despite these widespread misinterpretations of the PDA, Verrilli recommended against the Court taking the case.[29]

The reason was twofold: First, echoing many of the women's rights groups that had counseled against seeking Court review, he opined that pregnant women seeking accommodations could qualify as "disabled" under the amended ADA's new, more generous definition of what constitutes a disability under the ADA; and second, Verrilli noted that the EEOC was expected to soon issue a new "Guidance" on the issue of accommodating pregnancy that would "diminish" the need for a Court ruling.[30]

With the Court term coming to an end in a little over a month, Bagenstos and Gustafson began the vigil of watching its online calendar, which flags when a case is to be discussed by the justices. On June 3, there was a notice that Peggy Young's petition would be on the agenda at the June 19 meeting. But June 19 came and went without any news. On June 23, it was listed for review at the June 26 conference. But on June 26—still nothing. On June 30, the last day of the term, there was a notice the petition was being considered that day. On July 1—the day *after* the official end of the term—the news popped up: "Petition Granted."

The irony in the timing of the Court's decision wasn't lost on Bagenstos, who had been so bullish on a PDA case's chances before this Court: The day before, it had issued its opinion in *Burwell v. Hobby Lobby Stores, Inc.,*[31] ruling five to four that employers claiming a religious objection didn't have to provide contraceptive coverage to female employees under their health care plans—exposing, in the words of Justice Ruth Bader Ginsburg, a "blind spot" on women's issues.[32]

WHATEVER RESERVATIONS had existed among women's rights advocates about seeking Supreme Court review of Peggy Young's case were put in the rearview mirror after *cert* was granted. To Bagenstos's and Gustafson's gratification, there was aggressive mobilization around submitting a well-orchestrated chorus of friend of the court briefs in support of Young. There were a few key themes to hit: Illustrate the tangible economic cost of pregnancy discrimination to women and their families, explain the medical realities that cause women to need modification of job duties, and show the Court that there was broad consensus in favor of reading the PDA to require such accommodations.

The ACLU Women's Rights Project and A Better Balance, among others, submitted briefs on the first topic, emphasizing women's growing role as heads of households and sole caregivers for children.[33] A coalition of groups representing women of color, led by the Black Women's Health Imperative, also weighed in to emphasize that population's growing role as family breadwinners and their disproportionate presence in low-wage, physically demanding jobs.[34] To address the second theme, the National Partnership for Women and Families amassed groups of doctors, other medical providers, and groups focused on maternal and child health.[35] And in the third category, *amici* included unions,[36] the business-friendly Women's Chamber of Commerce,[37] members of Congress who had been involved in enacting the PDA,[38] and a bipartisan group of state and local lawmakers.[39]

Also in this third category was a coalition of twenty-three antiabortion organizations, which submitted a brief contending, accurately, that without on-the-job accommodation, some desperate women will have abortions so that they can keep their jobs.[40] Although social conservatives can show a more pro-business bent, that's not always the case when women's family and work responsibilities collide; indeed, women's advocacy community and "pro-life" organizations had come together to help enact the PDA in the late 1970s and the FMLA in the late 1980s and early 1990s. *Young v. UPS* offered a chance to, as Bagenstos put it, "get the team back together." Bagenstos and Gustafson were themselves emblematic of this "Care Caucus," as one commentator termed it,[41] with Bagenstos, the former Ginsburg law clerk and Obama administration official, allied with Gustafson, who was both deeply religious and an anti-abortion activist. Indeed, it was her connections among abortion opponents that helped yield such an impressive roster of *amicus* brief signatories. With these voices, Bagenstos hoped to reach the more conservative members of the Court—the chief justice and Justices Scalia, Thomas, Kennedy, and Alito.

Young also had the Obama administration on her side. Despite his prior recommendation against granting *certiorari,* Solicitor General Donald Verrilli joined a brief in support of Young, along with officials from the Justice Department and the EEOC.[42] (As predicted by Verrilli, the EEOC had recently issued its new formal Guidance interpreting the PDA[43] and had specifically disapproved the Fourth Circuit's decision in Young's case.) The government had to contend with one sticky wicket which it addressed in a footnote: The U.S. Postal Service itself refused to grant modified duty to its own employees, extending such benefits only to workers injured on the job. As to this apparent double standard, the government could only assure the Court that the postal service was "considering its options."[44]

Throughout the summer and fall of 2014, in addition to amassing friends of the court and drafting briefs outlining Young's case against UPS, Bagenstos set about preparing for the oral argument, scheduled for December 3. He followed a grueling schedule of moot courts. There were three: one at the University of Michigan (mainly his faculty colleagues, drawn from across the ideological spectrum), one at Georgetown's Supreme Court Institute (a mix of scholars and practitioners), and one at consumer rights group Public Citizen (litigators from a variety of specialties).

Young watched these fevered preparations from the sidelines, awed by the press coverage that the case was receiving and the outpouring of public support. There was one bittersweet note, though: A few months before the argument, when UPS filed its opposition brief in October 2014, it disclosed that it had changed its accommodation policy to include pregnancy as of January 1, 2015. UPS claimed it made the change not because the PDA required it but simply to make the company's life easier as it became subject to a growing patchwork of new state and local pregnancy accommodation laws. (At the time of the brief, nine states had such laws on the books.) If the company had intended some sort of image boost from the policy revision, it had miscalculated; most observers wrote off the change of heart as an eleventh-hour public relations stunt that only made its refusal to accommodate Young seem shoddier.

Young was gratified that her lawsuit might have helped make things better for thousands of women at UPS in the future, but, of course, the policy change came far too late to help her. A few months earlier, her daughter had had her seventh birthday.

"THAT'S PEGGY YOUNG! She's here!" Young recalled hearing the whispers as she walked through the hallways of the Supreme Court. Young had some protection from the stares, with Sharon Gustafson by her side, along with three of Gustafson's daughters, but she was still unnerved by the attention. "I'm nobody!" she said with a laugh. "It was just so real that actually, maybe this will make a difference for women, you know?" As for Bagenstos, although it was his third time before the Court, "I had never been so nervous before," he admitted later. "This was a case that had drawn so much public attention that I really felt acutely, if I screw this up, everybody's going to know!"

At the argument, Bagenstos went first. He had barely gotten past his opening sentences—"If Peggy Young had sought an accommodation for a twenty-pound lifting restriction that resulted from any number of conditions, whether acquired on or off the job, . . . UPS would have granted that accommodation. But because Peggy Young's twenty-pound lifting restriction resulted from her pregnancy and not from one of those conditions, UPS rejected her request."[45]—before Justice Kennedy grumpily interjected. "Well, you make it sound as if the only condition that was not accommodated was a lifting restriction because of pregnancy, and . . . I did not understand that to be the case. . . . It seems to me that you started out by really giving a misimpression." Bagenstos gently disagreed, noting: "UPS has not been able to point to a single driver who has a lifting restriction similar to my client, Peggy Young's, who didn't get accommodated who was not pregnant."[46] Kennedy didn't respond. One vote gone, Bagenstos thought.

The remainder of Bagenstos's time was consumed with parsing the question he had predicted would be most salient to the justices, the one that had consumed much of the discussion at all three of his moot court sessions: Where there are *two* groups of non-pregnant employees who are "similar in their ability or inability to work" to pregnant employees—and one group gets accommodation and the other group doesn't—which group of workers is the yardstick, for PDA purposes? Whom must pregnant workers be treated the "same" as—the group that gets the good deal or the group that gets the bad deal? Where was the dividing line that makes pregnant workers more "similar" to the favored group than to the disfavored group (or vice versa)?

As always, the justices posed hypotheticals to test the boundaries of the principles at stake. Suppose an employer gave employees with the most seniority the perk of getting driven to work if they were unable to drive themselves, asked Justice Scalia. Did the company have to drive pregnant employees too? No, answered Bagenstos, unless the pregnant employee qualified for the program based on her own seniority.[47] Justice Breyer was next: What if an employer gave employees in a particular job category a cash benefit of $1,000 per week if they were injured on the job? Did it have to pay it to pregnant women too? No, said Bagenstos, where an employer makes an "idiosyncratic" decision vis-à-vis a small group of employees, that wouldn't trigger the requirement to treat pregnant women the same. A few minutes later, Justice Alito jumped in. How about if an employer offers accommodations to employees who only *occasionally* have to lift, and they have lots of coworkers around to help them, but it doesn't do the same for employees who do heavy lifting most of the time, and primarily work alone? Must pregnant workers be given accommodation, regardless of what kind of job they hold? No, answered Bagenstos. If a pregnant worker's main duty is to lift all the time by herself, she is not "similar" to employees who almost never have to lift and have lots of colleagues to help them on the few occasions when they do.[48]

Bagenstos returned time and again to his main theme: The UPS policy violated the PDA because it accommodated so many non-pregnant employees in a whole range of job categories while still excluding pregnant women. It wasn't just a few workers with the most seniority, or just those with a particular job title, or just those whose jobs were the most physical; in his words (at various times during the argument), it was "very broad classes" of workers, "its employees generally," "many of its employees," "such large classes of employees," "three very large classes."[49] What did the second clause of the PDA even mean, asked Bagenstos, if not to be sure that pregnant employees were not treated *worse* than such large segments of a company's workforce?

"Congress was doing something with the second clause," he argued. And what it was doing, specifically, was roundly rejecting the Court's ruling in the *General Electric Co. v. Gilbert* decision, which had upheld precisely the kind of distinction UPS was arguing for here, and had prompted passage of the PDA.[50] Just as GE had decided to give disability benefits to workers with a whole host of conditions that just happened to exclude pregnancy, Bagenstos explained, UPS's decision to grant accommodations to three categories of impairments just happened to carve out pregnancy for worse treatment.[51]

As Bagenstos sat down, he couldn't tell where he stood with the centrist to conservative parts of the bench, his target audience. Justice Breyer had been the most active questioner, and he seemed favorably inclined toward Young—just unsure about where to draw the line for future cases. After Justice Kennedy's testy start, he'd remained silent. Chief Justice Roberts hadn't asked anything. Justice Alito had asked a few questions but not seemed overtly hostile. Justice Scalia, though, appeared to be a "no" vote, having repeatedly characterized Young as seeking "most favored nation" status for pregnancy—that is, favored over all of the other off-the-job medical conditions to which UPS denied accommodation.[52] The phrase came straight out of UPS's brief. Justice Thomas, predictably, hadn't said anything. (He had, at one point, summoned a clerk to bring him what appeared to be a dictionary.)

When it was UPS's turn, Caitlin Halligan rose to speak. An experienced appellate litigator with the white-shoe firm of Gibson Dunn, Halligan was a former solicitor general for the State of New York and had clerked for Justice Breyer. She also had been put forward by President Obama for a seat on the D.C. Circuit Court of Appeals, which has been described as the "most prestigious and important" of the federal appeals courts;[53] after prolonged inaction on the nomination, including a filibuster by Republican senators, Obama had withdrawn Halligan's name at her request. The *Young* case marked her sixth Supreme Court argument.

Halligan's time at the lectern was dominated by questions from Justices Kagan and Ginsburg. As Adam Liptak of *The New York Times* later noted, each asked as many questions as all of the other justices combined during the rest of the session.[54] Halligan had just gotten out a few sentences before Kagan began. "So, your reading of the statute basically makes everything [in the second clause of the

PDA] completely superfluous." She then added dryly, "And I think you would agree with that, wouldn't you?"[55] Halligan did not agree. The second clause defined the appropriate employees to whom pregnant workers should be compared, and, in this case, those were workers with off-the-job injuries or illnesses. And Halligan picked up on Scalia's "most favored nation" theme: Young's position meant that if a woman could point to even just one non-pregnant worker who got an accommodation, all pregnant women were entitled to that benefit.[56] But, she protested, that's not what the PDA intended; the statute doesn't say pregnant women must be treated "the same as *any* other person." Justice Ginsburg jumped in. "Well, [your position] is least favored nation, right?" she asked. "Mr. Bagenstos has told us that there is not in this record a single instance of anyone who needed a lifting dispensation who didn't get it except for pregnant people." Halligan demurred, stating there were workers with off-the-job injuries who didn't get the accommodations they wanted.[57]

What the PDA forbade—and what UPS did not do—argued Halligan, was to "single out pregnancy for adverse treatment." To ask for any more was to ask for a different statute, which is precisely what Young and her advocates should do, Halligan explained. Alluding to the pending federal Pregnant Workers Fairness Act and the enactment of state and local laws providing more generous accommodations to pregnant women, she noted that "this is an area where the democratic process is working as it should."

"Well, Ms. Halligan, for the democratic process to work as it should, the PDA has to be given a fair reading," Justice Kagan responded tartly. "And what we know about the PDA is that it was supposed to be about removing stereotypes of pregnant workers as marginal workers. It was supposed to be about ensuring that they wouldn't be unfairly excluded from the workplace. And what you are saying is that there's a policy that accommodates some workers but puts all pregnant women on one side of the line."[58] Before Halligan could say much, Justice Ginsburg had a few more questions that paralleled the questioning Bagenstos had received—so as long as *any* non-pregnant employee gets treated as poorly as pregnant women do, then there's no discrimination?—and then, Halligan's time was up.

Bagenstos stood for a brief rebuttal. He made the most of his time, using Kagan's and Ginsburg's questions to Halligan as the roadmap for his final points. Yes, Justice Ginsburg, the evidence in the case was that the only workers not accommodated by UPS were the pregnant ones.[59] Yes, Justice Kagan, your assessment of UPS's flawed interpretation of the PDA's second clause is correct. Yes, Justice Ginsburg, UPS's reading of the law would give pregnancy "least favored nation" status, and yes, Justice Kagan, "the purpose of this statute was to say to employers . . . you have to treat pregnant workers as just as valued employees as anybody else."[60] And then, the chief justice said the words that close every oral argument: "The case is submitted."

Outside on the steps of the Court, throngs of supporters were waiting for Young, chanting "We stand with Peggy!" Someone handed her a bouquet of pink, purple, and red flowers. Grassroots organization MomsRising presented her with a bound volume of fan mail and thousands of signatures gathered from people around the country. A man took her aside to confide that his wife also had been forced off the job because she couldn't get light duty. Young had been prepared for lots of reporters, but not the supporters and activists. Overwhelmed, wrapped in a beige coat with a furry collar and cuffs, she stepped to a bank of microphones. A small gold cross was visible on a chain around her neck. "I just want all the women out there to know that you have a voice and you need to use it," she said. "We want to start our families, we should be able to start our families and continue to work at the same time."[61]

Then she and Gustafson headed to Gustafson's husband's office for lunch, and later to MSNBC's studios for an interview with reporter Andrea Mitchell. Bagenstos joined his family—his wife and fifteen-year-old twins—at a nearby restaurant to celebrate before heading to the airport for the trip home to Ann Arbor. None of them felt they could tell which way the Court would rule, but that was itself a good sign.

ON THE MORNING of March 25, 2015, Gustafson called Young. The Court had reversed the Fourth Circuit's decision by a vote of six to three. Even Chief Justice Roberts and Justice Alito had joined the majority (with Alito submitting a separate concurring opinion); only Scalia, Thomas, and Kennedy had dissented. When Gustafson told her the news, Young cried. "I was crying because it was joy," she recalled. "Because, you know, this is big for everybody."

"Viewing the record in the light most favorable to Young, there is a genuine dispute as to whether UPS provided more favorable treatment to at least some employees whose situation cannot reasonably be distinguished from Young's," wrote Justice Breyer, on behalf of the majority. "[W]hy, when the employer accommodated so many, could it not accommodate pregnant women, as well?"[62] Because the Fourth Circuit hadn't considered that question, the case would be sent back for a second look.

As for what test the Fourth Circuit—and all future courts—should use in deciding where the line was between legal and illegal, the Court came close to delivering a total victory to Young but didn't quite. Justice Breyer explained that the Court needed to take an approach that would allow employers to *sometimes* grant certain workers with job modifications without opening the floodgates to accommodation claims by all pregnant workers. "We agree with UPS to this extent: We doubt that Congress intended to grant pregnant workers most-favored-nation status."[63] However, the Court refused to adopt UPS's argument—that because it used neutral criteria to decide who got accommodations, then there was no pregnancy discrimination. That was the same reasoning that led to the Court's approval of GE's disability plan, and Congress had rejected that reasoning by passing the PDA.

Going forward, said Breyer, the Court would apply to PDA failure-to-accommodate cases the same framework used in other Title VII cases where there wasn't a "smoking gun" showing bias. That analysis, named the *McDonnell Douglas* framework after the 1973 case in which it first arose, would require pregnant employees to show that "many" workers were treated better than they were and that the employer's reason for that differential treatment was in fact a "pretext" for discrimination. And the way a pregnant worker would prove pretext would be to show that the employer's policies "impose a significant burden on pregnant workers" without good reason. That reason, noted Breyer, "cannot consist simply of a claim that it is more expensive or less convenient to add pregnant women to the category of those ('similar in their ability or inability to work') whom the employer accommodates."[64]

Justice Scalia authored the dissent, and did not disappoint. "Faced with two conceivable readings of the Pregnancy Discrimination Act, the Court chooses neither," he wrote. "It crafts instead a new law that is splendidly unconnected with the text and even the legislative history of the Act."[65] With his trademark sarcasm in rare form—"It takes only a few waves of the Supreme Wand to produce the desired result. Poof!"; "The fun does not stop there."; "But (believe it or not) it gets worse."—Scalia wrote off the majority's decision as a "policy-driven compromise between possible readings of the law, like a congressional conference committee reconciling House and Senate versions of a bill."[66]

Perhaps wishing to set himself apart from Scalia's disdainful tone, Kennedy wrote a separate, brief dissent. It appeared that the "Care Caucus" had reached at least one of the conservative justices after all. "There must be little doubt that women who are in the work force—by choice, by financial necessity, or both—confront a serious disadvantage after becoming pregnant," he conceded.[67] He then went on to cite with approval two *amicus* briefs submitted in support of Young, one by the U.S. Women's Chamber of Commerce and the other by a coalition of law professors and civil rights groups.[68] Kennedy closed by pointing to the state laws that had been enacted specifically to accommodate pregnancy-related conditions, regardless of the protections afforded other employees. "These Acts honor and safeguard the important contributions women make to both the workplace and the American family."

A FEW WEEKS after the Court decision, Young sat in Gustafson's cozy living room at her home just outside Washington, DC, reflecting on more than seven years of litigation and the emotional high of its culmination. Her daughter Triniti busied herself serving tea and snacks using Gustafson's flowered china, excitedly reporting an impending trip to the Air and Space Museum.

Young still works two part-time jobs, one at Olive Garden and the other at a government contractor, where she helps manage office equipment inventory for various federal agencies. She and Gustafson were waiting to see what happened in the case; although technically the next step was for the Fourth Circuit to review the case again and issue a new decision, the parties could also decide to call it a day and settle. (A few months later, in October 2015, they did. The terms of agreement were confidential.[69])

Though she was slowly starting to appreciate the enormity of the case's significance—"I do realize it is big, but I try not to make it out that big"—it was for her daughters, she said, that she was most gratified by the case's outcome. "I don't want them to have to experience this kind of degradation of women, or motherhood," she said. "It shouldn't be like that."

epilogue

THE LEGAL AND CULTURAL CHANGE EFFECTED BY TI-
tle VII has been nothing short of revolutionary. The right to remain
employed during pregnancy, the right to be a working mother, the
right to hold a job historically deemed for "men only," the right to
be assessed on one's own merit rather than group traits, the right to
be free from the indignity of sexual harassment, the right to look and
act like *oneself*, whether that's traditionally "feminine" or something
else—all of these advances and more are owed to Title VII, and to
the cases profiled here. It's not an overstatement to say that the law,
in transforming what it means to be a woman who works, also transformed what it means simply to be a woman.

———————————

SO HOW DO the landmark cases profiled here continue to affect the
law today? How does employment discrimination still hold women
back? And what can the law do about it?

This book began with the story of Ida Phillips, who fought to hold
a job as the mother of a preschooler, and it makes sense to begin with
her here, too. Motherhood still remains one of the most impenetrable
barriers to women's equality. It propels them out of the workforce,[1]
inhibits their return to it,[2] and diminishes their pay and opportunities
while on the job.[3] (A recent headline from the satirical website *The
Onion* was so spot-on it hardly even qualified as a joke: "Company
Flat Out Asks Female Candidate How Much Mileage They Can Get
Out of Her Before She Has a Baby."[4])

In 1966, when Phillips applied to Martin Marietta, only about
25 percent of mothers with children under six were in the workforce.

Today, that number has more than doubled to nearly 65 percent.[5] And in 40 percent of households with children of any age, the mother is the sole or primary breadwinner.[6] But mothers' increased responsibility for families' economic well being hasn't translated into greater support for them at work. Much of this comes down to failures of policy, not antidiscrimination law. Those failures include the United States' shameful lack of job-protected paid leave (for both parents),[7] the absence of universal, affordable child care,[8] the culture of "overwork" that expects all-hours devotion to one's job[9]—or, in the case of low-wage workers, the need to work two jobs or pivot their delicately constructed, Jenga-esque child care regime on a dime due to last-minute shift assignments and cancellations, a practice known as "just-in-time" scheduling.[10]

Blatant bias against mothers, though, is still a big part of the problem. Legal scholars, aided by social scientists, have documented a "maternal wall" obstructing working mothers' paths, long before they bump up against the famed "glass ceiling."[11] Joan Williams, the scholar who coined the term in 2003, described the constellation of stereotypes that the maternal wall comprises:

> When a childless woman is not in the office, she is presumed to be on business. An absent mother is often thought to be grappling with child care. Managers and coworkers may mentally cloak pregnant women and new mothers in a haze of femininity, assuming they will be empathetic, emotional, gentle, nonaggressive—that is, not very good at business. If these women shine through the haze and remain tough, cool, emphatic, and committed to their jobs, colleagues may indict them for being insufficiently maternal.[12]

So what's the legal solution? The EEOC has recognized maternal wall bias as "caregiver discrimination" (also known as "family responsibilities discrimination") that is actionable sex discrimination under Title VII. In 2007, the agency issued a formal Guidance on the issue,[13] and private litigation has seen a concurrent explosion in such cases. The Center for WorkLife Law, founded by Williams, documented an almost 400 percent increase in such lawsuits between 1999 and 2008, and such cases have a much higher success rate than other discrimination cases.[14] One reason is that, while employers might have learned not to say, "We don't want a mother in this sales position," they are not nearly so discreet about voicing supposedly benevolent sentiments, such as, "We figured you wouldn't be interested in traveling so much anymore, with the new little one at home." As *Price Waterhouse* confirmed, such stereotypes—even if intended to be helpful—are just as discriminatory "because of sex" as an outright ban on mothers.

Social science has further documented that working fathers face penalties when they step out of their approved "manly" role by caring too openly about parenthood.[15] As Joan Williams told one reporter, "I've talked to people called wusses for asking for part time or taking leave."[16] Courts have recognized that such stereotyping discriminates as much "because of sex" as maternal wall bias does. CNN reporter Joshua Levs made headlines when he sued parent company Time Warner for extending a paltry two weeks' paid paternity leave to biological fathers while offering up to ten weeks to biological mothers and to all adoptive parents. The company later agreed to change its policy to provide up to six weeks for all new parents, with additional time off for women recovering from childbirth.[17] In one highly publicized lawsuit, a male Boston lawyer sued his firm for firing him shortly after he returned from FMLA leave spent caring for his newborn and mentally ill wife; he blamed a "macho" firm culture that devalued male caregivers.[18] The case settled before trial, but the problem won't be going away anytime soon. Sports radio host Mike Francesa gave a vivid illustration of the ridicule awaiting male caregivers when he lit into New York Met Daniel Murphy in the spring of 2014, after Murphy announced he was taking off the first two games of the season to be with his newborn son. Boasting that he never took any time off for his own kids' births and calling paternity leave a "gimmick" and a "scam,"[19] Francesa made fun of Murphy for twenty minutes. "What are you gonna do," Francesa said, addressing Murphy *in absentia*. "I mean, you gonna sit there and look at your wife in a hospital bed for two days?"[20]

LIKE BIAS against mothers, pregnancy discrimination remains one of the most pernicious barriers to working women's equality. Between 1997 and 2011, the number of charges filed with the EEOC and related agencies increased by nearly 50 percent, though that figure has decreased a bit in the last few years.[21] Illegal conduct that is head-scratchingly blatant still persists—the "no pregnancy in the workplace" policy recently implemented by Houston's United Bible Fellowship Ministries, for instance, prompting an EEOC lawsuit that later settled[22]; or Autozone's demoting and cutting the pay of a female manager whose pregnancy prompted her supervisor to comment, "Congratulations . . . I guess," and "I feel sorry for you." A jury later awarded the manager $185 million in back pay and damages for the company's three-year campaign to get rid of her.[23]

Women of color and those working in low-wage jobs in the retail, service, and health care sectors are especially vulnerable to such bias.[24] The U.S. Census recently reported that between 2006 and 2008, Latina first-time mothers were fired when they became pregnant at nearly 200 percent the rate of whites, and African American first-time mothers, at almost 150 percent.[25] The Center for WorkLife Law has documented a broad range of explicitly discriminatory conduct faced by low-wage workers upon announcing their pregnancies, ranging from immediate termination to chidings that they should abort their pregnancies.[26] Of course, harassment related to pregnancy isn't just limited to women surviving on the lowest rungs: A former executive with the New York Mets recently sued the franchise, claiming its Chief Operating Officer repeatedly humiliated her for being pregnant and unmarried (and then fired her in retaliation for complaining about it).[27]

Thankfully, the explicit, overbroad fetal protection policies like the one at issue in *Johnson Controls* are a thing of the past. The paternalism that motivated those policies still rears its head, though, particularly for women working in low-wage and physically strenuous jobs dominated by men.[28] A few years ago I had a client, a law enforcement officer, whose employer had a policy of deeming all pregnant women, no matter their job duties or stage of pregnancy, "at risk of abdominal injury" and immediately removing them from their duties. The employer eventually agreed to change its policy and the case settled.[29]

While it's largely uncontroversial to deem these varieties of pregnancy discrimination unlawful, the trickier realm is the one just navigated by the Supreme Court in *Young v. UPS*—namely, how an employer must respond to a pregnant worker who actually *does* need to modify her job duties in order to have a healthy pregnancy. It remains to be seen how lower courts will apply the Supreme Court's directives. Although the PDA requires that an employer treat pregnant women the same as employees "similar in their ability or inability to work," *Young* held that that duty is triggered only if "many" other workers are accommodated, and the failure to accommodate pregnancy poses a "significant burden." As with Title VII's minimalist "because of sex" language, it will take future court rulings about the lived experiences of pregnant working women to give meaning to those terms.

At the same time that they will be litigating such cases in the post-*Young* world, women's advocates also are seeking a more direct fix: amending the PDA entirely. The Pregnant Workers Fairness Act would require "reasonable accommodation" of pregnancy, regardless of how an employer treats other workers with similarly limiting conditions. Ironically, some of the PWFA's most vocal supporters include organizations that opposed California's pregnancy-leave law in *Cal Fed*. In July 2015, 148 organizations—including "equal treatment" stalwarts like the ACLU WRP, the National Women's Law Center, NOW, Legal Momentum (formerly NOW Legal Defense and Education Fund), and the National Partnership for Women and Families (formerly the Women's Legal Defense Fund)—sent a letter to Congress urging passage of the law. The reason for the change of heart, from opposing to supporting a pregnancy-only benefit? In contrast to the late 1970s and early 1980s when *Cal Fed* was being litigated, federal law now protects disabled workers on a gender-neutral basis; the Americans with Disabilities Act, enacted in 1991, requires "reasonable accommodations" including job modifications and job-protected leave. With pregnant women struggling to be found "similar" to those workers to win accommodation under the PDA, they're now the ones left unprotected.[30] In this climate, the movement to protect pregnant women's jobs is no longer seen as stigmatizing "special treatment." It's become the new "equal treatment."

Unless and until the PWFA is enacted, and while the courts figure out how to apply *Young v. UPS*, the states have started filling the gaps—a development that Lillian Garland's 1982 visit to the California Department of Fair Employment and Housing made possible. As of late 2015, fifteen states and four cities have enacted laws requiring employers to provide reasonable accommodations like the one requested by Peggy Young. Some of these also protect nursing mothers who want to pump milk at work—a need that, incredibly, many courts have ruled doesn't qualify under the PDA as a "medical condition" that is "related to" pregnancy and childbirth.[31] In this way, state and local governments have built some *Cal Fed*–style high "ceilings" for pregnant women, above the federal law's unstable "floor."

———

ALTHOUGH THE BIASES against assertive women that were on display in *Price Waterhouse* remain maddeningly entrenched, at least no one appears to be denying their existence anymore. Working women's double bind—assert yourself and get labeled a ballbuster, soften your tone and get dismissed as a pushover—was propelled out of business school white papers[32] and into the mainstream media in 2013, when Facebook Chief Operating Officer Sheryl Sandberg exhorted women to "lean in" to their careers.[33]

As a strategy for effecting tangible change, "leaning in" has gotten mixed reviews.[34] For one thing, many point to structural inequalities on the job—posed not just by gender but also race and class—that make it seem downright craven to suggest that the gender gap persists because women aren't trying hard enough; indeed, millions are leaning in so far they're about to fall over.[35]

Critics also say the real world penalties incurred by being assertive also are just too high for many women to risk the social experiment. An especially brutal cautionary tale was the widely publicized (and ultimately unsuccessful) 2015 discrimination lawsuit by Silicon Valley venture capitalist Ellen Pao, who was depicted at trial as having earned poor reviews due to her "sharp elbows" and who had been fired—she claimed—in retaliation for objecting to sexual harassment at the firm.[36] Another episode that had the Internet buzzing in the spring of 2014 was a blog post by a junior academic detailing how a job offer that she'd had in hand was withdrawn when she asked for a higher salary; the university told her it doubted her ability to "fit in."[37]

As Pao's loss shows, translating these attitudinal realities into evidence of discriminatory intent in a lawsuit is no easy feat. Indeed, decisionmakers may not even be conscious that they hold such biases at all.[38] (Research shows that employers can help root them out before they lead to litigation by, for instance, forcing supervisors to explain negative assessments of women's interpersonal skills.[39]) But at the very least, spokeswomen like Sandberg, Pao, the junior academic-turned-blogger, and all manner of other commentators,[40] have made women—and perhaps more important, men[41]—start talking frankly about the tension between likeability and competence that all working women face, no matter how high they ascend. And thanks to Ann Hopkins and *Price Waterhouse,* if a plaintiff can meet the challenge of showing that such biases harmed the "terms, conditions, or privileges" of her employment, she now has a legal remedy.

IT'S NOT JUST "masculine" women, like Ann Hopkins, who have been protected by *Price Waterhouse.* "Effeminate" men also have used it to win Title VII cases. Among them is Brian Prowel, a gay man who worked at Wise Business Forms' plant in western Pennsylvania. It was undisputed, including by Prowel, that he had a high voice and other stereotypically "feminine" mannerisms. Among other abuse, his coworkers ridiculed him as "Rosebud" and "Princess," and left a feathered pink tiara at his work station. The trial court dismissed Prowel's case, finding it to be a claim for discrimination "because of sexual orientation," which is not covered by Title VII.[42] But in 2008 the U.S. Court of Appeals for the Third Circuit reversed, finding that *Price Waterhouse* protected Prowel: "There is no basis in the statutory or case law to support the notion that an effeminate *heterosexual* man can bring a gender stereotyping claim while an effeminate *homosexual* man may not," said the court. "As long as the employee—regardless of his or her sexual orientation—marshals sufficient evidence such that a reasonable jury could conclude that harassment or discrimination occurred 'because of sex,'" the case should go to a jury.[43]

Another group that has seen some benefit from *Price Waterhouse* in recent years is transgender employees. In 2012, the EEOC made headlines when it ruled that Mia Macy, who had presented as a man when first applying to work at the U.S. Bureau of Alcohol, Tobacco, and Firearms, was denied the position after she told ATF that she was transitioning to being female.[44] Invoking *Price Waterhouse,* the EEOC held that Title VII didn't just ban discrimination "because of *biological* sex." It found that Macy's case qualified as sex discrimination because she was not dressing and behaving and living as ATF believed a biological man should dress and behave and live. (It further found that because ATF hired a man instead of Macy, her case also qualified as a more traditional example of sex discrimination.) In a 2015 ruling, the EEOC found discrimination on the basis of sexual orientation to be illegal discrimination "because of sex," as well. The EEOC has adhered to this interpretation of Title VII in its own litigation on behalf of individual employees, too. And in April 2015, President Obama issued an executive order barring federal contractors from discriminating on the basis of sexual orientation and gender identity.[45]

Until there is universal recognition by the courts that "sex" encompasses gender identity and sexual orientation, though, LGBT advocates continue to ask Congress to amend Title VII to explicitly include sexual orientation and gender identity as protected traits under the law. It's nonsensical that *Price Waterhouse* has been widely extended to protect employees who "seem" gay but won't protect those whose claim arises solely from the fact that they actually are. (After all, isn't being gay, lesbian, or bisexual the ultimate failure to conform with sex stereotype—that is, the idea that men should be attracted only to women and vice versa?) Advocates now hope that the Supreme Court's 2015 decision recognizing same-sex marriage as a constitutional right will provide the momentum needed to amend Title VII, and have thrown their weight behind the Equality Act, which would do just that. As Senator Jeff Merkley of Oregon said regarding his intention to fight for the law's passage, "People are going to realize that you can get married in the morning and fired from your job . . . in the afternoon. That is unacceptable."[46]

DESPITE MOSTLY positive steps forward for workers who don't look or act the way their employers think they "should," there is one area in which the *status quo* has barely budged in the years since Title VII was enacted: employer-mandated grooming and appearance codes. Such policies invariably require women employees to conform to a hyper-feminine, even hyper-sexualized, standard, far beyond that imposed upon Ann Hopkins. And although there are exceptions, they are usually approved by the courts, out of exaggerated deference to business's interest in building its brand.[47]

Notorious among these is the 2009 case of Darlene Jespersen, a bartender at Harrah's Casino in Reno. Despite having performed her job well for two decades, Jespersen was fired for refusing to conform to the casino's new "Personal Best" policy, which required that she wear face powder, blush, mascara, lipstick, and nail polish, and to wear her hair down at all times, either "teased, curled, or styled." (Male employees, on the other hand, were forbidden from wearing makeup or wearing their hair below their shirt collars.) "I had to become a sex object," Jespersen later wrote. "Although it had nothing to do with mixing drinks and handling customers, keeping my job became more and more about meeting Harrah's extreme and outdated idea of what a woman should look like."[48]

The Ninth Circuit Court of Appeals approved Harrah's policy. It wasn't enough, found the court, to show that requiring women to wear heavy makeup obviously reinforced a sex stereotype of women as a decorative sex object. Instead, a woman had to make (the almost impossible) showing that the casino actually had the specific intent to relegate women to that marginalized role.[49] Decisions like Jespersen's—or a New Jersey court's 2015 decision (under the state law modeled on Title VI) upholding Borgata Casino's policy banning its scantily clad cocktail servers, dubbed "Borgata Babes," from gaining more than 7 percent of their body weight[50]—bring to mind Representative Martha Griffiths's unminced words from nearly fifty years ago: She famously challenged an executive of United Airlines for hiring only young, thin, unmarried women to carry out the duties of flight attendant, demanding, "What are you running, an airline or a whorehouse?"[51]

Women of color face distinct hurdles when it comes to employer appearance codes. Such codes not only traffic in stereotypical notions of what's feminine; they also rest upon whiteness as the norm. How to style one's hair has become a particular locus of anxiety—and conflict—for working women of color, who fear that looking "too ethnic" will hold them back.[52] Indeed, the "Personal Best" policy at issue in *Jespersen* plainly presumed that female employees were white, stating that in addition to requiring that hair be "teased, curled, or styled," it also "must be worn down at all times, no exceptions."[53] As one scholar commented about *Jespersen,* "For most black women, wearing their hair 'down' would require that their hair be straightened, either by a hot comb or a chemical relaxer."[54]

Other hairstyles commonly worn by black women, from braids to two-strand twists to dreadlocks to finger waves, have been banned by employers as "too ethnic," "too wild," or—especially inscrutable—too "eye-catching," and courts have approved those narrow standards.[55] In one of the earliest cases, Renee Rogers, an American Airlines employee, challenged the airlines' rule against wearing her hair in cornrows.[56] The court dismissed the case because both men and women were prohibited from wearing their hair in braids. Moreover, because she would have been allowed to wear her hair in an Afro, the court saw no race discrimination in prohibiting the hairstyle most comfortable to Rogers, as a black woman.[57] The U.S. Army tried to impose similar limitations in March 2014 when it issued new appearance guidelines that forbade most black women's hairstyles, including braids, twists, and even Afros.[58] But after it was deluged with criticism from the public, members of the armed services, and the Congressional Black Caucus, the Army rescinded the rule a few months later.[59]

Employer appearance codes' harsh impact on women of color reflect a larger failing of antidiscrimination law: its tendency to treat employees as having a single identity—male, female, white, black, Asian, Latino, straight, gay, and so on—rather than acknowledging the intersections that make us human, and that trigger almost limitless forms of bias. For instance, Asian women, Latinas, and other women of color encounter specific animus that is distinct among each of them, and that white women will never face. Older women, whatever their race, fight against invisibility in a workplace that prizes women for their youth. Pregnant women are told by the law that they are comparable to employees who are blind or use wheelchairs or have cancer, but of course all of those conditions are distinct and carry distinct cultural weight.

Complete legal answers to these myriad problems are beyond the scope of this book. But the law must take better account for how, in the endlessly diverse real world, bias is manifested—including the fact that much of the bias that causes discriminatory decisionmaking is unconscious. It's no less real, though, for those who are subjected to it.

THE COMBINED effect of *Dothard v. Rawlinson, Price Waterhouse v. Hopkins,* and *UAW v. Johnson Controls* has been to help propel more women into fields historically held by men. Also invaluable was a 1987 Supreme Court decision approving sex-based affirmative action by employers when a particular job has a "conspicuous" gender imbalance.[60] Millions of women, especially those in historically all-male jobs, now have affirmative action to thank for their paychecks.[61] (Like so many workplace gains, though, it's white women who have reaped the most benefits from such policies.[62])

The *Dothard* disparate impact model has been especially valuable in tackling poorly constructed physical tests used by employers to screen applicants in some historically male jobs, especially police and fire departments.[63] Between the time *Dothard* was decided, in 1977, and 2012, more than half the legal challenges to such departments' physical examinations were successful.[64] Those successful cases, like Brenda Mieth's and Kim Rawlinson's forty years ago, turned on the employer's inability to show that the test actually made for better first responders.

Still, progress is slow. Though one 2008 study found that women make up more than 10 percent of firefighters in some of the nation's largest departments like Milwaukee, San Francisco, and Miami-Dade[65]—with women having served as fire chiefs in a number of them—in other departments, the numbers have remained pitifully low; more than half of the country's fire departments have no women members at all.[66] Women in law enforcement have fared slightly better: In 2014, roughly 12 percent of police and sheriff's patrol officers nationwide were women and 21 percent were detectives and criminal investigators were women, while 16 percent of the supervisors in those jobs are women, too. Women also make up close to 30 percent of correctional officers, bailiffs, and jailers.[67]

Merely having the legal right to enter previously men-only jobs, of course, doesn't mean women are going to be welcomed there.

Harassment of women in such settings is common, and can be especially vicious, dissuading many from staying on the job and thus maintaining the segregated *status quo*. Such harassment may be hyper-sexual, such as in displaying pornography or graphic graffiti, reminding women that they are welcome in the workplace only as sex objects, not co-workers; conversely, the harassment may be non-sexual, but still deeply hostile and even dangerous, taking the form of abusive epithets, assault, or sabotage of work materials.[68] Sheila White's futile efforts to get consistent on-the-job training after she was punitively transferred to track work, as well as her frequent assignment to perform tasks meant for two or more people and her lack of access to sanitary restroom facilities, all illustrate this phenomenon. Indeed, a recent study of the nation's women firefighters found that more women had experienced shunning and invasions of privacy in the firehouse's locker room facilities than had been subjected to pornography or sexual advances—though more than 30 percent had faced those abuses, too.[69]

The nation's first sexual harassment class-action lawsuit, *Jenson v. Eveleth Taconite Company*[70]—later the subject of a book[71] and then a movie, *North Country*[72]—helped cement that principle, on a larger scale than ever before. The case provided an especially vivid depiction of what can happen when a few women enter an environment where they're vastly outnumbered by men (as they were in the Eveleth Mines by 400 to 4). On plaintiff Lois Jenson's first day on the job, a male employee cornered her and leaned in close. "You fucking women don't belong here," he said. "Why don't you go home?"[73] Jenson and her three female colleagues also were subjected to stalking, nooses hung over their work stations, and semen deposited on their clothes.[74] (Frankly, it's stunning—not to mention stomach-turning—how often such bodily fluids are used to harass women in traditionally male settings, as if, on some very primal level, to mark certain territory. I've heard from more than one female firefighter about finding feces inside her boots, and once represented an auto mechanic, the only woman out of about 200 coworkers, who arrived at work one day to discover that all of her tools had been soaked in urine.)

The good news is that all of those behaviors do qualify as unlawful harassment, assuming they meet the "severe or pervasive" test established in *Vinson* and clarified in *Harris*. That principle was cemented by the Supreme Court's 1998 ruling that same-sex harassment also constitutes discrimination "because of sex."[75] Oil rig employee Joseph Oncale endured vicious harassment at the hands of his (heterosexual) male coworkers, who, among other "hazing" and abuse, assaulted him and threatened him with rape. Wrote Justice Scalia for a unanimous Court: "[H]arassing conduct need not be motivated by sexual desire to support an inference of discrimination on the basis of sex."[76]

In addition to women laboring in male-dominated fields, women working in low-wage workplaces—disproportionately women of color—regularly run a gauntlet of harassment. One such group is tipped workers, of whom 60 percent are women, and earn just $2.13 per hour.[77] A recent study by New York's Restaurant Opportunities Center found that a staggering 80 percent of tipped restaurant employees had experienced harassment by customers.[78] And although those workers are just 7 percent of the nation's employees, they account for 37 percent of sexual harassment charges filed with the EEOC.[79]

Title VII has been interpreted by courts and the EEOC to require employers to protect employees from customers' abuse, but that doesn't stop restaurant managers from encouraging or even instructing female servers to sexualize themselves in order to attract business.[80] Waitstaff are in a catch-22 when it comes to alerting managers to the gropes, leers, and propositions of customers, on whose goodwill they depend for the bulk of their income. For this reason, increasing tipped workers' base pay—thereby lessening the financial pressure to grin and bear guests' wandering hands—has become a rallying cry for women's advocates.[81]

Farmworkers are another population for whom sexual harassment remains commonplace. Women and girls make up about a quarter of the nation's roughly 2 million agricultural workers,[82] the majority of whom are immigrants, mostly Latina, and of whom at least half, according to conservative estimates, are undocumented.[83] A 2012 report by Human Rights Watch found that "sexual violence and sexual harassment experienced by farmworkers is common enough that some farmworker women see these abuses as an unavoidable condition of agricultural work."[84] Studies by other advocacy groups have reached the same conclusion.[85] A senior EEOC official who has litigated many farmworker abuse cases reported that one California company operated a site known as "field de *calzon*"—"field of panties"—because so many workers had been raped there.[86]

Far away from family support networks, often toiling in remote locations, not yet proficient in English, and fearing deportation should they complain, female farm laborers are among the most vulnerable in the American workforce. Title VII doesn't require employees to be citizens in order to invoke the law's protections, but to an undocumented worker—even one lucky enough to know about Title VII at all—the notion of approaching a U.S. government agency to file a charge of discrimination is unthinkable.

For this reason, the EEOC has made it a priority to educate workers and employers alike about Title VII, and to target these abuses through its litigation program (thus freeing the farmworkers from having to find their own attorneys).[87] It has brought several high-profile cases resulting in recovery of millions of dollars for workers;[88] one of the biggest came in September 2015, when a jury awarded $17 million to five women at Moreno Farms packing plant in Miami who were terrorized and raped by three company personnel, and ultimately fired.[89] Slowly but surely, such large awards are increasing awareness among agricultural employers about their obligations under the law. Some states have taken it upon themselves to protect this especially vulnerable group. California passed a law in 2015, for instance, requiring that personnel at all farming businesses—not just the largest ones—as well as labor contractors train their personnel in antiharassment policies.[90]

———

DESPITE THE CONTINUED prevalence of sexual harassment in the workplace, the Supreme Court has in recent years made it more difficult to hold employers liable. The Court's 1998 *Faragher* and *Ellerth* rulings allowed an employer to defeat a claim of supervisor hostile environment harassment by showing that it had taken reasonable steps to prevent and remedy such misconduct. (On the other hand, if the supervisor engaged in quid pro quo harassment—firing or demoting or otherwise tangibly punishing an employee who resists him—then, *Faragher* and *Ellerth* held, the employer would be automatically liable.)

In the nearly twenty years since the Court created the "*Faragher-Ellerth* defense," it unquestionably has encouraged well-intentioned employers to discover supervisor harassment and to fix it. But in many instances, judges tend to focus their *Faragher-Ellerth* inquiry less on how the employer did or didn't respond to the misconduct than on whether the harassed worker tried hard enough to complain. Shifting the burden to the *employee* to prove she's done enough to avoid a lawsuit turns on its head what was supposed to be the *employer*'s burden of showing it took action against predatory supervisors. Moreover, it gives employers an incentive to adopt what one advocacy group has termed "file cabinet compliance"[91]: Publish a policy against harassment, conduct a one-time sensitivity training (and collect employees' signatures affirming they attended it), and then sit back and wait to hear about any violations.

Even when an employee does step forward to file a complaint, some courts have found the most perfunctory investigations sufficient to satisfy the *Faragher-Ellerth* defense.[92] An employer may simply interview the accuser, then the accused, decide it's a he said–she said toss-up, and put the investigation paperwork back in that filing cabinet. That is, until the accuser sues, and the paperwork is brought out to show a judge just how diligently the employer addressed her complaint. Case dismissed.

Holding employers liable for supervisor harassment recently got harder still, and calls for a legislative remedy. In 2013's *Vance v. Ball State University,*[93] the Court—in a 5–4 opinion authored by Justice Alito—narrowed the definition of who even qualifies as a "supervisor" under *Faragher-Ellerth.* It found that only those employees with formal authority to hire, fire, and make similar decisions are supervisors; authority to merely decide someone's schedule or oversee her daily tasks, Alito wrote, would not be enough. Instead, such harassers would be considered coworkers. And coworker harassment is much harder for a plaintiff to prove, requiring a showing that the employer was negligent—that is, that it actually "knew or should have known" of the harassment and did nothing.

Justice Ginsburg, joined by Justices Breyer, Sotomayor, and Kagan, wrote a bitter dissent. The Court's new, crabbed definition of a supervisor, she wrote, "ignores the conditions under which members of the work force labor."[94] In today's workplace, there may be several tiers of supervisors who exert varying degrees of control over an employee's daily life, even though they lack the ultimate power to hire or fire. As Ginsburg explained, "An employee who confronts her harassing supervisor risks, for example, receiving an undesirable or unsafe work assignment or an unwanted transfer." Alternatively, "She may be saddled with an excessive workload or with placement on a shift spanning hours disruptive of her family life."[95] Ginsburg urged Congress to step in to correct *Vance,* just as it had in 1991 to amend Title VII and overrule a number of recent "wayward" Court decisions. "The ball is once again in Congress' court," she said, "to correct the error into which this Court has fallen, and to restore the robust protections against workplace harassment the Court weakens today."[96] Since *Vance* was decided, the Fair Employment Protection Act has been introduced in Congress to do just that.

Justice Ginsburg's prediction that *Vance* would pose insurmountable burdens to plaintiffs has proved prescient. In the fall of 2014, a little over a year after the case was decided, the National Women's

Law Center tallied up 43 sexual harassment cases that had been dismissed because the harasser didn't meet the stringent new supervisor standard and the plaintiff couldn't prove employer negligence, either.[97]

ON THE SAME day that the Supreme Court decided *Vance,* it issued another ruling that circumscribed employees' rights under Title VII—and earned another outraged dissent from Justice Ginsburg, joined again by Justices Breyer, Sotomayor, and Kagan. In *University of Texas Southwestern Medical Center v. Nassar,* the Court ruled that the "mixed-motive" proof structure was not available to employees alleging retaliation. Whereas a majority of the Court in *Price Waterhouse* had ruled that an employee who brought a discrimination claim could win even if the employer had an alternative, valid motivation for its actions—a holding confirmed by the 1991 Civil Rights Act—in *Nassar,* the conservative wing of the Court led by Justice Anthony Kennedy held retaliation plaintiffs to a higher standard. For those individuals, from now on the only way to win would be to show that retaliation was the employer's *only* motivation.

Nassar represented a U-turn by a Court that previously had read Title VII's anti-retaliation protection extremely broadly. Most notable, of course, had been *Burlington Northern*'s holding in 2006 that illegal retaliation included any action "likely to dissuade" an employee from complaining about bias. But the Court also had ruled in the years before and since that Title VII protected former employees from retaliation, as well as employees who gave corroborating evidence in support of another worker's complaint,[98] and family members of complaining employees who worked for the same company.[99] (In the latter case, a female employee's discrimination complaint prompted the company to fire her fiancée who also worked there.)

The popular wisdom held that the Court was moved to restrict retaliation claims because of the steady increase in their prevalence; by the time *Nassar* was argued, retaliation charges accounted for nearly 40 percent of filings with the EEOC, up from roughly 30 percent when the Court heard *Burlington Northern.* More cynical observers, though, thought that Justice Kennedy, who had objected to the mixed-motive framework created by *Price Waterhouse,* relished the opportunity to deal a backhanded blow to that decision.[100] Justice Ginsburg certainly implied as much. "Today's opinion," she wryly observed, "rehashes arguments rightly rejected in *Price Waterhouse.*"[101]

Ginsburg closed her dissent in *Nassar* with another plea for corrective action by Congress: "Today's misguided judgment, along with the judgment in [*Vance*], should prompt [an amendment of Title VII]."[102] In response, the Protecting Older Workers Against Discrimination Act has been introduced to remedy both *Nassar* and a similar decision relating to mixed-motive cases under the Age Discrimination in Employment Act.

WHEN IT COMES to women and retirement savings, *Manhart* and *Norris* have remained undisturbed. *Manhart* in particular remains a popular touchstone for the larger principles that Title VII requires employers to treat employees as individuals, not members of a group. Indeed, their significance has been diminished by employers' move away from pensions—fueled in part by the demise of unionized workplaces—and toward 401(k)s and related vehicles. But that shift has not remedied women's lagging far behind men in retirement savings. With retirement tethered to actual earnings, the persistent wage gap—77 cents on the dollar for white women, and much worse for women of color, ultimately costing women an average of $530,000 less over their lifetimes—means that women get less from Social Security and put away less in their 401(k)s.[103]

The Supreme Court has revisited the pension issue just once since *Norris,* in 2009, and it was not a happy outcome for the women involved. Noreen Hulteen, Eleanora Collet, Linda Porter, and Elizabeth Snyder all were long-term employees of AT&T Corporation and its associated predecessor companies, who in the late 1960s and early 1970s took leaves of absence to have their kids. Under the company's policy at the time, employees who took time off for temporary disability earned service credit—which eventually would be used to calculate their pension benefits when they retired—for the entire duration of their absence. Like so many other employer policies of the time, women who took time off for pregnancy and childbirth received no such service credit for most of their leave.

After Congress passed the PDA in 1978, AT&T adopted a new policy that did away with the old system for calculating years of service, and awarded the same credit for pregnancy leave as for temporary disability leave taken for other reasons. But the company did not restore any of the lost credit for women who had taken time off under the old policy. At the time they retired, the women brought suit, alleging that even though AT&T no longer denied service credit to its current employees who took maternity leave, its continued reliance on the pre-PDA system in calculating their present-day benefits was ongoing discrimination.

The Court disagreed, ruling that AT&T's unequal pension calculations could be considered ongoing discrimination only if the *original* policy of denying service credits also was discriminatory. And the Court concluded it wasn't. Why? Because pregnancy discrimination was not illegal until 1978 when Congress passed the PDA, long after any of the *Hulteen* plaintiffs took their leaves.

Justice Ginsburg wrote an impassioned dissent that Justice Breyer joined. After reviewing the history of how the law, aided by the Supreme Court in the years before Title VII, consistently had used women's biological capacity for pregnancy to marginalize women at work, she lamented that the Court was reviving that ignominious tradition and thumbing its nose at congressional authority. In so doing, the Court essentially was allowing AT&T to continue punishing its women employees for having had children.

————   ——

THE *HULTEEN* decision bore a remarkable resemblance to another controversial decision issued just two years earlier, decided by the same Court, which also concerned the question of whether and how to address present-day effects of past employer decisions: *Ledbetter v. Goodyear Tire & Rubber Company*.[104] Lilly Ledbetter worked for close to twenty years at a Goodyear tire plant in Alabama, where she was the only woman manager. Shortly before she left the company she received an anonymous note informing her that she was paid less than all the other male managers. Investigation revealed that the unknown tipster was correct, and Ledbetter filed suit. The Court ruled that the mere fact that Goodyear today paid Ledbetter lower paychecks as a result of her employer's past unfair decisions was not enough to trigger Title VII liability. Instead, the discrimination actually occurred years earlier, when the company decided to pay her less than her male colleagues and the statute of limitations on that claim had long since expired. That she didn't know it then, was just her bad luck.

Congress acted to negate the *Ledbetter* ruling, just as it had acted in 1978, passing the PDA to repudiate *Gilbert,* and in 1991, enacting the Civil Rights Act to correct a variety of other Court decisions. In 2008 it enacted the Lilly Ledbetter Fair Pay Act, which made clear that the "clock" starts on a new discrimination claim every time an employer issues an unequal paycheck, regardless of when the original decision was made. Advocates also continue to push for passage of the Paycheck Fairness Act, which would undo many court rulings that have de-fanged the 1963 Equal Pay Act as a weapon for combating the gender pay gap. Among its terms is one that would have been especially helpful to Ledbetter and the millions of women like her before and since: a provision permitting coworkers to openly discuss, and compare, their wages.

LILLY LEDBETTER'S determination to right the wrong done to her, even though she ultimately never saw a dime from Goodyear, is a cheering reminder of the difference one woman can make. She has rightfully become a household name because of her tenacious crusade.

The past fifty years have seen an abundance of such heroines, from Ida Phillips to Peggy Young, and we should remember their names, too. As we plot our next steps forward through the muck of inequality, in Congress, in the courts, and on the job, we also must work as hard as they did to overcome the occasional step backward, and to keep the law moving forward—slowly, surely, inexorably.

notes

Introduction

1. Todd Purdum, *An Idea Whose Time Has Come: Two Presidents, Two Parties, and the Battle for the Civil Rights Act of 1964* (New York: Henry Holt & Co., 2014), 195.
2. Caroline Bird, *Born Female* (New York: Pocket Books, 1968), 5.
3. Ibid., 4. See also Gail Collins, *When Everything Changed* (New York: Little, Brown & Co., 2009), 76.
4. Bird, *Born Female*, 4.
5. Clay Risen, "The Accidental Feminist," *Slate*, February 7, 2014, http://www.slate.com/articles/news_and_politics/jurisprudence/2014/02/the_50th_anniversary_of_title_vii_of_the_civil_rights_act_and_the_southern.html.
6. Quoted in Sheryl James, "Civil Rights, Women's Rights," *Law Quadrangle* (Fall 2014), http://quadrangle.law.umich.edu/features/civil-rights-womens-rights/.
7. Ibid.
8. Ibid.
9. Bird, *Born Female*, 5.
10. Louis Menand, "The Sex Amendment," *The New Yorker,* July 21, 2014, http://www.newyorker.com/magazine/2014/07/21/sex-amendment.
11. Clay Risen, *The Bill of the Century: The Epic Battle for the Civil Rights Act* (New York: Bloomsbury Press, 2014), 160; Purdum, *An Idea Whose Time Has Come,* 196–197; Collins, *When Everything Changed,* 76–77, 78–79; Risen, *The Accidental Feminist.*
12. Risen, *The Bill of the Century,* 161; Menand, "The Sex Amendment."
13. Because it was a "teller vote" and not a roll call vote, a precise accounting of who voted for and against wasn't possible. But Martha Griffiths was one of the "tellers" and reported on the breakdown of the yeas and nays. See Jo Freeman, "How 'Sex' Got into Title VII: Persistent Opportunism as a Maker of Public Policy," *Women, Law and Public Policy,* 2004, http://www.jofreeman.com/lawandpolicy/titlevii.htm.
14. Risen, *The Bill of the Century,* 160; Purdum, *An Idea Whose Time Has Come,* 198.
15. 42 U.S.C. § 2000e-2(a).
16. See, e.g., Cary Franklin, "Inventing the 'Traditional Concept' of Sex Discrimination," *Harvard Law Review* 125 (April 2012): 1307; Freeman, "How 'Sex' Got into Title VII"; Carl M. Brauer, "Women Activists, Southern Conservatives, and the Prohibition of Sex Discrimination in Title VII of the 1964 Civil Rights Act," *Journal of Southern History* 49, Issue 1 (February 1983): 37; Michael Evan Gold, "A Tale of Two Amendments: The Reasons Congress Added Sex to Title VII and Their Implication for Comparable Worth," *Duquesne Law Review* 19 (1981): 453.
17. U.S. Department of Labor, Women's Bureau, *1965 Handbook on Women Workers,* Bulletin 290 (Washington, DC: 1965), 2, https://fraser.stlouisfed.org/docs/publications/women/b0290_dolwb_1965.pdf.

18. Pauli Murray and Mary O. Eastwood, "Jane Crow and the Law: Sex Discrimination and Title VII," *George Washington Law Review* 34 (1965): 232.

19. U.S. Department of Labor, Women's Bureau, *Issue Brief,* June 2016, at 1, https://www.dol.gov/wb/resources/WB_WorkingMothers_508_FinalJune 13.pdf.

20. Catalyst, "Women Leaving and Re-entering the Workforce," March 28, 2013, http://www.catalyst.org/knowledge/women-leaving-and-re-entering-workforce#footnote ref1_pks1j3w.

21. Stephanie Coontz, *A Strange Stirring: The Feminine Mystique and American Women at the Dawn of the 1960s* (New York: Basic Books, 2011), 14. Today nearly a quarter of federal judges are women. Dina Refki, Abigya Eshete, and Selena Hajiani, "Women in Federal and State-Level Judgeships," A Report by the Center for Women in Government and Civil Society/Rockefeller College of Public Affairs and Policy at University of Albany (2012), http://www.albany.edu/womeningov/publications/summer2012_judgeships.pdf.

22. Menand, "The Sex Amendment"; Risen, "The Accidental Feminist."

23. Hugh Davis Graham, *The Civil Rights Era: Origins and Development of National Policy 1960–1972* (New York: Oxford University Press, 1990), 223.

24. John Herbers, "For Instance, Can She Pitch for Mets?" *The New York Times,* August 20, 1965.

25. Ibid.

26. "Shaping Employment Discrimination Law," U.S. Equal Employment Opportunity Commission, *EEOC History: 35th Anniversary: 1965–2000,* http://www.eeoc.gov/eeoc/history/35th/1965-71/shaping.html.

27. Caroline Frederickson, *Under the Bus: How Working Women Are Being Run Over* (New York: Free Press, 2015), 40.

28. See, e.g., Shelley J. Correll, Stephen Benard, and In Paik, "Getting a Job: Is There a Motherhood Penalty?," *American Journal of Sociology* 112, No. 5 (March 2007).

29. American Association of University Women, *The Simple Truth About the Gender Wage Gap,* Fall 2015 edition, 11 (Fig. 4), http://www.aauw.org/files/2015/09/The-Simple-Truth-Fall-2015.pdf.

30. Catalyst, "Statistical Overview of Women in the Workplace: Women at the Top," Mar. 3, 2014, http://www.catalyst.org/knowledge/statistical-overview-of-women-workplace.

31. Kathleen Peratis, "Severe and Pervasive," in Amy Richards and Cynthia Greenberg, eds., *I Still Believe Anita Hill* (New York: The Feminist Press, 2011), 157.

One

Unless otherwise indicated, direct quotes, biographical and historical details, and mental impressions come from the following sources: Interview with Reese Marshall in Jacksonville, Florida on April 21, 2015; interview with Ida Phillips's children—Peggy Brandt, Vera Tharp, and Al McAlister—in Jacksonville, Florida on April 21, 2015; interview with Bill Robinson in Washington, DC, on April 6, 2015.

1. September 6, 1966, letter from Ida Phillips to President Lyndon Johnson, "It Happened Here: Phillips v. Martin Marietta" (2010) (on display at George C. Young United States Courthouse, Orlando, FL).

2. Richard Burnett, "Missiles Spark Half-Century of High-Tech," *The Orlando Sentinel,* September 24, 2006, http://articles.orlandosentinel.com/2006-09-24/news/MARTIN24_1_1_martin-central-florida-orlando.

3. Ibid.

4. September 6, 1966 letter from Phillips to Johnson, "It Happened Here."

5. Serena Mayeri, *Reasoning from Race: Feminism, Law, and the Civil Rights Revolution* (Cambridge, MA: Harvard University Press, 2011), 51.

6. Judith Michaelson, "The Justices Saw It Her Way," *The New York Post,* January 30, 1971.

7. Quoted in ibid.

8. September 6, 1966, letter from Phillips to Johnson, "It Happened Here."
9. Quoted in Michaelson, "The Justices Saw It Her Way."
10. Ibid.
11. Appendix at 9a-10a, Phillips v. Martin Marietta Corp., 400 U.S. 542 (1971) (No. 73).
12. Michaelson, "The Justices Saw It Her Way."
13. Appendix at 11a-12a, Phillips v. Martin Marietta Corp., 400 U.S. 542 (1971) (No. 73).
14. Quoted in Michaelson, "The Justices Saw It Her Way."
15. Ibid.
16. Ibid.
17. 347 U.S. 483 (1954).
18. Gail Collins, *When Everything Changed: The Amazing Journey of American Women from 1960 to the Present* (New York: Little, Brown & Co., 2009), 86.
19. Phillips v. Martin Marietta Corp., No. 67-290-ORL-Civil, 1968 U.S. Dist. LEXIS 8595 (M.D. Fla. July 9, 1968).
20. Ibid. at *2.
21. Allison Herren Lee, William W. Shakely, and J. Robert Brown Jr., "Judge Warren L. Jones and the Supreme Court of Dixie," *Louisiana Law Review* 59 (1998): 209 & n.4.
22. 29 C.F.R. § 1604.1(a)(1)(i) (1965).
23. Ibid. § 1604.1(a)(1)(ii).
24. Ibid. § 1604.3(a).
25. Phillips v. Martin Marietta Corp., 411 F.2d 1, 4 (5th Cir. 1969).
26. Ibid.
27. Appendix, Phillips v. Martin Marietta Corp., 400 U.S. 542 (1971) (No. 73).
28. Phillips v. Martin Marietta Corp., 416 F.2d 1257 (5th Cir. 1969). One of the judges in the majority, G. Harold Carswell, may have come to regret his decision. Feminists bitterly contested his later—unsuccessful—nomination to the Supreme Court because of his vote against Ida Phillips. Testifying against him before the Senate Judiciary Committee, NOW founder Betty Friedan dubbed him "unusually blind in the matter of sex prejudice." Betty Friedan, *It Changed My Life* (New York: Random House, 1976), 170.
29. Phillips, 416 F.2d at 1259 (Brown, J., dissenting).
30. Ibid. at 1260.
31. Ibid.
32. 372 U.S. 335 (1963).
33. Anthony Lewis, *Gideon's Trumpet* (New York: Random House, 1964), 25.
34. Timothy S. Bishop, Jeffrey W. Sarles, and Stephen J. Kane, "Tips on Petitioning for *Certiorari* in the U.S. Supreme Court," *The Circuit Rider,* June 2007, https://www.mayerbrown.com/files/Publication/34891e80-a15d-4b25-84a2-d3c8573d23da/Presentation/PublicationAttachment/5f64270f-6be0-4cec-8cc8-10e6bed6988b/ART_CIRCUITRIDER_JUN07.PDF, 28.
35. Ibid.
36. Petition for Certiorari at 7–8, Phillips v. Martin Marietta Corp., 400 U.S. 542 (1971) (No. 73).
37. Phillips, 1968 U.S. Dist. LEXIS 8595 at *2.
38. Petition for Certiorari at 6, Phillips v. Martin Marietta Corp., 400 U.S. 542 (1971) (No. 73).
39. Ibid. at 7.
40. Ibid. at 11.
41. Ibid. at 10–11.
42. Ibid. at 10.
43. Michaelson, "The Justices Saw It Her Way."
44. Quoted in ibid.
45. Quoted in Elizabeth Heddericg, "Florida Woman's Discrimination Case May Open Up Jobs," *The St. Petersburg Times,* May 4, 1970.

46. Brief of the American Civil Liberties Union, Amicus Curiae at 14, Phillips v. Martin Marietta Corp., 400 U.S. 542 (1971) (No. 73).
47. Ibid.
48. Ibid.
49. See, e.g., Bart Landry, *Black Working Wives: Pioneers of the American Family Revolution* (Oakland: University of California Press, 2002).
50. Brief Amicus Curiae for National Organization for Women at 8–9, Phillips v. Martin Marietta Corp., 400 U.S. 542 (1971) (No. 73).
51. Ibid. at 9.
52. Brief of the American Civil Liberties Union, Amicus Curiae at 8, Phillips v. Martin Marietta Corp., 400 U.S. 542 (1971) (No. 73).
53. Collins, *When Everything Changed*, 20.
54. American Airlines advertisement, *DC Magazine*, Vol. 1, Issue 1, June 12, 1965, 2.
55. Amicus Curiae Brief of Air Line Stewards and Stewardesses Association in Support of Petitioner at 3–4, Phillips v. Martin Marietta Corp., 400 U.S. 542 (1971) (No. 73).
56. Timothy R. Johnson, Paul J. Wahlbeck, and James F. Spriggs, "The Influence of Oral Arguments on the U.S. Supreme Court," *American Political Science Review* 100 , No. 1 (February 2006), 99, 101 (internal citations omitted) (emphasis in original), http://home.gwu.edu/~wahlbeck/articles/Johnson-Wahlbeck-Spriggs%202006%20APSR.pdf.
57. 401 U.S. 424 (1971).
58. Michaelson, "The Justices Saw It Her Way."
59. Quoted in ibid.
60. Oral Argument at 15; 7:16; 8:15; 9:24; 10:27; 10:50; 9:40, Phillips v. Martin Marietta Corp., 400 U.S. 542 (1971) (No. 37), available at http://www.oyez.org/cases/1970-1979/1970/1970_73.
61. Ibid. at 11:30.
62. Ibid. at 11:40.
63. Ibid. at 21:25; 25:38; 26:14.
64. Ibid. at 5:26; 5:50.
65. Ibid. at 23:41.
66. Ibid. at 34:18; 34:35.
67. Ibid. at 46:22.
68. Ibid. at 49:44; 48:06; 48:52; 49:30.
69. Ibid. at 74:50; 75:25; 75:39; 75:46.
70. Quoted in Mayeri, *Reasoning from Race*, 53.
71. Oral Argument at 76:42, Phillips v. Martin Marietta Corp., 400 U.S. 542 (No. 37), available at http://www.oyez.org/cases/1970-1979/1970/1970_73.
72. August 11, 2015, email message from Reese Marshall to author.
73. Phillips v. Martin Marietta Corp., 400 U.S. 542, 544 (1971) (per curiam).
74. Ibid.
75. Ibid. at 543.
76. Ibid. at 545 (Marshall, J., concurring).
77. Ibid. at 545–546.
78. Bob Woodward and Scott Armstrong, *The Brethren* (New York: Simon & Schuster, 1979), 123.
79. Ibid.
80. Quoted in Mayeri, *Reasoning from Race*, 53–54.
81. Michaelson, "The Justices Saw It Her Way."
82. Quoted in ibid.
83. United Press International, "Woman Rightist Plans Spending," *The St. Petersburg Times,* July 30, 1971.
84. Quoted in ibid.
85. Quoted in Michaelson, "The Justices Saw It Her Way."
86. Ibid.

Two

Unless otherwise indicated, direct quotes, biographical and historical details, and mental impressions come from the following sources: Interview with John Carroll in Birmingham, Alabama on August 8, 2014; interview with Pamela Horowitz in Washington, DC, on September 29, 2014; interview with Joe Levin in Montgomery, Alabama, on August 7, 2014; interview with Brenda Mieth in Amissville, Virginia, on September 26, 2014 and by phone with the author on November 26, 2014; and interview with Kim Rawlinson in Montgomery, Alabama, on August 6, 2014, and by phone with the author on October 21, 2014.

1. Associated Press, "E.C. Dothard, State Trooper, 58," December 17, 1989, http://www .nytimes.com/1989/12/17/obituaries/e-c-dothard-state-trooper-58.html. According to a colleague, Dothard was "still barking out orders while on the ground after being shot." Ibid.

2. Dothan Area Convention & Visitors Bureau website, dothanalcvb.com.

3. Bureau of Labor Statistics, "Labor Force Statistics from the Current Population Survey: A Databook," Bulletin 2096 (September 1982): 657.

4. Carl Nink, "Women Professionals in Corrections: A Growing Asset," MTC Institute (August 2008), available at https://www.mtctrains.com/sites/default/files/Women ProfessionalsInCorrections-Aug08.pdf, 3.

5. "Unhired Women Sue Alabama on Minimum Sizes for Officers," *The New York Times,* December 10, 1975, http://timesmachine.nytimes.com/timesmachine/1975/12 /10/80101361.html?pageNumber=50.

6. Jerome J. Suich, "Height Standards in Police Employment and the Question of Sex Discrimination: The Availability of Two Defenses for a Neutral Employment Policy Found Discriminatory Under Title VII," *Southern California Law Review* 47 (1974): 586–587.

7. Ibid. at 585, 587 n.9.

8. Jo Freeman, "The Revolution for Women in Law and Public Policy," in Jo Freeman, ed., *Women: A Feminist Perspective,* 5th ed. (Mountain View, CA: Mayfield, 1995), 356–404.

9. See, e.g., Bart Landry, *Black Working Wives* (Oakland: University of California Press, 2002).

10. Bradwell v. Illinois, 83 U.S. 130, 141–142 (1872).

11. Muller v. Oregon, 208 U.S. 412, 421 (1907).

12. Goesaert v. Cleary, 335 U.S. 464 (1948).

13. Ibid. at 466. While the law's official rationale was that women needed a male authority figure's protection from lascivious, alcohol-fueled bar patrons, some scholars say the less chivalrous reality was that the male-dominated bartenders' union had lobbied hard for the law in order to keep those lucrative jobs for themselves. Amy Holtman French, "Mixing It Up: Michigan Barmaids Fight for Civil Rights," *Michigan Historical Review* 40, No. 1 (Spring 2009): 27–48.

14. See, e.g., Nink, *Women Professionals in Corrections;* James B. Jacobs, "The Sexual Integration of the Prison's Guard Force: A Few Comments on 'Dothard v. Rawlinson,'" *Toledo Law Review* 10 (Winter 1979): 389; Suich, "Height Standards in Police Employment and the Question of Sex Discrimination."

15. Equal Employment Opportunity Act of 1972, Public Law 92-261 (86 Stat. 103).

16. Jordan v. Wright, 417 F. Supp. 42 (M.D. Ala. 1976).

17. 401 U.S. 424 (1971).

18. Ibid. at 428.

19. Ibid. at 432.

20. Ibid. at 431.

21. Ibid. at 431, 432.

22. Ibid. at 431–432.

23. Ibid. at 430.

24. Officers for Justice v. Civil Service Comm'n, 395 F. Supp. 378 (N.D. Cal. 1975). The court also found the five-foot-six-inch height minimum to have an illegal disparate impact against Latinos and Asian Americans. Both are groups in which both men and women tend to be shorter than white or black men.

25. Ibid.

26. The remainder of the state's correctional facilities were work camps or work-release centers, plus the state's one juvenile detention center and one women's prison.

27. James v. Wallace, 406 F. Supp. 318 (M.D. Ala. 1976).

28. McCray v. Sullivan, 399 F. Supp. 271 (S.D. Ala. 1975).

29. Newman v. Alabama, 349 F. Supp. 278 (M.D. Ala. 1972).

30. James, 406 F. Supp. at 323–324.

31. Ibid. at 324.

32. Ibid. at 325. Judge Johnson further observed, "Guards rarely enter the cell blocks and dormitories, especially at night when their presence is most needed. The extremely high inmate-to-staff ratio makes personal interaction between the two virtually impossible because staff members must spend all their time attempting to maintain control or to protect themselves." But the guards also were to blame for these heightened tensions, said the court; they were virtually all white—whereas the inmates were mostly African American—and a "number of witnesses testified that staff members address black inmates with racial slurs, further straining already tense relations." Indeed, among the comprehensive remedies imposed by Judge Johnson were mandates that the Board of Corrections not only hire enough guards and adequately train them but also ensure that the guards better reflect the "racial and cultural" makeup of the inmate population. James, 406 F. Supp. at 325, 335.

To say that Alabama resisted implementing these directives is an understatement. Governor Wallace scoffed that the court wanted to create a "hotel atmosphere" in the state's prisons. "U.S. Relinquishes Alabama Prisons," The New York Times, January 15, 1989, http://www.nytimes.com/1989/01/15/us/us-relinquishes-alabama-prisons.html. Three years later, the court found the state to be in contempt of its orders and placed the prison system in receivership. Newman v. Alabama, 466 F. Supp. 628 (M.D. Ala. 1979). It wasn't until 1989 that the state finally was released from the court's oversight. "U.S. Relinquishes Alabama Prisons."

In early 2014, however, a Justice Department investigation found constitutional violations at Alabama's women's prison stemming from pervasive sexual abuse and harassment of inmates by prison guards. Eric Tucker, "Justice Department Reports on Abuse of Female Inmates, Questions Alabama's Work," The Washington Post, October 5, 2014, http://www.washingtonpost.com/politics/justice-department-reports-on-abuse-of-female-inmates-questions-alabamas-work/2014/10/05/c260adde-4caa-11e4-8c24-487e92bc997b_story.html. Federal intervention also recently was sought to address overcrowding and rampant abuse throughout the rest of the system. Kala Kachmar, "Justice Department Asked to Investigate State Prisons," Montgomery Advertiser, November 11, 2014, http://www.montgomeryadvertiser.com/story/news/local/alabama/2014/11/11/justice-department-asked-investigate-state-prisons/18891299/.

33. Phillips v. Martin Marietta, 400 U.S. 542, 545 (1971) (Marshall, J., concurring).

34. Bowe v. Colgate-Palmolive Co., 416 F.2d 711 (7th Cir. 1969).

35. Weeks v. Southern Bell Tel. & Tel. Co., 408 F.2d 228 (5th Cir. 1969).

36. Diaz v. Pan American World Airways, Inc., 442 F.2d 385 (5th Cir. 1971).

37. Rosenfeld v. Southern Pacific Co., 444 F.2d 1219 (9th Cir. 1971).

38. Mieth v. Dothard, 418 F. Supp. 1169, 1173 (M.D. Ala. 1976).

39. Ibid. at 1182.

40. Brief in Opposition by Respondent at 53, Dothard v. Rawlinson, 433 U.S. 321 (1977) (No. 76-422).

41. Brief of Petitioners at 6, Dothard v. Rawlinson, 433 U.S. 321 (1977) (No. 76-422).

42. Ibid., 7.

43. Dothard v. Rawlinson, 433 U.S. 321, 335 n.22 (1977).

44. Brief of Petitioners at 11, Dothard v. Rawlinson, 433 U.S. 321 (1977) (No. 76-422).
45. Brief in Opposition by Respondent at 53-54, Dothard v. Rawlinson, 433 U.S. 321 (1977) (No. 76-422).
46. See, e.g., Jacobs, "The Sexual Integration of the Prison's Guard Force."
47. Peter B. Bloch and Deborah Anderson, "Policewomen on Patrol: Final Report" (Washington, DC: Police Foundation, May 1974), http://files.eric.ed.gov/fulltext/ED102369.pdf.
48. Ibid. at 2.
49. Ibid. at 61.
50. Ibid. at 3. Notably, although both men and women had to meet a minimum height of five foot seven, the report noted that "the taller an officer was, the more likely he or she was to be rated poorly on performance." Ibid. at 60.
51. Thomas W. White and Peter B. Bloch, "Police Officer Height and Selected Aspects of Performance" (Washington, DC: Police Foundation, International Association of Chiefs of Police, and Urban Institute, October 1975), http://www.policefoundation.org/wp-content/uploads/2015/08/206509288-White-T-W-Bloch-P-B-Police-Officer-Height-And-Selected-Aspects-Of-Performance.pdf.
52. Ibid.
53. Mieth, 418 F. Supp. at 1184.
54. Less reticent was Governor George Wallace, with whom Mieth and her husband had stumbled into an unlikely social acquaintance. A few days after the lawsuit was filed, she was startled to answer the phone and find the governor on the line. He was livid. "Dammit, you've sued me! Why would you do that?" It took a few moments for Mieth to digest that a lawsuit against the Alabama Department of Public Safety was, however indirectly, a lawsuit against Wallace. Red-faced at her naivete, she apologized—and then reiterated her desire for a state trooper job. Wallace simply told her that he understood that she was doing what she needed to do, and the conversation ended there.
55. Quoted in Clare Cushman, ed., *Supreme Court Decisions and Women's Rights: Milestones to Equality* (Washington, DC: CQ Press, 2001), 26.
56. 347 U.S. 483 (1954).
57. It was Judge Brown who, seven years earlier, had bitterly dissented from the Fifth Circuit's refusal to reconsider its dismissal of Ida Phillips's sex discrimination case against Martin Marietta.
58. Armstrong v. Board of Education, 323 F.2d 333, 353 n.1 (5th Cir. 1963). See also Jack Bass, "The 'Fifth Circuit Four': How Four Federal Judges Brought the Rule of Reason to the South," *The Nation*, May 3, 2004, https://www.thenation.com/article/fifth-circuit-four.
59. 142 F. Supp. 707 (M.D. Ala. 1956), aff'd, 352 U.S. 950 (1956).
60. Quoted in Robert D. McFadden, "Frank M. Johnson Jr., Judge Whose Rulings Helped Desegregate the South, Dies at 80," *The New York Times*, July 24, 1999, http://www.nytimes.com/1999/07/24/us/frank-m-johnson-jr-judge-whose-rulings-helped-desegregate-the-south-dies-at-80.html
61. Quoted in ibid.
62. Mieth, 418 F. Supp. at 1182.
63. Ibid. at 1181.
64. Ibid. at 1179.
65. Ibid. at 1183.
66. Ibid. at 1180.
67. Serena Mayeri, *Reasoning from Race* (Cambridge, MA: Harvard University Press, 2011), 132.
68. Mayeri details the bumpy aftermath of *Mieth v. Dothard* for women hoping to become Alabama state troopers. Nearly two years later, no women had been hired. John Carroll and the Southern Poverty Law Center petitioned the court to suspend the veterans' preferences, but the motion was denied. Ibid., 132-133.

69. "Patrolling Alabama's Highways," *Ebony*, December 1979, 55.
70. 411 U.S. 677 (1973).
71. Ibid. at 684.
72. Reed v. Reed, 404 U.S. 71 (1971).
73. See, e.g., *Sisters in Law: How Sandra Day O'Connor and Ruth Bader Ginsburg Went to the Supreme Court and Changed the World* (New York: HarperCollins, 2015), 71-73; Fred Strebeigh, *Equal: Women Reshape American Law* (New York: W. W. Norton, 2009), 50-52. Letters between the lawyers of the ACLU WRP and the SPLC make clear that the former believed Levin had "reneged" on a promise to give Ginsburg and her staff control of the case. See, e.g., Hirshman, *Sisters in Law,* 71; Strebeigh, *Equal,* 51. Levin concedes that he had a change of heart as to who would handle the briefing, but as to the oral argument, his memory is that Ginsburg's taking the lead had only been raised as a possibility, not expressly agreed. In any event, Levin felt that relative peace was achieved in time for the argument, noting that he and Ginsburg, along with her late husband, Martin, had dinner in Washington the night before the argument.
74. Brief Amicus Curiae of American Civil Liberties Union, Dothard v. Rawlinson, 433 U.S. 321 (1977) (No. 76-422).
75. Linda Greenhouse, *Becoming Justice Blackmun: Harry Blackmun's Supreme Court Journey* (New York: Henry Holt & Co., 2005), 106.
76. Ibid.
77. Joan Biskupic, "Enforcing the Sartorial Code," *The Washington Post,* December 6, 1999, http://www.washingtonpost.com/wp-srv/WPcap/1999-12/06/008r-120699-idx.html.
78. Ibid.
79. Oral Argument at 2:56, Dothard v. Rawlinson, 433 U.S. 321 (1977) (No. 76-422), available at http://www.oyez.org/cases/1970-1979/1976/1976_76_422.
80. Ibid. at 17:31; 18:48; 18:57; 20:53.
81. Ibid. at 33:21; 33:28.
82. Ibid. at 35:24, 35:39; 35:50; 38:14.
83. Ibid. at 45:18; 50:23; 49:03.
84. Dothard v. Rawlinson, 433 U.S. 321, 331 (1977).
85. Ibid. at 330.
86. Ibid. at 332.
87. Ibid. at 335–36.
88. Ibid. at 341 (Marshall, J., concurring in part and dissenting in part).
89. Ibid. at 342.
90. Ibid. at 345.
91. Ibid. at 346.
92. Dothard, 433 U.S. at 335.
93. February 6, 2015, e-mail from Bob Horton, Alabama Department of Corrections, Public Information Officer, to author.

Three

Unless otherwise indicated, direct quotes, biographical and historical details, and mental impressions come from the following sources: Phone interview with Robert Dohrmann on July 24, 2014; interview with Bob Dohrmann in Los Angeles on February 13, 2015.
1. Kenneth A. Kochanek, M.A., Elizabeth Arias, Ph.D., & Robert N. Anderson, Ph.D., "How Did Cause of Death Contribute to Racial Differences in Life Expectancy in the United States in 2010?," NCHS Issue Brief, No. 125, July 2013, Centers for Disease Control and Prevention, http://www.cdc.gov/nchs/data/databriefs/db125.htm. Race-based mortality tables were long used by the life insurance industry but abandoned by the late 1960s due to a combination of forces, including "[p]ressure from civil rights organizations, a transformation in scientific and societal views about race after

World War II, post-war marketplace changes, the development of standardized race-merged tables by professional actuarial organizations, private party litigation, and late twentieth century investigations by state insurance departments." Mary L. Heen, "Nondiscrimination in Insurance: The Next Chapter," *Georgia Law Review* 49 (Fall 2014): 12.

2. Appendix at 45, Manhart v. City of Los Angeles Dep't of Water & Power, 435 U.S. 702 (1977) (No. 76-8610).

3. "In Memory," DWP Retirees Newsletter, Vol. 14, No. 5, Nov./Dec. 1995, case files of Schwartz, Steinsapir, Dohrmann & Sommers.

4. Dec. 17, 1968 letter from Alice Muller to Board of Administration, Water and Power Employees Retirement Plan, case files of Schwartz, Steinsapir, Dohrmann & Sommers: "In Memory," DWP Retirees Newsletter.

5. Appendix at 45, Manhart v. City of Los Angeles Dep't of Water & Power, 435 U.S. 702 (1977) (No. 76-8610).

6. May 3, 1973 letter from Alice Muller to Ruth Blanco, case files of Schwartz, Steinsapir, Dohrmann & Sommers.

7. Appendix at 44, Manhart v. City of Los Angeles Dep't of Water & Power, 435 U.S. 702 (1977) (No. 76-8610).

8. Ibid.

9. Undated note from Alice Muller, case files of Schwartz, Steinsapir, Dohrmann & Sommers.

10. Appendix at 17, Manhart v. City of Los Angeles Dep't of Water & Power, 435 U.S. 702 (1977) (No. 76-8610).

11. November 30, 1972, letter from Margaret D. Davis to Secretary to the Retirement Board, DWP Board of Commissioners, case files of Schwartz, Steinsapir, Dohrmann & Sommers.

12. November 30, 1972, letter from Carol J. Rastall to Allan F. Larson, Secretary of the Retirement Board, DWP Board of Commissioners, case files of Schwartz, Steinsapir, Dohrmann & Sommers.

13. Appendix at 1314, Manhart v. City of Los Angeles Dep't. of Water & Power, 435 U.S. 702 (1977) (No. 76-8610).

14. Hugh Davis Graham, *The Civil Rights Era: Origins and Development of National Policy* (New York: Oxford University Press, 1990), 229.

15. See, e.g., Caroline Bird, *Born Female: The High Cost of Keeping Women Down* (New York: Pocket Books, 1969), 64–65. The same assumption—that all men were primary breadwinners and all women did not work outside the home and were dependent on their husbands—was reflected in Social Security rules that paid lower survivorship benefits to men than to women; indeed, widowers were subject to onerous eligibility standards, whereas widows received benefits automatically. These requirements was invalidated in the 1970s by the Supreme Court, in a pair of cases litigated by then Columbia Law School professor and now Supreme Court Justice Ruth Bader Ginsburg. Califano v. Goldfarb, 430 U.S. 199 (1977); Weinberger v. Wiesenfeld, 420 U.S. 636 (1975).

16. 29 C.F.R. § 1604.9(f) (1972).

17. Robert Reinhold, "Opening New Freeway, Los Angeles Ends Era," *The New York Times,* October 14, 1993, http://www.nytimes.com/1993/10/14/us/opening-new-freeway-los-angeles-ends-era.html?pagewanted=print.

18. Ibid.

19. Editorial, "Sex-Segregated Actuarial Tables Discriminate," *The Las Vegas Sun,* June 16, 1974.

20. EEOC Decision No. 74-118 at 3–4 (1974).

21. Manhart v. City of Los Angeles Dep't of Water & Power, 387 F. Supp. 980, 982 (C.D. Cal. 1975).

22. 110 Congressional Record 13663–64 (June 12, 1964), quoted in Defendant's Memorandum in Opposition to Motion for Preliminary Injunction, Manhart v. City of Los Angeles Dep't of Water & Power, 387 F. Supp. 980 (C.D. Cal. 1975).

23. Manhart, 387 F. Supp. at 980, 983.
24. Ibid. at 983–984.
25. Ibid. at 984.
26. Ibid.
27. Flyer dated June 23, 1975, case files of Schwartz, Steinsapir, Dohrmann & Sommers.
28. Manhart v. City of Los Angeles Dep't of Water & Power, 553 F.2d 581, 590–591 (9th Cir. 1976).
29. Ibid. at 588.
30. Ibid. at 592.
31. Quoted in Robert Rawitch, "Appeals Court Backs Women on Pensions," *The Los Angeles Times*, December 1, 1976.
32. 429 U.S. 125 (1976).
33. "DWP to Fight Ruling on Employe Pensions," *The Los Angeles Times*, December 9, 1976.
34. Brief Amici Curiae of American Civil Liberties Union and American Association of University Professors, City of Los Angeles Dep't of Water & Power v. Manhart, 435 U.S. 702 (1977) (No. 76-1810).
35. Brief for the United States and the Equal Employment Opportunity Commission as Amici Curiae, City of Los Angeles Dep't of Water & Power v. Manhart, 435 U.S. 702 (1977) (No. 76-1810).
36. Brief for the International Union, United Automobile, Aerospace and Agricultural Implement Workers of America (UAW) and American Federation of Labor and Congress of Industrial Organizations as Amici Curiae, City of Los Angeles Dep't of Water & Power v. Manhart, 435 U.S. 702 (1977) (No. 76-1810).
37. Brief for the Association for Women in Mathematics and the Women's Equity Action League as Amici Curiae at 7-8, City of Los Angeles Dep't of Water & Power v. Manhart, 435 U.S. 702 (1977) (No. 76-1810).
38. Ibid., 9.
39. Brief Amici Curiae of American Civil Liberties Union and American Association of University Professors at 7-8, City of Los Angeles Dep't of Water & Power v. Manhart, 435 U.S. 702 (1977) (No. 76-1810).
40. Brief of American Nurses' Association, as Amicus Curiae, in Support of Respondents, City of Los Angeles Dep't of Water & Power v. Manhart, 435 U.S. 702 (1977) (No. 76-1810).
41. Brief of Teachers Insurance and Annuity Association of America and College Retirement Equities Fund, as Amici Curiae, in Support of Petitioners, City of Los Angeles Dep't of Water & Power v. Manhart, 435 U.S. 702 (1977) (No. 76-1810).
42. Brief Amicus Curiae of American Council of Life Insurance on Behalf of Petitioners at 3, City of Los Angeles Dep't of Water & Power v. Manhart, 435 U.S. 702 (1977) (No. 76-1810) (emphasis in original).
43. Brief of the State of Oregon as Amicus Curiae, in Support of Defendants-Petitioners; Brief of the City of New York as Amicus Curiae; and Brief for the New York State Teachers' Retirement System as Amicus Curiae, City of Los Angeles Dep't of Water & Power v. Manhart, 435 U.S. 702 (1977) (No. 76-1810).
44. Oral Argument at 7:10; 11:35; 1:57; 18:48, City of Los Angeles Dep't of Water & Power v. Manhart, 435 U.S. 702 (1977) (No. 76-1810), available at http://www.oyez.org/cases/1970-1979/1977/1977_76_1810.
45. Ibid. at 5:05; 7:13; 9:38; 2:10.
46. Ibid. at 27:49; 42:54: 43:00; 37:54.
47. Ibid. at 35:30; 36:35; 37:10; 37:20; 37:25.
48. Ibid. at 41:40.
49. Ibid. at 61:46.
50. City of Los Angeles Dep't of Water & Power v. Manhart, 435 U.S. 702, 711 (1977).
51. Ibid. at 709.
52. Ibid. at 711.
53. Ibid. at 714.

54. Ibid. at 717-718.

55. Ibid. at 726, 728 (Burger, C. J., dissenting).

56. Mary L. Heen, "Sex Discrimination in Pensions and Retirement Annuity Plans after Arizona Governing Committee v. Norris: Recognizing and Remedying Employer Non-Compliance," *Women's Rights Law Reporter* 8 (Summer 1985): 156, n.5, http://scholarship.richmond.edu/cgi/viewcontent.cgi?article=1260&context=law-faculty-publications.

57. 463 U.S. 1073 (1983).

58. Ibid. at 1081.

59. Mary L. Heen, "Nondiscrimination in Insurance: The Next Chapter," *Georgia Law Review:* 49 (Fall 2014): 49, http://scholarship.richmond.edu/cgi/viewcontent.cgi?article=2049&context=law-faculty-publications.

60. Ibid., 50, 54.

Four

Unless otherwise indicated, direct quotes, biographical and historical details, and mental impressions come from the following sources: Interview with Patricia Barry in Los Angeles, California, on February 16, 2015; phone interview with Judith Ludwic on June 23, 2015; phone interview with John Marshall Meisburg on June 23, 2015.

1. Quoted in Fred Strebeigh, *Equal: Women Reshape American Law* (New York: W. W. Norton & Co., 2009), 213.

2. Ibid., 213.

3. Mary Battiata, "Mechelle Vinson's Long Road to Court," *The Washington Post,* August 12, 1986, http://www.washingtonpost.com/archive/lifestyle/1986/08/12/mechelle-vinsons-long-road-to-court/b5fa7c5b-c0cf-412b-b40f-a3811e042884/.

4. Quoted in ibid.

5. Ibid.

6. Quoted in Kathy Hacker, "A Bank-Sex Case Becomes Cause Celebre," *The Philadelphia Inquirer,* June 1, 1986, http://articles.philly.com/1986-06-01/living/26042804_1_teller-case-caps.

7. Quoted in Battiata, "Mechelle Vinson's Long Road to Court."

8. Joint Appendix at 14, Meritor Sav. Bank, FSB v. Vinson, 477 U.S. 57 (1986) (No. 84-1979).

9. Vinson v. Taylor, No. 78-1793, 1980 U.S. Dist. LEXIS 10676 *3-*4 (D.D.C. Feb. 26, 1980); Hacker, "A Bank-Sex Case Becomes Cause Celebre."

10. Vinson, 1980 U.S. Dist. LEXIS 10676 at *4. In the court opinions in Mechelle Vinson's case, a distinction is drawn between the dozen or so occasions when Taylor "raped" Vinson and the rest of the occasions when they had intercourse that Vinson did not want but submitted to out of fear. Given Vinson's asserted lack of consent to any sex with Taylor, this is a distinction without a difference, and all intercourse will be described here as rape.

11. Quoted in Mary Battiata, "Mechelle Vinson's Tangled Trials," *The Washington Post,* August 11, 1986, http://www.washingtonpost.com/archive/lifestyle/1986/08/11/mechelle-vinsons-tangled-trials/40688848-d73c-4856-8a41-cff3e74277ba/.

12. Hacker, "A Bank-Sex Case Becomes Cause Celebre."

13. Philip Hager, "Supreme Court to Rule on Sexual Harassment at Work," *The Los Angeles Times,* June 8, 1986, http://articles.latimes.com/1986-06-08/news/mn-9645_1_supreme-court-ruling.

14. Quoted in Battiata, "Mechelle Vinson's Tangled Trials."

15. Strebeigh, *Equal,* 218-225.

16. Ibid., 225, 223.

17. Quoted in Enid Nemy, "Women Begin to Speak Out Against Sexual Harassment at Work," *The New York Times,* August 19, 1975.

18. Ibid. See also Strebeigh, *Equal,* 232–233; Carrie N. Baker, "He Said, She Said: Popular Representations of Sexual Harassment and Second-Wave Feminism," in Sherrie

A. Inness, ed., *Disco Divas: Women and Popular Culture in the 1970s* (Philadelphia: University. of Pennsylvania Press, 2003), 42–43.

19. Rhoda Koenig, "An Ardent Plea for Sexual Harassment," *Harper's,* February 1, 1976, 90.

20. Mary Bralove, "A Cold Shoulder: Career Women Decry Sexual Harassment by Bosses and Clients," *The Wall Street Journal,* January 29, 1976.

21. Baker, "He Said, She Said," 43.

22. Ibid., 49.

23. Augustus B. Cochran III, *Sexual Harassment and the Law: The Mechelle Vinson Story* (Lawrence: University of Kansas Press, 2004), 47.

24. Baker, "He Said, She Said," 49.

25. Barnes v. Train, No. 1828-73, 1974 U.S. Dist. LEXIS 7212 at *3 (D.D.C. Aug. 9, 1974), rev'd sub nom, Barnes v. Costle, 561 F.2d 983 (D.C. Cir. 1977).

26. Corne v. Bausch & Lomb, Inc., 390 F. Supp. 161, 163 (D. Ariz. 1975), rev'd, 562 F.2d 55 (1977).

27. Miller v. Bank of America, 418 F. Supp. 233, 236 (N.D. Cal. 1976), rev'd, 600 F.2d 211 (9th Cir. 1979).

28. Tomkins v. Public Service Electric & Gas Co., 422 F. Supp. 553, 556 (D.N.J. 1976), rev'd, 568 F.2d 1044 (3d Cir. 1977).

29. Fred Strebeigh provides a thorough account of how the activism of Lin Farley, Susan Meyer, and Karen Sauvigne on behalf of Carmita Wood dovetailed with the genesis of MacKinnon's book, which she began as an independent research project while a student at Yale Law School. Strebeigh, *Equal,* 225–234.

30. Catharine MacKinnon, *Sexual Harassment of Working Women* (New Haven, CT: Yale University Press, 1979), 89–90.

31. Ibid., 60, 63–74, 75–77.

32. Williams v. Saxbe, 413 F. Supp. 654, 658 (D.D.C. 1976), rev'd in part, vacated in part sub nom, Williams v. Bell, 587 F.2d 1240 (D.C. Cir. 1978).

33. See, e.g., Garber v. Saxon Bus. Prods., Inc., 552 F.2d 1032 (4th Cir. 1977); Heelan v. Johns-Manville Corp., 451 F. Supp. 1382 (D. Colo. 1978); Munford v. James T. Barnes & Co., 441 F. Supp. 459 (E.D. Mich. 1977).

34. In reversing *Barnes,* one of the three judges on the D.C. Circuit panel agreed that Paulette Barnes had been illegally harassed, but disagreed with the majority's ruling that an employer was absolutely liable for its supervisors' harassment. That judge was George MacKinnon—Catharine MacKinnon's father.

35. As MacKinnon described the phenomenon in *Sexual Harassment of Working Women* at page 33: "To date, all of the legally successful suits for sexual harassment have alleged some form of the trilogy of unwanted advances, rejection, retaliation."

36. Ibid., 32–40.

37. Ibid., 40, 44.

38. Battiata, "Mechelle Vinson's Tangled Trials."

39. Quoted in ibid.

40. Transcript of Trial, January 22, 1980 at 33, 34, Vinson v. Taylor, No. 78-1793, 1980 U.S. Dist. LEXIS 10676 (D.D.C. Feb. 26, 1980).

41. Strebeigh, *Equal,* 211–212.

42. Opposition of Plaintiff to Defendant's Motion to Dismiss, Declaration of Christine Malone, Vinson v. Taylor, No. 78-1793, 1980 U.S. Dist. LEXIS 10676 (D.D.C. Feb. 26, 1980).

43. Plaintiff's Motion to File First Amended Complaint and to Add Parties, Declaration of Mary Levarity, Vinson v. Taylor, No. 78-1793, 1980 U.S. Dist. LEXIS 10676 (D.D.C. Feb. 26, 1980).

44. Joint Appendix at 14-15, Meritor Sav. Bank, FSB v. Vinson, 477 U.S. 57 (1986) (No. 84-1979).

45. Quoted in Hacker, "A Bank-Sex Case Becomes Cause Celebre."

46. Title VII includes this "pattern or practice" language, which is generally used to bring class action discrimination claims involving large numbers of employees. Relying on

it was Barry's effort to ground her "condition of work," a/k/a hostile environment claim, not yet recognized in any federal court, in the text of the statute.

47. Transcript of Trial, January 23, 1980 at 16, 22, Vinson v. Taylor, No. 78-1793, 1980 U.S. Dist. LEXIS 10676 (D.D.C. Feb. 26, 1980).

48. 347 U.S. 483 (1954).

49. Adam Bernstein, "U.S. District Court Judge John Garrett Penn, 75," *The Washington Post*, September 12, 2007. http://www.washingtonpost.com/wp-dyn/content /article/2007/09/11/AR2007091102335.html.

50. Strebeigh, *Equal*, 263–264.

51. Ibid.; Cochran, *Sexual Harassment and the Law*, 70–71.

52. Strebeigh, *Equal*, 264.

53. Cochran, *Sexual Harassment and the Law*, 70–71.

54. Answers of Plaintiff to Interrogatories Propounded by Defendant at 23, Vinson v. Taylor, No. 78-1793, 1980 U.S. Dist. LEXIS 10676 (D.D.C. Feb. 26, 1980).

55. Battiata, "Mechelle Vinson's Tangled Trials."

56. Transcript of Trial, January 22, 1980 at 82, Vinson v. Taylor, No. 78-1793, 1980 U.S. Dist. LEXIS 10676 (D.D.C. Feb. 26, 1980).

57. Transcript of Trial, January 31, 1980 at 8, Vinson v. Taylor, No. 78-1793, 1980 U.S. Dist. LEXIS 10676 (D.D.C. Feb. 26, 1980).

58. Cochran, *Sexual Harassment and the Law*, 71.

59. Transcript of Trial, January 31, 1980 at 14, Vinson v. Taylor, No. 78-1793, 1980 U.S. Dist. LEXIS 10676 (D.D.C. Feb. 26, 1980).

60. Jane H. Aiken, "Protecting Plaintiffs' Sexual Pasts," *Emory Law Journal* 51 (2002): 561–563.

61. Vinson, 1980 U.S. Dist. LEXIS 10676 at *23.

62. Ibid. at *20.

63. Strebeigh, *Equal*, 268–269.

64. 29 C.F.R. § 1604.11(c) (1980) (rescinded Oct. 29, 1999).

65. Ibid. § 1604.11(a) (1980) (emphasis added).

66. 641 F.2d 934 (D.C. Cir. 1981).

67. Ibid. at 945.

68. Philip Smith, "Court Eases Rule on Sex Harassment," *The Washington Post*, January 26, 1985, http://www.washingtonpost.com/archive/local/1985/01/26/court-eases -rule-on-harassment/6c4eaf93-a091-4b46-bcc1-88f360effa8c/.

69. Eric Pace, "Spottswood W. Robinson 3d, Civil Rights Lawyer, Dies at 82," *The New York Times*, October 13, 1988, http://www.nytimes.com/1998/10/13/us/spotts wood-w-robinson-3d-civil-rights-lawyer-dies-at-82.html.

70. Barnes v. Costle, 561 F.2d 983 (D.C. Cir. 1977). Fred Strebeigh makes a strong case that Judge Robinson received an early version of MacKinnon's *Sexual Harassment of Working Women* (when it was still just a research paper) at the time the D.C. Circuit was deciding *Barnes*. MacKinnon's father, Judge George MacKinnon, was on the panel with Robinson, and MacKinnon happened to be visiting her father's chambers doing research when an unidentified woman, believed to be one of Robinson's clerks, borrowed the paper. See Strebeigh, *Equal*, 241–245, 250–258.

71. Marjorie Hunter, "Judge J. Skelly Wright, Segregation Foe, Dies at 77," *The New York Times*, August 8, 1988, http://www.nytimes.com/1988/08/08/obituaries/judge -j-skelly-wright-segregation-foe-dies-at-77.html.

72. Ibid.

73. Ruth Bader Ginsburg, "Four Louisiana Giants in the Law," Judge Robert A. Ainsworth Jr. Memorial Lecture, February 4, 2002, Loyola University New Orleans School of Law, http://www.supremecourtus.gov/publicinfo/speeches/sp_02-04-02 .html.

74. Strebeigh, *Equal*, 269.

75. Hacker, "A Bank-Sex Case Becomes Cause Celebre."

76. Strebeigh, *Equal*, 269.

77. Vinson v. Taylor, 753 F.2d 141, 145 (D.C. Cir. 1985) (emphasis in original).

78. Ibid. at 146.
79. Ibid.
80. Ibid. at 146 & n.36.
81. Ibid. at 150.
82. Ronald J. Ostrow, "Law Center Opposes Nomination: Bork Termed a Peril to the Rights of Women," *The Los Angeles Times,* August 19, 1987, http://articles.latimes .com/1987-08-19/news/mn-826_1_judge-robert-h-bork.
83. M. L. Nestel, "Conservative Scold Ken Starr Got a Billionaire Pedophile Off," *The Daily Beast,* January 30, 2015, http://www.thedailybeast.com/articles/2015/01/30 /conservative-scold-ken-starr-got-a-billionaire-pedophile-off.html.
84. Vinson v. Taylor, 760 F.2d 1330, 1331 (D.C. Cir. 1985) (per curiam) (Bork, J., dissenting).
85. Ibid.
86. Ibid.
87. Hacker, "A Bank-Sex Case Becomes Cause Celebre."
88. Georgia Dullea, "Sexual Harassment at Work: A Sensitive and Confusing Issue," *The New York Times,* October 24, 1980, http://timesmachine.nytimes.com/times machine/1980/10/24/111303733.html?pageNumber=20.
89. *9 to 5* (Twentieth Century Fox, 1980).
90. Rebecca Traister, "If You Want to See What Revolutionary Workplace Policies Really Look Like, Watch '9 to 5,'" *The New Republic,* May 13, 2015, http://www.new republic.com/article/121785/enduring-relevance-9-5.
91. Hacker, "A Bank-Sex Case Becomes Cause Celebre."
92. Battiata, "Mechelle Vinson's Tangled Trials."
93. As Fred Strebeigh details, Thomas had helped write a memo to the Reagan transition team advocating against vigorous enforcement of the Guidelines. "[T]he elimination of personal slights and sexual advances which contribute to an 'intimidating, hostile or offensive working environment' is a goal impossible to reach," he wrote. "Expenditure of the EEOC's limited resources in pursuit of this goal is unwise." Strebeigh, *Equal,* 283.
94. Ibid., 282–284.
95. Ibid., 283.
96. Barry told Fred Strebeigh, however, that her poor showing was an example of "self-sabotag[e]" motivated by insecurity. Quoted in Strebeigh, *Equal,* 290.
97. Interview with Carin Clauss, Madison, Wisconsin, August 26, 2014.
98. Lehman v. Nakshian, 453 U.S. 156 (1981).
99. Oral Argument at :33, Meritor Sav. Bank, FSB v. Vinson, 477 U.S. 57 (1986) (84-1979), available at http://www.oyez.org/cases/1980-1989/1985/1985_84_1979.
100. Ibid., 13:18; 13:52; 14:25; 21:30.
101. Ibid., 7:10; 8:10; 9:37; 9:47.
102. Ibid., 26:40.
103. Ibid., 28:20, 35:52.
104. Ibid., 36:12; 37:48; 47:33.
105. Ibid., 56:00.
106. Strebeigh, *Equal,* 299.
107. Meritor Sav. Bank, FSB v. Vinson, 477 U.S. 57, 64 (1986).
108. Ibid. at 67.
109. Ibid.
110. Ibid.
111. Ibid. at 68.
112. Ibid. at 69. Although this part of the decision was dispiriting to women's advocates, its impact was somewhat blunted by later changes to the Federal Rules of Evidence. In 1994, the rules applying to civil cases were changed to import the so-called rape shield law from criminal cases. Under Rule 412 of the Federal Rules of Evidence, the dress and behavior of the victim of an alleged sexual offense is irrelevant, except as toward the alleged offender himself. Under such a standard, much of the disputed

evidence about Mechelle Vinson would likely have been excluded. Notably, Justice Rehnquist wrote to Congress to object to the rape shield rule's extension to civil cases precisely because it would conflict with the "welcomeness" defense left available to defendants under *Vinson* ("[S]ome Justices expressed concern that the proposed amendment [to extend Rule 412 to civil cases] might encroach on the rights of some defendants"). See Aiken, "Protecting Plaintiffs' Sexual Pasts," at 573 (and citations contained therein).

113. Meritor, 477 U.S. at 72. Justice Marshall, in an opinion joined by Justices Brennan, Blackmun, and Stevens, filed a concurrence that disagreed with the Court's ruling on employer liability. The Court of Appeals' strict liability standard, which imported the EEOC Guidelines, was correct, Marshall wrote. The EEOC's (and solicitor general's) brief backing away from those Guidelines, said Marshall, was "untenable." 477 U.S. at 76 ("A supervisor's responsibilities do not begin and end with the power to hire, fire, and discipline employees, or with the power to recommend such actions. Rather, a supervisor is charged with the day-to-day supervision of the work environment and with ensuring a safe, productive workplace. There is no reason why abuse of the latter authority should have different consequences than abuse of the former.").

114. Meritor, 477 U.S. at 72–73.

115. Battiata, "Mechelle Vinson's Tangled Trials."

116. Quoted in ibid.

117. Ibid.

118. Ibid.

119. Ibid.

120. Judith Resnik, "Old and New Depictions of Justice: Reflections, Circa 2011, on Hill-Thomas," in Amy Richards and Cynthia Greenberg, eds., *I Still Believe Anita Hill* (New York: The Feminist Press, 2013), 53.

121. Catharine MacKinnon, "Voice, Heart, Ground," in Richards and Greenberg, *I Still Believe Anita Hill*, 72 (citations omitted).

122. United States v. Taylor, 867 F. 2d 700 (D.C. Cir. 1989).

123. Tanya Kateri Hernandez, "'What Not to Wear'—Race and Unwelcomeness in Sexual Harassment Law: The Story of Meritor Savings Bank v. Vinson," in Elizabeth M. Schneider and Stephanie M. Wildman, eds., *Women and the Law: Stories* (New York: Thomson Reuters/Foundation Press, 2011), 293.

124. Quoted in Sheila Weller, "These Women Changed *Your* Life," *Glamour,* September 2005, 268.

Five

Unless otherwise indicated, direct quotes, biographical and historical details, and mental impressions come from the following sources: Interview with Carin Clauss, Madison, Wisconsin, August 25, 2014; interview with Lillian Garland, Dale City, Virginia, April 8, 2015; interview with Patricia Shiu, Washington, DC, April 9, 2015; and phone interview with Linda Krieger, June 1, 2015.

1. Quoted in Tamar Lewin, "Maternity Leave: Is It Leave, Indeed?" *The New York Times,* July 22, 1984, http://www.nytimes.com/1984/07/22/business/maternity-leave -is-it-leave-indeed.html?pagewanted=all.

2. Ibid.

3. Montgomery Brower, "A Working Mother's Fight for Job Security Goes to the Last Round," *People,* February 10, 1986.

4. Quoted in Carol Kleiman, "Court Victory in War on Sex Bias Was Not Without Serious Casualties," *The Chicago Tribune,* June 22, 1987.

5. Brower, "A Working Mother's Fight."

6. Kleiman, "Court Victory in War on Sex Bias."

7. Amy Wilentz, "Garland's Bouquet," *Time,* January 26, 1987.

8. Kleiman, "Court Victory in War on Sex Bias."

9. 42 U.S.C. § 2000e(k).

10. Henry Weinstein, "Controversial Federal Judge Steps Down from L.A. Post," *The Los Angeles Times,* January 7, 1994, http://articles.latimes.com/1994-01-07/news/mn -9326_1_chief-judge.

11. Carol J. Williams, "Critics Want to Bench Judge Manuel L. Real," *The Los Angeles Times,* August 16, 2009, http://articles.latimes.com/2009/aug/16/local/me-judge -real16.

12. Weinstein, "Controversial Federal Judge Steps Down."

13. Ibid.

14. Ibid.

15. Terry Carter, "Real Trouble," *ABA Journal,* September 1, 2008, http://www.aba journal.com/magazine/article/real_trouble.

16. Bill Farr, "Contempt Charges Against Flynt Dismissed," *The Los Angeles Times,* March 29, 1985, http://articles.latimes.com/1985-03-29/local/me-20456_1_larry -flynt.

17. United States v. Flynt, 756 F.2d 1352 (9th Cir. 1985).

18. *The People vs. Larry Flynt* (Columbia Pictures, 1996).

19. The preemption doctrine stems from the Constitution's Supremacy Clause, which provides that the "Constitution and the laws of the United States . . . shall be the supreme law of the land . . . anything in the constitutions or laws of any State to the contrary notwithstanding." U.S. Constitution, Article VI.

20. California Federal Sav. & Loan Ass'n v. Guerra, No. 83-4927R, 1984 U.S. Dist. LEXIS 18387 at *2 (C.D. Cal., Mar. 21, 1984).

21. Ibid.

22. Jack Jones, "Court Overturns Maternity Leave Job Protection," *The Los Angeles Times,* March 20, 1984.

23. Lewin, "Maternity Leave: Is It Leave, Indeed?"

24. Linda J. Krieger and Patricia N. Cooney, "The Miller-Wohl Controversy: Equal Treatment, Positive Action and the Meaning of Women's Equality," *Golden Gate University Law Review* 13 (1983): 515.

25. Patricia A. Shiu and Stephanie M. Wildman, "Pregnancy Discrimination and So-cial Change: Evolving Consciousness About a Worker's Right to Job-Protected, Paid Leave," *Yale Journal of Law & Feminism* 21 (2009): 134.

26. Mont. Code Ann. §§ 39-7-201 (pre-1983 amendment).

27. Wendy W. Williams, "Equality's Riddle: Pregnancy and the Equal Treatment/Special Treatment Debate," *N.Y.U. Review of Law and Social Change* 13 (1984–85): 325.

28. Ibid., 327.

29. *60 Minutes: Maternity Leave* (CBS television broadcast, December 2, 1984).

30. Krieger and Cooney, "The Miller-Wohl Controversy," 518–519 (internal citations omitted).

31. Ibid., 519 (internal citation omitted).

32. See Fred Strebeigh, *Equal: Women Reshape American Law* (New York: W. W. Nor-ton & Co., 2009).

33. Krieger and Cooney, "The Miller-Wohl Controversy," 520 (internal citation omitted).

34. Ibid., 519.

35. Katharine T. Bartlett, "Pregnancy and the Constitution: The Uniqueness Trap," *Cali-fornia Law Review* 62 (1974): 1532.

36. Muller v. Oregon, 208 U.S. 412 (1907).

37. Quoted in Gail Collins, *When Everything Changed* (New York: Little, Brown & Co. 2009), 70.

38. Ibid.

39. At the time, Carin Clauss was a young lawyer at the Labor Department. (She later was appointed its Solicitor.) She recalled the dismay registered by Peterson, by then the Department's Special Assistant for Consumer Affairs, when Smith proposed add-ing "sex" to Title VII:

> Esther Peterson burst into my office. "Carin, you have to do something. Con-gress is about to pass a law that will undo all of our protective legislation!" [She]

had been at [former Secretary of Labor] Francis Perkins' side when the Triangle Shirtwaist fire [happened, killing 145 young female sweatshop workers], and they had worked so hard. . . ."They're gonna repeal all these laws, you gotta do something!"

40. Williams, "Equality's Riddle," 325.
41. See, e.g., Rosenfeld v. Southern Pacific Co., 444 F.2d 1219, 1223 (9th Cir. 1971); Bowe v. Colgate-Palmolive Co., 416 F.2d 711 (7th Cir. 1969); Weeks v. Southern Bell Tel. & Tel. Co., 408 F.2d 228 (5th Cir. 1969).
42. See, e.g., Deborah A. Widiss, "Gilbert Redux: The Interaction of the Pregnancy Discrimination Act and the Amended Americans with Disabilities Act," *University of California Davis Law Review* 46 (2013): 979–980 (and citations contained therein).
43. See General Elec. Co. v. Gilbert, 429 U.S. 125, 142 (1976) (internal citation omitted).
44. Ibid. at 143 (internal citation omitted).
45. Strebeigh, *Equal,* 116.
46. Ibid., 116–118.
47. 29 C.F.R. § 1604.10(a)–(b) (1973). Moreover, if a pregnant woman needed time off and she had exhausted any available leave under whatever policy the employer had in place for such absences, the employer had to allow the additional leave if refusing it would have a "disparate impact" on pregnant women—that is, if it would result in pregnant women's being disproportionately fired as compared to other employees who needed temporary leaves. Ibid. § 1604.10(c).
48. Cleveland Bd. of Educ. v. LaFleur, 414 U.S. 632 (1974).
49. Turner v. Department of Employment Security, 423 U.S. 44 (1975).
50. Nashville Gas Co. v. Satty, 434 U.S. 136 (1977).
51. Deborah L. Brake and Joanna L. Grossman, "Unprotected Sex: The Pregnancy Discrimination Act at 35," *Duke Journal of Gender Law & Policy* 21 (2013): 73.
52. Geduldig v. Aiello, 417 U.S. 484 (1974).
53. 429 U.S. 125 (1976).
54. Widiss, "Gilbert Redux," 993.
55. Deborah Dinner, "The Costs of Reproduction: History and the Legal Construction of Sex Equality," *Harvard Civil Rights-Civil Liberties Law Review* 46 (2011): 469–470.
56. 42 U.S.C. § 2000e(k).
57. Ibid.
58. Coleman v. Court of Appeals, 132 S. Ct. 1327, 1342 (2012) (Ginsburg, J., dissenting).
59. Troupe v. May Dep't Stores Co., 20 F.3d 734, 738 (7th Cir. 1994).
60. Shiu and Wildman, "Pregnancy Discrimination and Social Change," 129 (internal citation omitted).
61. Miller-Wohl Co. v. Commissioner of Labor and Industry, 692 P.2d 1243 (Mont. 1984), vacated by 479 U.S. 1050 (1987), remanded to 744 P.2d 871 (Mont. 1987).
62. 387 F. Supp. 980 (C.D. Cal. 1975).
63. Bruce Weber, "Warren J. Ferguson, 87, Federal Judge, Is Dead," *The New York Times,* July 12, 2008, http://www.nytimes.com/2008/07/12/washington/12ferguson.html.
64. Just the Beginning—A Pipeline Organization, "Earl B. Gilliam," http://www.jtb.org /index.php?src=directory&view=biographies&srctype=detail&refno=66.
65. California Federal Sav. & Loan Ass'n v. Guerra, 758 F.2d 390, 393 (9th Cir. 1985).
66. Ibid. at 396.
67. Mark Guerra was the director of California's Department of Fair Employment and Housing at the time Cal Fed filed its lawsuit, making him the named representative of the state.
68. Stephanie M. Wildman, "Pregnant and Working: The Story of California Federal Savings & Loan Association v. Guerra," in Elizabeth M. Schneider and Stephen M. Wildman, eds., *Women and the Law: Stories* (New York: Thomson Reuters/Foundation Press, 2011), 267.
69. Coleman, 132 S. Ct. at 1341 (Ginsburg, J., dissenting).

70. Margaret Wolf Freivogel, "Woman Wins Her Fight for Job Rights," *St. Louis Post-Dispatch,* December 13, 1987.
71. 133 S. Ct. 2562 (2013).
72. Kenji Yoshino, *Speak Now: Marriage Equality on Trial—The Story of Hollingsworth v. Perry* (New York: Crown Publishers, 2015), 23.
73. Oral Argument at 3:27-6:07; 22:35, 23:18-24:30, California Federal Sav. & Loan Ass'n v. Guerra, 479 U.S. 272 (1987) (85-494), available at http://www.oyez.org/cases/1980-1989/1986/1986_85_494#argument.
74. Ibid. at 8:20, 8:42-9:29; 9:55-10:17.
75. Ibid. at 28:53-29:15; 34:13-34:27; 34:45-34:56.
76. Ibid. at 37:20-38:09.
77. Ibid. at 40:33-41:02.
78. Ibid. at 50:34-50:48.
79. Patt Morrison, "Job Litigant Asked God to Guide Justices," *The Los Angeles Times,* January 14, 1987, http://articles.latimes.com/1987-01-14/news/mn-3375_1_custody.
80. California Federal Sav. & Loan Ass'n v. Guerra, 479 U.S. 272, 285 (1987).
81. Ibid. at 289.
82. Ibid. at 290 (emphasis in original) (citation omitted).
83. Quoted in Al Kamen, "Court Upholds Pregnancy Leave Laws," *The Washington Post,* January 14, 1987, http://www.washingtonpost.com/archive/politics/1987/01/14/court-upholds-pregnancy-leave-laws/89065d62-c58a-4517-bcd2-9f9eac4fda43/.
84. Quoted in Wilentz, "Garland's Bouquet."
85. Quoted in Kamen, "Court Upholds Pregnancy Leave Laws."
86. Quoted in ibid.
87. Steven K. Wisensale, "Two Steps Forward, One Step Back: The Family and Medical Leave Act as Retrenchment Policy," *Review of Policy Research* 20, No. 1 (March 2003): 135.
88. "Clinton Signs His First Legislation," *The New York Times,* February 6, 1993, http://www.nytimes.com/1993/02/06/us/clinton-signs-his-first-legislation.html; Felicity Barringer, "Family-Leave Bill: Peace of Mind Issue," *The New York Times,* February 4, 1993, http://www.nytimes.com/1993/02/04/garden/family-leave-bill-peace-of-mind-issue.html.
89. Bill Clinton, "Remarks at the Signing of the Family and Medical Leave Act" (February 5, 1993), The Miller Center, University of Virginia, http://millercenter.org/president/clinton/speeches/speech-4562.
90. Family and Medical Leave Act of 1993, Pub. L. No. 103-03, 107 Stat. 6 (codified as amended at 29 U.S.C. §§ 2601-2654 (2006)).
91. Lauren Sandler, "Taking Care of Our Own," *The New Republic,* May 18, 2015, http://www.newrepublic.com/article/121822/paid-leave-goes-progressive-pipe-dream-political-reality.
92. Clinton, "Remarks."
93. Barringer, "Family-Leave Bill."
94. Wilentz, "Garland's Bouquet."

Six

Unless otherwise indicated, direct quotes, biographical and historical details, and mental impressions come from the following sources: Iinterview with Ann Hopkins, Washington, DC, September 30, 2014; interview with Doug Huron, November 7, 2014; May 5, 2015 e-mail from Doug Huron to author; phone interview with Susan Fiske, Ph.D., April 15, 2015.
1. Quoted in Tamar Lewin, "Winner of Sex Bias Suit Set to Enter Next Arena," *The New York Times,* May 19, 1990, http://www.nytimes.com/1990/05/19/us/winner-of-sex-bias-suit-set-to-enter-next-arena.html.
2. Ann Branigar Hopkins, *So Ordered: Making Partner the Hard Way* (Amherst: University of Massachusetts Press, 1996), 9.

3. Quoted in Dorothy Storck, "Beating Men at Their Own Game: Ann Hopkins Is Not a Feminist. But She Shook Up the Old Boys in the Boardroom When She Decided to Fight for Her Rights," *The Philadelphia Inquirer,* May 22, 1990, http://articles .philly.com/1990-05-22/news/25885434_1_ann-hopkins-discrimination-suit-courts.

4. Hopkins, *So Ordered,* 4.

5. *Makers: Women in Business* (PBS television broadcast, October 28, 2014), www .makers.com/documentary/womeninbusiness.

6. Hopkins, *So Ordered,* 25.

7. August 18, 2015, email message from Ann Hopkins to author.

8. Hopkins v. Price Waterhouse, 825 F.2d 458, 462 (D.C. Cir. 1987).

9. Hopkins, *So Ordered,* 216.

10. Today, due to mergers and bankruptcies, the group is known as the "Big Four." See, e.g., Paul Danos, "Back to the Big Eight Again," Forbes.com, Apr. 12, 2007, http:// www.forbes.com/2007/04/12/danos-accounting-bigeight-oped-cx_pd_0413danos .html.

11. Eric N. Berg, "The Big Eight: Still a Male Bastion," *The New York Times,* July 12, 1988, http://www.nytimes.com/1988/07/12/business/the-big-eight-still-a-male-bas tion.html.

12. Hopkins, *So Ordered,* 137.

13. Ibid., 140.

14. Ibid.

15. Hopkins v. Price Waterhouse, 618 F. Supp. 1109, 1113, 1116-1117 (D.D.C. 1985).

16. Ibid. at 1116.

17. Ann Branigar Hopkins, "Price Waterhouse v. Hopkins: A Personal Account of a Sexual Discrimination Plaintiff," *Hofstra Labor & Employment Law Journal* 22 (Spring 2005): 361.

18. Hopkins, *So Ordered,* 138, 147.

19. Hopkins, 618 F. Supp. at 113.

20. Hopkins, 825 F. 2d at 462.

21. Hopkins, *So Ordered,* 152.

22. *Makers: Women in Business.*

23. Hopkins, *So Ordered,* 153.

24. Ibid., 138.

25. Ibid., 153–154.

26. Hopkins, "A Personal Account of a Sexual Discrimination Plaintiff," 368.

27. Hopkins, *So Ordered,* 156.

28. Ibid., 163.

29. Hopkins, 618 F. Supp. at 1117.

30. Ibid.

31. Timothy S. Robinson, "Sparks May Fly as Lawyers Pick Best, Worst Federal Judges," *The Washington Post,* May 30, 1980, http://www.washingtonpost.com/archive /business/1980/06/30/sparks-may-fly-as-lawyers-pick-best-worst-us-federal-judges /cd265f9a-06ab-4805-a1af-3fccd452acd4/.

32. Quoted in Bruce Lambert, "Judge Gerhard Gesell Dies at 82; Oversaw Big Cases," *The New York Times,* February 21, 1993, http://www.nytimes.com/1993/02/21/us /judge-gerhard-gesell-dies-at-82-oversaw-big-cases.html?pagewanted=1.

33. "Gerhard A. Gesell; Iran-Contra Judge," *The Los Angeles Times,* February 21, 1993, http://articles.latimes.com/1993-02-21/news/mn-752_1_arnold-gesell.

34. The clinic's name later was changed to the Yale Child Study Center. http://medicine .yale.edu/childstudy/about/history.aspx. Additionally, a New Haven, Connecticut, nonprofit devoted to the study and promotion of healthy child development, the Gesell Institute of Child Development, is named for Dr. Gesell. See http://www.gesell institute.org.

35. Bart Barnes, "James Heller Dies," *The Washington Post,* November 28, 2001, http://www.washingtonpost.com/archive/local/2001/11/28/james-heller-dies/416ee 2f3-4efc-4c77-9cd8-66843c2324fc/.

36. Quoted in Hopkins, *So Ordered*, 211.
37. Ibid., 212.
38. Hopkins, "A Personal Account of a Sexual Discrimination Plaintiff," 366.
39. Hopkins, *So Ordered*, 197.
40. Ibid., 221.
41. Ibid., 225.
42. Joint Appendix at 14, Price Waterhouse v. Hopkins, 490 U.S. 228 (1989) (No. 87-1167).
43. Ibid. at 20–33.
44. Ibid. at 58–59.
45. Hopkins, 618 F. Supp. at 1120.
46. Ibid. at 1118–1120.
47. Ibid. at 1114.
48. Ibid. at 1120.
49. Ibid. at 1121.
50. Hopkins, 825 F.2d at 466, 472.
51. Ibid. at 473.
52. Quoted in Lewin, "Winner of Sex Bias Suit Set to Enter Next Arena."
53. Hopkins, 825 F.2d at 477, 478 (Williams, J., dissenting).
54. Petitioner's Brief at 73, Price Waterhouse v. Hopkins, 490 U.S. 228, 251 (1989) (No. 87-1167).
55. Brief for Amicus Curiae American Psychological Association in Support of Respondent at 37, Price Waterhouse v. Hopkins, 490 U.S. 228 (1989) (No. 87-1167).
56. Quoted in Brief of Amici Curiae NOW Legal Defense and Education Fund, et al., in Support of Respondent at 16, Price Waterhouse v. Hopkins, 490 U.S. 228 (1989) (No. 87-1167).
57. Hopkins, "A Personal Account of a Sexual Discrimination Plaintiff," 369.
58. Oral Argument at 1:35-2:50; 15:44-17:14, Price Waterhouse v. Hopkins, 490 U.S. 228 (1989) (No. 87-1167), available at http://www.oyez.org/cases/1980-1989/1988/1988_87_1167.
59. Ibid. at 9:15.
60. Ibid. at 19:00–19:30.
61. Ibid. at 27:30–32:03.
62. Ibid. at 32:06–32:24.
63. Ibid. at 29:47–30:23.
64. Ibid. at 43:37.
65. Hopkins, *So Ordered*, 293, 294, 296.
66. Price Waterhouse v. Hopkins, 490 U.S. 228, 251, 256 (1989). What the six couldn't agree on, though, was how much evidence of bias the plaintiff needed to show in order to shift the burden to the defendant to prove it would have made the same decision anyway. When Congress amended Title VII in 1991, it clarified this standard—and minimized the burden of proof on the plaintiff.
67. Hopkins, *So Ordered*, 310.
68. Ibid., 350.
69. Lewin, "Winner of Sex Bias Suit Set to Enter Next Arena."
70. Hopkins v. Price Waterhouse, 737 F. Supp. 1202, 1210-11 (D.D.C. 1990).
71. Quoted in Tamar Lewin, "Partnership in Firm Awarded to Victim of Sex Bias," *The New York Times*, May 16, 1990, http://www.nytimes.com/1990/05/16/us/partnership-in-firm-awarded-to-victim-of-sex-bias.html.
72. Hopkins, *So Ordered*, 377.
73. Ibid., 381.
74. *Makers: Women in Business*.
75. Hopkins, "A Personal Account of a Sexual Discrimination Plaintiff," 412.
76. "The 100 Best Companies for Working Mothers," *Working Mother*, October 2002, 108.

77. Quoted in Reed Abelson, "If Wall Street Is a Dead End, Do Women Stay to Fight or Go Quietly?" *The New York Times*, August 3, 1999, http://www.nytimes.com/1999/08/03/business/if-wall-street-is-a-dead-end-do-women-stay-to-fight-or-go-quietly.html.

Seven

Unless otherwise indicated, direct quotes and biographical and historical details come from the following sources: interview with Joan Bertin, January 8, 2015, New York, New York; interview with Carin Clauss, Madison, Wisconsin, August 25 and 26, 2014; interview with Miriam Horwitz, Milwaukee, Wisconsin, August 25, 2014; interview with Marley Weiss, October 3, 2014, Bethesda, Maryland; interview with Patricia Shiu, April 9, 2015; phone interview with Judith Nason, July 15, 2015.

1. Joint Appendix at 106, International Union, UAW v. Johnson Controls, Inc., 499 U.S. 187 (1991) (No. 89-1215).
2. Ibid. at 88.
3. Quoted in Eileen McNamara, "Factory and Fertility Suit Raises Issues of Bias, Fetal Rights," *The Boston Globe*, October 17, 1989.
4. Peter T. Kilborn, "Employers Left with Many Decisions," *The New York Times*, March 21, 1991.
5. Quoted in McNamara, "Factory and Fertility Suit Raises Issues of Bias."
6. Quoted in Florence Estes, "Supreme Friends: Battery Workers Pulled Together to Pursue the Right to Their Jobs," *The Chicago Tribune*, April 28, 1991, http://articles.chicagotribune.com/1991-04-28/features/9102070557_1_johnson-controls-fetal-protection-policy-supreme-court.
7. David L. Kirp, "Fetal Hazards, Gender Justice, and the Justices: The Limits of Equality," *William & Mary Law Review* 34 (Fall 1992): 105.
8. Tamar Lewin, "Battery Manufacturer Loses a Bias Case," *The New York Times*, March 3, 1990.
9. 29 C.F.R. § 1910.1025 (1978). The Preamble to the Lead Standard appears at 43 Fed. Reg. 52952 (1978) and the Attachments appear at 43 Fed. Reg. 54353 (1978).
10. 29 C.F.R. § 1910.1025, Appendix A, Section II.B.2.
11. Ibid.
12. 43 Fed. Reg. at 52959–60, 52966.
13. 43 Fed. Reg. 52966.
14. 29 C.F.R. § 1910.1025(d)–(j).
15. Carin Ann Clauss, Marsha Berzon, and Joan Bertin, "Litigating Reproductive and Developmental Health in the Aftermath of UAW Versus Johnson Controls," *Environmental Health Perspectives Supplements* 101, Suppl. 2 (1993): 207.
16. Ibid., 207.
17. Mary E. Becker, "From Muller v. Oregon to Fetal Vulnerability Policies," *University of Chicago Law Review* 53 (1986): 1226; Gail Bronson, "Chemical Companies Move to Protect Women from Substances That May Harm Fetuses," *The Wall Street Journal*, November 7, 1977.
18. Becker, "From Muller v. Oregon to Fetal Vulnerability Policies."
19. Ibid.
20. Gail Bronson, "Bitter Reaction: Issue of Fetal Damage Stirs Women at Chemical Plants," *The Wall Street Journal*, February 9, 1979.
21. Deborah Stone, "Fetal Risks, Women's Rights: Showdown at Johnson Controls," *The American Prospect* (Fall 1990), http://prospect.org/article/fetal-risks-womens-rights-showdown-johnson-controls.
22. National Governors Association Center for Best Practices, Issue Brief, "Healthy Babies: Efforts to Improve Birth Outcomes and Reduce High Risk Births," June 28, 2004, http://www.nursefamilypartnership.org/assets/PDF/Journals-and-Reports/NGAHealthyBabiesBrief; Associated Press, "Poverty and Infant Mortality," February

21, 1982, http://www.nytimes.com/1982/02/21/style/poverty-and-infant-mortality.html.

23. Bronson, "Bitter Reaction."

24. Kirp, "Fetal Hazards, Gender Justice, and the Justices"; Becker, "From Muller v. Oregon to Fetal Vulnerability Policies."

25. Centers for Disease Control and Prevention, "Reproductive Health and the Workplace," http://www.cdc.gov/niosh/topics/repro/solvents.html.

26. Jim Morris, "A Toxic Legacy," *Slate*, July 2, 2015., http://www.slate.com/articles/business/moneybox/2015/07/toxic_substances_in_electronics_manufacturing_the_u_s_does_tragically_little.html.

27. National Institute for Occupational Safety and Health, "The Effects of Workplace Hazards on Female Reproductive Health," Publication No. 99-104 (February 1999), 4; Kirp, "Fetal Hazards, Gender Justice, and the Justices."

28. Susan Faludi, *Backlash: The Undeclared War on American Women* (New York: Crown Publishers, 1991), 438; Kirp, "Fetal Hazards, Gender Justice, and the Justices," 116.

29. See, e.g., Becker, "From Muller v. Oregon to Fetal Vulnerability Policies"; Carolyn Marshall, "An Excuse for a Workplace Hazard," *The Nation*, April 25, 1987, 532.

30. Quoted in McNamara, "Factory and Fertility Suit Raises Issues of Bias."

31. Ibid.

32. Ibid.

33. Bronson, "Bitter Reaction."

34. Faludi, *Backlash*, 439.

35. Jane E. Brody, "Sperm Found Especially Vulnerable to Environment," *The New York Times*, March 10, 1981, http://www.nytimes.com/1981/03/10/science/sperm-found-especially-vulnerable-to-environment.html.

36. Brody, "Sperm Found Especially Vulnerable to Environment"; Becker, "From Muller v. Oregon to Fetal Vulnerability Policies," 1237.

37. Joint Appendix at 84, International Union, UAW v. Johnson Controls, Inc., 499 U.S. 187 (1991) (89-1215).

38. See, e.g., Duren v Missouri, 439 U.S. 357 (1979); Califano v. Goldfarb, 430 U.S. 199 (1977); Weinberger v. Wiesenfeld, 420 U.S. 636 (1975); Kahn v. Shevin, 416 U.S. 351 (1974); Frontiero v. Richardson, 411 U.S. 677 (1973).

39. Joint Appendix at 75-88, International Union, UAW v. Johnson Controls, Inc., 499 U.S. 187 (1991) (No. 89-1215).

40. Ellen Goodman, "The Easy Way Out," *The Baltimore Sun*, October 16, 1990.

41. 410 U.S. 113 (1973).

42. Faludi, *Backlash*, 441.

43. Bill Richards, "Women Say They Had to Be Sterilized to Hold Jobs," *The Washington Post*, January 1, 1979, http://www.washingtonpost.com/archive/politics/1979/01/01/women-say-they-had-to-be-sterilized-to-hold-jobs/74f7104e-8449-48d2-9592-c52d496dfffc/.

44. Faludi, *Backlash*, 448.

45. Bronson, "Bitter Reaction"; Faludi, *Backlash*, 447.

46. Oil, Chem. & Atomic Workers Int'l Union v. American Cyanamid Co., 741 F.2d 444, 447, 450 (D.C. Cir. 1984).

47. Ibid.

48. Christman v. American Cyanamid Co., 92 F.R.D. 441 (N.D. W. Va. 1981).

49. See, e.g., Jim Morris, "How Politics Gutted Workplace Safety," *Slate*, July 7, 2015, http://www.slate.com/articles/business/moneybox/2015/07/osha_safety_standards_how_politics_have_undermined_the_agency_s_ability.html; Clauss, Berzon, and Bertin, "Litigating Reproductive and Developmental Health," 206 ("[T]he Department of Labor, after 1980, refused to take an active role in opposing fetal protection policies").

50. Julianna Gonen, *Litigation as Lobbying: Reproductive Hazards and Interest Aggregation* (Columbus: Ohio State Press, 2003), 38.

51. International Union, UAW v. Johnson Controls, Inc., 680 F. Supp. 309, 310 (E.D. Wisc. 1988).

52. Wolfgang Saxon, "Robert W. Warren, Wisconsin Federal Judge," *The New York Times,* August 22, 1998, http://www.nytimes.com/1998/08/22/us/robert-w-warren-72-wisconsin-federal-judge.html.

53. U.S. Equal Employment Opportunity Commission, "Policy Statement on Reproductive & Fetal Hazards Under Title VII," Fair Employment Practice Manual (BNA) 401: 6013, 6015 n.11 (October 3, 1988).

54. Ibid. at 6015–16 (footnotes omitted).

55. Jan Uebelherr, "Courtroom Revealed the Passionate Side of Judge Coffey," *The Milwaukee Journal-Sentinel,* November 13, 2012, http://www.jsonline.com/news/obitu aries/courtroom-revealed-the-passionate-side-of-coffey-pl7k0ju-179121421.html.

56. Quoted in Kirp, "Fetal Hazards, Gender Justice, and the Justices," 119.

57. International Union, UAW v. Johnson Controls, Inc., 886 F.2d 871, 896 (7th Cir. 1989) (en banc).

58. Ibid. at 898–899.

59. Ibid. at 871, 920 (7th Cir. 1989) (Easterbrook, J., dissenting).

60. Ibid. at 912.

61. Ibid. at 912–913.

62. U.S. Equal Employment Opportunity Commission, "Policy Guidance on United Auto Workers v. Johnson Controls, Inc.," No. 915-1047, EEOC Compliance Manual (CCH) Vol. II § 624 (January 24, 1990).

63. Caroline Bettinger-Lopez and Susan Sturm, "International Union, U.A.W. v. Johnson Controls: The History of Litigation Alliances and Mobilization to Challenge Fetal Protection Policies," Columbia Law School Public Law & Legal Theory Working Group, Paper No. 07-145 (2007), http://www2.law.columbia.edu/ssturm/pdfs/John son_Controls_4.22.07.pdf.

64. Brief Amici Curiae of Equal Rights Advocates, NOW Legal Defense and Education Fund, National Women's Law Center, and Women's Legal Defense Fund in Support of Petitioners, International Union, UAW v. Johnson Controls, Inc., 499 U.S. 187 (1991) (No. 89-1215).

65. McNamara, "Factory and Fertility Suit Raises Issues of Bias."

66. Oral Argument at 13:23-13:52, International Union, UAW v. Johnson Controls, Inc., 499 U.S. 187 (1991) (No. 89-1215), available at http://www.oyez.org/cases/1990 -1999/1990/1990_89_1215#argument.

67. Ibid. at 2:30–2:54; 1:02–1:20.

68. Ibid. at 6:30–6:57.

69. Ibid. at 10:00–10:50.

70. Before 2004, transcripts of oral arguments did not identify the questioner. Some voices—such as Justice O'Connor's—are immediately recognizable from the audio recording of the argument. Others may be identified because the attorney addresses the justice by name in answering.

71. Ibid. at 16:29–19:40.

72. Ibid. at 24:03–25:20.

73. Ibid. at 28:00–29:54.

74. Ibid. at 31:13–31:53.

75. Ibid. at 38:10–39:15.

76. Ibid. at 44:04–46:46.

77. Ibid. at 51:19–51:54.

78. International Union, UAW v. Johnson Controls, Inc., 499 U.S. 187, 204 (1991).

79. Ibid. at 199.

80. Ibid. at 206.

81. Ibid. at 203.

82. Ibid. at 223 (Scalia, J., concurring).

83. Ibid. at 223 (Scalia, J., concurring).

84. Ibid. at 211.

Eight

Unless otherwise indicated, direct quotes and biographical and historical details come from the following sources: interview with Teresa (Harris) Wilson and Irwin Venick, Nashville, Tennessee, May 19, 2012.

1. Joint Appendix at 47, 50–52, Harris v. Forklift Sys., Inc., 510 U.S. 17 (1993) (No. 92-1168).
2. Ibid., 44–46.
3. Ibid., 52–53.
4. 477 U.S. 57 (1986).
5. Ibid. at 67.
6. 805 F.2d 611 (6th Cir. 1986).
7. Ibid. at 623–624.
8. Ibid. at 619–621.
9. Harris v. Forklift Sys., Inc., No. 3:89-0557, 1990 U.S. Dist. LEXIS 20115 at *5, *11 (M.D. Tenn. Nov. 28, 1990).
10. Ibid. at *18.
11. Quoted in Ellen Goodman, "Insensitive Man or Oversensitive Woman?" *The Baltimore Sun,* October 12, 1993, http://articles.baltimoresun.com/1993-10-12/news /1993285101_1_harassment-teresa-harris-charles-hardy.
12. Harris v. Forklift Sys., Inc., Nos. 91-5301, 5871, 5822, 1992 U.S. App. LEXIS 23779 (6th Cir. Sept. 17, 1992).
13. 401 U.S. 424 (1971).
14. Petition for Certiorari at 10-12, Harris v. Forklift Sys., Inc., 510 U.S. 17 (1993) (No. 92-1168).
15. Marcia D. Greenberger, "What Anita Hill Did for America," CNN.com, October 22, 2010, http://www.cnn.com/2010/OPINION/10/21/greenberger.anita.hill/.
16. Brief for the United States and the Equal Employment Opportunity Commission as Amici Curiae at 20-22, Harris v. Forklift Sys., Inc., 510 U.S. 17 (1993) (No. 92-1168).
17. Brief for Amicus Curiae American Psychological Association in Support of Neither Party at 6-17, Harris v. Forklift Sys., Inc., 510 U.S. 17 (1993) (No. 92-1168).
18. Ibid., 18-20.
19. Oral Argument at 15:28–17:21, Harris v. Forklift Sys., Inc., 510 U.S. 17 (92-1168), available at http://www.oyez.org/cases/1990-1999/1993/1993_92_1168.
20. Ibid. at 18:16–19:04.
21. Ibid. at 30:06–30:40.
22. Ibid. at 30:49–35:52.
23. Ibid. at 39:02–41:39.
24. Ibid. at 46:10–46:33.
25. Ibid. at 46:42–51:25.
26. Harris v. Forklift Sys., Inc., 510 U.S. at 17, 22 (1993).
27. Ibid.
28. Ibid. at 25–26. (Ginsburg, J., concurring). See, e.g., Irin Carmon and Shana Knizhnik, *Notorious RBG: The Life and Times of Ruth Bader Ginsburg* (New York: Dey Street Books, 2015: Linda Hirshman, *Sisters in Law: How Sandra Day O'Connor and Ruth Bader Ginsburg Went to the Supreme Court and Changed the World* (New York: HarperCollins, 2015).
29. Harris, 510 U.S. at 22–23.
30. Ibid. at 23.

Nine

Unless otherwise indicated, direct quotes and biographical and historical details come from the following sources: interview with Sheila White, Memphis, Tennessee, August 5, 2014.

1. Shaila Dewan, "Forklift Driver's Stand Leads to Broad Rule Protecting Workers Who Fear Retaliation," *The New York Times*, June 24, 2006, http://www.nytimes.com/2006/06/24/us/24white.html.
2. Burlington Northern & Santa Fe Rwy. Co. v. White, 364 F.3d 769, 792 (6th Cir. 2004).
3. Quoted in Dewan, "Forklift Driver's Stand Leads to Broad Rule."
4. Transcript of Trial, August 31, 2000 at 292-293, White v. Burlington Northern & Santa Fe Rwy. Co., No. 99-2733, 2000 U.S. Dist. LEXIS 22799 (W.D. Tenn. Aug. 28, 2000).
5. Ibid. at 154.
6. March 5, 1998 note from D. Annice Golden, Ph.D., Exhibit 11, Marvin Brown Deposition, White v. Burlington Northern & Santa Fe Rwy. Co., No. 99-2733, 2000 U.S. Dist. LEXIS 22799 (W.D. Tenn. Aug. 28, 2000).
7. November 4, 1998 note from D. Annice Golden, Ph.D., Exhibit 14, Marvin Brown Deposition, White v. Burlington Northern & Santa Fe Rwy. Co., No. 99-2733, 2000 U.S. Dist. LEXIS 22799 (W.D. Tenn. Aug. 28, 2000).
8. Louis Graham, "Lawyer Examines McCalla's Behavior; Sixth Circuit Looks into Judicial Conduct," *The Commercial Appeal*, July 15, 2001.
9. United States v. Whitman, 209 F.3d 619, 624 (6th Cir. 2000).
10. Transcript of Trial, September 1, 2000 at 521, 537, White v. Burlington Northern & Santa Fe Rwy. Co., No. 99-2733, 2000 U.S. Dist. LEXIS 22799 (W.D. Tenn. Aug. 28, 2000).
11. Ibid. at 519.
12. Ibid., 479-480, 555-560.
13. 42 U.S.C. § 2000e-2(a)(1)–(2).
14. White v. Burlington Northern & Santa Fe Rwy. Co., No. 99-2733, 2000 U.S. Dist. LEXIS 22799 at *15 (W.D. Tenn. Aug. 28, 2000).
15. Transcript of Trial, September 1, 2000 at 697–698, White v. Burlington Northern & Santa Fe Rwy Co., No. 99-2733, 2000 U.S. Dist. LEXIS 22799 (W.D. Tenn. Aug. 28, 2000).
16. White v. Burlington Northern & Santa Fe Rwy. Co., No. 99-2733, 2000 U.S. Dist. LEXIS 22798 at *5, *6 (W.D. Tenn. Nov. 16, 2000).
17. White v. Burlington Northern & Santa Fe Rwy. Co., 310 F.3d 443, 451 (6th Cir. 2002).
18. Ibid. at 454.
19. Sheila White, *Fighting the Giant: From the Railyards of Tennessee All the Way to the Supreme Court* (Los Gatos, CA: Robertson Publishing, 2007), 54.
20. EEOC Compliance Manual § 8-II.D.3 (May 20, 1998).
21. Ibid.
22. Donald J. Donati, "Insights from an Advocate: Burlington Northern & Santa Fe Railway Co. v. White," *University of Memphis Law Review* 41 (Summer, 2011), 713.
23. Edward Feisenthal, "Beach Dispute May Bring a Pivotal Harassment Ruling," *The Wall Street Journal*, January 7, 1998, http://www.wsj.com/articles/SB88412603 2492704000.
24. Faragher v. City of Boca Raton, 864 F. Supp. 1552, 1557 (S.D. Fla. 1994).
25. Faragher v. City of Boca Raton, 524 U.S. 775, 780 (1998).
26. Ellerth v. Burlington Indus., 912 F. Supp. 1101, 1106–1109 (N.D. Ill. 1996).
27. Ellerth v. Burlington Indus., 524 U.S. 742 (1998); Faragher v. City of Boca Raton, 524 U.S. 775 (1998).
28. U.S. Equal Employment Opportunity Commission, "Sexual Harassment Charges, EEOC and FEPAs Combined: FY 1997–FY 2014," http://www.eeoc.gov/eeoc/statistics/enforcement/sexual_harassment.cfm.
29. U.S. Equal Employment Opportunity Commission, "EEOC Charge Statistics: FY 1997 through FY 2014," http://www.eeoc.gov/eeoc/statistics/enforcement/charges.cfm.

30. Quoted in Bartholomew Sullivan, "Memphian Has Day at Supreme Court—Harassment Case May Be Precedent-Setting," *The Commercial Appeal,* April 16, 2006.

31. Tony Mauro, "Appellate Lawyer of the Week: Eric Schnapper, University of Washington Law School," *The National Law Journal,* October 27, 2010, http://www.law .washington.edu/News/Articles/Appellate_Lawyer_of_the_Week.pdf.

32. Donald A. Donati, Remarks, National Employment Lawyers Association, 2014 Annual Conference, "Blazing the Trail: Courage, Challenge, Change," June 26, 2014, Boston, MA.

33. Ibid.

34. Oral Argument at :13-:49, Burlington Northern & Santa Fe Rwy. Co. v. White, 548 U.S. 53 (2006) (No. 05-259), available at http://www.oyez.org/cases/2000-2009 /2005/2005_05_259.

35. Ibid. at 3:27–3:35.

36. Ibid. at 5:05–5:25.

37. Ibid. at 15:45–16:58.

38. Ibid.

39. Ibid. at 8:24–8:33.

40. Ibid. at 8:56–9:31.

41. Ibid. at 48:43.

42. Ibid. at 34:11.

43. Ibid. at 41:33.

44. Ibid. at 38:26–39:01.

45. Donald A. Donati, Remarks, National Employment Lawyers Association, 2014 Annual Conference, June 26, 2014, Boston, MA.

46. Oral argument at 35:59–36:27, Burlington Northern & Santa Fe Rwy. Co. v. White, 548 U.S. 53 (2006) (No. 05-259), available at http://www.oyez.org/cases/2000-2009 /2005/2005_05_259.

47. Ibid. at 56:20–57:35.

48. White, *Fighting the Giant,* 57.

49. Ibid.

50. Burlington Northern & Santa Fe Rwy. Co. v. White, 548 U.S. 53, 68 (2006).

51. White, *Fighting the Giant,* iv.

52. Ibid., 58.

Ten

Unless otherwise indicated, direct quotes, biographical and historical details, and mental impressions come from the following sources: Telephone interview with Sam Bagenstos on April 22, 2015; interview with Sharon Gustafson and Peggy Young in Arlington, Virginia, on April 10, 2015.

1. Rebecca Traister, "Labor Pains," *The New Republic,* February 3, 2015, http://www .newrepublic.com/article/120939/maternity-leave-policies-america-hurt-working -moms.

2. Plaintiff's Memorandum in Opposition to Defendant's Motion for Summary Judgment at 22, Young v. United Parcel Service, Inc., No. DKC 08-2586, 2011 U.S. Dist. LEXIS 14266 (D. Md. February 14, 2011).

3. Ibid.

4. Ibid.

5. U.S. Department of Labor, Women's Bureau, "Facts Over Time: Labor Force Participation Rates—Labor Force Participation Rates by Sex and Race or Hispanic Ethnicity, 1972-2012," http://www.dol.gov/wb/stats/facts_over_time.htm.

6. Jeanette M. Cleveland, Margaret Stockdale, and Kevin Murphy, *Women and Men in Organizations: Sex and Gender Issues at Work* (New York: Psychology Press, 2000), 208.

7. Lynda Laughlin, "Maternity Leave and Employment Patterns of First Time Mothers: 1961-2008," U.S. Census Bureau, Current Population Reports, P7-128 (October 2011) at 6-7 & Table 4, http://www.census.gov/prod/2011pubs/p70-128.pdf.

8. See, e.g., Joanna L. Grossman and Gillian L. Thomas, "Making Pregnancy Work: Overcoming the Pregnancy Discrimination Act's Capacity-Based Model," *Yale Journal of Law & Feminism*: 21 (2009): 19-22.

9. Lydia DiPillis, "Under Pressure, Wal-Mart Upgrades Its Policy for Helping Pregnant Workers," *The Washington Post*, April 5, 2014, http://www.washingtonpost.com/blogs/wonkblog/wp/2014/04/05/under-pressure-walmart-upgrades-its-policy-for-helping-pregnant-workers/.

10. Bryce Covert, "Pregnant Worker at Pier 1 Put on Unpaid Leave Even Though She Wanted to Continue Working," *ThinkProgress*, April 17, 2014, http://thinkprogress.org/economy/2014/04/17/3427898/pregnant-worker-pier-1/.

11. Leahy v. Gap, Inc., No. 07-2008, 2008 U.S Dist. LEXIS 58812 (E.D.N.Y. July 29, 2008).

12. Rachel L. Swarns, "Doctor Says No to Overtime; Pregnant Worker's Boss Says No Job," *The New York Times*, October 19, 2014, http://www.nytimes.com/2014/10/20/nyregion/doctors-letter-spells-end-of-job-for-pregnant-employee.html?smprod=nytcore-iphone&smid=nytcore-iphone-share; Brigid Schulte, "Pregnant Women Fight to Keep Jobs via 'Reasonable Accommodations,'" *The Washington Post*, August 4, 2014, https://www.washingtonpost.com/national/health-science/pregnant-women-fight-to-keep-jobs-via-reasonable-accommodations/2014/08/04/9eb13654-1408-11e4-8936-26932bcfd6ed_story.html; Rachel L. Swarns, "Placed on Unpaid Leave, a Pregnant Worker Finds Hope in a New Law," *The New York Times*, February 2, 2014, http://www.nytimes.com/2014/02/03/nyregion/suspended-for-being-pregnant-an-employee-finds-hope-in-a-new-law.html?ref=rachellswarns&_r=1.

13. National Partnership for Women & Families, "Listening to Mothers: The Experiences of Expecting and New Mothers in the Workplace," January 2014, http://www.nationalpartnership.org/research-library/workplace-fairness/pregnancy-discrimination/listening-to-mothers-experiences-of-expecting-and-new-mothers.pdf, 3.

14. U.S. Equal Employment Opportunity Commission, "Charge Statistics: FY 1997 Through FY 2014," http://www.eeoc.gov/eeoc/statistics/enforcement/pregnancy.cfm.

15. Brigid Schulte, "New Statistics: Pregnancy Discrimination Claims Hit Low-Wage Workers Hardest," *The Washington Post*, August 5, 2014, http://www.washingtonpost.com/blogs/she-the-people/wp/2014/08/05/new-statistics-pregnancy-discrimination-claims-hit-low-wage-workers-hardest/.

16. 42 U.S.C. § 2000e(k).

17. Ibid.

18. Ensley-Gaines v. Runyon, 100 F.3d 1220 (6th Cir. 1996).

19. Peter Baker, "Once More, Bush Turns to His Inner Circle," *The Washington Post*, October 4, 2005, http://www.washingtonpost.com/wp-dyn/content/article/2005/10/03/AR2005100301781.html; see also Elisabeth Bumiller, "Court in Transition: The President; An Interview By, Not With, the President," *The New York Times*, July 21, 2005, http://query.nytimes.com/gst/fullpage.html?res=9800E5DC153CF932A15754C0A9639C8B63.

20. Clarence Thomas, *My Grandfather's Son: A Memoir* (New York: Harper Collins, 2007).

21. Nomination of Judge Clarence Thomas to Be Associate Justice of the Supreme Court of the United States, Day 1, Before the Committee on the Judiciary, 102nd Cong. 38 (1991) (Testimony of Anita F. Hill, Professor of Law, University of Oklahoma, Norman, OK), http://www.loc.gov/law/find/nominations/thomas/hearing-pt4.pdf.

22. U.S. Equal Opportunity Employment Commission, "Written Testimony of Emily Martin, Vice President and General Counsel, National Women's Law Center," Meeting of the Commission, February 15, 2012, http://www.eeoc.gov/eeoc/meetings/2-15-12/martin.cfm.

23. U.S. Equal Opportunity Employment Commission, "Written Testimony of Judith L. Lichtman, Senior Advisor, National Partnership for Women and Families," Meeting of the Commission, February 15, 2012, http://www.eeoc.gov/eeoc/meetings/2-15-12/lichtman.cfm.

24. U.S. Equal Opportunity Employment Commission, "Written Testimony of Sharon Terman, Senior Staff Attorney, Gender Equity and LGBT Rights Program, Legal Aid Society-Employment Law Center," Meeting of the Commission, February 15, 2012, http://www.eeoc.gov/eeoc/meetings/2-15-12/terman.cfm.

25. U.S. Equal Opportunity Employment Commission, "Written Testimony of Maryann Parker, Associate General Counsel, Service Employees International Union," Meeting of the Commission, February 15, 2012, http://www.eeoc.gov/eeoc/meetings/2-15-12 /parker.cfm.

26. U.S. Equal Opportunity Employment Commission, "Written Testimony of Joan C. Williams, Professor of Law & Director, Center for WorkLife Law, UC-Hastings," Meeting of the Commission, February 15, 2012, http://www.eeoc.gov/eeoc/meet ings/2-15-12/williams.cfm.

27. National Women's Law Center and A Better Balance, "It Shouldn't Be a Heavy Lift: Fair Treatment for Pregnant Workers," June 18, 2013, http://www.nwlc.org/sites/de fault/files/pdfs/pregnant_workers.pdf.

28. Ledbetter v. Goodyear Tire & Rubber Co., 550 U.S. 618 (2007).

29. Brief for the United States as Amicus Curiae, Young v. United Parcel Service, Inc., 135 S. Ct. 1338 (2015) (No. 12-1226).

30. Ibid. at 32–34.

31. 134 S. Ct. 2751 (2014).

32. Sean Sullivan, "Justice Ruth Bader Ginsburg Says Male Justices Have a 'Blind Spot' on Women's Issues," The Washington Post, July 31, 2014, http://www.washington post.com/blogs/post-politics/wp/2014/07/31/justice-ruth-bader-ginsburg-says-male -justices-have-a-blind-spot-on-womens-issues/.

33. Amicus Curiae Brief of the American Civil Liberties Union and A Better Balance, et al., in Support of Petitioner, Young v. United Parcel Service, Inc., 135 S. Ct. 1338 (2015) (No. 12-1226).

34. Brief of Amicus Curiae Black Women's Health Imperative, Joined by Other Black Women's Health Organizations, in Support of Petitioner, Young v. United Parcel Service, Inc., 135 S. Ct. 1338 (2015) (No. 12-1226).

35. Brief of Health Care Providers, National Partnership for Women & Families, and Other Organizations Concerned with Maternal and Infant Health as Amici Curiae in Support of Petitioner, Young v. United Parcel Service, Inc., 135 S. Ct. 1338 (2015) (No. 12-1226).

36. Brief of Amicus Curiae National Education Association, et al. in Support of the Petitioner, Young v. United Parcel Service, Inc., 135 S. Ct. 1338 (2015) (No. 12-1226).

37. Brief of U.S. Women's Chamber of Commerce, et al. as Amici Curiae Supporting Petitioner, Young v. United Parcel Service, Inc., 135 S. Ct. 1338 (2015) (No. 12-1226).

38. Brief of Members of Congress as Amici Curiae in Support of Petitioner, Young v. United Parcel Service, Inc., 135 S. Ct. 1338 (2015) (No. 12-1226).

39. Brief of Bipartisan State and Local Legislators as Amici Curiae in Support of Petitioner, Young v. United Parcel Service, Inc., 135 S. Ct. 1338 (2015) (No. 12-1226).

40. Brief of Amici Curiae 23 Pro-Life Organizations, et al. in Support of Petitioner Peggy Young, Young v. United Parcel Service, Inc., 135 S. Ct. 1338 (2015) (No. 12-1226).

41. Naomi Schoenbaum, "When Liberals and Conservatives Agree on Women's Rights," Politico, March 31, 2015, http://www.politico.com/magazine/story/2015/03/supreme -court-pregnancy-discrimination-coalition-116559.html#.VUJ2ZaZN3zJ.

42. Brief for the United States as Amicus Curiae Supporting Petitioner, Young v. United Parcel Service, Inc., 135 S. Ct. 1338 (2015) (No. 12-1226).

43. U.S. Equal Employment Opportunity Commission, Enforcement Guidance: Pregnancy Discrimination and Related Issues, July 14, 2014, superseded by Enforcement Guidance: Pregnancy Discrimination and Related Issues, June 25, 2015, http://www .eeoc.gov/laws/guidance/pregnancy_guidance.cfm,

44. Brief for the United States as Amicus Curiae Supporting Petitioner, Young v. United Parcel Service, Inc., 135 S. Ct. 1338 (2015) (No. 12-1226).

45. Oral Argument at :08–:32, Young v. United Parcel Service, Inc., 135 S. Ct. 1338 (2015) (No. 12-1226), available at http://www.supremecourt.gov/oral_arguments /audio/2014/12-1226.
46. Ibid. at 49–1:02.
47. Ibid. at 3:01–5:35.
48. Ibid. at 6:57–8:45.
49. Ibid. at 5:38–5:43; 11:43–11:46; 12:00.
50. 429 U.S. 125 (1976).
51. Ibid. at 10:00–11:08.
52. Ibid. at 2:33–2:50.
53. Carl Hulse, "Blocked Bids to Fill Judgeships Stirs New Fight on Filibuster," *The New York Times,* March 8, 2013, http://www.nytimes.com/2013/03/09/us/politics/filibus ter-stirs-a-new-battle-on-us-judges.html.
54. Adam Liptak, "UPS Suit Hinges on an Ambiguous Pregnancy Law," *The New York Times,* December 3, 2014, http://www.nytimes.com/2014/12/04/us/politics/in-ups -case-justices-tackle-ambiguity-in-pregnancy-law.html.
55. Ibid. at 27:54–28:05.
56. Ibid. at 28:10–28:29.
57. Ibid. at 30:30.
58. Ibid. at 54:46–55:39.
59. Ibid. at 57:57.
60. Ibid. at 1:10:20–1:02:44.
61. "Andrea Mitchell Reports: SCOTUS Hears Pregnancy Discrimination Case" (MS-NBC television broadcast, December 3, 2014).
62. Young v. United Parcel Service, Inc., 135 S. Ct. 1338, 1354 (2015).
63. Ibid. at 1350.
64. Ibid.
65. Ibid. at 1361 (Scalia, J., dissenting).
66. Ibid. at 1364, 1365, 1366.
67. Ibid. at 1367 (Kennedy, J., dissenting).
68. Brief of Law Professors and Women's and Civil Rights Organizations as Amici Curiae in Support of Petitioner, Young v. United Parcel Service, Inc., 135 S. Ct. 1338 (2015) (No. 12-1226).
69. Ben James, "UPS Settles Pregnancy Bias Case That Went to High Court," *Law360,* October 2, 2015, http://www.law360.com/employment/articles/709843?nl_pk=8924 1183-ba46-425a-818a-12d046b8fc9b&utm_source=newsletter&utm_medium=ema il&utm_campaign=employment.

Epilogue

1. See, e.g., Claire Cain Miller and Liz Alderman, "Why U.S. Women Are Leaving Jobs Behind," *The New York Times,* December 12, 2014, http://www.nytimes .com/2014/12/14/upshot/us-employment-women-not-working.html.
2. See, e.g., Sylvia Ann Hewlett and Carolyn Buck Luce, "On-Ramps and Off-Ramps: Keeping Talented Women on the Road to Success," *Harvard Business Review,* March 2005, https://hbr.org/2005/03/off-ramps-and-on-ramps-keeping-talented-wo men-on-the-road-to-success; Paulette Light, "Why 43 Percent of Women with Children Leave Their Jobs, and How to Get Them Back, *The Atlantic,* April 19, 2013, http://www.theatlantic.com/sexes/archive/2013/04/why-43-of-women-with-chil dren-leave-their-jobs-and-how-to-get-them-back/275134/.
3. See, e.g., Claire Cain Miller, "The Motherhood Penalty v. The Fatherhood Bonus: A Child Helps Your Career, If You're a Man," *The New York Times,* September 6, 2014, http://www.nytimes.com/2014/09/07/upshot/a-child-helps-your-career-if -youre-a-man.html.
4. "News in Brief," *The Onion,* July 30, 2015, http://www.theonion.com/article /company-flat-out-asks-female-candidate-how-much-mi-50963.

5. U.S. Department of Labor, Women's Bureau, "Latest Annual Data—Mothers' Participation in the Labor Force," 2013 annual averages, http://www.dol.gov/wb/stats/recentfacts.htm.

6. Wendy Wang, Kim Parker, and Paul Taylor, "Breadwinner Moms: Mothers Are the Sole or Primary Provider in Four-in-Ten Households with Children; Public Conflicted About Growing Trend," Pew Research Center, May 29, 2013, http://www.pewsocialtrends.org/files/2013/05/Breadwinner_moms_final.pdf, 1.

7. See, e.g., Sharon Lerner, "The Real War on Families: Why the U.S. Needs Paid Leave Now," *In These Times,* Aug. 18, 2015, http://inthesetimes.com/article/18151/the-real-war-on-families; Rachel Gillette, "'I Didn't Feel Appreciated': Inside the 'Backwards' Reality of Taking Unpaid Maternity Leave in America," *Business Insider,* June 20, 2015, http://www.businessinsider.com/the-reality-of-unpaid-maternity-leave-in-america-2015-6; Rebecca Traister, "Labor Pains," *The New Republic,* February 3, 2015, http://www.newrepublic.com/article/120939/maternity-leave-policies-america-hurt-working-moms.

8. Jonathan Cohn, "The Hell of American Day Care," *The New Republic,* April 16, 2013, http://www.newrepublic.com/article/112892/hell-american-day-care.

9. Anne Marie Slaughter, "A Toxic Work World," *The New York Times,* Sept. 18, 2015, http://www.nytimes.com/2015/09/20/opinion/sunday/a-toxic-work-world.html.

10. Caroline Frederickson, *Under the Bus: How Working Women Are Being Run Over* (New York: The New Press, 2015), 117-120, 174.

11. Joan C. Williams, "Beyond the Maternal Wall," *Harvard Women's Law Journal* 77 (2003), http://www.law.harvard.edu/students/orgs/jlg/vol26/williams.pdf.

12. Joan C. Williams, "The Maternal Wall," *Harvard Business Review,* October 2004, https://hbr.org/2004/10/the-maternal-wall.

13. U.S. Equal Employment Opportunity Commission, "Enforcement Guidance: Unlawful Discrimination of Workers with Caregiving Responsibilities," May 23, 2007, http://www.eeoc.gov/policy/docs/caregiving.html.

14. Joan C. Williams & Stephanie Bornstein, "Caregivers in the Courtroom: The Growing Trend of Family Responsibilities Discrimination," *University of San Francisco Law Review* 41 (2006): 71.

15. Scott Coltrane, Elizabeth C. Miller, Tracy DeHaan, and Lauren Stewart, "Fathers and the Flexibility Stigma," *Journal of Social Issues* 69, Vol. 2 (June 2013): 279.

16. Quoted in Becky Beaupre Gillespie and Hollee Schwartz Temple, "A Lawsuit Claims 'Macho' Culture Led to Associate Dad's Firing," *ABA Journal,* March 1, 2011, http://www.abajournal.com/magazine/article/not_mans_work_a_lawsuit_claims_macho_culture_led_to_associate_dads_firing/.

17. Noam Scheiber, "Attitudes Shift on Paid Leave: Dads Sue, Too," *The New York Times,* Sept. 15, 2015, http://www.nytimes.com/2015/09/16/business/attitudes-shift-on-paid-leave-dads-sue-too.html?_r=0. See also Joshua Levs, *All In: How Our Work-First Culture Fails Dads, Families, and Businesses—and How We Can Fix It Together* (New York: HarperCollins, 2015).

18. Gillespie and Temple, "A Lawsuit Claims 'Macho' Culture Led to Associate Dad's Firing."

19. "Radio Host Mike Francesa Stands by Daniel Murphy Paternity Leave Comments After Heavy Criticism," cbsnews.com, April 4, 2014, http://www.cbsnews.com/news/sports-talk-radio-host-mike-francesa-stands-by-dan-murphy-paternity-leave-comments-after-heavy-criticism/.

20. Jennifer Ludden, "More Dads Want Paternity Leave. Getting It Is a Different Matter," NPR, August 13, 2014, http://www.npr.org/2014/08/13/333730249/more-dads-want-paternity-leave-getting-it-is-a-different-matter.

21. U.S. Equal Employment Opportunity Commission, "Pregnancy Discrimination Charges, EEOC & FEPAs Combined: FY1997-FY2011," http://www.eeoc.gov/eeoc/statistics/enforcement/pregnancy.cfm.

22. Bryce Covert, "Nonprofit Ordered to Pay $75,000 Over 'No Pregnancy in Workplace' Policy," *ThinkProgress,* May 29, 2015, http://thinkprogress.org/economy/2015/05/29/3663986/no-pregnancy-policy/.

23. Bryce Covert, "Company to Pay Record-Breaking Damages for Telling Pregnant Woman She Couldn't Do Her Job Anymore," *ThinkProgress,* July 23, 2015, http://thinkprogress.org/economy/2015/07/23/3683910/autozone-pregnancy-case/.

24. Brigid Schulte, "New Statistics: Pregnancy Discrimination Claims Hit Low-Wage Workers the Hardest," *The Washington Post,* Aug. 5, 2014, http://www.washington post.com/blogs/she-the-people/wp/2014/08/05/new-statistics-pregnancy-discrimina tion-claims-hit-low-wage-workers-hardest/.

25. Lynda Laughlin, "Maternity Leave and Employment Patterns of First Time Mothers: 1961-2008," U.S. Census Bureau, Current Population Reports, P7-128 (October 2011) at 11-12 & Table 7, http://www.census.gov/prod/2011pubs/p70-128.pdf.

26. Stephanie Bornstein, "Poor, Pregnant, and Fired: Caregiver Discrimination Against Low-Wage Workers," Center for WorkLife Law, University of California-Hastings School of Law, 2011, http://worklifelaw.org/pubs/PoorPregnantAndFired.pdf.

27. Kristie Ackert and Oren Yaniv, *New York Daily News,* March 14, 2015, http://www.nydailynews.com/sports/baseball/mets/mets-settle-sex-discrimination-suit-filed-ex-team-exec-article-1.2148501.

28. See, e.g., Bornstein, "Poor, Pregnant, and Fired."

29. U.S. Department of Justice, U.S. Attorney's Office, Eastern District, Press Release, "United States Settles Pregnancy Discrimination Action Against Triborough Bridge and Tunnel Authority," November 10, 2015, http://www.justice.gov/usao-edny/pr/united-states-settles-pregnancy-discrimination-action-against-triborough-bridge-and.

30. July 15, 2015 Pregnant Workers Fairness Act Coalition Letter to Members of Congress, http://www.nationalpartnership.org/research-library/workplace-fairness/preg nancy-discrimination/pregnant-workers-fairness-act-coalition-letter.pdf.

31. National Partnership for Women and Families, "Reasonable Accommodations for Pregnant Workers: State and Local Laws," July 2015, http://www.nationalpartner ship.org/research-library/workplace-fairness/pregnancy-discrimination/reasonable -accommodations-for-pregnant-workers-state-laws.pdf. See, e.g., Amanda Marcotte, "Breast-Feeding Mom Loses Case Because Men Can Lactate Too," *Slate,* Feb. 4, 2015, http://www.slate.com/blogs/xx_factor/2015/02/04/angela_ames_sex_discr imination_case_breast_feeding_mom_loses_because_men.html.

32. See, e.g., Theresa K. Vescio, "Sugar-Coated Sexism," Harvard Business School, Research Symposium, Gender & Work: Challenging Conventional Wisdom, 2013, http://www.hbs.edu/faculty/conferences/2013-w50-research-symposium/Docu ments/vescio.pdf.

33. Sheryl Sandberg, *Lean In: Women, Work, and the Will to Lead* (New York: Knopf, 2013).

34. See, e.g., Cheryl Alter, "Here's What Anne-Marie Slaughter Has to Say About Sheryl Sandberg," *Time,* September 26, 2015, http://time.com/4050404/anne-marie-slaugh ter-unfinished-business-sheryl-sandberg/; Susan Faludi, "Facebook Feminism," *The Baffler,* No. 23 (2013), http://thebaffler.com/salvos/facebook-feminism-like-it-or-not.

35. See, e.g., Frederickson, *Under the Bus,* 4-7.

36. Annie Lowrey, "Ellen Pao and the Sexism You Can't Quite Prove," *New York Magazine,* March 30, 2015, http://nymag.com/daily/intelligencer/2015/03/ellen-pao-and-the-sexism-you-cant-quite-prove.html.

37. Maria Konnikova, "Lean Out: The Dangers for Women Who Negotiate," *The New Yorker,* June 10, 2014, http://www.newyorker.com/science/maria-konnikova/lean-out-the-dangers-for-women-who-negotiate.

38. See, e.g., Vauhini Vara, "The Ellen Pao Trial: What Do We Mean by 'Discrimination'?," *The New Yorker,* March 14, 2015, http://www.newyorker.com/business/currency/the-ellen-pao-trial-what-do-we-mean-by-discrimination.

39. See, e.g., Rex Huppke, "The Roots of Workplace Gender Bias," *The Chicago Tribune,* July 27, 2014, http://www.chicagotribune.com/business/careers/ct-biz-0707-work-advice-huppke-20140707-column.html.

40. Farhad Manjoo, "Ellen Pao Disrupts How Silicon Valley Does Business," *The New York Times,* March 27, 2015, http://mobile.nytimes.com/2015/03/28/technology

/ellen-pao-disrupts-how-silicon-valley-does-business.html?referrer=&_r=0; Kathleen Davis, "The One Word Men Never See in Their Performance Reviews," *Fast Company,* August 27, 2014, http://www.fastcompany.com/3034895/strong-female-lead/the-one-word-men-never-see-in-their-performance-reviews; Jessica Bennett, "Why We Need to Stop Calling Powerful Women 'Bitches,'" *Cosmopolitan,* March 8, 2014, http://www.cosmopolitan.com/career/advice/a5890/powerful-women-names/.

41. Hannah Seligson, "Page by Page, Men Are Stepping Into the 'Lean In' Circle," *The New York Times,* November 1, 2013, http://www.nytimes.com/2013/11/03/fashion /Page-by-Page-Men-Are-Stepping-Into-sheryl-sandbergs-lean-in-circle.html.

42. Prowel v. Wise Bus. Forms, No. 2:06-cv-259, 2007 WL 2702664 at *5, *8 (W.D. Pa. Sept. 13, 2007).

43. No. 07-3997, 2009 U.S. App. LEXIS 19350 at *19 (3d Cir. Aug. 28, 2009).

44. Macy v. Holder, EEOC Appeal No. 0120120821 (Apr. 20, 2012).

45. See Baldwin v. Foxx, EEOC Doc. 0120133080, 2015 WL 4397641 at *5 (EEOC July 15, 2015); U.S. Equal Employment Opportunity Commission, Press Release," EEOC Sues Detroit Funeral Home Chain for Sex Discrimination Against Transgender Employee," September 25, 2014, http://www.eeoc.gov/eeoc/newsroom/release /9-25-14d.cfm; Jeff Guo, "America Might Have Accidentally Banned Transgender Discrimination in 1964," *The Washington Post,* November 11, 2015, https:// www.washingtonpost.com/news/wonk/wp/2015/11/11/america-might-have-acciden tally-banned-transgender-discrimination-in-1964/.

46. Quoted in Erik Eckholm, "Next Fight for Gay Rights: Bias in Jobs and Housing," *The New York Times,* June 27, 2015, http://www.nytimes.com/2015/06/28/us/gay -rights-leaders-push-for-federal-civil-rights-protections.html.

47. Joanna L. Grossman, "Hit the Gym, Borgata Babes," *Verdict,* September 29, 2015, https://verdict.justia.com/2015/09/29/hit-the-gym-borgatababes.

48. Darlene Jespersen, "Case Is About Civil Rights and Sex Bias," *Reno Gazette-Journal,* February 5, 2004, 11A.

49. Jespersen v. Harrah's Operating Co., Inc., 444 F.3d 1104 (9th Cir. 2006) (en banc).

50. Martin DeAngelis and Maxwell Reil, "Appeals Judges Uphold Borgata Weight Rules," *Press of Atlantic City,* September 18, 2015, http://www.pressofatlanticcity.com /business/appeals-judges-uphold-borgata-weight-rules-in-babes-suit/article_0d11e d7a-5d4e-11e5-9716-6ffff54a2988.html.

51. Kathleen Berry, *Femininity in Flight: A History of Flight Attendants* (Durham: Duke University Press, 2007), 137.

52. Ashleigh Shelby Rosette and Tracy Dumas, "The Hair Dilemma: Conform to Mainstream Expectations or Emphasize Racial Identity," *Duke Journal of Gender Law & Policy* 14 (2007), http://scholarship.law.duke.edu/cgi/viewcontent.cgi?art icle=1119&context=djglp.

53. Jespersen, 444 F.3d at 1107.

54. Angela Onwuachi-Willig, "Another Hair Piece: Exploring New Strands of Analysis Under Title VII," *The Georgetown Law Journal* 98 (2010): 1085.

55. Rosette and Dumas, 408-09.

56. Rogers v. American Airlines, 527 F. Supp. 229 (D.C.N.Y. 1981).

57. Ibid. at 233.

58. Helen Cooper, "Army's Ban on Some Popular Hairstyles Raises Ire of Black Female Soldiers," *The New York Times,* April 20, 2014, http://www.nytimes.com /2014/04/21/us/politics/armys-ban-on-some-popular-hairstyles-raises-ire-of-black -female-soldiers.html.

59. Maya Rhodan, "U.S. Military Rolls Back Restrictions on Black Hairstyles," *Time,* August 13, 2014, http://time.com/3107647/military-black-hairstyles/.

60. Johnson v. Transportation Agency, 480 U.S. 616, 640 (1987).

61. Sally Kohn, "Affirmative Action Has Helped White Women More Than Anyone," *Time,* June 17, 2013, http://ideas.time.com/2013/06/17/affirmative-action-has-helped -white-women-more-than-anyone/.

62. Ibid.

63. See, e.g., "Justice Department Files Lawsuit Against Corpus Christi, Texas Police Department for Sex Discrimination," Press Release, U.S. Dep't of Justice, Office of Public Affairs, July 3, 2012, http://www.justice.gov/opa/pr/justice-department-files-lawsuit-against-corpus-christi-texas-police-department-sex (challenging physical ability test for entry-level police officers, later settled); E.E.O.C. v. Dial Corp., 469 F.3d 735 (8th Cir. 2006) (invalidating strength test at meatpacking plant); United States v. City of Erie, 411 F. Supp. 2d 524 (W.D. Pa. 2005) (striking physical ability test for police applicants); Berkman v. City of New York, 536 F. Supp. 177 (E.D.N.Y. 1982) (invalidating physical ability test for firefighter candidates).

64. Yiyang Wu, "Scaling the Wall and Running the Mile: The Role of Physical Selection Procedures in the Disparate Impact Narrative," *University of Pennsylvania Law Review* 160 (2012): 1212-13, n.82.

65. Denise M. Hulett, Marc Bendick, Jr., Sheila Y. Thomas and Fran Moccio, "A National Report Card on Women in Firefighting," at 1, April 2008, https://i-women.org/wp-content/uploads/2014/07/35827WSP.pdf.

66. Ibid.

67. Bureau of Labor Statistics, Household Data, Annual Averages, Table 11, "Employed Persons by Detailed Occupation, Sex, Race, and Hispanic or Latino Ethnicity," 2014, http://www.bls.gov/cps/cpsaat11.pdf, 4.

68. See, e.g., Vicki Schultz, "Telling Stories About Women and Work: Judicial Interpretations of Sex Segregation in the Workplace in Title VII Cases Raising the Lack of Interest Argument," *Harvard Law Review* 103, No. 8 (June 1990); Gregory Pratt, "Country Club Hills Lawsuit Alleges Porn in Fire Station, Sexual Harassment," *The Chicago Tribune*, Aug. 20, 2015, http://www.chicagotribune.com/suburbs/daily-southtown/news/ct-sta-country-club-firefighters-suit-st-0820-20150819-story.html; "Female Firefighter Files Sex Discrimination Lawsuit," *Florida Times-Union*, Aug. 22, 2014, http://www.firerescue1.com/fire-department-management/articles/1968958-Female-firefighter-files-sex-discrimination-lawsuit/.

69. Hulett, Bendick, Jr., Thomas and Moccio, "A National Report Card on Women in Firefighting," April 2008 at 3.

70. 824 F. Supp. 847 (D. Minn. 1993).

71. Clara Bingham and Laura Leedy Gansler, *Class Action: The Landmark Case That Changed Sexual Harassment Law* (New York: Doubleday, 2002).

72. *North Country* (Warner Brothers, 2005).

73. Suzanne Goldenberg, "'It Was Like They'd Never Seen a Woman Before,'" *The Guardian*, Feb. 3, 2006, http://www.theguardian.com/film/2006/feb/03/gender.world.

74. Ibid.

75. Oncale v. Sundowner Offshore Services, Inc., 523 U.S. 75, 77 (1998).

76. 523 U.S. 75, 77 (1998).

77. "The Glass Floor: Sexual Harassment in the Restaurant Industry," Restaurant Opportunities Center United, Oct. 7, 2014, http://rocunited.org/new-report-the-glass-floor-sexual-harassment-in-the-restaurant-industry/.

78. Ibid.

79. Saru Jayaraman, "It's Not a Tip Credit, It's a Tip Penalty," *The Stranger*, Apr. 9, 2014, http://www.thestranger.com/seattle/its-not-a-tip-credit-its-a-tip-penalty/Content?oid=19234278.

80. Jillian Berman, "80 Percent of Female Restaurant Workers Say They've Been Harassed by Customers," *The Huffington Post*, Oct. 8, 2014, http://www.huffingtonpost.com/2014/10/08/sexual-harassment-restaurants_n_5948096.html.

81. "The Glass Floor."

82. Human Rights Watch, "Cultivating Fear: The Vulnerability of Immigrant Farmworkers in the U.S. to Sexual Violence and Sexual Harassment," May 5, 2012, https://www.hrw.org/report/2012/05/15/cultivating-fear/vulnerability-immigrant-farmworkers-us-sexual-violence-and-sexual.

83. Ibid.

84. Ibid.

85. Southern Poverty Law Center, "Injustice On Our Plates: Immigrant Women in the U.S. Food Industry," November 2010, https://www.splcenter.org/news/2010/11/23/injustice-our-plates.

86. William R. Tamayo, "The Role of the EEOC in Protecting the Civil Rights of Farmworkers," *University of California-Davis Law Review* 33 (Summer 2000): 1075.

87. Liz Jones, "Farm Worker Harassment Draws Increased Scrutiny," KUOW, May 12, 2013, http://kuow.org/post/farm-worker-harassment-draws-increased-scrutiny; *Frontline*, "Rape in the Fields," PBS Broadcast (June 25, 2013), http://www.pbs.org/wgbh/pages/frontline/social-issues/rape-in-the-fields/transcript-46/; Sasha Khokha, "Down on the Farm, Sexual Harassment Claims Finally Surface," *The California Report*, July 24, 2006, http://audio.californiareport.org/archive/R607240850/a.

88. U.S. Equal Employment Opportunity Commission, "Selected List of of Pending and Resolved Cases Involving Farmworkers from 1999 to the Present," June 2015, http://www.eeoc.gov/eeoc/litigation/selected/farmworkers_august_2014.cfm.

89. Esther Yu-Hsi Lee, "5 Female Farmworkers Will Be Awarded $17 Million After Facing Rape and Harassment," *ThinkProgress*, September 11, 2015, http://thinkprogress.org/immigration/2015/09/11/3700839/female-farmworkers-17-million-verdict/.

90. Ibid.

91. Equal Rights Advocates, "Moving Women Forward: On the 50th Anniversary of Title VII of the Civil Rights Act, A Three-Part Series, Part One: Sexual Harassment Still Exacting a Heavy Toll," Oct. 9, 2014, 8-9, http://www.equalrights.org/wp-content/uploads/2014/11/ERA-Moving-Women-Forward-Report-Part-One-Sexual-Harassment-Oct-2014.pdf.

92. See, e.g., Joanna Grossman, "The U.S. Court of Appeals for the Eleventh Circuit Undercuts Sexual Harassment Victims' Rights: How the Decision Underlines Problems with the Supreme Court's Approach to Hostile Environment Harassment," *FindLaw*, Apr. 3, 2007, http://writ.news.findlaw.com/grossman/20070403.html.

93. 133 S. Ct. 2434 (2013)

94. Ibid. at 2455 (Ginsburg, J., dissenting).

95. Ibid. at 2456 (Ginsburg, J., dissenting).

96. Ibid. at 2466 (Ginsburg, J., dissenting).

97. Bryce Covert, "Exclusive: 43 Harassment Cases That Were Thrown Out Because of One Supreme Court Decision," *Think Progress*, Nov. 24, 2014, http://thinkprogress.org/economy/2014/11/24/3596287/vance-sexual-harassment/.

98. Crawford v. Metropolitan Gov't of Nashville and Davidson County, Tenn., 129 S. Ct. 846 (2009).

99. Thompson v. North American Stainless, LP, 131 S. Ct. 863 (2011).

100. See, e.g., Linda Hirshman, *Sisters in Law: How Sandra Day O'Connor and Ruth Bader Ginsburg Went to the Supreme Court and Changed the World* (HarperCollins, 2015), 284-85.

101. 133 S. Ct. 2517, 2546 (2013) (Ginsburg, J., dissenting).

102. Ibid.

103. Bryce Covert, "The Lifelong Effects of the Gender Wage Gap," *ThinkProgress*, Sept. 3, 2015, http://thinkprogress.org/economy/2015/09/03/3698300/gender-retirement-gap/.

104. 127 S. Ct. 2162 (2007).

index